Java®
Application Strategies
for the AS/400

About the Cover: The cover of this book sports a large, strong oak tree. Oak was the first name given to the language now known as Java. Sun Microsystems dropped the name Oak after they learned that it is trademarked. While at a coffee shop, the designers of Oak renamed their language Java. Regardless of its name, this modern language is now strong enough to support large AS/400 business applications.

Conventions Used in This Book: Java is a case-sensitive language. For example, invalidstateexception and InvalidStateException are two different variables. To emphasize keywords, the convention used in this book is to employ small capitals for the lowercase letters and large capitals for uppercase words. Thus, the two example variables are emphasized as INVALIDSTATEEXCEPTION and INVALIDSTATEEXCEPTION.

Java®
Application Strategies
for the AS/400

Don Denoncourt

First Edition

Second Printing—March 2000

Every attempt has been made to provide correct information. However, the publisher and the author do not guarantee the accuracy of the book and do not assume responsibility for information included in or omitted from it.

IBM and AS/400 are trademarks of International Business Machines Corporation. All other product names are trademarked or copyrighted by their respective manufacturers.

© 1999 Midrange Computing
ISBN: 1-883884-61-6

Midrange Computing
5650 El Camino Real, Suite 225
Carlsbad, CA 92008
www.midrangecomputing.com

V4R2

To my wife and my personal editor, may she forgive my long sentences and my long nights; my short instructions and my short temper; my missing references and my forgotten promises.

Suzanne, thank you.

CONTENTS

INTRODUCTION

With more than 600 Java books now in print, why would the computer industry need yet one more? *Java® Application Strategies for the AS/400* is written specifically for the AS/400 RPG programmer. For the most part, the myriad of available Java books presume a readership replete with C++ or at least C programming experience.

Also, many Java books include no discussion whatsoever about business programming. Written for AS/400 business programmers, IBM's Java Redbooks serve as an important reference resource; yet, they don't provide a straightforward discussion on strategies for Java application design and programming.

This book gives you real-world strategies for the development of AS/400 Java applications. *Java® Application Strategies for the AS/400* is divided into five sections:

- An Introduction to Java for RPG Programmers.
- Object-Oriented Design.
- Accessing Your AS/400.
- Object-Oriented Strategies for Mapping DB2/400 to Java.
- Graphical User Interface.

The first section, An Introduction to Java for RPG Programmers, acquaints you with Java from the perspective of an RPG programmer. This section of the book introduces you to not just the structure of the Java language but also the intent of the language. Learning Java as just another programming language is easy; but if you develop Java applications using the same structured techniques that you've employed in RPG applications, those Java applications will fail. This inevitable failure arises from Java's intrinsic design as an object-oriented rather than a structured programming language. The benefits of Java can be achieved only through the use of proper object-oriented programming strategies.

The second section, Object-Oriented Design, provides seven chapters on object-oriented programming with Java, the first viable object-oriented language for business programming. Not just a fad, object-oriented programming is a proven methodology that has been widely used on most computing platforms for more than 10 years. Even the AS/400 has hosted object-oriented programming for a half-dozen years with IBM's VisualAge for C++ and VisualAge for Smalltalk. Finally, however, with the power and simplicity of Java, the AS/400 has an object-oriented language that doesn't require a computer science degree to understand. Section II of the book provides you with complete coverage of the Java language's implementation of object-oriented programming.

The third section, Accessing Your AS/400, details the use of the utilities that IBM Rochester delivers with its Java Toolbox for the AS/400. These utilities provide record-level and SQL access to DB2/400, legacy program interoperability, and data queue support. The curious thing about this section comes to light in the closing paragraphs, which point out that my own Java examples are poor illustrations of object-oriented programming. For ease of understanding, these examples were developed using structured techniques that RPG programmers will find familiar. But, as mentioned earlier, a successful Java application must be properly designed using object-oriented techniques. The fourth section of this book gives you the strategies you'll need to do that.

Section IV, Object-Oriented Strategies for Mapping DB2/400 to Java, provides instruction on how to develop Java classes that encapsulate access to business entities stored in DB2/400. This section also provides a framework of Java classes, the purpose of which is twofold. First, it furnishes a complete example of the development of object-oriented Java business classes. Second, it provides a framework of classes that you can use in the development of your own business classes. Both IBM and Inprise have object-to-relational utilities (*wizards* or *smartguides*, as they prefer to call them) that produce Java classes that map your DB2/400 data to Java. The resulting classes that are generated from these utilities function much the same as the frameworks presented in Section IV so the coverage in this section still applies, regardless of the object-to-relational tool used. The frameworks presented in this section and the Java classes generated from Inprise or IBM primarily differ in that Inprise's and IBM's classes use SQL for data access and mine use record-level access. Record-level access, as you know, is faster than SQL.

Users want a graphical user interface. They've wanted one since Windows first became popular. A GUI empowers users, puts them in the driver's seat. For years, they have worked with the user interface of the 5250 where the programmer had control. Java encompasses some very elegant GUI programming strategies; and Section V, Graphical User Interface, provides a tutorial on how to develop Java GUIs using those strategies. The first chapter within this section covers basic Java GUI programming using Java's package of GUI classes known as the Abstract Windowing Toolkit (AWT). The second chapter details the design of several Java GUIs that present DB2/400 data that is accessed from the example business classes developed in Section IV. One constant theme throughout this section is the separation of UI (graphical or otherwise) code from the code that maintains your business entities.

Ah, subfiles. What will replace AS/400 subfiles? The final chapter of this book provides a tutorial on the replacement paradigm for AS/400 subfiles—*grids* or, more specifically, the JTable grid component from Sun Microsystems' Java Foundation Classes (JFC). The chapter not only provides a tutorial on JFC's JTable, but it also introduces you to the JFC GUI classes for the development of advanced business GUIs. This last chapter contains a tutorial on how to use JFC's JTree component and JFC's JTabbedPane. JFC's JTree uses the visual metaphor of a tree such as is used with Windows Explorer. JFC's JTabbedPane component is used for the creation of tabbed dialogs. The GUI of robust business applications requires sophisticated components such as grids, trees, and tabbed dialogs; this section tells you how to develop those GUI applications using Sun's JFC.

Ultimately, by reading *Java® Application Strategies for the AS/400,* you will:

- Learn the structure and intent of the Java programming language.

- Gain an understanding of the power of object-oriented programming.

- Learn standard strategies for object-oriented design.

- Know how to access DB2/400.

- Have strategies for interoperating Java applications with your legacy applications.

- Have a strategy and a framework for the development of business classes.

- Know how to develop Java GUIs complete with a replacement paradigm for AS/400 subfiles.

SECTION I

~

AN INTRODUCTION TO JAVA FOR RPG PROGRAMMERS

1

JAVA FOR RPG PROGRAMMERS

The structures of RPG programs and Java programs are, in many ways, similar, even though the intended program design strategies of the RPG and Java languages greatly differ. This chapter compares the structure of a Java program with the structure of an RPG program. It then provides a quick overview of the general syntax of Java statements and follows with a discussion of basic Java data types. The chapter concludes with coverage of the looping constructs of Java.

AS/400 LIBRARIES AND JAVA PACKAGES

Figures 1.1 and 1.2 contain the source for the sample Java and RPG programs used to compare structure. Java *program* here is a misnomer intentionally adopted for the sake of comparing Java and RPG structures; Figure 1.1 actually contains a *class* (explained in detail later in this chapter) as there is no such thing as a Java program.

```
package Sales;
import SomeOtherPackage;
class Customer {
   String LSTNAM;
   int CSTNUM;
   float BALDUE;

   /* function prototypes are not necessary in Java */
   public static void main(String[] pList)
   {
      BALDUE = CalcBal(102.58);
   }
   Customer ()// constructor
   {
      LSTNAM = "";
   }
   float calcBal(float payment)
   { // function begin
      // local variables
      float localBal = 0.0;
      // calculations
      localBal = BALDUE - buy;
      // return value
      return localBal;
   } // function end
} // class's closing curly brace
```

Figure 1.1: The CUSTOMER Java class.

Right from the start, the Java program in Figure 1.1 uses a keyword, PACKAGE, that RPG programmers don't recognize. Yet, the concept behind Java packages is not foreign to those who code primarily in RPG. Consider the program in Figure 1.2. For the purpose of this discussion, assume that this RPG program will compile to an AS/400 library named SALES. Most AS/400 libraries contain programs and database files that collectively make up one application.

Similarly, with Java, a program is assigned as part of a *package*—essentially a library of Java programs (or, more accurately, classes) that make up an application. The first statement of the Java source in Figure 1.1 says that the compiled version of this file is to become a member of the package of Java programs (classes) called SALES.

```
 * Program Name: SLS023
FCUSTMAST
D*external file definition

 * function prototype
D CalcBal    PR     9P 2
D   localBal        9P 2 VALUE
 * Mainline
C *ENTRY  PLIST Parms
C                  EVAL BALDUE = CalcBal(102.58)

C   *INZSR     BEGSR
C* set state of pgm variables
C                  ENDSR
P CalcBal    B
D              PI  9P 2
D    payment      9P 2 VALUE

D  localBal S     9P 2 INZ(0)

C                  EVAL localBal = BALDUE-buy

C                  RETURN      localBal

P CalcBal    E
* end of program source
```

Figure 1.2: The CUSTOMER RPG program.

One distinction between Java and RPG lies in the manner in which a class or program is assigned to a package or library. Unfortunately, the AS/400's library system provides no automatic control over which programs or files go into a library. An RPG program can be compiled to one library, a new version of that program can be compiled to a different library, and later that same program might be moved to yet another library. However, you can't move a compiled Java program (class) to any other package. The only way to make this class available in another Java package entails changing the package statement at the top of the source file and recompiling the class.

On a side note, the AS/400 library system goes just one level deep whereas Java packages are kept in hierarchical file systems such as that of DOS, Windows, or the Integrated File System (IFS) of your AS/400. The Java package statement typically qualifies several levels of directories. The qualification uses a dot as the separator rather than the slash of DOS or Windows. IBM's Java Toolbox for the AS/400, for instance, has a package of Java classes that enables AS/400 connectivity. Each of the classes that comprise the AS/400 package has the following package statement as the first statement of its Java source file:

```
package com.ibm.as400.access;
```

IMPORT

The second statement of the Java source in Figure 1.1 is an IMPORT statement that specifies the name of another package of Java classes. You might jump to the conclusion that the IMPORT statement must work like a /COPY in RPG. Not so. The code of the Java classes contained within the package specified in the IMPORT statement is not bound or copied into the Java program at compile time. A Java import statement more closely compares with the CL Add Library List Entry (ADDLIBLE) command.

At compile time for an RPG program, the specifications for the fields of the files used in that program are retrieved from database files that reside in various application libraries. When you code your RPG programs, you assume the field attributes of a file are available even if you did not describe them in the program. To make sure the external file specifications are available to the compiler, you use the ADDLIBLE command for interactive compiles or you add the additional libraries to the job description that you use for a batch compile.

Java's import statement is used to make the classes of other packages available at compile time. As you code your Java class, you use the import statement to make sure the compiler knows where to find the attributes of classes that are in another package. When you use IBM's Java Toolbox for the AS/400 in your Java applications, for instance, you always have the following import statement just after your package statement:

```
import com.ibm.as400.access.*;
```

The Java class of Figure 1.1, then, is a part of the Java application contained in a Java package called SALES. That particular Java class uses the classes of

SOMEOTHERPACKAGE. The implementation is nice and clean, with the location of the Java class explicitly coded, as is the location of other packages used to develop that particular Java class. The RPG implementation involves a bit more effort. You have to compile the RPG program to the proper library and you must be sure that the library list of the OS/400 job performing the compile has entries for the libraries that contain the files (and their external field descriptions) used in the RPG program.

A PROGRAM WITH CLASS

The third statement of the Java source of Figure 1.1 is the Java class statement. The word CLASS is a Java reserved word just like PACKAGE and IMPORT. A Java application is comprised of Java classes, each of which represents one entity complete with its fields and functions. In RPG, the fields are represented in DB2/400 and the functions reside in various RPG programs.

The class statement clearly identifies the class name as CUSTOMER. When the Java source is compiled, the resulting class will bear the name CUSTOMER. Looking at the RPG program in Figure 1.2, can you determine the name of the compiled program object? Of course, the opening comment says it's to be called SLS023, which might lead you to assume that the name of that particular member of the RPG source file is SLS023. But can you be sure?

Normally, when you compile an RPG program, the name of the source member also serves as the name of the program. However, programs frequently get copied and renamed, often causing programmers to lose track of the original source. Of course, you can use the Display Object Description (DSPOBJD) command to obtain the source file and member name, but that's just so you can clean up after programs get misplaced.

LET'S START HERE...

The next point of interest in the Java program is the curly brace that follows the class name declaration. This curly brace essentially marks the beginning of the program.

Blocks of code are delimited in Java with sets of curly braces. RPG programmers delimit blocks of code with pairs of op codes such as BEGSR/ENDSR, IF/ENDIF, and SELECT/ENDSL. An RPG subroutine—a block of code itself—often contains other blocks of code such as nested IF clauses.

Because an RPG source member can contain only one program, the start of the program is simply the first statement of the source file and the end of the program is the last statement of the source member. A Java source file, however, can have more than one class (which you can still think of as a program, for the sake of comparison). A Java class, therefore, is demarcated with an opening curly brace and, after the complete code for the class, a closing curly brace.

The Java class can contain many other curly-braced blocks of code nested inside the class's set of curly braces. The first inner level of curly-braced sections of code within a Java class demarcates the functions of that class. Subsequent curly-braced sections are the conditional code blocks.

SUBROUTINES AND FUNCTIONS

The ILE RPG programming language now has not only subroutines but also functions and procedures. While everybody is familiar with RPG subroutines, many programmers still feel uncomfortable with RPG's functions and procedures. Functions and procedures represent a great enhancement to RPG and it's important you know why.

One of the biggest problems with RPG III is that all program variables are global. In other words, all the variables that you define in an RPG program are accessible from the mainline and all the subroutines. ILE brings modular programming to the AS/400.

There are two levels of modular programming: modular design within a single source member and modular design within a group of source members that are compiled into modules and bound together with the Create Program (CRTPGM) command. I encourage you to explore the second level, but the most effective comparison of Java class to RPG construct makes me focus your attention on modular design within one ILE program. Before continuing with this comparison, you should have an understanding of ILE RPG functions. Before continuing with this comparison, you should have an understanding of ILE RPG functions.

ILE RPG functions have *local variables.* If you define a variable in an RPG function, the scope of that variable is limited to that function—neither the mainline nor the other subroutines and functions of that program may access that variable. By limiting the scope of variables, you decrease the complexity of a program. One commonly used software metric calculates the complexity of a program with a simple algorithm that counts, among other things, the amount of variables in a code block. Based on this software metric, the complexity of a standard small RPG III program (say, 5,000 lines) would be extremely high. By decreasing the amount of global variables through the use of local variables, you greatly reduce the complexity of functions and hence the program's overall complexity.

DENONCOURT'S *RPG*

Had IBM approached me and said, "Don, design some improvements to the RPG programming language," I would have redesigned subroutines to be modular. First I would have wanted RPG subroutines to have local variables. I probably would have implemented that by allowing I-specs to be specified within the context of a single RPG subroutine as shown in Figure 1.3.

```
C     SUBX        BEGSR
ILOCAL                    9S2
C* some complex calculations
C                 ENDSR
```

Figure 1.3: My suggestions for RPG subroutines would include local I-specs.

Then, because that subroutine has to share the results of its calculations, I would have enhanced the RETURN op code to return a value from that souped-up subroutine to the line of code that invoked the subroutine with EXSR as shown in Figure 1.4.

```
C          SUBX        BEGSR
ILOCAL                          9S2
C* some complex calculations
C                       RETURN LOCAL
C                       ENDSR
```

Figure 1.4: My suggestions would include subroutines returning values just like functions in other languages.

Further, now that all the subroutines are being secretive about their local variables, the subroutine would need to accept parameters so that it could operate like a mini-program as shown in Figure 1.5.

```
C          SUBX        BEGSR
C                      PARM                    INPUT 9 2
ILOCAL                          9S2
C                      MULT    INPUT      LOCAL
C* some complex calculations
C                      RETURN LOCAL
C                      ENDSR
```

Figure 1.5: My improved subroutines would also accept parameters.

IBM's RPG

Apparently, IBM didn't use my RPG enhancement. Instead of improving RPG subroutines, IBM added functions and procedures to enable modular programming within an RPG program. It also replaced the familiar I-specs with the far more powerful D-specs. ILE RPG's functions, unlike subroutines, can have their own set of D-specs. Any variables defined in the D-specs of an RPG function are local to that function. The CALCBAL function shown in Figure 1.6 uses local D-specs for the declaration of a variable called LOCALBAL.

But those two D-specs that precede the declaration of LOCALBAL—what are they all about? The first D-spec declares the data type of the value that is returned from that function. The second D-spec declares the data type of the input parameter. ILE RPG functions will only ever have one return value, but they can have zero or more input parameters.

```
P CalcBal       B
D               PI  9P 2
D payment           9P 2 VALUE
D localBal S        9P 2 INZ(0)
C               EVAL localBal = BALDUE-buy
C               RETURN      localBal
P CalcBal       E
```

Figure 1.6: ILE RPG procedures and functions have local variables that are declared in D-specs within the enclosing P-specs.

One last point about ILE RPG functions is function prototypes. To be able to use a function in RPG, you must declare a *function prototype*. Function prototypes are specified in the program-level D-specs at the top of the program. Their purpose is to declare to the compiler the number and data type of the function's parameters as well as its return data type. The following is the prototype for the CALCBAL function:

```
D CalcBal       PR   9P 2
D    localBal        9P 2 VALUE
```

The characters PR of the above prototype means PROTOTYPE ; and the 9, P, and 2 tell the compiler that the function called CALCBAL returns a packed decimal number with a length of nine that has two decimal positions. The second D-spec line indicates that the CALCBAL function requires one input parameter that is a packed decimal number. In the same line, the keyword value says that the parameter is passed by VALUE rather than by reference. (With RPG, you can use either parameter-passing strategy.) Also note that the parameter name (LOCALBAL in the example) is optional; the only purpose for adding it is to give programmers some idea what kind of information the parameter is to store.

With that quick summary of ILE functions complete, I can compare them to Java functions. Java, just like any modern programming language for the last 15 or 20 years, includes functions that accept multiple parameters, locally scoped variables, and return values.

The Java version of the CALCBAL function is much easier to read and understand than its RPG version. The return type of a Java function is specified first, followed by the function name. You specify the parameters for a function within parentheses after the function name. If the function has no parameters, the parentheses are still required; they just have no arguments specified within them.

The data type in Figure 1.1 is FLOAT, which holds a floating-point number. (Later, this chapter introduces you to Java's version of a fixed-point decimal number called BIGDECIMAL, but for now the floating-point data type makes the code easier to understand.) Notice that the opening curly brace marks the beginning of the function and the closing curly brace denotes the end of the function. With the ILE RPG function in Figure 1.2, the function begins with the new P-spec that has a lone B character (for *begin*, I guess) and the function ends with the next P-spec and the E character for the *end* specification.

The Java function, just like the RPG function, declares a local variable called LO-CALBAL and assigns it an initial value. The CalcBal function then performs some computations and returns the value of LOCALBAL to whatever other function invokes this one.

Despite the similarities pointed out so far, you won't see a Java equivalent of the RPG program's prototype for the CALCBAL function. Java does not require function prototypes as ILE RPG, C, and even C++ programs do.

GLOBAL VARIABLES

In the ILE RPG program of Figure 1.2, the F-spec declares an externally described file. Compiling the source automatically pulls the field attributes of that file into the compiled version of the program. Realize that RPG is a data-driven language designed to manipulate database files. Java is not tightly coupled to any database so a Java class must describe the attributes of the business entities that it operates on. Just after the class statement in Figure 1.1, you can see the declaration for three fields:

```
String LSTNAM;
int CSTNUM;
float BALDUE;
```

The naming convention used for these three fields of the Java class should look familiar to you since they seem to adhere to the six-character convention of RPG

III variables. Java has no such restriction; in fact, a standard naming convention for Java variables is to spell out the variable in mixed case, with the initial letter of all but the first word in uppercase:

```
String lastName;
int customerNumber;
float balanceDue;
```

This naming convention differentiates variable names from Java class names, since the first letter of a class name's first word is also uppercase. Although I prefer the standard Java naming convention, in this case I chose to retain the same variable names used in the DB2/400 file. Programmers who are familiar with the six-character naming of DB2/400 fields will find Java code easier to read and understand if they see field names they've used for years in RPG.

Note that the three variables are not within the context of a function; they fall within the context of the class. Those variables can be considered as global to the class because all the functions of that class may reference those variables. The global variables of the customer class are just like the fields of the ILE RPG program (Figure 1.2) that come from the externally defined file.

You might consider it a real step backward to have to describe the fields of a file internally to your Java program, and it will be—that is, if you don't follow the strategies outlined in Section IV of this book.

PROGRAM ENTRY

ILE RPG programs are capable of accepting parameters. You probably already know that program arguments enter an RPG program via the entry parameter list (*ENTRY PLIST). The entry parameter list of an ILE RPG program describes the number and type of required parameters for the RPG program. When you develop ILE modules, only one of the many modules that make up the bound RPG program needs to have an entry parameter list. OS/400's CRTPGM command prompts you for the name of the module it is to use as the entry point for the program.

Java classes, just like ILE modules, do not have to specify an entry point. If a class has no specified entry point, it cannot be invoked as an application. But a

Java class does specify an entry point is considered a Java application and can be invoked from the command line.

The Java equivalent to an RPG program's entry parameter list and mainline is a Java function called MAIN. All Java MAIN functions have the following syntax:

```
public static void main(String[] pList)
```

By the end of Section II of this book, you'll be very comfortable with the Java reserved words that precede the function name. For now you'll receive just a quick overview.

The keyword PUBLIC indicates that the function that follows may be called from outside the context of this class. It's the external entry point that allows a user to invoke the MAIN function from a DOS window or AS/400 command line. The keyword STATIC says that an object of this class need not exist to be able to call this function. Such a brief explanation on the STATIC keyword might throw you, but Section II elaborates on the use of STATIC more fully.

The keyword VOID merely serves as a placeholder for the data type of the value returned from this function. The special Java function called MAIN does not return any data value and the VOID keyword tells the compiler as much. Then the function name of MAIN is declared, followed by its parameter list. A MAIN function can only have one parameter, which will always be an array of strings. I called that string array PLIST but you can call it whatever you like. C programmers tend to call it ARGS for arguments, but PLIST works just as well for those with an RPG background.

It seems that the string array parameter is a limitation of Java. You might wonder how you can be sure that the data types of the external parameters are correct? The Java class that contains a MAIN function is usually just the starting point for a Java application. Special Java functions known as *constructors* are used more often than MAIN functions for initialization parameters, and those parameters are strongly typed. (The chapter on object-oriented basics in Section II covers constructors in more detail.)

*INZSR AND CONSTRUCTORS

A Java constructor is a special Java function that has the same name as its class. In the CUSTOMER class of Figure 1.1, the function called CUSTOMER is the class's constructor function. The ILE RPG analogy to Java constructors—the initialization subroutine (*INZSR)—sets the initial state of an RPG program's variables upon the first invocation of that program in a user job. OS/400 allocates the storage required for the RPG program memory in the Process Access Group (PAG), and the initialization subroutine sets the initial values of the variables of that program. *INZSR can also be used to retrieve values from data areas and pre-open files.

A Java constructor serves the same purpose; it sets the initial state of the global fields of a Java class the first time that class is used after Java allocates storage in main memory for the fields of that class. A Java constructor can also open database files. At this point, however, the similarities of RPG and Java begin to fade. You see, a Java class is actually the definition for an abstract data type. The example CUSTOMER class can be used as the data type in the declaration of a variable in a function of other Java classes.

```
Customer aCust;
```

The first time an instance of the CUSTOMER class is created in main memory, the class's constructor function sets its initial state—similar to the initialization subroutine's invocation the first time an RPG program is called. Subsequent calls to that RPG program will use the same main memory storage area. In Java, subsequent uses of the same instance of the CUSTOMER class as referenced through the ACUST variable will use the same memory that the constructor function allocated and initialized.

The ACUST variable declared above (whose data type is of the customer class) has not had any memory allocated for it yet. It is allocated when you use Java's NEW operator over the CUSTOMER class's constructor function:

```
aCust = new Customer();
```

At that point, the ACUST variable becomes an object instance of the CUSTOMER class. You could think of Java objects as being little PAGs for classes, with each PAG referring to a different instance of the CUSTOMER class.

The declaration for the CUSTOMER constructor function in Figure 1.1 differs from all the other constructor functions in that it does not specify a return type. The return type of a constructor function is implicitly the class itself. The customer constructor returns a CUSTOMER object that you can think of as having its own little PAG.

JAVA VIRTUAL MACHINE

Java source files all have the suffix of .JAVA, and compiled Java classes are contained in files that have suffixes of .CLASS. On the AS/400, Java source files and Java compiled class files are kept in the IFS. If you use SEU to enter Java source, you have to copy that source to the IFS with the Copy to Stream File (CPYTOSTMF) command. Then you can compile that Java source file with the JAVAC command, specifying the source file as its parameter:

```
javac Customer.java
```

If no errors surface, the compile produces a .CLASS file. Java is an interpreted language; the .CLASS file contains what is known as Java byte code. To execute the Java .CLASS file (the compiled code), you run the JAVA command:

```
java Customer
```

The JAVA command starts the Java Virtual Machine (JVM), which reads the Java byte code of the compiled class file and then executes those byte code instructions using the low-level, machine-specific instruction set of the current platform. It is important to understand that a class file produced on any platform can be copied to and then executed on any other platform that has a Java Virtual Machine—no recompilation required. Consequently, you can develop Java applications on your PC and then copy the Java class files to the AS/400 and they are ready to execute.

JOB CONTROL

RPG applications typically have CL drivers that set up the job's library list. When calls are made to programs that do not reside in the current library, OS/400 uses the library list to search for those programs. Java applications go through similar motions by employing a *class path*. The class path resembles a library list in that as functions of a Java class attempt to use classes contained in other Java packages, the JVM looks for classes by searching the directories specified in the classpath environment variable. The classpath environment variable works just like the path environment variable in DOS. To set up a class path, you use the set command and then specify the directory paths to the various Java packages that your Java applications use:

```
SET CLASSPATH=C:\WorkingApps\Sales;
```

One technique that I use in my DOS batch files is to enclose a reference to the classpath environment variable within a set of percent symbols:

```
SET CLASSPATH=%CLASSPATH%C:\WorkingApps\Sales;
```

That SET command then effectively operates like OS/400's ADDLIBLE because it takes the existing class path and appends to it an additional directory path.

On the AS/400, the classpath environment variable is set with the Add Environment Variable (ADDENVVAR) command or the Work with Environment Variable (WRKENVVAR) command. OS/400's Java class path uses a colon as the separator character rather than the semicolon found in a DOS path or classpath environment variable.

You have one other task to complete before your Java application can execute: You must make sure that the path environment variable (not classpath, but *path*) specifies the path to the directory containing the JVM. For instance, my Java Development Kit (JDK) is located on my C drive in the BIN directory underneath the JDK1.1.6 directory:

```
SET PATH=%PATH%C:\java\JDK1.1.6/Bin;
```

SUMMARY

Java is not a difficult language to learn when you begin to compare it to ILE RPG. The advantages of Java stem not from its syntax but from its integrated, object-oriented architecture. It is the primary intent of this book to provide object-oriented strategies for developing AS/400 Java applications.

The next chapter introduces you to the concepts of object-oriented programming through a language that you are already comfortable with: RPG. Chapter 3 covers Java syntax in more detail and chapter 4 covers the three major Java programming models: applets, applications, and servlets.

Section II includes seven full chapters of object-oriented programming concepts. Section III covers the use of IBM's Java Toolbox for the AS/400 for DB2/400 access and integration with legacy RPG applications. In Section IV, you'll learn strategies for encapsulating access to DB2/400 files. Finally, in Section V, you can take advantage of a tutorial on Java GUI programming.

The book maintains a constant theme of adhering to the tenets of object-oriented programming. RPG has worked well for the careers of AS/400 programmers, but Java represents the future.

2

OBJECT-ORIENTED RPG

The first chapter pointed out the similarities in the structure of an RPG program and a Java class. But when those structures are used in the construction of Java applications, following the design strategies intended for Java, the similarities between RPG and Java begin to disappear. Java is an object-oriented language whereas RPG is structural. In Java, one class represents one business entity, and processing is event-driven. In contrast, a single RPG program often opens dozens of files. In fact, many AS/400 shops eagerly awaited ILE RPG not for its modular programming capabilities but for its support for more than 50 files. The RPG programming language was developed with the sole intent of processing relational databases whereas the base Java language doesn't even know about relational databases.

The design of RPG applications and programs is based on algorithmic decomposition, which results in a hierarchy of systems and programs. RPG is a procedural language: Each program's mainline drives the processing of business entities stored in DB2/400 in what is often referred to as the *big loop*. In general, Java classes don't loop; they are event-driven rather than data-driven. With Java, an entity's behavior is tightly coupled with its data in a Java class. The interface to the entities of a database file is retrieved through the functions of the Java class that is designed to represent those entities. The Java class encapsulates database access through its lists of functions while hiding the complexity of that class's implementation.

RPG++

It's difficult enough to learn a new language without learning a whole new philosophy of application design. To bridge that paradigm shift, this chapter introduces you to the concepts of object-oriented programming using the RPG programming language rather than Java. Because RPG was not designed as an object-oriented language, effective illustration of object-oriented principles through RPG examples involved changing the intent of RPG. I invented some hypothetical extensions to RPG and called this new language RPG++; just as C++ is an object-oriented C, RPG++ is an object-oriented RPG. I considered calling this extended language Postum as a word play on Java because Postum is a coffee substitute—it's not "real" and neither are my hypothetical extensions to RPG.

The first big change with the RPG++ language lies in each program maintaining one business entity. For example, each program invocation operates on one customer—no looping. "Now how's that going to work?" you wonder. Bear with me. Java classes, as covered in the first chapter, have a *constructor* that initializes the state of the fields of that class. A customer class in Java might have a constructor function containing an integer argument, which the constructor uses as a key to retrieve the values of a customer record from a relational database file.

RPG already utilizes an initialization subroutine that is similar in concept to a constructor. However, *INZSR does not accept parameters. The RPG++ language's *INZSR does accept parameters. The customer program shown in Figure 2.1 includes an initialization subroutine with a parameter for the customer number. That customer number parameter is then used as the key to retrieve information about that customer from the customer master file.

```
FCUSTMAST U F
 * code omitted
C      *INZSR    BEGSR
```

Figure 2.1: The hypothetical RPG++ customer program maintains only one customer at a time. (Part 1 of 2)

```
C               PARM            CustNo    5 0
C     Cust      Chain  CustRec
C               ENDSR
 *
C     getLSTNAM BEGSR
C               Return          LSTNAM
C               ENDSR
 *
C     getBALDUE BEGSR
C               return          BALDUE
C               ENDSR
 *
C     putBALDUE BEGSR
C               PARM            NewBal    5 0
C               z-add  NewBal   BALDUE
C               ENDSR
 *
C     putLSTNAM BEGSR
C               PARM            NewNam 20
C               move   NewNam   LSTNAM
C               ENDSR
 *
C     update    BEGSR
C               Update CustRec
C               ENDSR
 *
C     write     BEGSR
C               Write  CustRec
C               ENDSR
 *
C     next      BEGSR
C               READ   CustMast
C               MOVE   CSTNUM   custNo
C               NEW    'Customer' aCust
C               PARM            custNo
C               RETURN aCust
C               ENDSR
 *
C     *INZSR    BEGSR
C               PARM            CustNo    5 0
C     Cust      Chain CustRec
C               ENDSR
```

Figure 2.1: The hypothetical RPG++ customer program maintains only one customer at a time. (Part 1 of 2)

The whole purpose of invoking the customer program is to maintain the customer associated with the number that was passed to its initialization subroutine. But how do you pass parameters to the initialization subroutine? My RPG++ language has a new op code called NEW. When other RPG programs want to retrieve information about a customer, they do not open the customer master file for update; rather, they use the NEW op code with the name of the customer program in factor two and a parameter that contains the customer number:

```
C               NEW   'Customer'   aCust
C               PARM  148          custNo
```

The NEW op code does not call the customer program's mainline, and the customer number parameter is not sent to the *ENTRY PLIST. The new op code invokes the *INZSR of the customer program, and the customer number parameter is used to obtain the associated customer master record with a chain operation. Like any RPG initialization subroutine, the RPG++ customer program's *INZSR sets up its own Process Access Group (PAG) for this new program invocation. Every use of RPG++'s NEW op code over the customer program causes another program invocation with its own separate PAG.

Note the variable name in the result field that follows the NEW invocation of the customer program. The data type of that variable, ACUST, is the customer program. Customer is now a data type with operations, just as a packed decimal data type has operations of ADD, SUBTRACT, MULTIPLY, DIVIDE, and ASSIGNMENT. The customer program is an abstract data type complete with operations of UPDATE, WRITE, NEXT, and a variety of GET and PUT operations for the retrieval and modification of the attributes of a customer entity. The customer program shown in Figure 2.1 has a number of subroutines that can be directly invoked from other RPG programs. Figure 2.2 lists those externally invocable subroutines.

The subroutines of the customer program can be invoked from a variable that holds a reference to the customer program invocation like the ACUST variable created earlier. That ACUST variable, which is declared in a program other than the customer program, is used, along with the dot operator, to qualify a function name of the customer program:

```
C               EVAL  bal = aCust.getBALDUE ()
C               EVAL  aCust.putBALDUE(bal)
C               EVAL  aCust.update()
```

```
C     getLSTNAM  BEGSR
C     getBALDUE  BEGSR
C     putBALDUE  BEGSR
C     putLSTNAM  BEGSR
C     update     BEGSR
C     write      BEGSR
C     next       BEGSR
```

Figure 2.2: The customer program has a number of subroutines that can be invoked from other RPG programs.

When an RPG++ program needs to work with another customer, it must use the NEW op code to access another customer program because, as you'll recall, the *INZSR retrieves that customer's record from the customer master file:

```
C              NEW    'Customer'   aCust
C              PARM   148          custNo
```

PROCESSING SETS

This scenario works fine in an interactive program that iteratively prompts the user for a customer number to instance a new customer program. But what if the other RPG++ program wants to sequentially process all the customers? One way to handle that is to add a subroutine to the customer program to create another customer program invocation. That's what subroutine NEXT does in the customer program shown in Figure 2.3. It reads a record from the customer master and then uses the customer number in the parameter that follows the NEW op code. As I already covered, the NEW op code calls the *INZSR of the customer program to create a new program instance. That customer program instance is then returned to the other programs that invoke the customer program's NEXT function.

```
C     next   BEGSR
C            READ   CustMast
C            MOVE   CSTNUM     custNo
C            NEW    'Customer' aCust
C            PARM              custNo
C            RETURN aCust
C            ENDSR
```

Figure 2.3: The NEXT subroutine creates a new customer program from a sequentially retrieved customer master record.

The example DO loop shown in Figure 2.4 demonstrates how another RPG program would loop through and then process customers. Within the DO loop, the program uses the customer program's NEXT function to retrieve customers sequentially. If the ACUST variable (which is a handle to the customer program invocation that holds the state of the first customer) is zero, the loop aborts; otherwise, a new balance is calculated for that customer and the SETBALDUE function of the customer program is invoked through the ACUST variable. The change is carried through to DB2/400 by a call to the customer program's UPDATE function.

```
C                 DO
C                 EVAL      aCust = Customer.next()
C        aCust    IFEQ         0
C                 LEAVE
C                 ENDIF
C* calculate balance due
C                 EVAL      aCust.setBALDUE (balance)
C                 EVAL      aCust.update()
C                 ENDDO
```

Figure 2.4: Other RPG++ programs can loop through customers by iteratively calling the customer program's NEXT subroutine.

BUSINESS OBJECTS

Whether you program in Java, C++, or Smalltalk (or even RPG++), the access and manipulation of your business entities—customers, invoices, purchase orders, items, and so forth—should be done through a class. With a well-designed relational database, the classes map directly to record formats. The fields of that class correspond to the fields of a record format. When a class is used to create an instance of an entity (which is stored as a record in DB2/400), that instance is known as an object.

This chapter introduced you to an op code called NEW; Java, too, has an operator called NEW that you use to construct an object from a class. The class is an abstract data type used to define variables. Java access to entities takes place through the class that represents that entity. Only the Java class that is designed to represent an entity should open the DB2/400 file that stores the state of that entity. When other classes need to retrieve, modify, or create an entity, they do it solely through the functions of that entity's class.

It's easy to learn Java and then begin to design structured Java applications, but the benefits of Java will only come from object-oriented programming. In fact, as you'll see in Section III, the effort involved to access DB2/400 files and fields makes it almost impossible to code in the same manner as you do with RPG. But when you design your Java applications by following the basic strategies of object-oriented programming, you will reap the rewards of code reuse, application adaptability, and improved programmer productivity.

3

AN INTRODUCTION TO BASIC JAVA SYNTAX

Even though this book is not intended as a complete introduction to Java's syntax, this chapter nevertheless provides you with a quick overview of the language's basic syntax. This chapter should provide enough coverage of the basic syntax of Java so that you can follow along with the object-oriented strategies presented in other sections of this book. I encourage you, however, to pick up and read an introductory book on Java if you find the concepts of this chapter confusing.

LOOPS

When your business applications inevitably have to process sets of data, they use looping constructs. Java has three looping constructs: *while, do/while,* and *for.* The do/while loop is used to perform a block of code at least once:

```
do {
} while (x > 5 && y == 8 || z == 0);
```

The condition of the do/while is specified within parentheses following the WHILE keyword. That condition is a Boolean statement, which means that you can create a complex Boolean statement with ANDs and ORs. Java's AND operator, by the way, consists of a double ampersand; the OR operator is the double bar. The single ampersand and the single bar are used for bitwise ANDS and ORs, which business programmers do not use all that often. The EQUAL operator in Java is the double equal sign because the single equal sign is used for assignment.

The do/while of Java represents an improvement over the equivalent operation in RPG. RPG uses the Do Until (DOU) op code for a do/while. The conditional clause in an RPG DOU is specified at the top of the loop even if it isn't checked until the loop executes once. At least ILE RPG now allows the use of complex Boolean statements rather than multiple lines of AND and OR conditions:

```
C                     DOU   (x > 5 & y = 8 | z = 0)
C                     ENDDO
```

The WHILE statement in Java simply consists of the WHILE keyword followed by the parenthetical conditional statement:

```
while (x == 5)
{
}
```

The RPG equivalent operation is the Do While (DOW) op code as shown in Figure 3.1.

```
C          X          DOWEQ 5
C                     ENDDO
 * or
C                     DOW   (X = 5)
C                     ENDDO
```

Figure 3.1: RPG's Do While operation tests the loop condition before executing the loop.

No matter how carefully you code your while and do/while loops, whether in Java or RPG, sometimes you just want to get the heck out of there. In RPG to abort a DOU or a DOW construct, you use the LEAVE op code. In Java, the reserved keyword of BREAK accomplishes the same task.

Sometimes you also want to skip processing one occurrence of a loop. RPG's ITER op code tells a program to ignore the rest of the statements in the loop and continue at the top. Java programmers use the CONTINUE keyword as ITER's equivalent.

A third looping construct of Java that I particularly like is the FOR loop. Java's FOR loop has three clauses: initialization, while condition, and iteration. The first and second clauses end with semicolons and the last ends with the closing parenthesis as shown in the example of Figure 3.2.

```
for (Record rec = file.readFirst();
     rec != null;
        rec = file.readNext())
{
     // process record
}
```

Figure 3.2: Java's FOR loop has three clauses: initialization, while, and iteration.

The above example, excerpted from one of the Java classes in the chapter on record-level access, illustrates how to loop through records of a DB2/400 file. The initialization clause gets a record from a file with the READFIRST function. The while clause is then checked to see if the read function successfully returned a record object (remember, in its own little PAG) to the REC variable. The REC variable will have a null value if no record was retrieved and the while clause of the FOR loop then causes the loop to terminate.

The third clause of the FOR loop, the iterator clause, does not execute immediately after the while clause, as you might think. Instead, the code within the FOR loop's curly braces executes before the iterator clause does. So, on the first pass of the FOR loop, the initialization clause executes, followed by the while clause. The iteration clause is skipped and the FOR loop's code executes. On subsequent iterations of the FOR loop, the iterator executes, followed by the while clause—the initialization clause does not execute again. The RPG example in Figure 3.3 provides the same effect.

```
C* rec externally defined
C                          READ        Record    98
C         *IN98            DOWEQ       *OFF
C*   process record
C                          READ        Record    98
C                          ENDDO
```

Figure 3.3: RPG file processing typically initializes the loop just before the do/while clause.

The READ at the top of the loop parallels the Java initialization clause, the DOW corresponds to Java's while clause, and the READ at the bottom of the loop parallels the Java iteration clause. The problem that I have with this RPG looping strategy is that the initialization is not a discrete part of the loop; with Java's FOR loop, it is.

CASE

RPG finally supplied a case construct a few years ago. Unfortunately, the language's developers overloaded the use of the term *case* with RPG's compare and execute subroutine (CAS) op codes so their new case construct is select/when, as shown in Figure 3.4.

```
C                          SELECT
C                          WHEQ variable = 1
C                          OREQ  variable = 2
*  process 1 and 2
C                          WHEQ variable = 3
*  process 3
C                          OTHER
*    fall through
C                          ENDSL
```

Figure 3.4: RPG's case statement is called SELECT.

Java inherited its case statement from the C programming language. It starts with the Java reserved word of SWITCH, followed by a variable within parentheses. The Java reserved word CASE is then used to specify the value to compare against the switch clause's variable, as shown in Figure 3.5.

```
switch (variable) {
    case 1:
    case 2:
        // process 1 and 2
        break;
    case 3:
        // process 3
    break;
  default:
        // fall through
}
```

Figure 3.5: A Java case statement is enclosed within a switch block.

The Java case statement of Figure 3.5 processes the same way as the RPG SE-LECT statement in Figure 3.4. The first two case clauses check to see if the variable has a value of 1 or 2. The default clause of the case statement is equivalent to the OTHER op code of RPG's SELECT. RPG's SELECT and Java's CASE primarily differ in Java's use of the BREAK statement. The switch block, you'll notice, contains several break statements. If those breaks were not there, the code would drop through the next case and then the default clause would execute. That presents a problem because the default clause is typically coded to handle an error condition.

RPG programmers expect that, once a case is true, the code within that particular case clause executes and then processing continues after the switch statement's closing curly brace. Java's seemingly strange syntax was inherited from C and C++. The point being emphasized here is to make sure you always insert those break statements within each case clause of the switch blocks.

CONSTANTS

Around the same time that RPG's SELECT statement became available, constants were also added. Today, ILE RPG's D-specs also allow you to specify constant values:

```
D DaysInWeek              C   7
```

The character C in the D-spec means constant, and the initialization value follows. In Java you specify that a variable is to be a constant with Java's reserved word of FINAL:

```
final int DaysInWeek = 7;
```

Now why would the designers of the Java language use FINAL as the keyword to mean *constant*? Why not use CONST like C or C++ does? It turns out that C++ had three different meanings for its reserved word of CONST. Since Java borrowed much of its syntax from C++, Sun's designers wanted to remove the ambiguity for their CONSTANT keyword so they used the synonym *final*. Whenever you see the keyword FINAL, just think CONST.

ARRAYS

Arrays in both RPG and Java are statically sized. RPG III used E-specs to define an array and now ILE RPG uses D-specs:

```
D ints           S          2I 0 DIM(10)
```

In Java, you declare an array by defining a variable name of some data type followed by a pair of brackets:

```
int bunchOfIntegers[];
```

The BUNCHOFINTEGERS variable is a handle to an array of integers. In fact, the BUNCHOFINTEGERS variable does not yet have a bunch of integers to provide a handle to. How could it? The declaration above doesn't even specify the size of the array. If, at this point, a function uses BUNCHOFINTEGERS, your Java application would get a runtime error. To create an array, you use Java's NEW operator followed by the data type of the array. You place the size of the array within brackets:

```
bunchOfIntegers = new int[10];
```

That syntax should look a little familiar to you by now because it closely resembles the instancing of a Java class, like the CUSTOMER object example presented in chapter 2:

```
Customer aCust = new Customer();
```

Remember that in the construction process of an object instance of a Java class, the Java Virtual Machine (JVM) allocates storage in memory for the fields of the class. The creation of the array is similar because the NEW operator tells the JVM to allocate storage for 10 integers to be referenced by the BUNCHOFINTEGERS variable. A shorter form of the creation of an array combines the array declaration with the creation of the array:

```
int bunchOfIntegers[] = new int[10];
```

Java arrays, by the way, all have an attribute called LENGTH that contains the number of elements. The length attribute is often used to spin through the elements of an array. The FOR loop of Figure 3.6, for instance, spins through all the elements of the BUNCHOFINTEGERS array and prints their value:

```
for (int element = 0; element < bunchOfIntegers.length; element++)
{
    System.out.println("The value of array element " + element +
" is: " + bunchOfIntegers[element]);
}
```

Figure 3.6: Java's FOR loop is often used to spin through the elements of an array.

COMPILE-TIME ARRAYS

Sometimes RPG programmers use compile-time arrays, in which the elements of the array are defined at compile time. As the example in Figure 3.7 shows, the CTDATA keyword in the D-spec specifies that the array's elements are located in the program source, and the array elements are specified after a double asterisk at the bottom of the program.

```
D DaysOfWeek S 8A DIM(7)CTDATA
C* the RPG program source
**
Sunday
Monday
Tuesday
Wednesday
Thursday
Friday
Saturday
```

Figure 3.7: RPG's compile-time array values are given at the bottom of its source.

To define a compile-time array in Java, you declare an array and then use the NEW operator followed by the data type of the array to create. But instead of specifying the size of the array in the brackets, you leave the brackets empty. Then, between a pair of curly braces that follows the empty brackets, you define each element of the array, using commas to separate the elements. Figure 3.8 shows the declaration and creation of an array called DAYSOFWEEK.

```
String daysOfWeek[] =
      new String[]
      {"Sunday",
       "Monday",
       "Tuesday",
       "Wednesday",
       "Thursday",
       "Friday",
       "Saturday"};
```

Figure 3.8: Java allows you to initialize the elements of an array.

STATIC

Java's reserved word of STATIC is known as the static modifier because it changes or modifies the scope of a class's field or function. Its purpose is to declare that the value of a field or function in a particular class is to be shared among all object instances of that class.

Remember that you use the name of your application's classes as an abstract data type for the declaration of a variable type. Then you use Java's NEW operator followed by the class's constructor function so that Java can allocate storage for the variable whose data type is of that constructor's class. The variable then refers to a specific instance of an object of that class in memory. Each additional construction of a variable of that class has its own separate storage (like the activation group of an RPG program). The following two Java statements create two instances of a CUSTOMER class:

```
Customer aCust = new Customer();
Customer anotherCust = new Customer();
```

The attributes for each customer will vary, with different customer numbers and probably different last names. That works fine because each invocation of a customer has its own storage area allocated for its field. Sometimes, however, a field (or *attribute*, in object-oriented parlance) of a class has a value that should be shared among all object instances of that class. The value of that field should be stored in one memory location that is referenced by all of the object instances of that field's class.

As an example, consider a CUSTOMER class whose attributes are stored in a DB2/400 file. The CUSTOMER class's constructor function would have to open the customer master DB2/400 file so it can retrieve and subsequently modify the values of various customers. Unfortunately, you'll need to process many instances of the CUSTOMER class; and, if each instance opens the DB2/400 file during its construction, the Java application will perform poorly. The solution is to specify the CUSTOMER class's file field as static so that all instances of the class will share the same file open.

The following Java statement declares a variable to be of the KEYEDFILE data type. The static modifier tells the JVM to share the storage for that variable across all instances of customers:

```
static KeyedFile customerMaster;
```

The best RPG analogy to Java's STATIC modifier exists in the AS/400 *data area*. A data area is essentially a one-record file, and the values of a data area's fields are shared among multiple RPG programs at the same time. To make the analogy work, you need to assume that the data area is created in the QTEMP library of a job. That's because the values of static Java fields are not sharable across job boundaries like data areas are unless the data area resides in the QTEMP library.

BASIC DATA TYPES

My earlier explanation of Java as a completely object-oriented language is slightly inaccurate; Java has a set of basic data types that aren't object-oriented at all. Most of them are numeric, but two—CHAR and BYTE—are not. Table 3.1 lists Java's basic data types.

These basic data types, commonly re-ferred to as the *Java primitives*, are not object-oriented. When you declare a variable of a primitive data type, the storage for that variable is automati-cally allocated—no new operator and construction invocation required. The following code will work fine:

```
int anInt;
anInt = 1;
```

You can initialize the value of a vari-able of one of the basic data types as shown:

```
int anInt = 0;
```

Table 3.1: Java's Basic Data Types.

Basic Data Type	Description
Int	4-byte integer
Long	8-byte number
Float	4-byte floating-point number
Double	8-byte floating-point number
Char	2-byte Unicode to sup-port the character sets of all languages
Byte	1-byte raw value

Java has a couple of curious mathematical operators. The double plus, for in-stance, when specified after a variable whose type is a numerical primitive, incre-ments that variable by one; the double minus decrements it:

```
anInt++;
anInt--;
```

The RPG analogy to these mathematical operators employs the ADD or SUB op code with no factor one and the number one in factor two:

```
C                 ADD   1        anInt
C                 SUB   1        anInt
```

Another numerical operator is the plus equal:

```
anInt += 2;
```

This syntax adds two to the integer variable called ANINT. When you think about it, this syntax is very similar to RPG's ADD op code with no factor one:

```
C                 ADD   2        anInt
```

Most RPG programmers prefer the previous form of RPG's ADD operation to the form of the following, where the variable name in factor one is the same as the variable name in the result field:

```
C     anInt       ADD   2        anInt
```

Preference for the first form is common because with the latter form, at first glance, the programmer's instinct expects the variable name in factor one to be different from the variable name in the result field. The same confusion might happen with the following valid Java statement:

```
anInt = anInt + 2;
```

NUMERICAL JAVA CLASSES

Java also has a set of numerical classes, the names of which correspond to the data type of the numerical value that the class contains. Note too that the class name starts with an uppercase character and the name is fully spelled out:

- INTEGER
- LONG
- DOUBLE
- FLOAT
- BIGINTEGER
- BIGDECIMAL

Because these numerical data types are classes, if you declare a variable of one of the above classes, that variable must be constructed before it can be used. The first of the statements that follow declares a variable to be of the INTEGER class and then the next statement attempts to use that variable:

```
Integer anInt;
anInt.toString(); // runtime error, variable contains a null
reference
```

The Java application that contains the above two statements would receive a runtime error stating that the ANINT variable contains a null reference. The variable called ANINT is a handle to an INTEGER object. Before that handle is assigned a reference to an instance of an INTEGER object, its value is considered null (empty). The ANINT INTEGER variable can be set to reference an existing INTEGER object:

```
anInt = anExistingInteger;
```

The ANINT INTEGER variable can also be set to reference the INTEGER object that is created by calling the INTEGER class's constructor with Java's NEW operator:

```
anInt = new Integer(5);
```

However, once you construct an INTEGER (or LONG or FLOAT or DOUBLE) object, you can't change the numerical value of that object. Java's numerical classes are basically containers or wrappers around Java's primitive data types. Further, the value that the numerical classes contain is immutable—it can't be changed unless you convert the numerical value to its corresponding primitive and then re-create another numerical class using the primitive in the numerical class's constructor:

```
int i = anInt.intValue();
i +=4;
anInt = new Integer(i);
```

So why would you ever want to use Java's numerical classes when you can't do mathematical operations over them? First, many of the classes that are delivered as a standard part of Java have function interfaces that require numerical objects rather than primitives. Second, if you intend to send business objects that have numerical fields over the Internet, those fields need to be typed as a numerical class and not a Java primitive. Although you can get around that requirement, it entails the extra coding effort of implementing the serializable interface.

I follow a simple rule for numeric values: When designing a business class, never define the global fields of that class as Java primitives. Otherwise, go ahead and use the Java primitives.

FIXED DECIMAL ARITHMETIC

Java's BIGDECIMAL class, however, does have mathematical operations. It has functions called ADD, SUBTRACT, MULTIPLY, and DIVIDE as well as a number of other useful functions such as MIN, MAX, and SETSCALE. The BIGDECIMAL class became available in Java 1.1 to provide a numerical class that could handle fixed-point decimal arithmetic. Without the use of BIGDECIMAL, in Java 1.0, you had to use the FLOAT or DOUBLE classes or Java's float or double basic data types to hold your application's decimal data (e.g., monetary values). Floating-point numbers present a problem in that, even if they can hold decimal values, they have strange rounding behaviors that accountants and customers find unacceptable.

For business programming, proper fixed-point decimal arithmetic is a must; and, when you program with Java, that's enabled with the BIGDECIMAL class. When this book begins to cover AS/400 access in Section III, you'll see that IBM's Java Toolbox for the AS/400 converts DB2/400's zoned and packed numbers with BIGDECIMAL objects.

The BIGDECIMAL class has not one but *four* constructors. One of its constructors allows you to build a BIGDECIMAL object with a STRING, one with a DOUBLE, one with a BIGINTEGER (another class you'll learn about in a moment), and one with a BIGINTEGER and an INT. The following lists the prototypes for BIGDECIMAL's four constructors:

```
BigDecimal(String fixedDecNum)
BigDecimal(double longFloatNum)
BigDecimal(BigInteger realLongNum)
BigDecimal(BigInteger realLongNum,int decimalCount)
```

With four constructors at your disposal, you can use whichever one accepts the data type or class of a variable that you have at hand. The following examples show how you'd create BIGDECIMAL objects from a string value and then from a DOUBLE value:

```
BigDecimal money1 = new BigDecimal("128.95");
BigDecimal money2 = new BigDecimal(128.95);
```

The two remaining BIGDECIMAL constructors take a BIGINTEGER object for a parameter. The BIGINTEGER class was also introduced in Java 1.1 to accommodate very long integer numeric values that neither the INTEGER nor the DOUBLE class would support. The following code shows how you would create two BIGDECIMAL objects using a BIGINTEGER object:

```
BigInteger aBigInt = new BigInteger("325");
BigDecimal threeHundred25Bucks = new BigDecimal(aBigInt);
BigDecimal threeBucksAndaQuarter = new BigDecimal(aBigInt, 2);
```

Note that the second BIGDECIMAL constructor includes a parameter for you to specify the decimal precision.

BIGDECIMAL is superior to the other numeric classes (INTEGER, LONG, DOUBLE, and FLOAT) because it has ADD, SUBTRACT, MULTIPLY, and DIVIDE functions. BIGDECIMAL has to have functions for numeric operations so that the decimal numeric precision is maintained. However, the use of those functions is, at first, counterintuitive. The following example shows the straightforward construction of a BIGDECIMAL object followed by the use of BIGDECIMAL's ADD function:

```
BigDecimal cash = new BigDecimal(128.12);
cash.add(0.25);
```

You would think that the value of cash, after adding 25 cents to it, would be $128.37, but the value of cash is still $128.12. What happened to that quarter? The ADD function returned a BIGDECIMAL object with a value equal to the sum of $128.12 and $.25. To add to that cash variable, you have to assign the returned BIGDECIMAL object back to the cash variable:

```
cash = cash.add(0.25);
```

You might think that the behavior of the ADD function is odd but you probably agree that the use of BIGDECIMAL's DIVIDE function should not change the value of that numeric object. The following code computes the average purchase amount of the 29 customers that contributed to total sales of $2,572.98:

```
BigDecimal totalSales = new BigDecimal(2572.98);
BigDecimal customers = new BigDecimal(29);
BigDecimal avg =
totalSales.divide(customers, BigDecimal.ROUND_HALF_DOWN);
```

Notice that BIGDECIMAL's DIVIDE function forces you to make clear specifications for rounding. It's understandable that the DIVIDE function would not change the value of the TOTALSALES variable. You would, however, want to change a total purchase cost by the state sales tax, so the following code assigns the results of calculating the state sales tax back into the TOTALSALES variable:

```
BigDecimal totalSale = new BigDecimal(76.32);
BigDecimal stateSalesTax = new BigDecimal(7.25));
totalSale = totalSale.multiply(stateSalesTax);
```

STRING HANDLING

ILE RPG provides some powerful string-handling functions such as %REPLACE, %SUBST, and %SIZE. RPG III also has a strong set of string-handling operations such as SCAN, CAT, and SUBST. But Java's string-handling capabilities far surpass any that you will find in RPG. Java's string class is called STRING (with an uppercase S). The STRING class has an extremely long list of functions that operate on the string values of STRING objects. The following code creates two STRINGS and then concatenates them to create a third:

```
String first  = new String("First");
String second = new String("Second");
String firstAndSecond = first + second;
```

Notice the use of the plus sign as the concatenation operator. The Java language added support for the plus symbol as the concatenate operator because strings are heavily used. For all other string operations, however, you'll have to use one of the STRING class functions that are listed in Table 3.2.

Table 3.2: String Manipulation Functions for Java's String Class. (Part 1 of 3)

Function	Description
charAt(int)	Returns the character at the specified index.
compareTo(String)	Compares two strings lexicographically.
concat(String)	Concatenates the specified string to the end of this string.
copyValueOf(char[ ])	Returns a string that is equivalent to the specified character array.
CopyValueOf(char[ ], int, int)	Returns a string that is equivalent to the specified character array.
endsWith(String)	Tests if this string ends with the specified suffix.
equals(Object)	Compares this string to the specified object.
equalsIgnoreCase(String)	Compares this string to another object.
getBytes()	Converts this string into bytes according to the platform's default character encoding, storing the result in a new byte array.
GetBytes(int, int, byte[ ], int)	Copies characters from this string into the destination byte array. Deprecated.
getBytes(String)	Converts this string into bytes according to the specified character encoding, storing the result in a new byte array.
getChars(int, int, char[ ], int)	Copies characters from this string into the destination character array.
hashCode()	Returns a hashcode for this string.
indexOf(int)	Returns the index within this string of the first occurrence of the specified character.
indexOf(int, int)	Returns the index within this string of the first occurrence of the specified character, starting the search at the specified index.
indexOf(String)	Returns the index within this string of the first occurrence of the specified substring.
IndexOf(String, int)	Returns the index within this string of the first occurrence of the specified substring, starting at the specified index.
intern()	Returns a canonical representation for the string object.
lastIndexOf(int)	Returns the index within this string of the last occurrence of the specified character.

Table 3.2: String Manipulation Functions for Java's String Class. (Part 2 of 3)

Function	Description
LastIndexOf(int, int)	Returns the index within this string of the last occurrence of the specified character, searching backward starting at the specified index.
lastIndexOf(String)	Returns the index within this string of the rightmost occurrence of the specified substring.
LastIndexOf(String, int)	Returns the index within this string of the last occurrence of the specified substring.
length()	Returns the length of this string.
RegionMatches(boolean, int, String, int, int)	Tests if two string regions are equal.
RegionMatches(int, String, int, int)	Tests if two string regions are equal.
Replace(char, char)	Returns a new string resulting from replacing all occurrences of oldChar in this string with newChar.
startsWith(String)	Tests if this string starts with the specified prefix.
StartsWith(String, int)	Tests if this string starts with the specified prefix.
substring(int)	Returns a new string that is a substring of this string.
substring(int, int)	Returns a new string that is a substring of this string.
toCharArray()	Converts this string to a new character array.
toLowerCase()	Converts this string to lowercase.
toLowerCase(Locale)	Converts all of the characters in this string to lowercase using the rules of the given locale.
toString()	This object (which is already a string!) is itself returned.
toUpperCase()	Converts this string to uppercase.
toUpperCase(Locale)	Converts all of the characters in this string to uppercase using the rules of the given locale.
trim()	Removes white space from both ends of this string.
valueOf(char)	Returns the string representation of the char argument.

Table 3.2: String Manipulation Functions for Java's String Class. (Part 3 of 3)	
Function	**Description**
ValueOf(char[ ])	Returns the string representation of the char array argument.
ValueOf(char[ ], int, int)	Returns the string representation of a specific subarray of the char array argument.
valueOf(double)	Returns the string representation of the double argument.
valueOf(float)	Returns the string representation of the float argument.
valueOf(int)	Returns the string representation of the int argument.
valueOf(long)	Returns the string representation of the long argument.
valueOf(Object)	Returns the string representation of the object argument.

DEFAULT OUTPUT

The Java programming language has support for simple printing to what is known as the default output device. When running a Java application in a batch job on the AS/400, for instance, the default output device is the job log. When running a Java application in a DOS window on your Microsoft Windows 95 machine, the default output device is the DOS window itself. When running a Java application from a Java Integrated Development Environment (IDE) such as Inprise's JBuilder or IBM's VisualAge for Java, the default output device is a separate window, as shown in Figures 3.9 and 3.10.

If you want to change the default output device, you can easily redirect output to a file. To print to Java's default output device, you simply use the following syntax:

```
System.out.println(String);
```

To print my name, for instance, I would simply place "Don Denoncourt" inside the parentheses in the above statement. But since the print line function of SYSTEM.OUT accepts any string, I can also pass it a STRING variable, as shown:

```
String name = new String("Don Denoncourt");
System.out.println(name);
```

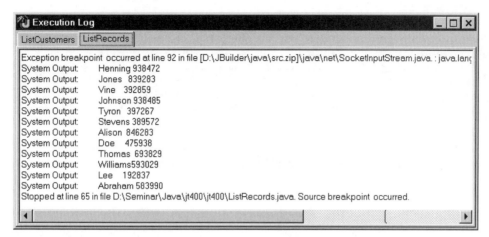

Figure 3.9: The default output device for Inprise's JBuilder is its EXECUTION LOG window.

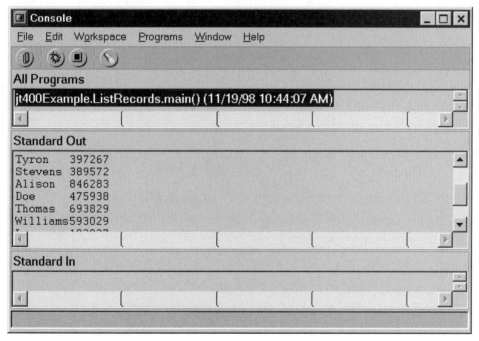

Figure 3.10: IBM's VisualAge for Java's default output device is its CONSOLE window.

Further, with the use of the plus concatenation operator and the STRING class's ability to convert the values of various object types to their string representation, you can dynamically build an output line:

```
int i = 28;
System.out.println("The value of " + "i plus 2 is: " + (i+2));
The resulting output would be as follows:The value of i plus 2 is:
30
```

Notice, however, the use of the inner parentheses to force the value contained within the variable *i* to be increased by two before the printing operation took place.

DYNAMIC ARRAYS

Earlier you read that Java arrays, like RPG arrays, are statically sized. However, the Java class called VECTOR is basically a dynamic array because you can add and remove elements from a VECTOR object at will. Table 3.3 shows all the functions of the VECTOR class.

An example of the use of vectors is shown in the Java code snippet in Figure 3.11. It begins by creating an array of 10 integers and a vector. The first FOR loop fills each of the INTEGER array elements with the integer value of the array index and the loop then adds the array element to the VECTOROFINTEGERS. The code finishes by listing all the entries of the vector.

```
Integer arrayOfIntegers[] = new Integer[10];
Vector vectorOfIntegers = new Vector();
for (int element = 0; element < arrayOfIntegers.length;
element++)
{
arrayOfIntegers[element] = new Integer(element);
    vectorOfIntegers.addElement(arrayOfIntegers[element]);
}
for (int entry = 0; entry < vectorOfIntegers.size(); entry++)
{
System.out.println(vectorOfIntegers.elementAt(entry));
}
```

Figure 3.11: Java's VECTOR class supports dynamically sizable arrays complete with insert and delete functions.

Table 3.3: Functions of the Vector Class. (Part 1 of 2)

Function	Description
Vector()	Constructs an empty vector.
Vector(int)	Constructs an empty vector with the specified initial capacity.
Vector(int, int)	Constructs an empty vector with the specified initial capacity and capacity increment.
addElement(Object)	Adds the specified component to the end of this vector, increasing its size by one.
capacity()	Returns the current capacity of this vector.
clone()	Returns a clone of this vector.
contains(Object)	Tests if the specified object is a component in this vector.
CopyInto(Object[ ])	Copies the components of this vector into the specified array.
elementAt(int)	Returns the component at the specified index.
elements()	Returns an enumeration of the components of this vector.
ensureCapacity(int)	Increases the capacity of this vector, if necessary, to ensure that it can hold at least the number of components specified by the minimum capacity argument.
firstElement()	Returns the first component of this vector.
indexOf(Object)	Searches for the first occurrence of the given argument, testing for equality using the equals method.
IndexOf(Object, int)	Searches for the first occurrence of the given argument, beginning the search at the specified index, and testing for equality using the equals method.
InsertElementAt(Object, int)	Inserts the specified object as a component in this vector at the specified index.
isEmpty()	Tests if this vector has no components.
lastElement()	Returns the last component of the vector.
lastIndexOf(Object)	Returns the index of the last occurrence of the specified object in this vector.
LastIndexOf(Object, int)	Searches backwards for the specified object, starting from the specified index, and returns an index to it.

Table 3.3: Functions of the Vector Class. (Part 2 of 2)

Function	Description
removeAllElements()	Removes all components from this vector and sets its size to zero.
removeElement(Object)	Removes the first occurrence of the argument from this vector.
removeElementAt(int)	Deletes the component at the specified index.
SetElementAt(Object, int)	Sets the component at the specified index of this vector to be the specified object.
setSize(int)	Sets the size of this vector.
size()	Returns the number of components in this vector.
toString()	Returns a string representation of this vector.
trimToSize()	Trims the capacity of this vector to be the vector's current size.

JAVA SYNTAX SUMMARY

This chapter quickly summarized the basic syntax of Java. It covered how to control the flow of Java functions with while and do/while constructs, the FOR loop, and the SWITCH statements. It listed the basic data types of Java as well as the numerical classes. The chapter detailed how to create arrays and, because Java arrays are statically sized, how to use the dynamic array capability of the VECTOR class. It further discussed the BIGDECIMAL class for fixed-point decimal values that AS/400 programmers have been storing in DB2/400 as packed and zoned numbers. It also covered the STRING class and provided a quick overview of printing to the default output device.

4

Java Programming Models:

Applets, Applications, and Servlets

Java has three basic programming models: applets, applications, and servlets. Java applets, or small applications that are run from within the context of a Web browser, actually propelled Java to fame. Applets contribute to the concept of thin-client strategy because they reside on the server and are dynamically downloaded to browsing clients. Java applications, on the other hand, more closely resemble traditional applications in that they are distributed through more traditional channels such as diskette distribution and FTP downloads. Java servlets, the third Java programming model, can be thought of as the opposite of Java applets because servlets run in the context of a Web server rather than a Web browser. This chapter introduces you to these three Java programming models so that you will understand which model best fits your company's requirements.

Applets

When a Java applet is downloaded to a Web browser, as shown in Figure 4.1, it executes from that browser's *sandbox*. The idea behind the sandbox is that the Java applet *plays* within the constraints of this sandbox so as not to infect the lo-

49

cal machine with viruses. As a further precaution, Java applets cannot perform any file I/O to the client Web browser's machine. The only machine to which an applet can perform file I/O is the host machine that originally served that applet.

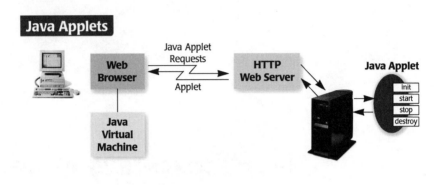

Figure 4.1: Java applets are downloaded from the Web server to remote Web browsers.

Java has a package of classes called java.applet. A class called APPLET within that package has four milestone functions: initialize (INIT), START, STOP, and DESTROY. When you develop a Java applet, you expand on the core APPLET class from the java.applet package. Table 4-1 shows all the functions of the APPLET class.

For your applet to be executed from a Web browser, it must implement its own version of the INIT function. The Web browser invokes the milestone functions of an applet after downloading it from the server and, if your applet doesn't have a custom INIT function, the APPLET class's version of INIT will be invoked—and won't do anything. You need to code your applet so that when the Web browser invokes the INIT function, your applet can perform program initialization such as opening a DB2/400 file and presenting a GUI to the applet user.

The Web browser invokes your applet's version of the start function, if you have coded one, each time the window of your applet becomes the active window. The Web browser invokes your applet's stop function when its window becomes in-active. You might, for instance, code a start function to begin animation and then code a stop function to end the complex calculations and screen painting required for animation when the applet is no longer the active window. The Web browser invokes your applet's destroy function before the applet is unloaded from the browser. Typically, you would code a destroy function to close files or otherwise free resources allocated during the life of the applet.

Table 4.1: Functions Associated with Java's Applet class. (Part 1 of 2)

Four milestone functions often reimplemented in custom applets:

init()	Called by the browser or applet viewer to inform this applet that it has been loaded into the system.
start()	Called by the browser or applet viewer to inform this applet that it should start its execution.
stop()	Called by the browser or applet viewer to inform this applet that it should stop its execution.
destroy()	Called by the browser or applet viewer to inform this applet that it is being reclaimed and that it should destroy any resources that it has allocated.

Various other functions useful to custom applets:

getAppletContext()	Determines this applet's context, which allows the applet to query and affect the environment in which it runs.
getAppletInfo()	Returns information about this applet.
getAudioClip(URL)	Returns the audio clip object specified by the URL argument.
getAudioClip(URL, String)	Returns the audio clip object specified by the URL and name arguments.
getCodeBase()	Gets the base URL.
getDocumentBase()	Gets the document URL.
getImage(URL)	Returns an image object that can then be painted on the screen.
GetImage(URL, String)	Returns an image object that can then be painted on the screen.
getLocale()	Gets the locale for the applet, if it has been set.
getParameter(String)	Returns the value of the named parameter in the HTML tag.
getParameterInfo()	Returns information about the parameters that are understood by this applet.

Table 4.1: Functions Associated with Java's Applet class. (Part 2 of 2)

Various other functions useful to custom applets, *continued*

isActive()	Determines if this applet is active.
play(URL)	Plays the audio clip at the specified absolute URL.
Play(URL, String)	Plays the audio clip, given the URL and a specifier that is relative to it.
resize(Dimension)	Requests that this applet be resized.
Resize(int, int)	Requests that this applet be resized.
setStub(AppletStub)	Sets this applet's stub.
showStatus(String)	Requests that the argument string be displayed in the status window.

Many applets only provide an implementation for the INIT function. Figure 4.2 shows the code for a Java applet that simply presents a To Do List GUI. The INIT function of TODOAPPLET creates three GUI components: a button, a text box, and a list box. When the user selects the ADD button, the applet gets the text that the user entered into the text field and adds it as an element to the list box.

```
import java.applet.*;
import java.awt.*;
import java.awt.event.*;
public class ToDoApplet extends Applet {
    Button add;
    TextField text;
    List toDoList;

    public void init() {
        text = new TextField(20);
        add = new Button("add");
        toDoList = new List();
```

Figure 4.2: The TODOLIST applet implements its own INIT function to present a To Do List GUI. (Part 1 of 2)

```
        add(new Label("Note: "));
        add(text);
        add(add);
        add(new Label ("To Do List:"));
        add(toDoList);

        add.addActionListener( new ActionListener() {
            public void actionPerformed(ActionEvent e) {
                toDoList.add(text.getText());
        }});
    }
}
```

Figure 4.2: The TODOLIST applet implements its own INIT function to present a To Do List GUI. (Part 2 of 2)

Figure 4.3 shows the resulting GUI in Internet Explorer. GUI programming will be covered in detail in Section V of this book.

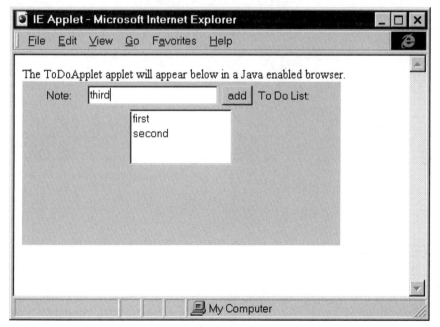

Figure 4.3: Internet Explorer invokes the TODOAPPLET applet's INIT function to be able to present a To Do List GUI.

INVOKING AN APPLET

How does a browser know to load an applet? Hypertext Markup Language (HTML) source files drive Web browsers. HTML is a simple language constructed with sets of tags. Figure 4.4 shows the HTML file used to present the GUI shown in Figure 4.3. Each new HTML tag in the file has a corresponding tag that begins with a slash. For instance, the complete HTML file of Figure 4.3 is enclosed within the tag pair of <html> and </html>.

The applet tag is used to inform the Web browser to run an applet. The CODE clause of the applet tag informs the browser of the name of the applet class. The WIDTH and HEIGHT clauses of the applet tag are used to tell the browser the size of the applet window.

```
<HTML>
<TITLE>To Do List Applet</TITLE>
<BODY>
The ToDoApplet applet will appear below in a Java enabled
browser.

<APPLET
 CODE="ToDoApplet.class"
 WIDTH=400 HEIGHT=200>
</APPLET>
</BODY></HTML>
```

Figure 4.4: The TODOAPPLET.HTML HTML file contains an applet tag that informs the Web browser to run an applet.

AS/400 APPLET SERVING

Java applets are stored on the Integrated File System (IFS) of your AS/400. To make your applets available from your AS/400's Web server, you must copy the Java class file and the HTML file from your PC-based Java development environment to a directory of your AS/400's IFS. You can use File Transfer Protocol (FTP) or, if you have Client Access, you can simply use the drag-and-drop feature of Windows Explorer.

Once the Java class and HTML source files are in the IFS, you need to set authorities for both the files and the directory of those files. To set those authorities, you can use the Work with Authority (WRKAUT) panel (which you obtain by selecting option 9 from the Work with Object Links [WRKLNK] panel) or you can directly enter the information with the Change Authority (CHGAUT) command. You'll need to give authority to the two default browser profiles of QTMHHTTP and QTMHHTP1 for both the HTML and the Java class files:

```
CHGAUT OBJ('/html/ToDoApplet.html') USER(QTMHHTTP) DTAAUT(*R)
CHGAUT OBJ('/html/ToDoApplet.html') USER(QTMHHTP1) DTAAUT(*R)
CHGAUT OBJ('/html/ToDoApplet.class') USER(QTMHHTTP) DTAAUT(*R)
CHGAUT OBJ('/html/ToDoApplet.class') USER(QTMHHTP1) DTAAUT(*R)
```

Also, your AS/400's HTTP server configuration file must contain a *pass directive* specifying the IFS directory that contains the HTML file. The Work with HTTP Configuration (WRKHTTPCFG) command displays a configuration file editor through which you can add the pass directive. The following pass directive enables the IFS path called HTML in the server configuration file:

```
Pass /html/*
```

Any modifications you make to the HTTP server configuration file take effect only after you restart the server:

```
STRTCPSVR SERVER(*HTTP) RESTART(*HTTP)+ HTTPSVR(DENONCOURT)
```

Finally– with the applet compiled and supporting HTML created; with the class and HTML files copied to the IFS; with the class's and HTML file's security set; and with the IFS path in a pass directive on your AS/400's Web server's configuration file—Web-browsing users can access the applet via the following syntax:

```
http://AS400Domain/html/ToDoApplet.html
```

JAVA APPLICATIONS

The incredible fervor that surrounded applets arose primarily because applets solved the problem of software distribution. Of course, AS/400 applications didn't suffer from a software distribution problem since 5250 terminals provided the user interface to application programs that actually ran on the AS/400. PC software, however, has created a real problem in terms of distribution and maintenance.

Applets elegantly solve that problem but nevertheless have fallen into disfavor due to bandwidth constraints. It takes time for a Web browser to download an applet from the server; the more robust and powerful the application is, the longer it takes to download. As with standard PC-based applications, Java applications must be installed on the PC. However, Java applications are not executable like most PC applications; they are interpreted and executed from a Java Virtual Machine (JVM). So, a Java applet runs from the context of a Web browser and a Java application runs from the context of a JVM.

Any hardware platform that wants to support Java develops a JVM. The JVM is implemented with the native architecture and language of each platform, but all of them are able to execute compiled Java classes. Furthermore, these machine-specific JVMs are able to execute Java classes regardless of where they were compiled. This means that you can develop a Java class with code that is in a .JAVA source file, compile it on your PC to a .CLASS file, copy that executable .CLASS file (also known as Java byte code) to the IFS of your AS/400, and execute it without recompilation.

That ability of the JVMs of various platforms to execute Java classes from any source represents one of the great strengths of Java. That's one of the reasons why Java is already a successful language. Powerful application software is being made available for the AS/400 on almost a daily basis simply because the AS/400 has a JVM. Many traditional C++ shops have switched to Java because it solves many of the cross-platform problems that they have had with C++ and C. Further, many traditional RPG-based application software providers are also switching to Java because it enables them to expand their market beyond the AS/400.

Figure 4.5 shows an application version of the To Do List that was presented earlier as an applet. Just as the Web browser automatically calls the INIT function to get an applet started, the JVM automatically calls a Java application's (here, TODOAPPLICATION's) MAIN function. To start the JVM and direct it to run a Java application, you use the JAVA command followed by the name of the Java class:

```
java ToDoApplication
import java.awt.*;
import java.awt.event.*;

public class ToDoApplication extends Frame {
    Button add;
    TextField text;
    List toDoList;

    public static void main(String[] pList) {
        ToDoApplication myApp = new ToDoApplication();
         myApp.show();
    }

    ToDoApplication () {
        super("To Do Application");
        setLayout(new FlowLayout());
        text = new TextField(20);
        add = new Button("add");
        toDoList = new List();
        add(new Label("Note: "));
        add(text);
        add(add);
        add(new Label ("To Do List:"));
        add(toDoList);

        add.addActionListener( new ActionListener() {
            public void actionPerformed(ActionEvent e) {
                toDoList.add(text.getText());
        }});
        addWindowListener( new WindowAdapter() {
            public void windowClosing(WindowEvent e) {
            System.exit(0);
        }});

    }
}
```

Figure 4.5: A Java application bootstraps itself from its MAIN function.

Notice that the MAIN function of the TODOAPPLICATION class creates an object whose data type is that of the application itself. In accordance with standard Java coding technique, the MAIN function bootstraps the application by creating an object of its own class type. The NEW operator invokes the constructor of the

TODOAPPLICATION where all of the setup for the application GUI is performed. The TODOAPPLICATION's GUI is shown in Figure 4.6.

The Java executable that starts the JVM and executes a Java application is available for free from both Sun and Microsoft either as a Java Development Kit (JDK) or a Java Runtime Environment (JRE). The JRE contains only those tools necessary to execute a Java application, whereas the JDK contains the tools used to run *and* develop Java applications. The AS/400's JVM comes as a free program product: 5769-JV1 AS/400 Developer Kit for Java.

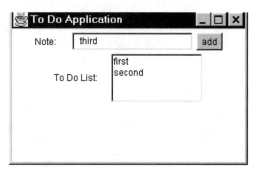

Figure 4.6: The JVM automatically invokes a Java application's MAIN function.

SERVLETS

Java servlets are to the Web server what applets are to the client. A servlet runs in the context of a Web server (see Figure 4.7) whereas applets run in the context of a Web browser. The Java servlet API was introduced formally at the JavaOne conference in San Francisco in April of 1998; yet, servlets are already in wide use. Why the sudden acceptance and use of such a new programming model? Servlets answered a real need.

Companies initially set up Web sites to deliver static information they stored in HTML files on the server's platform. For the most part, the first Web sites for many companies consisted merely of online marketing brochures. But many companies quickly saw the need for dynamic information. Federal Express's Web site, for instance, allows you to enter your tracking number to see where your package is. To enable the delivery of dynamic data, Web servers were extended with a feature called Common Gateway Interface (CGI). CGI allows you to use a legacy programming language such as RPG to respond to user queries from remote browsers by dynamically generating HTML files.

You can think of servlets as a CGI program written in Java, and you'd almost be correct in that thought. You would, however, be discounting the inherent power

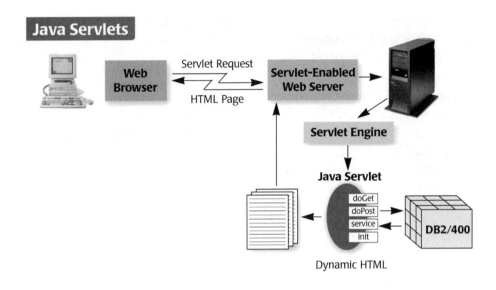

Figure 4.7: Servlets execute in the JVM of the Web server to dynamically construct HTML.

of object-oriented programming, the cross-platform capabilities of Java, and the efficiency of Web servers' integrated support for the Java servlet API. The implementation of CGI was a hack, a quickly developed kludge to solve the need for dynamic data. The Java servlet API, on the other hand, is a well-designed strategy for disseminating dynamic information across the Internet.

Some say the CGI is like providing drinking water for a city with one bucket—it used to work a couple of hundred years ago but no more. Each browser requires that the CGI program be reloaded, which means resolving the location of the program, allocating resources, and opening files. Java servlets, on the other hand, were designed to maintain state between requests.

The Web server requires a JVM to run servlets, just as a Web browser requires a JVM to run applets. V4R3 of OS/400 is the first release to support servlets, and the Web server that IBM bundles with OS/400 provides full support for servlets. Further, IBM's WebSphere application server (which performs more advanced application-serving features than does IBM's HTTP server) now comes bundled with OS/400 V4R4. Because of the availability of such powerful and yet free tools combined with the fact that the Java servlet API is designed to make servlets easy to use and implement, the use of servlets bears consideration for the deployment of AS/400 host-based Java applications.

Because the servlet-programming model has been so well received, a whole new crop of Web servers has been optimized for servlets. These new servers allow you to take advantage of Enterprise JavaBeans, Remote Method Invocation (RMI), and Common Object Request Broker Architecture (CORBA). Known as Web application servers, this new breed of Web servers enables the delivery of interactive business applications across the Internet. If you want a fast and robust Internet application, servlets—the comparative newcomer to the world of Java programming models—are your answer.

DISTRIBUTED OBJECTS

If the world has moved to object-oriented programming, why bother converting a Java object into HTML as a protocol? The list of the functions associated with a class is essentially a protocol. In another Java programming model, you use the API of your classes as the protocol for distributing objects across the Internet. There are three strategies for the Internet distribution of objects:

- DCOM—Microsoft's Distributed Common Object Model

- RMI—Sun's Java language's Remote Method Invocation

- CORBA—Object Management Group's (OMG's) Common Object Request Broker Architecture

Although the implementations of these three distributed-object communications strategies vary considerably, the basic concepts are the same: You develop your host application's interfaces using your language of choice, then you use a tool that creates all of the sockets programs required to handle the low-level TCP/IP Internet communications. Your application's host API is then accessible from remote applications—as if the host application were local to the remote machine (see Figure 4.8).

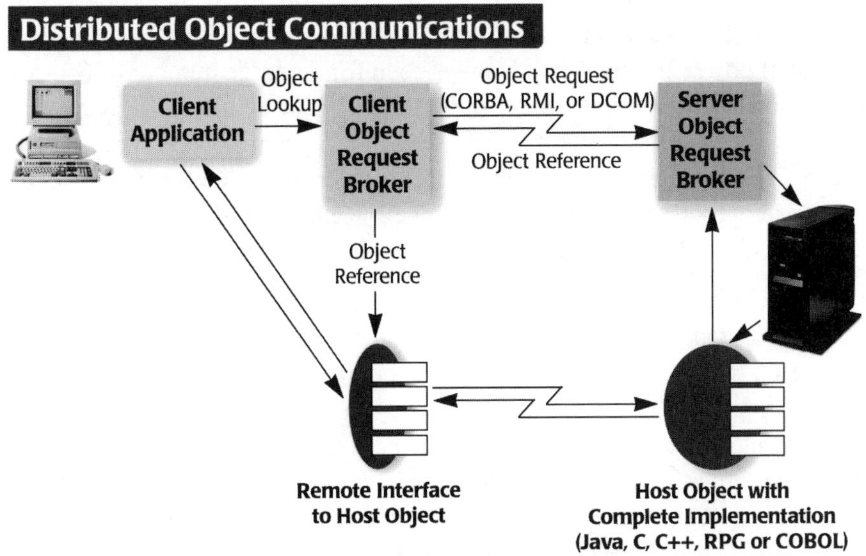

Distributed Object Communications

Object Lookup

Client Application

Object Request (CORBA, RMI, or DCOM)

Client Object Request Broker

Object Reference

Server Object Request Broker

Object Reference

Remote Interface to Host Object

Host Object with Complete Implementation (Java, C, C++, RPG or COBOL)

Figure 4.8: Java objects can communicate over the Internet using CORBA, RMI, or DCOM.

Without a distributed-object strategy, your remote applications would have to contain all of the code to maintain the application's data (with DB2/400) and to handle the low-level communications. With a distributed-object strategy, you develop the base components of your applications to remain on the AS/400. Then, you develop your application's remote programs with code that merely provides a GUI. Those remote GUI programs seamlessly access the host API after registering with a DCOM, RMI, or CORBA utility, passing to it the host machine's URL. Basically, your remote programs are *thin* clients with the *fat* server code remaining on the host. Isn't that what client/server is all about anyway?

Although similar in concept, the three models of distributed-object communications differ significantly in the way they operate. RMI, the simplest of the three, is a Java-to-Java strategy and, as such, is language dependent. Microsoft's DCOM is language independent; but even if, as rumored, an AS/400 DCOM is being developed, DCOM is still platform dependent. CORBA, also language independent, is truly *platform* independent as well.

CORBA is a set of standards for the implementation of Object Request Brokers (ORBs) by third-party vendors. Its architecture is designed by the OMG, a consortium of powerful, important businessmen from a large number of companies. In the short-term future, CORBA and RMI will have an increasingly closer relationship: The low-level protocol for CORBA has always been Internet Inter-ORB Protocol (IIOP, where ORB is Object Request Broker), and Sun has recently decided to adopt this protocol for RMI as well. Right now, this means little; but in the future, CORBA ORBs may be able to broker RMI requests and vice versa.

With distributed-object computing, the code base of all but the application GUI remains on the host. You take full advantage of your object-oriented application by extending it to the Web. Your Internet applications are then more scalable than with other Internet strategies. However, DCOM, RMI, and CORBA implementations quickly become complex; even the simplicity of Java's RMI becomes complex in actual deployment. As mentioned in the servlets discussion, a new breed of application servers is now being designed to work with all three of these distributed-object strategies to help manage some of their complexities of deployment. Also, solid implementations of the new Enterprise JavaBeans specification will go far in reducing the complexities of distributed-object communications.

APPLETS, APPLICATIONS, OR SERVLETS?

So what's it to be: applets, applications, or servlets? The remainder of this book concentrates on applications, but only because Java applications are easier to load and test than are applets or servlets.

Java applications might answer your needs so long as you don't mind taking control of application software distribution. Certain software products (Marimba, for example) are available that use the Internet to handle the distribution of Java applications. Java applets might be the answer if you want to enable Internet applications that provide a powerful GUI. However, download times can present a real issue with applets unless your clients have high-speed connections. Of course, you can always develop your applets to use minimal resources. If you don't mind limiting your users to the user interface of HTML, then servlets offer a powerful alternative to applets or applications. Optionally, you can use applets for a GUI front-end that communicates with servlets for the business-logic back-end—thus creating a lightweight GUI client and a heavyweight application server.

With a little extra work up front, the use of one of the three distributed-object technologies can prove very fruitful. The common strategy with all these programming models is Java and object-oriented programming. The purpose of this book is to introduce you to object-oriented strategies for Java applications; the strategies presented work well regardless of the programming model that you select.

SECTION II

~

OBJECT-ORIENTED DESIGN

5

OBJECT-ORIENTED PROGRAMMING WITH JAVA

What makes Java so hot? The source of that heat is object-oriented programming—not just a feature of Java but its basic foundation. Programmers can achieve the long-term benefits of writing business applications in Java only through sound, object-oriented design. This section of the book is designed to teach Java programming from the context of object-oriented design. This chapter in particular introduces the Unified Modeling Language (UML) for use as the standard graphical notation for object modeling. The chapter illustrates the use of UML through a sample purchase order application, which is explained from object design to Java code.

OBJECT-ORIENTED ANALYSIS—USE CASES

Just like structured applications, an object-oriented project begins with analysis and then moves into design. The first phase of object-oriented analysis involves the development of *use cases*. A use case is simply a written summary of a typical interaction between a user and a computer system to perform a discrete business task. An example of a use case follows:

> The order processor will search for the customer in the system first using the caller ID, as shown on the phone LCD. If the customer information is not found, the order processor will request the customer's number. If the customer does not know his number, the customer's company name will be used. If the customer information is still not found, the order processor will assume that the customer is not in the database and will then add that customer to the system.

These use cases are developed with the collaborative efforts of a domain expert—a user who is an expert in the business area of the proposed application—and an object-oriented programming and design expert. Initially, the object-oriented design team develops enough of these use cases to provide an overview into the scope of the application. Use cases should provide a clear understanding of what the user expects from the application. Often, the use cases become bargaining chips ("I can get the application done two weeks earlier if I drop this caller ID thing and we just force the customer to know his number"). And, as always, use cases enforce the idea of "getting it in writing."

OBJECT DISCOVERY

Armed with use cases to provide project scope, the application designer works closely with a domain expert to model the world (or at least their little part of it) by discovering the business objects that form the vocabulary of the problem domain (the application). The nouns of a use case suggest business objects and the verbs represent object responsibilities or behaviors.

A business object is nothing more than a business entity. As a legacy application programmer, you might ask, "Isn't this process of discovering business objects the same as the first step of relational database design?" Yes, the two processes are similar. The identification of business entities makes up a major part of both structured and object-oriented analysis. In the design phase, both object-oriented and structured methods define the attributes of entities and chart the relationships between those entities. But with object-oriented design, an entity's *behavior* as well as its attributes are designed to be an integral part of that entity.

Take a moment to look at the object model of Figure 5.1. Then look at the entity relation chart in Figure 5.2. Both of these graphics model the same business entities except for a few extra objects in the model of Figure 5.1—specifically, CONSUMER and COMPANY. Object-oriented analysis drills down further in the decomposition of entities by classifying them into hierarchies (more on that later). For now, understand that the identification of objects is the hardest part of object-oriented analysis and design. A well-designed object model is elegantly intuitive but, as Descartes once said, "The discovery of an order is no easy task. Yet, once the order has been discovered, there is no difficulty at all knowing it." To help clarify objects, you need a graphical design aid, which is where UML comes into play.

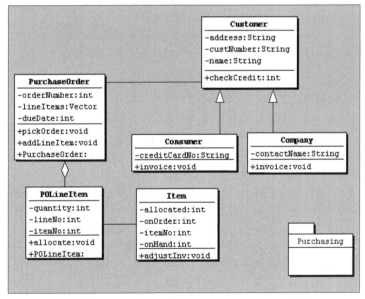

Figure 5.1: The purchasing application's object model uses UML to chart the collaboration among objects.

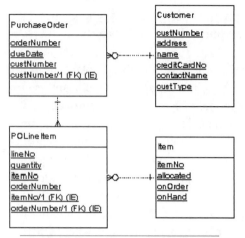

Figure 5.2: The purchasing application's ERD chart graphs the relationships and dependencies between files.

The object model of Figure 5.1 uses the notation specified by UML. For the past decade, each of the half-dozen leaders in the object-oriented programming industry had its own published design methodologies, complete with dissimilar notations. In 1997, three of them, Booch, Jacobson, and Rumbaugh (collectively known as "the three amigos"), got together and collaborated on a standard graphical notation—UML. The notation of UML is to be used to graphically express object-oriented designs. In the short time that UML has been available, the industry has already widely embraced it as the standard for object modeling. (For a complete description of UML, visit www.rational.com; for the shareware version of the UML utility used for this book, visit www.oi.com. Also recommended is the book *UML Distilled* by Fowler.)

THE PURCHASING PROBLEM DOMAIN

The purchasing application's UML in Figure 5.1 uses boxes to represent business entities or objects. Each object box has three sections. The top identifies the object, the middle lists the attributes of the object, and the bottom shows the operations (also called behaviors) associated with that object. The PURCHASEORDER object, for instance, has order number, line items, and due date attributes along with operations to add line items to the order and to allocate inventory for the order. It also has an operation with the same name as the object itself— PURCHASEORDER. Special operations such as these, known as *constructors*, are used to create an object and then set that object's initial state.

DESIGN WITH CLASS

A *class* is a set of objects that share a common structure and a common behavior. The Java implementation for the class of PURCHASEORDER objects is shown in Figure 5.3. The PURCHASEORDER class is the Java code designed to hold the attributes and behaviors of purchase orders. This Java class contains ORDERNUM-BER and DUEDATE, the attributes that are in the UML object model of Figure 5.1. Two other attributes—LINEITEMS and CUSTOMER—are defined in the class but are not explicitly defined in the UML. Those attributes relate the PURCHASE ORDER object to other objects—POLINEITEM and CUSTOMER. The UML graphically portrays these relationships with links to the other objects. Adding these objects as data members to the attribute section of the object box would be redundant and would also clutter up the object model during the initial iterations of object-oriented design.

```java
import java.util.Vector;

public class PurchaseOrder {
  // attributes (a.k.a. fields or class variables):
  private int orderNumber;
  private Vector lineItems;
  private int dueDate;
  private Customer customer;

  // operations (a.k.a. functions or methods):
  public void allocate(){
    for (int i = 0; i < lineItems.size(); i++) {
      POLineItem lineItem = (POLineItem)lineItems.elementAt(i);
      lineItem.allocate();
    }
  }
  public void addLineItem(int itemNo, int qty){
    POLineItem lineItem = new POLineItem(itemNo, qty);
    lineItems.addElement(lineItem);
  }
  // constructor function
  public PurchaseOrder(int due, Customer custNo){
    // set state of this PO object
    dueDate = due;
    customer = custNo;
    // create (instantiate) a dynamic array to
    // hold POLineItems
    lineItems = new Vector();
  }
}
```

Figure 5.3: The purchasing application's object model is implemented as Java classes. (Part 1 of 2)

```
public class POLineItem {  private int quantity;
   private int lineNo;
   private int itemNo;
   private static int lastLineNo = 0;
   Item item;
   public void allocate(){
     item.allocate();
   }
   public POLineItem(int itemNo, int qty){
   }
}

public class Item {
   private int itemNo;
   private int allocated;
   private int onOrder;
   private int onHand;

   public void allocate(){/*code */}
   public void adjustInv(int amount){/*code */}
}

public class Customer {
   private String address;
   private String custNumber;
   private String name;

   public int checkCredit(){
     return 10000;
   }
}

public class Consumer extends Customer {
   private String creditCardNo;
   public void invoice() {/*code */}
}

public class Company extends Customer {
   private String contactName;
   public void invoice(){/*code */}
}
```

Figure 5.3: The purchasing application's object model is implemented as Java classes. (Part 2 of 2)

Notice the diamond at the top of the link from PURCHASEORDER to POLINEITEM in Figure 5.1. The diamond represents aggregation; you have multiple line items for a purchase order. That's why, in the Java class code, the name of the array of POLINEITEMS (as represented with the Java dynamic array data type, VECTOR) is plural.

BEHAVIORAL RELATIONSHIPS

Let's compare the object model's PURCHASEORDER to POLINEITEM and CUSTOMER relationships (Figure 5.1) with the entity relation chart (Figure 5.2). The attributes of the PURCHASEORDER entity are represented with data fields of a record format in Figure 5.2. The CUSTNUMBER field of PURCHASEORDER is tagged as a foreign key to show the dependency to the CUSTOMER entity. The PURCHASEORDER entity of the entity relation chart has no POLINEITEMS array as the UML did—that is handled with the relational database design. The POLINEITEM entity contains the ORDERNUMBER foreign key to relate each line item to a specific purchase order.

The UML and the entity relation diagrams appear quite similar. They differ primarily in that the object model encapsulates an entity's behavior to an object. Therein lies the added value of object-oriented programming—the ability to encapsulate the definition of the procedures that manipulate that state of an entity within the same discrete storage location as its data.

In the UML diagram, the third section of an object box contains the operations of that object. These operations are the names of functions that will be defined in a Java class with the code that implements the computer simulation of the behaviors of an object. The Java class code of Figure 5.3 shows the function definitions for the operations of a purchase order: ALLOCATE, ADDLINEITEM, and PURCHASE ORDER. These functions are implemented to accept specific external parameters and then provide the object's behavioral code between the function's curly braces.

Unlike RPG and COBOL, Java uses no global variables. The functions that constitute a class have access only to those fields, those data members, those attributes (these three terms all mean the same thing) that are a part of that class. A class's only connection to the outside world is from the external parameters that are passed to those functions.

73

ABSTRACT DATA TYPES

The Java class definition of a purchase order object is known as an abstract data type. Most programmers are familiar with a number of general data types such as integers, floats, and the ubiquitous zoned-decimal and packed-decimal data types of RPG. These data types all have attributes: their numeric values and, for zoned and packed, their decimal count. Just like Java classes, these basic data types have operations associated with them—addition, subtraction, multiplication, division, and, of course, assignment. In RPG, COBOL, or CL, you define a variable as a particular data type. For example, with CL, you might have the following declaration of a decimal data type variable:

```
DCL &MONEY *DEC LEN(9 2)
```

The variable MONEY may then invoke the implicit addition and assignment operations:

```
CHGVAR &MONEY VALUE(&MONEY + 5.4)
```

With object-oriented programming languages, you define your own data types (except for a few built-in ones). You design these abstract data types to encapsulate the attributes that represent the state of an entity along with the operations that modify the state of that entity.

CONSTRUCTION

This chapter's definition of a purchase order Java class is an abstract data type. In other words, the fields and functions that make up a class form an abstraction of an entity. That Java class can then be used as a user-defined data type, hence the term *abstract data type*. For example, the Java PURCHASEORDER class name is used as an abstract data type to declare the type of a Java variable in the following statement:

```
PurchaseOrder poVariable;
```

Before you can use this purchase order variable, you must first create it with an object-oriented process known as *construction*. The POVARIABLE, until it is constructed, is considered a null object—it has not been assigned to represent a particular business entity, and it contains no data. It doesn't even have storage reserved to contain that data.

To construct a Java object, you use the class constructor of the abstract data type of the variable to be created. For the POVARIABLE class variable, you use the PURCHASEORDER constructor function, passing the required parameters, as shown in Figure 5.3 (remember that a constructor function has the same name as its class). That operation (or function) takes an integer order due date value and a customer object. Constructors are special functions because they are used to create an object instance of a class. In Java, an object is created by using the reserved word NEW followed by the name of the constructor function of the object to be created along with its required parameters:

```
poVariable = new PurchaseOrder(1298, aCustomerObject);
```

Java's NEW operator handles the storage allocation for the object, and the class's constructor function is implemented with the code necessary to set the object's initial state. For example, the purchase order constructor first sets its due date attribute to be equal to 12/98 and then sets its customer attribute to reference the passed customer object. The PURCHASEORDER constructor then creates the LINEITEMS vector attribute. Note that the VECTOR class is a base part of Java and provides an abstract data type of a dynamically sizable array. As you can see in Figure 5.3, the constructor function for the VECTOR class takes no parameters, and the NEW operator returns a reference to the object created by VECTOR's constructor. Likewise, when the PURCHASEORDER constructor completes, POVARIABLE is set to reference the newly created purchase order object.

CLASS VERSUS OBJECT

Throwing the terms *class* and *object* out to you in such a seemingly random fashion might make them appear arbitrary, but there is a difference between a class and an object. A Java class is the code that represents an entity, and an object is a specific instance of an entity. A class is an abstract data type that can be thought of as the mathematical set of all objects of that data type. An object, on the other hand, is one instance of an object of that set. A class is the definition (or pattern or template) for an object, and an object is the physical manifestation of that definition (or pattern or template). An object has its own state, behavior, and identity.

To use an AS/400 database analogy, a class could be compared to a record format. That record format, like a class, has fields for the representation of the attributes of entities. An object could be compared to a single record. The values of the fields in that record contain the state of a specific entity, and the key of that record holds the unique identity of that entity. The behavior of the entity...well, here the analogy breaks down. This is one of the advantages of object-oriented programming—the behaviors of an entity are encapsulated in the object that represents the entity.

No Object Is an Island

An object interacts with the outside world through its functions. Values and objects are passed as parameters, and the functions return an object. (Technically, a function can also return a simple data type like an integer or a float rather than an object.) The UML notation for operations shows the return data type following the colon that appears after the operation's name. For instance, in Figure 5.1, the CUSTOMER object's CHECKCREDIT function returns an integer. Some functions return nothing, which is represented with the Java keyword VOID.

Remember POVARIABLE? The routine that declared that class variable interacts with the PURCHASEORDER object by invoking the desired operation using the Java syntax of the variable name, the dot operator, and the function name, followed by any required parameters. For instance, look back at the purchase order class's ADDLINEITEM function in Figure 5.3. The purchase order's line items attribute, LINEITEMS, invokes the VECTOR class's ADDELEMENT() function. This function adds an element to the LINEITEM's dynamic array. That element will then reference the purchase order line item object passed to VECTOR's ADDELEMENT() function:

```
poVariable.addLineItem(289, 3);
```

In this first level of object-oriented programming with Java, you use classes as abstract data types to declare class variables. Through those variables, you can invoke the class functions that encapsulate the business rules for the entities represented by that class. A well-designed class encapsulates the operations of a business entity by hiding the complexity of the class implementation from other programmers who merely want to use that class. The user, in this case, is another programmer who uses the class as an abstract data type.

CLASS ASSOCIATION

Each object of the UML model of Figure 5.1 is associated with another object. The UML notation uses a simple line between object blocks to show relationship. The CUSTOMER object has relationship to a purchase order and the ITEM object has a relationship with a purchase order line item. The CONSUMER and COMPANY objects have an indirect association to the PURCHASEORDER object through their parent CUSTOMER class; you'll learn more about inheritance in chapter 7.

Each association line has two roles: One for each potential direction of the object association. The CUSTOMER object could have a direct association to the PURCHASEORDER object and the PURCHASEORDER object could have a direct association with the CUSTOMER object. These association roles in the purchasing object model may also have a notation for multiplicity or *cardinality*, which indicates how many objects participate in a relationship (e.g., a purchase order is always associated with one customer).

Figure 5.4 shows the UML notation for cardinality. This type of notation was omitted from the object model of Fig-

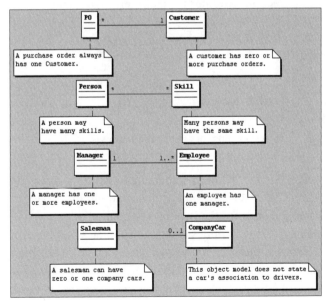

Figure 5.4: UML has a notation for cardinality to show the two-way relationship between objects.

ure 5.1 for simplicity. (Following this discussion, perhaps you should pencil in the appropriate notations for Figure 5.1.)

The customer-to-PO association represents a one-to-many relationship; the person-to-skill association represents a many-to-many relationship; and the manager-to-employee association is a one-to-one-or-more relationship. Take note of the last association example of Figure 5.4, which specifies cardinality for the salesman-to-company car association but not for the company car-to-salesman association. This signals a *unidirectional association* rather than a *bidirectional association* because the designer is not concerned with tracking the people associated with a car. If an object is not to have explicit qualification for multiplicity to the associated object, then the multiplicity notation is left out. This might happen, for instance, when the object's Java class implementation is from an external package where the class would have no inherent knowledge of your class.

The Java class code implementation directly reflects the cardinality of the associations in the object model. The PO class, for example, would have a function that returned the customer for an order:

```
Customer customer getCustomer() {…}
```

The CUSTOMER class might have a function that returned an array of open purchase orders for a customer:

```
Array POs getPurchaseOrders() {…}
```

Also, for the PO class to be able to get its associated customer, the designer must implement some method of maintaining that relationship. The most obvious method calls for the PO class to contain a CUSTOMER object, but a less obvious strategy is to simply store the customer's number from which the PO class could obtain a reference to the associated CUSTOMER object with some form of a lookup or query. On the other hand, the COMPANYCAR class, because it has no cardinality with the SALESMAN class, would have no function to return a salesman and therefore would not have to implement a method of maintaining a relationship to a salesman.

TIME SEQUENCE DIAGRAMS

As our PURCHASEORDER class demonstrates, Java classes themselves can contain other classes and can also receive object references as function parameters. The sequence of object function invocation can therefore become quite complex. To graph the intricacies of nested object function invocations, designers use a UML notation called time sequence diagrams. Time sequence diagrams (or, more succinctly, sequence diagrams) are used to graphically portray the collaboration of objects to provide some behavior—typically a single use case. Figure 5.5 shows the sequence of events that occur for the example purchasing system to allocate inventory.

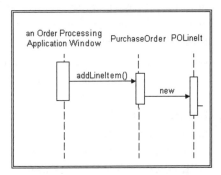

Figure 5.5: Time sequence diagrams graphically display the nested invocation of functions as objects collaborate in the implementation of one use case.

The vertical dashed lines symbolize the lifetime of an object. Each object that collaborates in the creation of a new line item has its own lifetime: purchase order, purchase order line item, and item. The rectangles represent an operation and the solid arrow connecting each object represents object interaction as identified by a function name (in fact, sequence diagrams are also known as interaction diagrams). The object collaboration line between the purchase order and the purchase order line item bears mention because the line is identified with the word NEW rather than a function name. Java's reserved word NEW is used for the creation of a new object, and its use in a sequence diagram clearly identifies the instantiation of an object—in this case, a purchase order line item.

The strength of sequence diagrams lies in the simplistic method by which they describe object collaboration. But their weakness is their inability to provide a computational, complete description of class functions. Object designers often add pseudo-code notes to a sequence diagram to meet that end. The UML notation for sequence diagrams is being extended to provide additional diagrammatic notations. However, as sequence diagrams become more complex, so too will they be more difficult to understand, thus losing some of their inherent strength of simplicity.

THREE LEVELS OF OBJECT-ORIENTED PROGRAMMING

The concepts of object-oriented programming are often broken down into three major areas: *encapsulation*, *inheritance,* and *polymorphism*. Encapsulation, already briefly covered, will be described in detail in the following chapter.

Inheritance relates to deriving a new class from the definition of an existing class, thus inheriting all the attributes and behaviors of its parent class. The new object definition then has more specific behavior added. The COMPANY and CONSUMER classes of Figure 5.1, for example, inherit the ADDRESS, CUSTNUMBER, and NAME attributes from the CUSTOMER class, as well as the CHECKCREDIT operation. You can think of the parent class as being a generalization of a related business entity and the derived classes as conforming to that generalized API.

Polymorphism, the most difficult concept of object-oriented programming to grasp, is when a program dynamically performs behavior specific to objects from various levels of an inheritance tree. Because inheritance is like a generalized API, polymorphism acts as a kind of substitution in which any object from an inheritance tree that conforms to the same generalized API can be substituted for a class variable of a related data type. Chapter 10 explains polymorphism in detail.

THINK OBJECTS

Through this brief overview of object-oriented design strategies, you have seen how the discovery of business entities in object-oriented design is very similar to the same process in database design. This chapter has introduced you to the use of basic UML for the clarification of an object model. You have also seen how a Java class is coded from the design of that object model, how a Java object is created, and how a Java object interacts with the outside world.

6

STANDARD
ENCAPSULATION STRATEGIES

Everyone knows how to use a clock; it has a simple interface. You wind it up and then rotate the hour and minute hands until they point to the appropriate time.

Yet, most people don't know about a clock's implementation— all the gears, wheels, and other gizmos inside that make the clock keep time. Your design of Java classes should work in a similar manner: You should separate the interface of a class from its implementation. In object-oriented programming, this separation process is known as encapsulation. This chapter details a strategy for encapsulating Java classes with a tutorial of the encapsulation process.

Encapsulation is the process of placing all the properties and behaviors of an entity into one place—a Java class definition—and exposing to users only what the designer feels they need to know about the class to use it. Encapsulation delivers two basic benefits:

- A class is easier to understand and use if the complexity of its implementation is hidden.

- If users of a class can't touch its implementation, they can't break it.

As covered in chapter 5, a Java class can be thought of as an abstract data type. When a class is used to define a variable's type (a process known as type declaration), that variable then has access to the interface of its class. Just like the user of a clock, that class variable can access the functions that the designer exposed for user manipulation.

The formal definition for a class's interface is the list of its public and protected fields and functions. You use PUBLIC and PROTECTED, two new Java keywords known as access specifiers, to selectively expose the functions and fields of a class. A third access specifier, PRIVATE, is used to hide fields and functions.

The CLOCK object model displayed in Figure 6.1 uses the notation of the Unified Modeling Language (UML). The top section of an object block contains the name of the object, the middle section lists the object's fields (or *attributes*), and the bottom section contains the functions or operations of that object. The plus (+), minus (-), or pound (#) symbol preceding every field or function signifies the access specified for that field or function. For instance, the plus symbol specifies public access, the minus symbol specifies private access, and the pound symbol specifies protected access.

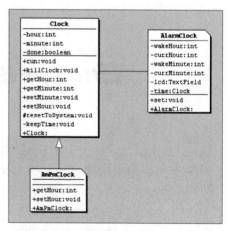

Figure 6.1: The UML of the CLOCK class shows the AMPMCLOCK inherits from CLOCK and ALARMCLOCK uses the CLOCK class.

Notice the access specifier use in Figure 6.1: All of the CLOCK object's functions are public except for KEEPTIME(), which is private, and RESETTOSYSTEM(), which is protected. Also, all of the fields associated with the CLOCK object are labeled as private. Just what purpose does each access specifier serve, and what determines a designer's choice of private, protected, or public access?

THE ALARM CLOCK INTERFACE

Class fields and functions specified as public are accessible to users of that class. Remember that a user of a class is a programmer who either extends that class in the design of a new class or uses that class for the type declaration of a class variable.

For instance, the TESTALARMCLOCK class at the bottom of Figure 6.2 types a variable in its MAIN() function to be of the ALARMCLOCK class (Label G). That variable, ALARM (after it is instantiated with Java's NEW operator and a call to ALARMCLOCK's constructor function), then has access to the interface of the ALARMCLOCK class.

```
import Clock.*;
import java.util.*;
import java.io.*;
import java.awt.*;              // Label D
import java.awt.event.*;

public class AlarmClock extends Frame {
   private int wakeHour, currHour;
   private int wakeMinute, currMinute;
   private TextField lcd;
   private Clock time;

   public AlarmClock () {
      // set up GUI components
      super("Alarm Clock");
      setSize(200, 60);
      setLayout(new BorderLayout(10,10));
      lcd = new TextField();
      lcd.setFont(
         new Font("Courier", Font.BOLD, 15));
```

Figure 6.2: The ALARMCLOCK class uses the CLOCK class as the data type for one of its fields. (Part 1 of 2)

```
    add(lcd);
    addWindowListener(new WindowAdapter() {
      public void windowClosing(WindowEvent e){
        ((Window)e.getSource()).dispose();
        System.exit(0);
      }
    });
    show();
  }
  public void set(int wakeHour, int wakeMinute,
                  int currHour, int currMin) {
    // create a clock and set its time
    time = new Clock();
    time.setHour(currHour);
    time.setMinute(currMin);
    // time.resetToSystem(); compile error  // Label E

    // set the time to get up
    this.wakeHour = wakeHour;
    this.wakeMinute = wakeMinute;
    // loop until it's time
    int lastMinute = 0;
    while (wakeHour   != time.getHour() ||
           wakeMinute != time.getMinute() ) {
      if (time.getMinute() != lastMinute)
        lcd.setText(time.getHour()+":"+
                    time.getMinute());
      lastMinute = time.getMinute();
    }
    lcd.setText("Wake Up");
    time.killClock();              // Label F
  }
}

public class testAlarmClock {
  public static void main (String[] args) {
      AlarmClock alarm = new AlarmClock();// Label G
    alarm.set(23, 12, 23, 11);
  }
}
```

Figure 6.2: The ALARMCLOCK class uses the CLOCK class as the data type for one of its fields. (Part 2 of 2)

The interface for the ALARMCLOCK class consists of the SET() function and the ALARMCLOCK constructor function, because they are the only public or protected fields or functions (as you can see from the UML of Figure 6.1). The ALARM object variable of the TESTALARMCLOCK class cannot access any of the ALARMCLOCK class fields, because they are all identified as private. If TESTALARMCLOCK class's main() function had attempted to access the private fields of the ALARMCLOCK class (Figure 6.3), it would not have compiled.

```
public static void main (String[] args) {
  AlarmClock alarm = new AlarmClock();
  alarm.wakeHour = 6;
  alarm.wakeMinute = 15;
  alarm.currHour = 23;
  alarm.currMinute = 11;
  alarm.set(6, 15, 23, 11);
}
Error: variable wakeHour has private access in class AlarmClock
Error: variable wakeMinute has private access in class AlarmClock
Error: variable currHour has private access in class AlarmClock
Error: variable currMinute has private access in class AlarmClock
```

Figure 6.3: Other Java classes that use the ALARMCLOCK class may not use the ALARMCLOCK's private fields.

The simplistic interface makes the ALARMCLOCK class easy to use. The user—in this case, the TESTALARMCLOCK application class—cannot break the ALARMCLOCK because it does not have access to its internals (its implementation). The ALARM CLOCK class is encapsulated. Figure 6.4 shows the resulting GUI of the ALARM CLOCK class as presented with the TESTALARMCLOCK application class.

PLAUSIBLE DENIABILITY

By now, you can see the fairly explicit purpose for private and public access specifiers. Public functions and fields are accessible to users of the class; private ones are not. When you declare a function private, you make it available only to the class that defined it; not even a *subclass* (a class that inherits or extends another class) can use that private function. For example, the AMPMCLOCK class—a subclass of CLOCK, as the triangle in Figure 6.1 denotes—cannot use CLOCK's KEEPTIME function. (The triangle is UML's symbol for derivation.)

The use of the private access specifier implements *information hiding,* because the designer basically says, "You don't need to know about these guys." Designing a class with private fields and functions allows *plausible deniability*. Although a private function might very well be integral to the implementation of the class, users cannot access that function and, moreover, usually do not even know it exists.

IRISH SETTERS

The design strategy for the CLOCK and ALARMCLOCK classes is a good example of standard encapsulation. The object model in Figure 6.1 shows that all of the CLOCK class's fields are declared with private access. The ALARMCLOCK class has all its fields declared as private, too. It is a standard technique to make all of a class's fields private.

But how can you retrieve or modify the values of a class's field? The standard encapsulation strategy is to explicitly make the values of class fields retrievable with GET functions and values modifiable with SET functions. These functions, known as getter and setter functions, employ a standard function-naming convention: prefixing the name of the field to be retrieved or modified with the word *get* or *set*.

The CLOCK class's interface includes the GETHOUR() and GETMINUTE() functions so users of the class can retrieve the time. The SETHOUR() and SET MINUTE() functions provide the capability to set the clock's time. You might think, "Wouldn't it be easier to make the hour and minute class fields public?" That certainly would work. However, the CLOCK class's code for the SETHOUR() function in Figure 6.5 performs some simple validation at Label C. Setter functions should always perform some sort of verification of the proposed new value, such as range checks, key verification, or date validation. The SETHOUR() function, for instance, includes validation of the value for the new hour. Maybe your boss thinks there are more than 24 hours in a day, but this SET function knows otherwise; it verifies the appropriateness of the new hour based on the length of an Earth day.

```
package Clock;

import java.util.*;
import java.io.*;

public class Clock extends Thread {   // Label A
   private int hour;
   private int minute;
   private boolean done = false;
   public Clock () {
      new Thread(this).start();     // Label B
   }
   public void run() {
      keepTime();
   }
   public void killClock () {
       done = true;
   }
   public int getHour () {return hour;}
   public int getMinute () {return minute;}
   public void setMinute (int minute) {
      if (minute > 60)
         return; // should throw an exception
      this.minute = minute;
   }
   public void setHour (int hour) {   // Begin Label C
      if (hour >  24)
         return; // should throw an exception
      this.hour = hour;
   }                                  // End Label C
   protected void resetToSystem () {
      Date now = new Date();
      hour = now.getHours();
      minute = now.getMinutes();
   }
   private void keepTime () {
      while (!done) {
         // wait a minute
         try {
             sleep(60000); // milliseconds
         } catch (InterruptedException error){}
         if (minute < 60) {
            minute++;
```

Figure 6.5: The CLOCK class has public functions as the interface to the clock and private functions for its hidden implementation of a clock. (Part 1 of 2)

```
      } else {
        minute = 0;
        if (hour == 24)
           hour = 0;
        hour++;
      }
    }
  }
}
```

Figure 6.5: The CLOCK class has public functions as the interface to the clock and private functions for its hidden implementation of a clock. (Part 2 of 2)

This, too, is a vital piece of encapsulation—setter functions ensure the integrity of an object's state by disallowing invalid values. By following this simple encapsulation strategy, you keep your company's business rules maintained in one place: the Java class code implementation.

Now contrast the use of proper encapsulation classes with legacy RPG programming. With RPG, once a program reads a record from a file opened for update, that program has complete control over the state of the business entity represented by that record. RPG programmers must, therefore, take care to add the proper code to verify compliance with business rules in every update program. Unfortunately, as you know, that doesn't always happen. Remember benefit #2 of encapsulation: if they can't touch it, they can't break it.

Note that none of the ALARMCLOCK class's fields have getter or setter functions, because they were not required for the class's user interface. The ALARM CLOCK's SET function does set the state of the fields contained within the CLOCK class, but it delegates the setting of those fields to the CLOCK class's SET functions. The ALARMCLOCK class, as you can see in the object model of Figure 6.1, contains CLOCK as the time field (also known as a *data member*). The ALARMCLOCK class can then invoke the public or private functions of the CLOCK class by using the time class field, the dot operator, and the name of the function, as shown:

```
time.setHour(hour);
```

INFORMATION HIDING

You may be wondering about CLOCK's private KEEPTIME() function. But beware—that function is moderately complex and is part of the private implementation of the CLOCK class. Remember plausible deniability? Well, I wrote the CLOCK class and, believe me, it's not a Timex. If this clock does not keep time well (and it won't), you can plausibly say, "It's not my code."

Seriously, though, the KEEPTIME() function was created for internal use of the CLOCK class. This design is an example of information hiding, because users of the CLOCK class require neither access to nor knowledge of the KEEPTIME() function to use the class. Consequently, the KEEPTIME() function remains excluded from CLOCK's user interface.

THE THREADS OF TIME

The gears, wheels, and other gizmos (otherwise known as the implementation) of the CLOCK class are the combination of Java's threads and a little code. A *thread* is the sequential flow of an execution of a process. Every Java applet or application has at least one thread process, but Java allows you to start multiple, simultaneously executing processes.

The CLOCK class had to implement a method of keeping time. The KEEPTIME() function (see Figure 6.5) accomplishes this task with a never-ending loop that waits 60 seconds and then increments the minutes field. That loop process is implemented with the use of a Java thread so that it does not impede the processing of any classes that might use a CLOCK object.

The KEEPTIME() function of the CLOCK class, therefore, runs as a background process—a thread. The CLOCK class *extends* Java's THREAD class. All classes that extend the THREAD class must provide a RUN() function. The clock's thread is created and the RUN() function is indirectly started in the clock's constructor function at Label B with the following:

```
new Thread(this).start();
```

The THIS keyword (a Java reserved word) is a reference to the CLOCK object itself. The THREAD object's START() function executes the RUN() function of the object specified as the parameter to the THREAD constructor (in this case, the CLOCK object). CLOCK's version of THREAD's RUN() function in turn executes the never-ending KEEPTIME() function. Actually, KEEPTIME() will end when the Boolean DONE variable is set to true with the KILLCLOCK() function, as the ALARMCLOCK class does at Label F (Figure 6.2).

To Serve and to Protect

For beginning and intermediate Java object-oriented programmers, the use of the private and public access specifiers should suffice. However, a cursory understanding of the protected access specifier can come in handy, since you might be using a class that contains protected fields or functions. Protected fields and functions of a class may be accessed only by one of the class's own functions or by a subclass. The AMPMCLOCK in Figure 6.6, for example, is designed to extend the CLOCK class (at Label H) to present a 12-hour clock interface. To do that, the AMPMCLOCK simply provides GETHOUR() and SETHOUR() functions, the code implementation of which handles the conversion to and from military time.

```
import Clock.*;

public class AmPmClock extends Clock { // Label H

  public AmPmClock() {
    resetToSystem();                    // Label I
  }
  public int getHour () {
    int hour = super.getHour();
    if (hour > 12)
      hour -= 12;
    return hour;
  }
  public void setHour (int hour, boolean PM) {
    if (PM)
      hour += 12;
    super.setHour(hour);
```

Figure 6.6: The AMPMCLOCK extends the CLOCK class to present a 12-hour interface.

Returning to the discussion of protected functions, because AMPMCLOCK is a subclass of CLOCK, its functions can invoke the protected RESETTOSYSTEM() function of its parent class, as it did in its constructor function at Label I. If, however, you try to reference the protected RESETTOSYSTEM() function outside of the AMPMCLOCK subclass, as attempted in the test class shown in Figure 6.7, you get a compilation error.

```
class testAmPmClock {
  public static void main (String[] args) {
    AmPmClock AM_PM = new AmPmClock();
    AM_PM.resetToSystem();
  }
}
```

Figure 6.7: A protected function cannot be accessed outside the context of its defining class or subclass.

Here's yet another example of invalid access to a protected function: When the ALARMCLOCK class attempted to invoke the protected function of CLOCK (as it did at Label E of Figure 6.3 before it was commented out), it resulted in the following compiler error.

```
Error: method resetToSystem() has protected access in class Clock
```

It is unlikely that your initial Java projects would call for the protected access specifier in your class design. You'll typically find the protected specifier in a nested hierarchy of classes for the exclusive use of trusted subclasses. Most intermediate Java programmers stick with single-level inheritance, which doesn't often warrant the use of protected access. You will, however, see it used in some of Java's base classes, as well as in toolkits and other third-party packages.

The rules for protected access might not be intuitive, but the rule for access of private fields and functions in derived classes is easy. Neither a derived class nor a user of that class can access private fields.

FRIENDLY FUNCTIONS

If a class's field or function has no access specifier, things get more difficult to explain. The use of a class occurs in one of two contexts:

- The class is used from within other classes of the same Java package.

- The class is used by another class that is not a member of the same Java package.

Consider the ALARMCLOCK class's use (see Figure 6.3) of Java's Abstract Window Toolkit (AWT) package of GUI components. AWT's FRAME and TEXTFIELD classes were made accessible to the ALARMCLOCK class with the IMPORT JAVA.AWT.*; statement at Label D. The ALARMCLOCK class is not a member of the AWT package. For a class to be a part of a package, its source must contain a package statement as the first statement of its source.

The AWT Java classes, for instance, each have the PACKAGE JAVA.AWT; statement at the top of their source files. You might have already noticed that my CLOCK class is identified as the CLOCK package with the PACKAGE CLOCK; statement. The other classes that use the CLOCK class all have IMPORT CLOCK.*; statements, so they can use all of the classes within the CLOCK package (of which there is only the CLOCK class).

This quick definition of Java packages aside, realize now that when you do not explicitly declare an access specifier for a class field or function, the default access is set to *package*. This default access of a field or function is often called *friendly* because that field or function is then accessible to all its "friends" (friends being classes of the same package).

Figure 6.8 gives a graphic summary of the scope of Java's default, public, protected, and private access specifiers. Notice that the UML symbol for friendly access is a blank, as used in the DEFAULTFUNC() of CLASSA.

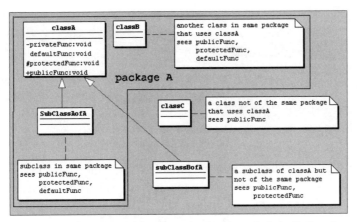

Figure 6.8: Access to the functions of a class is controlled with the private, protected, public, and default access specifiers.

CLASS SPECIFIERS

Fields and functions of a class are not the only elements of a Java class that can have access specifier qualification. Classes themselves may have explicit access specified. Notice that each of my classes has the public access specifier preceding the class declaration, as in the CLOCK class declaration at Label A of Figure 6.2. When a designer does not want a class exposed for use outside of the package, he specifies the whole class as private. Private classes are typically utility classes reserved for the exclusive use of other classes within the same package.

The set of public and protected functions of a class is considered the API of the class. Programmers can easily understand a well-crafted class simply by looking at its API. The JAVAP.EXE utility program that comes with the Java Development Kit (JDK) lists the public and protected functions of a class. I often use JAVAP's listing to help me quickly gain an understanding of a class. Figure 6.9, for instance, lists the JAVAP output from the CLOCK class.

```
public class Clock.Clock extends java.lang.Thread {
    public Clock.Clock();
    public void run();
    public void killClock();
```

Figure 6.9: The JAVAP listing shows the API of a class. (Part 1 of 2)

```
    public int getHour();
    public int getMinute();
    public void setMinute(int);
    public void setHour(int);
    protected void resetToSystem();
}
```

Figure 6.9: The JAVAP listing shows the API of a class.(Part 2 of 2)

Most of the Java reference manuals available consist merely of JAVAP listings along with a concise overview. These manuals are still worthwhile, with my recommendation being *Java in a Nutshell*.

JAVA ENCAPSULATION ENCAPSULATED

A well-crafted Java class encapsulates an entity by placing its state, identity, and behaviors in one place—a Java class—and exposing to users of that class an intuitive interface. This chapter covered the standard encapsulation strategy of making all class fields private and providing getter and setter functions for retrieval or modification of those fields only when they are required by users of that class.

You now know that the interface of a class is its list of public functions. Protected functions also make up part of a class's interface, but I suggest reserving the use of the protected access specifier for advanced Java programmers. The result of the proper encapsulation is a Java class with a simplified interface that shields its users from the complexities of its implementation.

Tell the users only what they need to know. If they can't see it, they can't break it.

7

INHERITANCE

The most often heralded benefit of Java and object-oriented programming is code reuse. Of course, legacy programmers already have two varieties of code reuse: cut and paste and copy code. With cut and paste (a technique used all too often), you copy good code examples into a new program and then tweak the code to perform the desired behavior. The copy code technique entails copying the code into a source member at compile time (rather than design time, when cut and paste is utilized) using \COPY statements. The use of copy code with COBOL and RPG programs is more productive than cut and paste, but it has limitations. Typically, copy code has been restricted to the definition of complex data structures; it has not been widely used for calculations.

Object-oriented programming gives us a method of code reuse far superior to cut and paste or copying code: object-oriented encapsulation. Encapsulation, as covered in the previous chapter, involves placing all the properties and behaviors of an entity into one place—a Java class definition—and exposing to users of that class only the information the designer feels they need to know about the class. As a Java programmer, when you use that class as the abstract data type in the declaration of a variable, you are, in effect, reusing the implementation of that class without touching its code.

In truth, you can achieve similar results with ILE modularization techniques. But what do you do when you find a Java class (or an ILE module, for that matter) that is almost, yet not quite, what you need? Your first impulse might lead you to fall back into the bad habit of cutting and pasting code in the design of a completely new Java class. Don't. There is a better way: the object-oriented mechanism known as inheritance. Unfortunately, ILE languages offer no such alternative.

THE ROLES OF INHERITANCE

Inheritance plays an even stronger role than mere code reuse– the role of abstraction. Object-oriented designers use the abstraction capabilities of inheritance to organize business entities into hierarchies of specialization.

When designers classify business entities, they seek to group them by their common characteristics or their common behaviors. Classification is nothing new; it's how we order knowledge. To understand the complexities and variations of things, we categorize them into clusters of generalized groups. Object-oriented programming directly supports our human nature to categorize by allowing us to build a hierarchy of classes in which specialized classes inherit the structure and behavior defined by more generalized classes.

Biology's classification of species is often used as an excellent example of classification. Carolus Linnaeus came up with the hierarchical categorization of genus and species in the 1700s, which modern biology has expanded to kingdom, phylum, class, order, family, genus, and species. Don Denoncourt belongs to the kingdom Animalia, phylum Chordata, class Mammalia, order Primates, family Hominidae, genus *Homo*, species *sapiens*.

At the start of application design, object-oriented designers seek to discover objects that model the problem domain. Often, they discover a variety of objects that share common characteristics. Rather than redundantly implementing those common characteristics as fields and functions in each of the various classes, the designer factors them out as generalizations into a base class.

The object model of Figure 7.1 shows a COMPANY and a CONSUMER class. Both of these objects have dissimilar characteristics, but they also have common characteristics that were factored out into the CUSTOMER class. The CONSUMER and COMPANY classes inherit their common characteristics and behaviors from the CUSTOMER class.

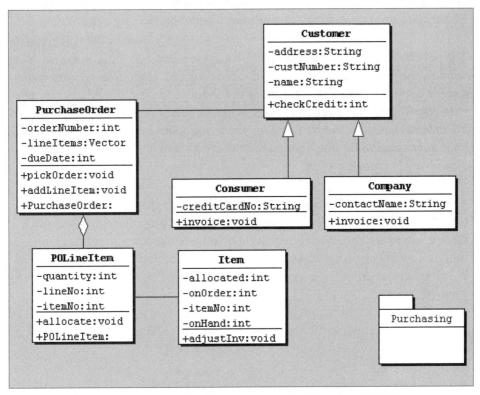

Figure 7.1: Both the CONSUMER and the COMPANY classes inherit from the CUSTOMER class.

The Unified Modeling Language (UML) notation graphically portrays inheritance with the line that descends to those two classes from the CUSTOMER class. (The diamond symbol represents inheritance.) The operative word here is *descends*. The CONSUMER and COMPANY classes are *descendants* of the

CUSTOMER class. Just as with humans, the CONSUMER and COMPANY classes inherit the characteristics of their parent. The difference is that a Java class can inherit from only one parent.

The CUSTOMER class provides an example of the abstraction capabilities of object-oriented design. However, programmers enhance existing applications and databases more frequently than they design new applications. At the workaday level, inheritance gives programmers a code-reuse mechanism. You build on top of existing classes by developing new ones that inherit the fields and functions of a base class; then you add the capabilities required by the new class.

The payoffs from object-oriented inheritance are numerous. First, you don't need to know the implementation details of a class's parent class. Second, you don't have to duplicate the efforts of writing and testing code that provides a service similar to something already provided in another class. Third, inheritance allows incremental development by allowing you to introduce new code without causing bugs in existing code, which might have occurred with the cut-and-paste techniques of RPG programming.

You get a fourth payoff from inheritance when the implementation of a base class is modified (which always happens in business programming), because those changes are immediately available to derived classes without recompilation. In an RPG application, for instance, if the original section of code that had been copied numerous times requires modification, so too do all the copied versions of that code. Use of RPG's \COPY creates less of a problem, but all of the affected programs still require recompilation. The payoffs from Java's code reuse alone should give you sufficient reason to consider moving from RPG to Java development.

THE BASICS OF INHERITANCE

All Java classes have some form of inheritance—even those classes that do not explicitly extend another class. That's because all Java classes inherit from Java's great grandparent of base classes: the OBJECT class. Figure 7.2 shows a UML diagram of the BIGDECIMAL class. BIGDECIMAL inherits from the NUMBER class, which inherits from the OBJECT class.

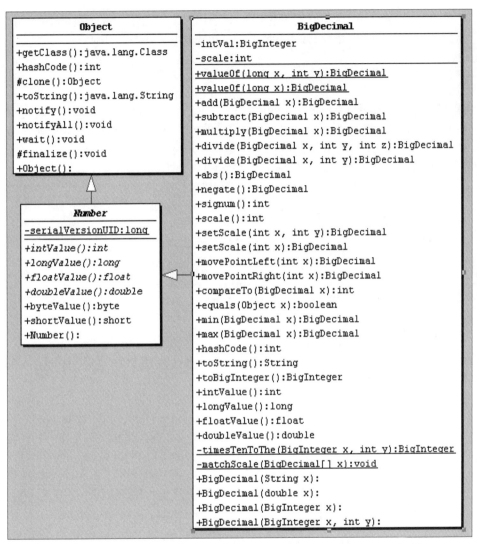

Figure 7.2: The UML diagram of Java's BIGDECIMAL class shows that it inherits from the NUMBER class, which in turn inherits from the OBJECT class.

The NUMBER class generalizes the behaviors of numbers, be they integers, long, float, double, or even the familiar zoned and packed numbers. In fact, you will use the BIGDECIMAL class to store those fixed decimal values that you've traditionally kept on the AS/400 as zoned or packed. The BIGDECIMAL class extends the NUMBER class with the following:

```
class BigDecimal extends Number {…}
```

If a Java class does not extend another class, the Java compiler implicitly assigns the OBJECT class to be its parent. Figure 7.3 shows two different declarations that create an identical NUMBER class.

```
class Number {
// fields and functions:
}
class Number extends Object {
// fields and function:
}
```

Figure 7.3: If a Java class does not specifically extend a class, by default it extends the OBJECT class.

The Java compiler automatically inserts EXTENDS OBJECT to the first implementation of the NUMBER class. The NUMBER class is—as all classes ultimately are—an extension of the OBJECT class.

A base class is also known as the *parent class* or *superclass*, and the derived class is also termed the *subclass*. The NUMBER class, as a subclass, picks up all the characteristics and behaviors of its parent—Java's OBJECT class. The NUMBER class then adds new behaviors to those derived from OBJECT. An instance of a BIGDECIMAL object can directly invoke functions that are a part of any of its ancestors, which includes Java's CLASS class:

```
BigDecimal money = new BigDecimal ();
Class moneyClass = money.getClass();
String str = money.toString();
```

When you derive a class, only those fields and functions designated in the parent class with the *public* or *protected* access specifiers are available for implementation by a derived class. (Chapter 6 covers the UML notation for the public, protected, and private access specifiers: the +, #, and – characters, respectively.)

PRIVATE fields and functions are not inherited by derived classes; they exist solely for the internal implementation of their classes.

When a function has an access specifier of *protected*, as explained in the previous chapter, it is accessible only from within other functions of that same class or from within functions of its subclasses. The *protected* functions, for instance, of the OBJECT class—CLONE() and FINALIZE()—are inherited by the PURCHASEORDER class and are available for its implementation, but they are not available to instance variables of the PURCHASEORDER class, as Figure 7.4 shows.

```
class PurchaseOrder extends Object {
    PurchaseOrder () {
            // internal use of a protected Object function
        clone();
    }
}
PurchaseOrder po = new PurchaseOrder();
// external use of Object's protected function
po.clone ();     // compile error, function inaccessible
po.finalize (); // compile error, function inaccessible
```

Figure 7.4: Protected functions can be used in the implementation of derived classes but not by users of that derived class.

Inheritance, as explained so far, is fairly straightforward. That is, you design a new class by extending an existing class, thereby inheriting all of its public and protected fields and functions. Then, you add additional fields and functions as required by the new class. Using only the concepts covered so far, you can define some fairly sophisticated object models. But, as always, you have to be concerned with a few other areas: namely, *overriding, overloading,* and *constructor invocation* in an inheritance tree.

OVERRIDING

In an object-oriented language, you would say that the CONSUMER object of Figure 7.1 IS-A CUSTOMER. The CONSUMER inherited all of the fields and functions of its parent class, so it *is* a CUSTOMER. But the CONSUMER class comprises more than just a CUSTOMER class because it was extended to include some additional consumer-specific functions.

In some situations, however, you might want to change behaviors inherited from a base class. When the inherited behaviors and characteristics of a base class are changed in a derived class, you say that the subclass IS-A-KIND-OF its base class. You use the IS-A-KIND-OF terminology because you have changed the subclass to have some but not all of the characteristics and behaviors of its base. Why would you want to do this?

You might want to change the implementation of a function inherited from a base class to adapt it to the needs of a new class. For instance, the FINALIZE() function implemented in Java's ubiquitous OBJECT class is often reimplemented in derived classes to perform class-specific cleanup, such as closing files when an object is garbage-collected (destroyed) by the Java Virtual Machine (JVM). That new, improved FINALIZE() function is automatically invoked when JVM's garbage collection facilities destroy an object.

HIDE AND SEEK

You can change the inherited behaviors of a superclass by defining a function in the subclass that has the same name, return type, order, and type of arguments as a function of its superclass. Characteristics inherited from a base class are changed simply by defining a field that has the same name as a field of the base class. This process of replacing the base class's characteristics and behaviors in a derived class is known as *overriding*.

When fields or functions of a base class are overridden in a derived class (subclass), the base versions of those fields and functions remain available to the derived class; they are simply hidden by the new versions in the derived class. You can still access the base class's overridden fields or functions by qualifying the reference with the Java SUPER keyword. (Think of the reserved word SUPER as a synonym for the base class name.) By specifying the overridden base class's function or field name qualified by SUPER, you force the Java compiler to reference the parent's version. The DOS Java executions shown in Figure 7.5 of the SUPERCLASS and SUBCLASS classes of Figure 7.6 show how a parent class's overridden fields and functions—THEINT and THEFUNC—may be accessed.

```
C:>java superClass
theInt:1 theFunc():1

C:>java subClass
theInt:2 theFunc():2
super.theInt:1 super.theFunc():1
```

Figure 7.5: A subclass may explicitly invoke an overridden function with the use of the SUPER qualifier.

```
class superClass {
    int theInt = 1;
    int theFunc() { return 1;}
    void print() {
        System.out.print("theInt: "+theInt+
      "theFunc():"+theFunc());
    }
    public static void main(String[] argv) {
    new superClass().print();
    }
}

class subClass extends superClass {
    int theInt = 2;
    int theFunc() { return 2; }
    void print() {
        System.out.print("theInt:"+
                theInt+" theFunc():"+theFunc());
        System.out.print("\nsuper.theInt:"+
            super.theInt+
          " super.theFunc():"+
            super.theFunc());
    }
    public static void main(String[] argv) {
        new subClass().print();
    }
}
```

Figure 7.6: A subclass that overrides a function of its base may still invoke that overridden function by qualifying the call with the SUPER keyword.

Functions are overridden far more often than attributes. The object designer might wish to extend the functionality of a given method without complicating the API by adding another public function. Frequently, the overridden method even calls the very function that it hid. A simple example is a technique often used to test the functions of a class: You derive a class that overrides each of the functions in the superclass, add test code such as profiling information, and then invoke the parent's implementation of the function so the parent class still works as designed. The process is shown in Figure 7.7.

```
class TestProfile extends VeryComplicatedClass {
    void veryComplicatedFunction() {
        System.out.print("got to veryComplicatedFunction()");
        super.veryComplicatedFunction();
    }
    ...
}
```

Figure 7.7: Often an overridden function itself invokes its parent's version by qualifying a call to that function with the SUPER keyword.

OVERLOADED FUNCTIONS

Java programmers can easily understand the functional interface of a well-designed class because it has descriptive function names, return types, and parameter lists. Often, business applications require interfaces that are similar in function but have a variety of argument options. For this reason, Java allows you to *overload* a function name by defining several functions with the same name but different signatures (a *signature* being the combination of function name, return type, number, and type of arguments).

In RPG (or even in a poorly designed Java class), programmers often create parameter lists by cramming in all the potential options; however, that practice makes it unclear which parameters are required. A well-designed Java class lets you create multiple functions that have the same name and accept the correct combinations of parameters needed.

The BIGDECIMAL class of Figure 7.2 uses function overloading because it has not one but four constructor functions. (You might recall that a constructor function has the same name as its class and no return type; it is used in conjunction with Java's NEW operator to instantiate an object of the constructor's class.) You can build an instance of a BIGDECIMAL object with a numerical string, a double value, another BIGINTEGER object, or a BIGINTEGER with specification for decimal precision, as shown in Figure 7.8.

```
BigDecimal money1 = new BigDecimal("128.95");
BigDecimal money2 = new BigDecimal(128.95);
BigInteger aBigInt = new BigInteger("325");
BigDecimal threeHundred25Bucks = new BigDecimal(aBigInt);
BigDecimal threeBucksAndaQuarter = new BigDecimal(aBigInt, 2);
```

Figure 7.8: Java's BIGDECIMAL objects can be created with any one of four constructors.

If you define a function in a derived class with the same function name as one in the base class (but with a different signature), it's considered an overloaded function. The base class's function of the same name is not overridden and is still directly available to the derived class. To override a function of the base class, you must specify the same signature in the function of the derived class.

You *override* a base class's function by defining a function of the same name and signature in the derived class. You *overload* a function by defining a function of the same name but with a different signature. Overriding a base class's function extends or modifies the behavior of the derived class and hides the base class's version. By overloading functions, you allow multiple methods to have the same descriptive name, but with different parameter requirements to provide an intuitive API.

IF YOU DO NOT HAVE A CONSTRUCTOR, ONE WILL BE APPOINTED FOR YOU

The initial state of an object is set by its constructor function. Every object in Java has a constructor function, whether you code one or not. If you do not code a constructor, Java creates one for you. You might think you don't need to learn anything more about class construction, since Java seems to handle everything for you. However, understanding class construction becomes more important when you start using inheritance.

When you create an object by invoking the NEW operator on a class's constructor, that constructor's code must call the constructor of its parent class. Why? Remember that you should not be concerned with the implementation details of parent objects and that private attributes and functions are not inherited. With that in mind, realize that a subclass's constructor should not be required to set the initial state for fields found in all levels of its inheritance tree. That's why the constructor of the parent class must be called. Again, Java helps out because, if you don't explicitly code a call to the parent's constructor in your subclass's constructor, Java will attempt to do it for you.

IMPLICIT CLASS CONSTRUCTION

Earlier, you learned how to use Java's SUPER keyword (e.g., SUPER.PARENT-FIELD) to qualify fields and functions to be from a subclass's parent. So, qualifying a subclass's constructor with SUPER() to reflect the parent's constructor should come as no surprise. Now the tricky part: If the first statement in a subclass's constructor is neither a call to SUPER() nor a call to another overloaded constructor of the same class, then Java implicitly inserts a function call to SUPER() as the first statement. For example, suppose you define the derived class as shown in Figure 7.9.

```
class MyDerivedClass extends MyParentClass {
    int i;
MyDerivedClass() {
        i = getIValue();
}
}
```

Figure 7.9: A constructor function is not able to initialize the state of the private fields of its parent class.

The Java compiler would create the Java byte code of the class with the inclusion of a call to MYDERIVEDCLASS's parent's constructor, as shown in Figure 7.10.

```
MyDerivedClass() {
    super();
    i = getIValue();
}
```

Figure 7.10: Java automatically inserts a call to the special SUPER function in the compiled version of the Java class.

Further, if you do not code a constructor, Java creates a default constructor for you that calls the class's immediate ancestor's constructor. If you let Java create constructors for you, don't go looking around for the default constructor code. Just trust that it will be in the *.CLASS byte code file. It will not be inserted into your *.JAVA source file. Nevertheless, the constructor code would look like this:

```
MyDerivedClass() {
  Super();
}
```

As you can see, the Java-appointed default constructor of the derived class does nothing but invoke the constructor of the base class. The Java-created constructor always has an empty parameter list. A constructor function that has no arguments is known as a *default* constructor. Once you code your own constructor function (regardless of whether or not it takes any arguments), Java no longer generates a default constructor for you.

EXPLICIT CLASS CONSTRUCTION

So far, Java does it all for you. Again, you might think you don't need to mess with construction because Java always seems to step in and call the parent's constructor for you, whether you define a constructor or not. But Java can help only if you derive your class from a base class that has a default constructor. If you derive your class from a class that has an explicit constructor (which takes arguments) and that class does not also have a default constructor (one that takes no arguments), then Java can't help. You must explicitly code your subclass to call that parameterized constructor.

Think of it this way: The designers of the superclass are forcing you to provide the parameters that the superclass requires to properly initialize itself. No matter; this is easily done with an explicit call using the SUPER() function, passing the appropriate parameter list:

```
super(argument1, argument2, ...);
```

107

THE SHOULDERS OF GIANTS

Your initial Java development efforts might not require the sophisticated design of hierarchical classes. Yet, those initial efforts will require the reuse of existing classes within standard packages such as Java's Abstract Window Toolkit (AWT) and third-party classes like IBM's Java Toolbox for the AS/400. When you first start to look at the classes that make up a package, you should also look at the accompanying online hypertext documentation. Each class within the package has its own hypertext document that lists its public fields and functions. To fully understand the use of a class, you should also look at the hypertext documentation of its superclass.

For instance, AWT has a GUI class called TEXTFIELD that allows the entry of characters into a Windows component. You would expect the TEXTFIELD class to define a method of retrieving its text with something like a GETTEXT function; but if you pull up the Java Development Kit's hypertext documentation for AWT's TEXTFIELD, you won't find any such function to retrieve TEXTFIELD's text. At the top of TEXTFIELD's hypertext document, however, you'll see the inheritance tree for TEXTFIELD. By clicking on its parent TEXTCOMPONENT class to browse that class's documentation, you'll find the GETTEXT function. Therefore, TEXTFIELD, by order of inheritance, also contains the GETTEXT function.

Inheritance allows programmers to create a new class based on an existing class without reimplementing the functionality of the existing class. You don't even need to know the implementation details of the base class. Through inheritance, you can incrementally develop Java applications by introducing new classes without causing bugs in an application's base classes. Further, Java's innovative method of handling inheritance at runtime allows modified base classes to be moved into production without the recompilation of derived classes. As you develop Java classes by using inheritance, you stand on the shoulders of the talented object designers who came before you.

8

Java Interfaces

Object-oriented programmers can take advantage of a new strategy called *designing to an interface*. Proponents of this strategy forget about using complex hierarchies of classes and instead focus on the common interfaces of classes. (Remember that a class's interface consists of its list of public and protected functions.) With inheritance, unlike interfaces, a base class passes its interface as well as its implementations on to its subclasses. However, Java classes don't always share the same functions *and* implementations of other classes. When your classes share functions of the same name but not necessarily the same implementations of other classes, using an interface can simplify your programming efforts.

When you design using Java's inheritance, you write your derived classes to use the functional interfaces of your base classes. Java's polymorphism then kicks in to call the proper subclass implementation of the base class's interface. If you feel as though you're pushing your understanding of object-oriented programming right now, don't worry; Java has an alternative approach, referred to as *designing to an interface*, that is more intuitive than inheritance. This chapter covers the approach to designing to an interface first with Java's intuitive method and then, after introducing you to the concepts of polymorphism, with the inheritance method.

Java has a construct that supports designing to an interface that is clearer than any other object-oriented language. Even with the sophisticated language of C++, programmers have to bend over backwards to simulate what Java does effortlessly. This Java construct is aptly called an *interface*. Java interfaces allow you to associate the names of functions that serve a similar or related purpose into a discretely named unit.

A Java interface and a Java class differ in that the functions of an interface are without implementations. The ITRANSACTION interface in Figure 8.1 is composed of functions typically associated with transactions, such as setting and getting the date, quantity, cost, and description of a transaction. At first glance, you'd think an interface is much the same as a class. But if you look more closely, you'll notice that the ITRANSACTION interface contains no code implementations for its functions. You might also notice that the interface does not declare the date, description, cost, or quantity fields that its functions presumably get and set.

```java
import java.util.Date;
public interface ITransaction {
    public Date getDate();
    public String getDescription();
    public int getQuantity ();
    public void setDate(Date date);
    public void setDescription(String desc);
    public void setQuantity (int qty);
}
public interface IPrint {
    public void printDetail();
    public void printFooter();
    public void printHeader();
}
```

Figure 8.1: The ITRANSACTION and IPRINT interfaces, as with all Java interfaces, have no code implementations.

A Java interface is a standard protocol that is used as a consistent API for behaviors that a variety of classes share. For instance, as you design an object model, you might find yourself defining the same printing functions in classes that represent dissimilar entities. So, you develop an IPRINT interface such as the one shown in Figure 8.1. That interface then serves two purposes. First, it defines the protocol for the implementation of a printable interface. Second, any object that has an implementation for the printable interface can be used as a runtime IPRINT object via polymorphism. Ah, that 10-dollar word resurfaces, and this chapter *does* address polymorphism eventually, but first you need to know how to implement an interface.

You can see in Figure 8.2 that the purchase order activity (POActivity) class *implements* the ITRANSACTION interface. When you design a class that implements an interface, you must provide code implementations for all of the functions inherited from that interface. As a result, the POACTIVITY class has code for all of the functions declared in the ITRANSACTION interface. To implement the ITRANSACTION interface, the POACTIVITY class must define functions with the same name, return type, and number and type of arguments—that is, the same signature—as the ITRANSACTION interface.

```
import java.util.Date;

public class POActivity
            extends RdbEntity
            implements ITransaction, IPrint
{
    private Date date;
    private String description;
    private int quantity;
    private String shipMethod;
    public java.util.Date getDate() {return date;}
    public String getDescription() {
        return description;}
    public int getQuantity() {return quantity;}
    public void printDetail() {
        System.out.println(getDescription());}
    public void printFooter() {
```

Figure 8.2: The POACTIVITY and the WOACTIVITY classes both implement the ITRANSACTION interface. (Part 1 of 3)

```
            System.out.println(
                "*** POActivity Footer ***");}
    public void printHeader() {
        System.out.println(
            "Purchase Order Activity:");}
    public void setDate(Date date) {
        this.date = date;}
    public void setDescription(String desc) {
        description = desc;}
    public void setQuantity(int qty) {
        quantity = qty;}
    public void setShipMethod(String shipMethod){
        this.shipMethod = shipMethod;}
}
public class WOActivity extends RdbEntity
        implements ITransaction, IPrint {

    private java.util.Date date;
    private String description;
    private int quantity;
    private int shift;
    private int badge;

    public java.util.Date getDate() {
        return date;
    }
    public String getDescription() {
        return date+" Badge: "+badge+" Desc: "+description;
    }
    public int getQuantity() {
        return quantity;
    }
    public void printDetail() {
        System.out.println(getDescription());
    }
    public void printFooter() {
        System.out.println("*** WO Footer *** ");
    }
    public void printHeader() {
        System.out.println("Work Order Activity:");
    }
    public void setBadge (int badge) {
        this.badge = badge;
```

Figure 8.2: The POACTIVITY and the WOACTIVITY classes both implement the ITRANSACTION interface. (Part 2 of 3)

```
    }
    public void setDate(Date date) {
        this.date = date;
    }
    public void setDescription(String desc) {
        description = desc;
    }
    public void setQuantity(int qty) {
        quantity = qty;
    }
    public void setShift (int shift ) {
        this.shift = shift;
    }
}
```

Figure 8.2: The POACTIVITY and the WOACTIVITY classes both implement the ITRANSACTION interface. (Part 3 of 3)

If you look at the Unified Modeling Language (UML) diagram in Figure 8.3, you'll notice that the POACTIVITY class declares those date, description, and quantity fields that the functions of the ITRANSACTION interface implied.

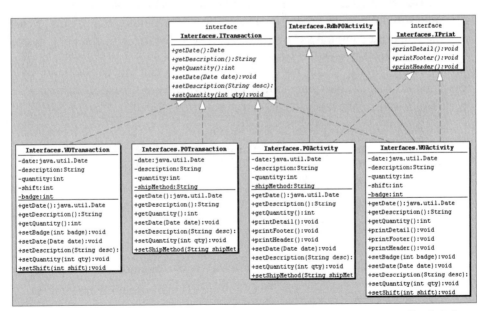

Figure 8.3: The UML object model shows how the same interface can be implemented in dissimilar objects.

Perhaps you think it would have been clearer to define those three fields directly in the ITRANSACTION interface, but Java interfaces don't support the declaration of fields. And, when you think about it, if you could put fields in an interface, you would in essence be defining an entity (that is, a real-world object that has a state and identity). An interface is not an entity; it is only a list of functions, merely a standard protocol for communicating. Because the creators of Java did not want interfaces to represent entities, an interface can never be instantiated as an object. You couldn't, for example, code the following:

```
ITransaction trans = new ITransaction();
```

Actually, you *can* declare a field in a Java interface, but that field is implicitly qualified as STATIC and FINAL. (Note that the fields and functions of an interface are also implicitly public.) The STATIC and FINAL qualifiers effectively make the fields of an interface constants because their values cannot be modified; they are immutable. Because fields of an interface are immutable, their values must be initialized as a part of the field declaration, as the class field called red in Figure 8.4's ICOLORS interface shows. Although the ICOLORS interface has fields, ICOLORS still does not represent an entity because the fields are constants. You'll find that the most common use of interface fields is for default values.

```
interface IColors {
    // implicit public static final
    int RED = 1;
    // the public static final qualifiers are not necessary
    // because they will be added by the compiler
    public static final int GREEN = 2;
    // implicitly public
    void int getColor();
    // the public qualifier is not necessary
    // because it will be added by the compiler
    public int setColor(int color);
}
```

Figure 8.4: A Java interface can declare fields but they are implicitly qualified as static, final, and public; therefore, they are effectively constants.

INHERITANCE VERSUS INTERFACES

The Java ITRANSACTION interface of Figure 8.1 could have been developed instead as a class called TRANSACTION, and that class could then have been a superclass for the work order (WOACTIVITY) and purchase order (POACTIVITY) classes. But as the object model in Figure 8.3 shows, the WOACTIVITY class already has a base class. Java classes can only have one parent, so WOACTIVITY couldn't extend a TRANSACTION class.

Even so, WOACTIVITY does implement two interfaces: ITRANSACTION and IPRINT. A big advantage of interfaces over inheritance is that, although a class can extend only one parent class, a class can implement multiple interfaces. The UML notation, by the way, for implementing an interface is a dotted line, and an interface is differentiated from a class with the word *interface* at the top of a box.

If you look at the Java code for the WOACTIVITY class's implementation of the ITRANSACTION interface in Figure 8.2, you'll notice that it varies from that of the POACTIVITY class. (Note that the integer representations for badge would probably have been implemented in a real system by an EMPLOYEE class that encapsulates the attributes and behaviors of an employee.) Such variations give programmers another reason to use interfaces rather than inheritance: When implementations of an interface will vary from class to class, it doesn't make sense to put code implementations for those functions in a base class. Chapter 7 revealed how Java allows you to override the implementation of a function inherited from a parent class, but inheritance works best when the code implementation of a base class fits the requirements of its subclasses.

WHAT'S THE BIG DEAL?

The ability to define a standard protocol with a Java interface is all well and good, but that ability alone is nothing more than an enforced naming convention. The big deal comes from the flexibility, extensibility, and pluggability that interfaces give you:

- *Flexible* because interfaces allow you to change the implementation of an interface based on varied requirements of classes.

- *Extensible* because you can string multiple interfaces in the definition of a class.

- *Plugable* because, as you'll see shortly, the classes that implement the same interface can be used interchangeably.

EXTENSIBILITY

Complex interfaces with lots of functions can often be simplified by dividing them into several small interfaces. The ITRANSACTION interface of Figure 8.1, for instance, could be further divided into IDATE, IDESCRIPTION, and IQUANTITY interfaces. The entirely new-looking (but functionally equivalent) ITRANSACTION interface shown in Figure 8.5 is a composite interface of ITRANSACTION's three components. This variety of interfaces also serves to further protect the internals of objects by giving other objects access only to a specific interface.

```
// example of a composite interface
interface IDate {
    Date getDate();
    void setDate(Date date);
}
interface IDescription {
    String getDescription();
    void setDescription(String desc);
}
interface IQuantity {
    int getQuantity ();
    void setQuantity (int qty);
}
interface ITransaction extends IDate, IDescription, IQuantity {}
```

Figure 8.5: Interfaces can be combined into one composite interface.

PLUGGABILITY

It follows that a class (such as the WOACTIVITY class) that implements an interface can then be instantiated as an object. That object can then invoke the functions that were implemented in that class but defined in the interface:

```
WOActivity woActive = new WOActivity();
woActive.setDescription("Widget polished");
```

The pluggability of the interfaces of WOACTIVITY will become evident when you see that you can assign the reference to that WOACTIVITY object to a variable that is typed as an interface:

```
ITransaction trans = woActive;
```

Earlier, you read that you can never instantiate an interface. You can, however, declare the type of a variable as an interface and assign to that interface variable a reference to any object whose class implemented that variable's interface. The interface variable may then invoke the functions that were defined in its interface.

For instance, the TRANS interface variable can invoke SETDESCRIPTION, but it cannot invoke PRINTHEADER. Even though PRINTHEADER is a part of the WOACTIVITY class that the WOACTIVE object was originally instantiated as, PRINTHEADER is not a part of the ITRANSACTION interface. The TRANS variable, constrained by the functions of its ITRANSACTION object type, cannot invoke the PRINTHEADER function. It may sound as if interface variables are used to limit the scope of objects, but they actually make Java more powerful. As you'll see, the ability to reference objects with an interface variable makes objects that implement interfaces very pluggable.

The Many Faces of an Interface

The TESTTRANSACTIONS application class of Figure 8.6 and the PRINTTRANS-ACTIONS class shown in Figure 8.7 demonstrate the pluggability of interfaces. The pluggability of interfaces illustrates Java *polymorphism*, which literally means "many forms." As I'll explain, the function implementations of the ITRANSACTION interfaces go through a metamorphosis several times in the TESTTRANSACTIONS class.

```
public class TestTransactions {
  public TestTransactions ( ) {

    // create a PO Activity object and invoke its
    // implementation of the setDescription function
```

Figure 8.6: Java's polymorphism adapts code at runtime to invoke the various implementations of interfaces by dissimilar objects. (Part 1 of 2)

117

```
        // inherited from the ITransaction class
        POActivity po = new POActivity();
        po.setDescription("purchase order shipped");

        // create a WO Activity object and invoke its
        // implementations of several of the inherited
        // functions of the ITransaction class
        WOActivity wo = new WOActivity();
        wo.setDescription("W/O routing step 110 completed");
        wo.setDate(new java.util.Date());
        wo.setBadge(928);

        // create two ITransaction variables and
        // set them to reference objects whose
        // class implemented the ITransaction interface
        ITransaction trans1 = po;
        ITransaction trans2 = wo;

        // print the description of the transaction
        // note that the implementation of the ITransaction
        // function will be of the object referenced
        System.out.println(trans1.getDescription());
        System.out.println(trans2.getDescription());

        // create an array and initialize it to the
        // PO and WO Activity objects
        IPrint[] printGroup = {po, wo};
        // create a print transaction object passing
        // an output medium and then print the transactions
        PrintTransactions print =
            new PrintTransactions(PrintTransactions.FILE);
        print.print(printGroup);
    }

    public static void main(java.lang.String[] args) {
        new TestTransactions();
    }
}
```

Figure 8.6: Java's polymorphism adapts code at runtime to invoke the various implementations of interfaces by dissimilar objects. (Part 2 of 2)

```
public class PrintTransactions {
    public static final String FILE = "FILE";
    public static final String PRINTER="PRINTER";

    PrintTransactions (String printer) {
        // create and open file here if "FILE"
        // passed else write to printer
    }
    public void finalize() throws Throwable {
        // flush file or printer
    }
    public void print(IPrint[] printGroup) {
        for (int i = 0; i < printGroup.length; i++)
        {
            printGroup[i].printHeader();
            printGroup[i].printDetail();
            printGroup[i].printFooter();
        }
    }
}
```

Figure 8.7: Utility classes can be coded to use Java interfaces without prior knowledge of the implementation of those interfaces.

The function main of the TESTTRANSACTIONS application bootstraps the application by creating itself. To do this, it invokes its constructor function with Java's NEW operator. The constructor function creates a POACTIVITY object and invokes its implementation of the SETDESCRIPTION function inherited from the ITRANSACTION class. Then it creates a WOACTIVITY object and invokes its implementations of several of the inherited functions of the ITRANSACTION class.

So far, no new Java strategies have arisen, but TESTTRANSACTIONS then creates two ITRANSACTION variables and sets them to reference objects whose class implemented the ITRANSACTION interface. Remember, you cannot instantiate an interface as an object:

```
ITransaction trans = new ITransaction();  // compile error
```

However, you *can* assign a reference to an object that was created from a class that implemented the same interface as a variable typecast as that interface:

```
POActivity po = new POActivity();
ITransaction trans1 = po;
```

In this process, sometimes called *downcasting*, the object referenced with the variable PO was typecast as member of the POACTIVITY class; but because the POACTIVITY class also is a type of ITRANSACTION, you can assign that object's reference to an ITRANSACTION variable. Because the TRANS interface variable was less than that of a POACTIVITY class variable, you can say that we downcast a POACTIVITY variable to an ITRANSACTION variable.

The TESTTRANSACTIONS function then prints the description of the transaction using the interface variables. It would have been easier to have simply invoked the GETTRANSACTION functions directly from the WO or PO variables:

```
System.out.println(wo.getDescription());
```

However, the use of the interface variables should have given you a glimpse of the power of interfaces and the polymorphic behavior of objects. You now can see that although the TRANS1 and TRANS2 variables are not of the POACTIVITY or WOACTIVITY class, they invoke the functions that were implemented in those classes.

The last three Java statements of the TESTTRANSACTIONS function further illustrate the polymorphic behavior of interfaces. The PRINTGROUP variable is an array that is typecast as IPRINT. The array is initialized to reference the two POACTIVITY and WOACTIVITY objects. Then a PRINTTRANSACTIONS object is instantiated. Note that the constructor for PRINTTRANSACTIONS opens the selected output medium. The PRINTGROUP array is then passed to PRINTTRANS-ACTIONS' print function, which spins through the array and invokes each of the functions of the IPRINT interface.

The PRINTTRANSACTIONS class and its PRINT function have been designed to an interface. Rather than writing a function to print work order transactions and writing another function to print purchase order transactions and then writing… well, you get the idea—you write one function that is designed to use the IPRINT interface. The PRINTTRANSACTIONS class can handle the printing of any class that implements the IPRINT interface. Figure 8.8 shows the result of running the TESTTRANSACTIONS application.

```
purchase order shipped
Mon Jun 15 21:23:27 EDT 1998 Badge: 928 Desc: W/O routing step
110 completed
Purchase Order Activity:
purchase order shipped
*** POActivity Footer ***
Work Order Activity:
Mon Jun 15 21:23:27 EDT 1998 Badge: 928 Desc: W/O routing step
110 completed
*** WO Footer ***
```

Figure 8.8: The Java Virtual Machine, via polymorphism, dynamically handles the behavior of various implementations of the ITRANSACTION and IPRINT interfaces.

THE POWER OF INTERFACES

Even if you never design a single Java interface, you will still use them. The implementation of Java itself makes heavy use of Java interfaces. Two areas in particular that employ interfaces are Java's GUI event-handling mechanism and Java's Remote Method Invocation (RMI) facility.

Many of the standard Java packages such as the Abstract Windowing Toolkit (AWT) make extensive use of Java interfaces When you develop a Java GUI with AWT, you group window components such as buttons, text boxes, and list boxes into a window. Each of these components can generate a variety of events, such as the clicking of buttons, the entry of text into the text box, or selection of a list box element with the mouse. Each of these events has an associated AWT interface.

You design your Java application to handle these events by creating classes that implement the standard AWT interfaces. Object instances of the classes that implement the AWT interfaces are then registered with a component so that it can react to events generated by that component. You don't code calls to those functions; the Java Virtual Machine (using polymorphism) automatically does that for you by invoking your class's code implementation of the AWT interface. Because these interfaces are common, you can obtain Java classes that implement these standard interfaces from a wide variety of sources—other teams, Internet freeware, and third-party suppliers—once again displaying the pluggability of interfaces.

RMI, Java 1.1's strategy for distributed computing, provides another example of the power and versatility of interfaces. Remote access to objects residing on host machines is enabled through an interface. You pull the functions of a host class that require remote access into a Java interface. Then, with the magic of RMI, a Java application on a client machine can declare a variable of the interface type and assign it a reference to the object on the host machine that implements the interface.

The other day my wife said to one of our sons: "That's what you get for being a member of my side of the family." She laughed and quickly corrected her statement because it sounded as if she were saying that my son had inherited attributes only from her. But I thought, hey, that's Java inheritance—only one parent. What, then, would be the human analogy to Java interfaces?

Human behaviors allow people to interface with others using character, style, and skill. These qualities are not inherited; they are acquired—you provide your own implementation of character, style, and skill. If my sons (who are trying to develop a class of their own) had adequate knowledge of Java and would actually listen to me, I would instruct them to implement a character, implement a style, and implement a skill (see Figure 8.9).

```
class Denoncourt
{
   int intelligence, creativity; // [editorial license]
}

class DonDenoncourt extends Denoncourt
implements
ICharacter, IStyle, IProgrammer, IWriter, IMakeSandwiches
{
    ...// implementations of interfaces
}

class JoshuaDenoncourt extends Denoncourt
implements ICharacter, IStyle, IArtist, IWriter
{
    // implementations of interfaces:
```

Figure 8.9: Individuals may inherit characteristics from their parents; but to interface with the world, they have to implement their own character, style, and skill. (Part 1 of 2)

```
    ...
// note that JoshuaDenoncourt's implementation of character,
style and writer
// are completely different from DonDenoncourt's, even if the
interface is the
// same. JoshuaDenoncourt also implements an artist interface
    ...
// interfacing with others,
// JoshuaDenoncourt usually uses the DonDenoncourt
implementation
// of IMakeSandwiches to get a sandwich but he also uses
// Subway or other IMakeSandwiches implementations
void getSandwich(IMakeSandwiches chef) {
        chef.getSandwich();
    }
}
```

Figure 8.9: Individuals may inherit characteristics from their parents; but to interface with the world, they have to implement their own character, style, and skill. (Part 2 of 2)

They already have the inherited attributes of intelligence and creativity, as well as self-preservation and desire. I could tell them to develop multiple interfaces so that, like a Java class, others would be able to interface with them in a variety of ways to satisfy their particular needs. For instance, I have my own implementations for the IPROGRAMMER, IWRITER, or IMAKESANDWICHES interfaces. When my sons use my IMAKESANDWICHES interface, they have only one need in mind. In other words, they don't care about my IPROGRAMMER implementation—they just want a good sandwich.

9

ABSTRACT CLASSES

The preceding chapter introduces you to the power of Java interfaces. Java interfaces allow you to associate a set of function names that serve a similar or related purpose into a discretely named unit. The functions of an interface are without implementations whereas the functions of a class must have code implementations.

Java interfaces work well when dissimilar entities exhibit a common behavior. You design a Java interface as a list of functions that represent common behaviors exhibited by dissimilar entities. You design Java classes to represent business entities. Each of those Java classes provides custom code implementation for the functions of the common interface. The idea is that classes of an application have a consistent interface, although the implementations of that interface vary from class to class.

But what do you do when you find yourself coding the same implementation over and over again for the functions of an interface? You might consider using a base class instead. Also, perhaps you might want to define some nonconstant fields (which interfaces do not support) so, once again, you consider developing a base class.

As covered in chapter 5, a base class allows you to provide fields for the general characteristics and functions for the general behaviors of a common group of entities. A derived class can then extend that base class to provide functions for the specialized behaviors and fields for the specialized characteristics of a subset of the group of entities generalized in the base class. Consider, as an example of a base class, a customer class. Some classes derived from the customer class might be consumer and company classes. Both of these classes inherit many of their attributes and behaviors from their common customer base class, but they also extend the base functionality of ancestry to provide behaviors specific to consumers or companies.

You can follow this rule of thumb for deciding whether to use a base class or an interface: Use a base class when the common functions are to share the same implementation, and use an interface when the common functions cannot share the same implementation. But what do you do when you have a mix? That is, perhaps some of your functions should have base class code implementations and some should be custom-coded in implementations of the derived class.

IMPLEMENTATIONS OF ABSTRACT CLASSES

Java's solution to this design dilemma comes in the form of an abstract class. Java abstract classes resemble Java interfaces in that they can define functions without providing implementations. An abstract class, like an interface, can never be instantiated. Unlike interfaces, however, abstract classes can optionally provide function implementations. It's sort of like your boss giving you a list of things for you to do– some of them he wants done his way; the others he just wants done, in whatever manner you choose to do them. Abstract classes and interfaces also differ in that an abstract class, unlike an interface, can have fields that are mutable (changeable).

A simple but very real example of an abstract class is Java's own NUMBER class (shown in Figure 9.1). Chapter 7's explanation of inheritance covers the NUMBER class but neglects to mention that NUMBER is an abstract class. The NUMBER class is a generalization of numbers—any number, be it integer, long, short, or floating-point or fixed-point decimal. Some of the functions of the NUMBER class have implementations and others do not, because they are abstract functions.

```
public abstract class Number  {
    public abstract int intValue();
    public abstract long longValue();
    public abstract float floatValue();
    public abstract double doubleValue();
    public byte byteValue();
    public short shortValue();
    public java.lang.Number();
}
class BigDecimal
      extends Number  {
    // code omitted
    public int intValue();
    public long longValue();
    public float floatValue();
    public double doubleValue();
    // code omitted
}
```

Figure 9.1: Java's BIGDECIMAL class provides code implementations for the abstract functions declared in its parent class, JAVA.LANG.NUMBER.

Many Java classes derive from the NUMBER class. Each of those classes defines implementations of NUMBER's abstract functions that are appropriate for manipulating the characteristics of that derived class's type of number. The BIGDECIMAL class, for instance, is derived from the NUMBER class to implement a fixed-point decimal class. Because the BIGDECIMAL class extends the abstract NUMBER class, it must provide code implementations for the four abstract functions of the NUMBER class (INTVALUE, LONGVALUE, FLOATVALUE, and DOUBLEVALUE). The two non-abstract functions of the NUMBER class (BYTEVALUE and SHORTVALUE) do not require implementation in the BIGDECIMAL class. If you create a BIGDECIMAL object, that object has SHORTVALUE and BYTEVALUE functions; the code implementation for those functions comes from BIGDECIMAL's parent NUMBER class.

The TRANSACTION class shown in Figure 9.2 provides another example of an abstract class. TRANSACTION implements the ITRANSACTION interface in the design of a base transaction class. Notice that the class definition begins with the Java keyword ABSTRACT, which states that this class is not to be considered a *concrete* data type. You cannot instantiate an ABSTRACT class; it is only to be used as a base class. You can't instantiate a NUMBER object, for example, with new NUM-BER() because NUMBER is an abstract class. Likewise, you cannot instantiate a TRANSACTION object.

```
import java.math.BigDecimal;
import java.util.Date;

abstract class Transaction extends RdbEntity
        implements IPrint, ITransaction {
  protected Date date;
  protected String description;
  protected int quantity;
  protected BigDecimal cost;
  // notice no implementation for IPrint interface

  // no implementation for the new getDescription function
  abstract    public String getDescription();

  // implementations for ITransaction interface
  public BigDecimal getCost () {return cost;}
  public Date getDate() {return date;}
  public int getQuantity () {return quantity;}
  public void setCost(BigDecimal cost) {
    this.cost = cost;}
  public void setDate(Date date) {
    this.date = date;}
  public void setDescription(String desc) {
    this.description = desc;}
  public void setQuantity (int qty) {
    this.quantity = qty;}
}
```

Figure 9.2: The TRANSACTION class is considered abstract because it has no implementation for its GETDESCRIPTION function.

When a class that is derived from an abstract class implements the null functions (functions that are implemented as a set of curly braces with no code between them) of its base, that class is then considered a *concrete* class. So you can create a BIGDECIMAL object (which IS-A NUMBER) with NEW BIGDECIMAL() because BIGDECIMAL is a concrete class.

The TRANSACTION class defines the modifiable fields of date, description, quantity, and cost. You might recall that Java interfaces only support constant fields, so the ITRANSACTION interface could not declare the four fields that are obviously part of any transaction. The TRANSACTION class implements the ITRANSACTION interface and defines those four fields.

The TRANSACTION class, however, is an abstract class because it has no implementations for one of its functions: GETDESCRIPTION. The GETDESCRIPTION function has the obligatory ABSTRACT keyword qualifier to tell the compiler that you do not want to provide code implementation for this function. Abstract classes are handy when some of the functions of an abstract class have general implementations that its derived classes can use but when other functions would best be implemented in the derived classes themselves. Consider the TRANSACTION class: The GETDATE function implementation will work fine for any class derived from the TRANSACTION base class. Those derived classes clearly would want to provide their own description for their transactions. Note that when one or more functions of a class are declared as abstract, the class definition also must be declared as abstract. The Java compiler then makes sure that any derived classes implement those abstract functions and that the abstract class is not instanced as an object.

The abstract TRANSACTION class serves as the base class for both the WOTRANSACTION and POTRANSACTION classes, as shown in Figure 9.3. Besides extending the characteristics and behaviors of the TRANSACTION base class with the BADGE field and SETBADGE function, WOTRANSACTION and POTRANSACTION both provide the required implementations for the abstract GETDESCRIPTION function.

```
public class POTransaction extends Transaction{
    private String shipMethod;
  // implementation of abstract function
    public String getDescription() {
      return " Ship via: " + shipMethod +
            " Desc: "+description;
```

Figure 9.3: The WOTRANSACTION and POTRANSACTION classes provide code implementations for the abstract SETDESCRIPTION function of their base TRANSACTION class and the IPRINT interface. (Part 1 of 2)

```
    }
    // implementation for IPrint interface
    public void printDetail() {
        System.out.println(getDescription());}
    public void printFooter() {
        System.out.println(
            "*** POTransaction Footer ***");}
    public void printHeader() {
        System.out.println(
            "Purchase Order Transaction:");}
}
public class WOTransaction extends Transaction{
    private int badge;
    // implementation of abstract function
    public String getDescription() {
        return date+" Badge: "+badge+" Desc: " +
            description;}
    // implementation for IPrint interface
    public void printDetail() {
        System.out.println(getDescription());}
    public void printFooter() {
        System.out.println("*** WO Footer *** ");}
    public void printHeader() {
        System.out.println("Work Order Trans:");}
    public void setBadge(int badge) {
        this.badge = badge;}
}
```

Figure 9.3: The WOTRANSACTION and POTRANSACTION classes provide code implementations for the abstract SETDESCRIPTION function of their base TRANSACTION class and the IPRINT interface. (Part 2 of 2)

The work order and purchase order transaction classes also implement functions for the IPRINT interface. Perhaps you noticed that the TRANSACTION class implemented the IPRINT interface. You might also wonder, then, why the TRANSACTION class didn't provide its own implementation of the IPRINT interface's functions. After all, the TRANSACTION class nicely provided implementations for all of the functions of the ITRANSACTION interface.

Abstract classes like TRANSACTION are not required to provide code for any of the functions that have the ABSTRACT keyword specified. All the functions of interfaces are implicitly tagged as abstract and the responsibility of implementing the code for abstract functions is delegated to those classes that implement that interface. The TRANSACTION class—because it is an abstract class—does not have to provide code for the functions of the IPRINT interface; it effectively delegates the responsibility for implementing the IPRINT interface to any classes that extend the TRANSACTION class—like the WOTRANSACTION class.

POLYMORPHISM

The beauty of base classes, abstract base classes, and Java interfaces is that you can design other Java classes to use the general design of the functions of those base classes and interfaces. You wouldn't, for instance, create separate print classes for WOTRANSACTION and POTRANSACTION. You would create a generic print class. The PRINTTRANSACTIONS class of Figure 9.4 can print information about any object whose class implements the IPRINT interface. This class should look familiar to you because chapter 8 uses it to print the IPRINT interface implementations of the WOACTIVITY and POAZ classes.

```java
public class PrintTransactions {
    public static final String FILE = "FILE";
    public static final String PRINTER="PRINTER";

    PrintTransactions (String printer) {
        // create and open file here if "FILE"
        // passed else write to printer
    }
    public void finalize() throws Throwable {
        // flush file or printer
    }
    public void print(IPrint[] printGroup) {
        for (int i = 0; i < printGroup.length; i++)
        {
            printGroup[i].printHeader();
            printGroup[i].printDetail();
            printGroup[i].printFooter();
        }
    }
}
```

Figure 9.4: The PRINTTRANSACTION class can print information about any object whose class implements the IPRINT interface.

The TESTABSTRACTTRANSACTION class of Figure 9.5 creates POTRANSACTION and WOTRANSACTION objects in its constructor. Both of these classes have the abstract base class of TRANSACTION. The PRINTGROUP array that holds objects of the TRANSACTION class is initialized to contain references to the PO and WO objects. Then the TESTABSTRACTTRANSACTION's constructor instantiates a PRINTTRANSACTIONS object. Note that the constructor for PRINTTRANSACTIONS is passed a constant value—a static final field from the PRINTTRANSACTIONS class—that tells the print utility class to print to a file. PRINTTRANSACTIONS' print function accepts an argument of the array of PRINTGROUP TRANSACTION objects.

```
public class TestAbstractTransaction {
  public TestAbstractTransaction ( ) {

    POTransaction po = new POTransaction();
    po.setDescription("purchase order shipped");

    WOTransaction wo = new WOTransaction();
    wo.setDescription(
        "W/O routing step 110 completed");
    wo.setDate(new java.util.Date());
    wo.setBadge(928);
    // create an array and initialize it to the
    // PO and WO Activity objects
    Transaction[] printGroup = {po, wo};
    PrintTransactions print =
     new PrintTransactions(
              PrintTransactions.FILE);
    print.print(printGroup);
  }
  public static void main(String[] args) {
    new TestAbstractTransaction();
  }
}
```

Figure 9.5: The TESTABSTRACTTRANSACTION class is designed to use the common interface of the TRANSACTION abstract base class and the IPRINT interface.

It is important to note that the PRINTTRANSACTIONS class's PRINT function does not take a reference to TRANSACTION, nor does it take a reference to PO-TRANSACTION or WOTRANSACTION. The function was designed to take an object whose class implemented the IPRINT interface—in other words, the PRINT function was designed to an interface. PRINTTRANSACTIONS' print function, at runtime, uses the object-oriented feature called polymorphism to invoke the function of the class for which the PRINTGROUP object was originally created. The listing of Figure 9.6 shows that the PRINTTRANSACTIONS class's PRINT function magically uses the appropriate implementations of the IPRINT interface.

```
Purchase Order Transaction:
 Ship via: null Desc: purchase order shipped
*** POTransaction Footer ***
Work Order Trans:
Tue Nov 03 14:15:10 EST 1998 Badge: 928 Desc: W/O routing step
110 completed
*** WO Footer ***
Purchase Order Transaction:
 Ship via: null Desc: purchase order shipped
*** POTransaction Footer ***
Work Order Trans:
Tue Nov 03 14:15:38 EST 1998 Badge: 928 Desc: W/O routing step
110 completed
*** WO Footer ***
```

Figure 9.6: The output of the TESTABSTRACTTRANSACTION class application demonstrates the results of designing to an interface using both abstract classes and interfaces.

DON'T DO TODAY WHAT YOU CAN PUT OFF UNTIL TOMORROW

You may be wondering how all this polymorphism stuff works. Let me give you the two-minute explanation.

You probably understand that with legacy programming languages like RPG, function calls are tied to their code implementation at compile time (either by reference or by copy). Consider, for instance, an ILE RPG program in which a driver module invokes another module. The code for that other module is bound to the program at compile time if you use the bind-by-copy method. All the code for the invoked module becomes an integral part of the compiled program because it is copied into the compiled version of the program. You would get the same effect if you copied the entire source of that module to within the driver module.

With Java, function calls are not bound at compile time; they are bound at runtime. When an object invokes a function, the Java Virtual Machine uses the object reference and calls the function that the object's class implemented. The code for the function is dynamically bound at runtime.

When you design to an interface, you declare your variables as either an interface or a base class. Those variables are known as object references because they are handles to object instances of any object whose class has implemented the interface (if the variable is typed as an interface) or extended the base class (if the variable is typed as a base class). When you use that object reference to invoke a function, the code for that function is bound at runtime, rather than at compile time, to the function implementation of the class that was used to instantiate the referenced object.

That's a difficult concept to grasp. It seems that if the function that uses the object knows it only as a base class or an interface, how can it know to invoke the function of a class? The secret is in the object reference; that reference is a handle to an object and the object knows what class it was created as and, hence, the appropriate function to call.

This runtime process does add overhead, which is one of the biggest reasons Java (and other object-oriented languages) runs slower than non-object–oriented languages like RPG and COBOL. But the pluggability of Java interfaces, classes, and abstract classes provides additional benefits, the value of which goes way beyond the cost of a few extra CPU cycles.

Twenty or thirty years ago, assembly language programmers were saying that third-generation languages like C, RPG, and COBOL consumed too many resources, but how many assembly language programmers do you know? We all know, however, that the industry moved to third-generation languages because they made programmers more productive. The industry at large has already moved on to object-oriented languages to raise programmers to yet a higher level of productivity. Now that Java provides us with a viable object-oriented business language, it's time AS/400 shops adopt the proven strategies of object-oriented design as well.

10

JAVA POLYMORPHISM

Polymorphism—what a cool-sounding, scientific term. When I first heard the term polymorphism, I thought back to the SAT vocabulary exam and remembered *poly* means *many* and *morph* means *form*. An image of my children's toys and of a couple of Saturday morning cartoons—"Transformers" and "Mighty Morphin Power Rangers"—popped into my head. The Transformer toys are robots with humanoid faces, hands, and feet. The Power Rangers are all teenage kids. The Transformers and the Power Rangers run around doing the things you would expect of robots and teenagers. But, whenever evil threatens the universe, the robots transform into different objects—like an elephant, a tank, or even a plane. The Power Rangers, on the other hand, morph into spandex-clad superheroes, each with a different superpower and weapon. For most of us, the term *polymorphism* still brings to mind visions of robots and silly teenage superheroes rather than a sophisticated programming concept.

When object-oriented programs use polymorphism, an object that some section of code believes is of an ordinary class responds to a function request by doing something other than what was expected of that object. The program creates the object as one type, but the object is changed to work like another object type.

There may even be a variety of reactions to the object's function call, because the object could be one of many different incarnations of some base class. A variety of objects appear to "morph" or transform into different objects at runtime. Let's look at these mighty morphin' business objects to find out the secrets behind their superpowers.

First, polymorphism involves no magic whatsoever. The technology is simply the result of a well-designed object model using simple inheritance. Code that is common to several classes is factored into a base class, and derived classes augment the behaviors of the base class to have more refined and specialized abstractions.

To understand polymorphism, you need to know how Java accesses objects. Except for the primitive data types (e.g., INT, CHAR, BOOLEAN), Java variables hold references to objects. A reference can be thought of as a *handle* for an object because the reference contains the storage address, and not the value, of that object. That address is usually the address assigned to the object when the object was originally created, but it can be changed.

The ordinary class mentioned above is the base class. The application code that uses the base class does so by declaring an object, specifying that base class as the object's type. The application code is written to use the API of the variable's type—the base class. (Look at Figure 10.1 to see the type declaration for the variable MYOBJ in the constructor USESMYOBJECT.)

```
import java.util.*;

// existing class
class MyObject {
    MyObject() {}
    void buggyFunction() {
        System.out.println("buggy section of code");
    }
}

// existing class
```

Figure 10.1: The capabilities of polymorphism are often used to test an existing class by extending it merely to provide test code. (Part 1 of 2)

```
class UsesMyObject {
    MyObject myObj;
    UsesMyObject(MyObject myObj) {
        this.myObj = myObj;
    }
    void doSomething() {
        myObj.buggyFunction();
    }
}

// debug class
class DebugMyObject extends MyObject {
    void buggyFunction() {
        super.buggyFunction();
        System.out.println("debug information");
    }
}

// debug class
class TestMyObject {
    public static void main(String args[]){
        DebugMyObject myDbgObj = new DebugMyObject();
        UsesMyObject useIt = new UsesMyObject(myDbgObj);
        useIt.doSomething();
    }
}
```

Figure 10.1: The capabilities of polymorphism are often used to test an existing class by extending it merely to provide test code. (Part 2 of 2)

But while the program is running, the variable that contains the reference to the base class is changed to refer instead to a class derived from the base class. At runtime, the application code is passed or retrieves an object reference that is not really of the base class but is, instead, one of the base class's derivations. Because the methods of the derived classes are used, the object now behaves like the derived class, not the base class.

USES OF POLYMORPHISM

When programmers new to object-oriented programming first begin to use derived classes, they often do not notice areas that experienced object-oriented programmers would see as obvious places for polymorphism. Once you understand the concepts of polymorphism and design your class inheritance properly, polymorphism just happens.

When and how can you use polymorphism? (I wish we could drop the term polymorphism—it's too technical sounding for how easy it is to implement.) Three uses come to mind right away: as a tool for debugging, as a simple method of enhancing existing software, and as a representation of complex business objects.

Debugging seems to be an awfully inelegant use of polymorphism, but it is a handy programming technique that exemplifies the simplicity of polymorphism. Suppose an object gives you trouble; let's call it MYOBJECT (see Figure 10.1). You derive a new class from that object called DEBUGMYOBJECT. Next you override the buggy function in the derived class. The new function is coded to call its parent's base class function to provide the same behavior, but then the new function also displays debugging information. So far, this is just simple inheritance; but when existing application code that uses MYOBJECT is passed a reference to DEBUGMYOBJECT, the derived function is magically called. How?

Again, looking at Figure 10.1, you see that the class USESMYOBJECT expects a reference to MYOBJECT, but the test class called TESTMYOBJECT instead passes a reference to DEBUGMYOBJECT. USESMYOBJECT doesn't choke on DEBUG-MYOBJECT, because it is derived from a MYOBJECT class. When USESMY-OBJECT requests a BUGGYFUNCTION() call of the variable typed as MYOBJECT, MYOBJECT's BUGGYFUNCTION() is not invoked. The runtime function request was made to a program variable that references DEBUGMYOBJECT, not MYOBJECT. It is the object itself that invokes functions, so DEBUGMYOBJECT. BUGGYFUNCTION() is called. This is the hook of polymorphism: Object-oriented languages have moved the responsibility of function invocation from calling code to the object. That's polymorphism.

From this example, you can see that the same technique can apply to enhancements to an existing application's object model. You can extend an existing class to provide an interface that is identical to its base but that is implemented to serve more specific requirements. Existing programs that use the original base class will function properly when processing objects that they think are of the base class but are really one of the newly derived classes. The classes that are users of the base class need no knowledge of the derived implementations. They do not even require recompilation.

In essence, Java and other object-oriented languages have moved the responsibility of function invocation from the calling code to the object as it was instantiated or created. (Remember that instantiation is an object-oriented term that refers to the process of creating an instance of an object with the Java operator NEW.)

THE OLD WAY

Let's consider how you would use RPG to solve a business problem that could be elegantly solved with Java objects using polymorphism. Suppose you have an inventory application that has an ITEM file with two fields: REORDPOINT and ONHAND. A daily process spins through all the ITEM records, checking the REORDPOINT value against the ONHAND value and calling a program to order more items if necessary (see Figure 10.2).

```
* Reorder all items that are apt to go out of stock
Fitem      IF   E          K DISK
 *
C     *In91          DowEq     *OFF

C                    Read   rItem

C     *In91          IfEq   *OFF

C     ReOrdPoint     IfGt   OnHand
C                    Call   'OrderMore'
C                    Parm   ItemNumber
C                    EndIf

C                    EndIf

C                    EndDo
```

Figure 10.2: An RPG inventory program might call another program when stock levels become low.

That seems simple enough. What would happen if your boss decided to implement a more sophisticated ordering system for a subset of the company's items? You would have to modify the ITEM file to add an additional field—item type—to identify the whether an item is to be reordered based on REORDPOINT or other requirements. You would also have to modify the daily reorder program to process the other requirements and REORDPOINT items differently. Items reordered according to other criteria require that you check arrival dates and quantities on existing purchase orders against forecasts and on-hand quantities. Your RPG program might look like the code in Figure 10.3.

```
FItemMstr IF    E           K DISK
 *
C     *In91       DowEq      *OFF

C                 Read       rItem                    91

C     *In91       IfEq       *OFF

C     ItemType    Select
C                 WhEq       'Requirements'
C                 Call       'CheckReq'
C                 Parm                    ItemNumber
C                 Parm                    OnHand
C                 Parm                    Order
C     Order       IfEq       'Y'
C                 Call       'OrderMore'
C                 Parm                    ItemNumber
C                 EndIf

C                 WhEq       'Basic'
C     ReOrdPoint  IfGt       OnHand
C                 Call       'OrderMore'
C                 Parm                    ItemNumber
C                 EndIf
C                 EndSl

C                 EndIf

C                 EndDo
```

Figure 10.3: An RPG program that implements requirements planning would have a system of programs coded to proactively order materials.

Notice how the case statements operate off the item type. This old method of handling variations of similar business entities has proliferated through legacy application code.

Now, consider the object-oriented, polymorphic approach. Before using polymorphism, your application would start off with a simple item class with only reorder point logic (Figure 10.4).

```
// these classes cannot be executed as
// the getItemCursor function requires
// a complex implementation using
// JDBC, DDM, serialization, or an OODB
class Item {
    private int number, reorderPoint, onHand;
    static Item getItemCursor() {
        // implementation not provided
    }
    public int shouldOrderMore() {
        if (reorderPoint > onHand)
            return 1;
        return 0;
    }
}

class ReqItem extends Item{
    ReqItem() {}
    public int shouldOrderMore() {
        return checkRequirements();
    }
}

class ReOrder {
    ItemCursor itemCur = Item.getItemCursor();

    public static void main(String args[]){
        for (Item item = itemCur.first(); item; itemCur.next())
{
            if (item.shouldOrderMore() == 1)
                System.out.println("Order More\n");
        }
    }
}
```

Figure 10.4: The requirements item class, ReqItem, extends the Item class by adding functionality specific to requirements planning.

On a daily basis, the REORDER class's MAIN() would be invoked to check for order requirements. When your boss decided to use a new order policy for a group of items, the REQITEM class was derived from ITEM. This class overrides the SHOULDORDERMORE() function, so existing code has to be modified. The REORDER class's code remains untouched and the daily run of MAIN() still spins through all items (some of which are REQITEMs masquerading as ITEMs). When REORDER.MAIN() calls ITEM.SHOULDORDERMORE(), if an item object reference was originally instantiated as a REQITEM, SHOULDORDERMORE() calls REQITEM's version of SHOULDORDERMORE().

Note that the implementation for getItemCursor() is not provided, as it would require a complex implementation using Java Database Connectivity, Distributed Data Management, Java serialization, or an object-oriented database. Section IV of this book, Object-Oriented Strategies for Mapping DB2/400 to Java, covers how to use DB2/400 for the storage of your business objects.

A REAL-WORLD EXAMPLE

Once you pick up the concepts of polymorphism, you will begin to design applications to indirectly invoke higher-level functions for a variety of objects at the base level. I wrote ASNA's EXTERMIN8 for Windows, a Windows-based RPG, COBOL, and Control Language Program (CLP) debugger for AS/400 programs, using an object-oriented language. The Windows client debugger downloads the source associated with the program selected for debugging. XT8WIN then instantiates one of three objects to display the program's source: an RPG source window (RPGSOURCEVIEW), a CLP source window (CLPSOURCEVIEW), or a COBOL source window (COBOLSOURCEVIEW). The classes of these three objects extend the behavior of their base class SOURCEVIEW. When a programmer double-clicks the left mouse button, XT8WIN captures the mouse event in code that was written to manipulate a SOURCEVIEW object. That generic code calls SOURCEVIEW's GETVARIABLESTRING() function to retrieve the variable name string the mouse is pointing to, or a null if the mouse is not on a variable. The version of GETVARIABLESTRING() that is called will vary depending on what derivation of the SOURCEVIEW class the object was originally instantiated as.

This use of polymorphism dramatically decreases the amount of coding, because figuring out if the mouse is pointing to a variable string depends on the programming language. RPG variables can reside in factor one, factor two, or the result column (not to mention F-, I-, and O-specifications); CL variables are preceded by ampersands; and COBOL variables have the added complexity of IN and OF qualifications that are potentially on multiple lines.

DYNAMIC METHOD LOOKUP VERSUS BINDING

Java uses a dynamic method to look up which function to invoke. This dynamic lookup, known as *late binding*, occurs at runtime. In traditional programming languages, calls are bound to function code not at runtime but at compile time, link time, or program-load time. ILE compilers on the AS/400 and C compilers on PCs bind to function calls at compile time if the function is contained within the same source file member. The binding process takes place at link time if a separate compile unit contains the function code. In ILE, for instance, the Create Program (CRTPGM) command resolves the binding of function calls to the modules specified in the CRTPGM module list. The bind may even be deferred until the program loads if the ILE program references a function that is contained within a service program. A Windows C program can accomplish the same load-time binding with Dynamic Link Libraries (DLLs).

Java does not bind to functions at compile time, at link time, or at program-load time. Java languages wait until that last possible moment and then dynamically bind (or *resolve*) a function call to the appropriate function code at runtime. As you have seen, the responsibility of resolving the function call has been delegated from statically coded, type-sensitive switch statements to Java's dynamic function lookup.

I WISH C++ HAD THAT...

The more I learn about Java, the more often I think, "Boy, I wish C++ had that." That thought resurfaced when I learned about the INSTANCEOF operator and of the class OBJECT. The INSTANCEOF operator is quite simple to describe and just as easy to use:

```
objectHandle instanceof Type
```

The INSTANCEOF operator returns the Boolean value of true if the object referenced by OBJECTHANDLE is of the same type as the class name TYPE. This operator comes in handy, but don't go using it in place of polymorphism by coding switch statements all over the place and then checking object types with the INSTANCEOF operator.

You'll also think, "Why doesn't C++ have that?" when you discover the class CLASS. No, that's not a typo. All Java classes are derived from a standard Java class named OBJECT, and OBJECT has a function called GETCLASS() that returns—you guessed it—the object CLASS.

Even your own classes implicitly derive from the OBJECT class. In Figure 10.1, CLASS MYOBJECT { is interpreted as and equivalent to CLASS MYOBJECT EXTENDS OBJECT {. The point is, you can call GETCLASS() on any object to return a CLASS object. The CLASS object has a number of methods, and a few of the more interesting ones deserve mention:

- GETNAME()—returns the name of the class.
- GETSUPERCLASS()—returns the superclass of the class.
- NEWINSTANCE()—creates a new instance of the class.

When you begin to use base-class typed variables to hold subclass instantiations, the CLASS functions come in handy if your code needs to know, at runtime, more about an object's specific subclass.

MANUAL CONTROL

All object-oriented programming languages have ways of stopping polymorphic function calls. In C++, for instance, for functions to be polymorphic, you must precede your function declaration with the keyword VIRTUAL. In Java, all functions are virtual (polymorphic) by default. To stop Java's polymorphic behavior, you can do one of four things.

First, you can declare functions *static* so they cannot be overridden. Second, you can declare a function *private* so that it can't be inherited. Third, you can declare a function *final*, which also prevents it from being overridden. Note that the use of *static* and *final* achieve two different purposes, the effect of which also happens to stop polymorphic behavior on a function.

144

The fourth way of stopping polymorphic behavior involves using an *explicit cast* on object variables. For instance, if you cast the DEBUGMYOBJECT object to be passed to the constructor of USESMYOBJECT, then TESTMYOBJECT.MAIN() will not call the DEBUGMYOBJECT version of BUGGYFUNCTION:

```
UsesMyObject useIt = new UsesMyObject((MyObject)DebugMyObject);
```

Just be aware that when you use casting, you in effect tell the compiler, "Trust me. I know what I am doing." Be sure that you do.

SUMMARY

Now you know that mighty morphin' business objects are simply the result of well-designed inheritance. Once you grasp polymorphism's concepts, polymorphism just happens.

Because your derived classes extend the behavior of a base class, you can type variables as the base. Such variables will then invoke the implementation of whatever derived class the variables happen to reference at runtime. Use of polymorphism substantially cuts down on the code bloat that is considered normal when RPG and COBOL applications must react to constant changes in the behavior of business entities.

11

JAVA ERROR HANDLING
FOR CL PROGRAMMERS

It's tough for RPG programmers to make the shift to Java. The methods of object-oriented programming starkly contrast the procedural methods of legacy AS/400 application programming. It doesn't help that most authors of introductory Java books write from the perspective of a C++ or C programmer. One area, however, where AS/400 programmers come out ahead of C programmers is in the understanding of error handling.

Most authors of introductory books on Java skirt the issue of error handling because they think readers lack the perspective from which to understand error handling. AS/400 legacy programmers do have that perspective. It turns out that the error handling that you've used for years on the AS/400 is very similar to Java's error handling. This chapter describes Java's mechanism for handling errors from the perspective of AS/400 error handling.

Consider the Java code snippet in Figure 11.1. If you squint your eyes (or look at Figure 11.2), you can almost see the equivalent CL code. In OS/400, errors are organized and categorized in message files. In Java, errors are objects. (Everything in Java is an object.) Program errors are generated in OS/400 with the Send Program Message (SNDPGMMSG) command. In Java, errors are created by instantiating an EXCEPTION object with Java's NEW operator. An OS/400 mechanism for handling errors consists of adding the Monitor Message (MONMSG) command in CL programs. In Java, the CATCH operation handles errors. The similarities between Java and OS/400 error handling are relatively straightforward. This chapter first describes how errors are designed, categorized, and generated; then it covers how to handle errors in Java applications.

```
try {
  aObject.SomeFunc();
  aObject.SomeOtherFunc();
} catch (SpecificExcp error) {
  System.out.println(exp.getMessage());
} catch(Exception error) {
  System.out.println(e.getMessage());
} finally {
  System.out.println("executes no matter what");
}
```

Figure 11.1: Java error handling utilizes a try/catch block, similar to the MONMSG command used in CL programs.

```
CRTWHATEVER THING(L/X)
MONMSG CPF1234 EXEC(DO)
  /* handle specific error */
  ENDDO
MONMSG CPF0000 EXEC(DO)
  /* handle generic error */
  ENDDO
```

Figure 11.2: CL programs use a MONMSG command to catch and handle explicit or generic errors.

DESCRIBING ERRORS

As you know, OS/400 errors are stored in message files. OS/400 indexes messages with a seven-digit number: a three-digit alphanumeric prefix followed by four hexadecimal digits. The three-character prefix is used to categorize messages. The four-character suffix is used to further break down the message category.

For instance, OS/400 message file QCPFMSG contains messages that begin with a prefix of CPF to identify them as operating system messages. (CPF stands for Control Program Facility—the operating system name of the AS/400's predecessor, the S/38.) CPF messages with a 12 heading up the hexadecimal portion of the index relate to AS/400 jobs and subsystems. The last two numbers in the message name identify a specific error. CPF1254, for instance, is the error message for a user not being authorized to an output queue in a particular library. The following three CPF messages use the four-digit numbers to identify all OS/400 messages, the 1200 series of messages, and a specific message:

- CPF0000—All OS/400 messages

- CPF1200—All job- and subsystem-related messages

- CPF1254—User &1 not authorized to output queue &2 in library &3

You'll find nothing new there; you already know this stuff. Java's errors are similar in design. Just like OS/400, Java gives you standard errors that you can use. And, just as in OS/400, you can create your own Java errors. The only difference is that Java errors will be objects rather than message file entries. To illustrate Java's and OS/400's error handling similarities, I've used simple inheritance to design a category of Java error message objects that is similar to OS/400's CPF 1200 series.

First, I created a generic Java message object to identify CPF messages and called that Java class CPFMSG. The CPFMSG error class uses inheritance because, as you can see in Figure 11.3, it extends the EXCEPTION class of Sun's JAVA.LANG package. All Java errors, known as *exceptions*, should inherit from the base exception class of JAVA.LANG.EXCEPTION. This class, just like all members of an OS/400 message file, contains a string that holds a description of the error message. By order of inheritance, CPFMSG also contains a string representation of the error. Note that CPFMSG does not truly extend JAVA.LANG. EXCEPTION by adding more fields and functions; I've used it just for categorization purposes. You would never actually create a CPFMSG exception object, but neither would you ever send a CPF0000 message; they are simply used as broad categories.

```
class CPFMsg extends java.lang.Exception
{
}
class CPFSbsJobMsg extends CPFMsg
{
}
class CPFUsrAuthOutq extends CPFSbsJobMsg
{
  String user;
  String outq;
  String lib;
  CPFUsrAuthOutq(String user, String outq, String lib)
  {
     this.user = user;
     this.outq = outq;
     this.lib =  lib;
  }
}
```

Figure 11.3: Java's *JAVA.LANG.EXCEPTION* error object class can be used as the base class for a hierarchy of custom errors.

To create a more generalized Java error object category to correspond to the CPF 1200 series of errors, I'll create a message class called CPFSBSJOBMSG. Note the obvious advantage of Java errors—their class names more clearly represent the errors than the alphanumeric code of OS/400 message members. (Did you really recall that CPF1200 was for jobs and subsystems?) CPFSBSJOBMSG extends the broad error category of CPFMSG; again, this class does not truly add any attributes to improve the family name but merely serves as a subcategory.

Finally, the CPFUSRAUTHOUTQ class defines a representation of a specific error; a user is not authorized to an output queue. Because this class extends CPFSBSJOBMSG, it inherits all the attributes of its father, its great-grandfather (CPFMSG), and its great-great-grandfather (JAVA.LANG.EXCEPTION). CPFUSRAUTHOUTQ then adds the string attributes required to hold the name of the user and the name of the output queue (and its library) that the user cannot access. Likewise, OS/400's CPF1254 message member holds the values for user, output queue, and library as message data values.

MESSAGE GENERATION

You already know how to generate errors with OS/400—you use the
SNDPGMMSG command:

```
SNDPGMMSG MSGID(CPF1254) MSGF(QCPFMSG) +
        MSGDTA('DENONCOURTINVPRT  INVLIB ') +
        MSGTYPE(*ESCAPE)
```

The SNDPGMMSG command looks fairly object-oriented to me. SNDPGMMSG creates an instance of an AS/400 error message. (Note: messages of the message type *ESCAPE are considered exceptions.) That error message will then contain information specific to the CPF1254 message from the values that were passed to the SNDPGMMSG command in the Message Data (MSGDTA) parameter: user name, output queue, and library. Consider the way you'd generate that error with my Java CPF class:

```
CPFUsrAuthOutq error = new CPFUsrAuthOutq("DENONCOURT", "INVPRT",
"INVLIB");
```

As are all Java variables, the error variable is a handle to an object that is instantiated by invoking Java's NEW operator on the class constructor function. CPFUSRAUTHOUTQ's constructor takes parameters for the user name, output queue, and library, just as the SNDPGMMSG command did in its MSGDTA prompt.

While the SNDPGMMSG command both creates and sends the error message, the Java error object involves an additional step. With Java errors, the object is explicitly sent with the THROW keyword:

```
throw error;
```

Java programmers will often concatenate the two operations into one Java statement to reduce the lines of code:

```
throw new CPFUsrAuthOutq("DENONCOURT", "INVPRT", "INVLIB");
```

This short form also removes the requirement for the temporary error object variable. You can be sure that the error object variable will not be used after the THROW operation because control returns to the calling function as a result of the THROW (as it does with an *ESCAPE message sent in a CL program on OS/400).

ERROR HANDLING

You now have an idea how Java error classes are designed and how to create (instantiate, in Java parlance) error objects. It's time to handle those errors that you've created.

In legacy OS/400 applications, you use the SNDPGMMSG command to generate errors and signal the calling program that an error occurred. When the error occurs and an *ESCAPE message is generated, that message is propagated (bubbles) up the invocation stack. An *invocation stack* is the list of functions or programs that stack up on top of one another as they call each other. The stack grows as functions are called and shrinks as functions return. In the case of error processing, functions implicitly return when a SNDPGMSG *ESCAPE type error message is generated. The calling program has the opportunity to handle the program error. If it doesn't, the error continues its trek up the invocation stack until a calling program handles it or it reaches the top of the call stack (or a control boundary in ILE) and a termination CPF message is generated by OS/400. Note that an error is *handled* with the CL's MONMSG command. That's some pretty deep stuff I just covered, but I'm confident you understand it because it's standard OS/400 error handling.

Java error handling uses Java's CATCH keyword rather than MONMSG. The CATCH is followed by the parenthetical phrase of the exception class and exception variable:

```
catch (SpecificExcp error)
```

Should a SPECIFICEXCP error object be thrown, the section of code inside the curly braces following the CATCH phrase will execute. For example, in Figure 11.1, the exception variable named ERROR will be the exception object created by either the SOMEFUNC or SOMEOTHERFUNC function.

The difference between CL's MONMSG and Java's CATCH clause is that the MONMSG statement relates only to the command that immediately precedes the MONMSG (with the notable exception of global monitors). In Java, the CATCH clause relates to all of the functions enclosed within the curly braces following Java's TRY keyword. Because the TRY and CATCH verbs go hand in hand, they are commonly referred to as *try/catch blocks*.

It is important that you understand the implicit power of Java exception objects. They are objects, and, as such, they have functions that may be invoked. Notice that, in Figure 11.1, the SPECIFICEXCP object variable, ERROR, is used to invoke the GETMESSAGE function (defined in the JAVA.LANG.EXCEPTION base class) to print the message text. You might code your own exception class to have a function that presents a complete GUI that allows the user to fix the problem. Note too the FINALLY clause of the try/catch block. Unlike CL's MONMSG, Java allows you to specify a section of code to execute regardless of whether an error occurs. This feature comes in handy for tasks that need to be done whether or not errors occurred, such as closing files or deallocating resources.

ENFORCED ERROR HANDLING

Java's error handling capability has one big improvement over OS/400's error handling feature—it enforces error handling. That's a big deal. Think about what often happens in your shop. You and your veteran cohorts create a sophisticated AS/400 application. You create an application-specific message file and design message IDs for a wide spectrum of application errors. Those messages are generated in your application and all of your CL programs have MONMSG commands that handle the errors. Then some hotshot kid straight out of college joins your team. She's pretty smart, and you give her some complex programs to write. She does a great job, and her programs go into production. Then things start to blow up. Your well-designed application is aborting and you see in the job log that your hot new coder failed to monitor for any of your carefully designed messages. You also see that she wasn't monitoring and handling what you and I know are standard OS/400 CPF messages. Unfortunately, your coder was not aware of these messages.

On the AS/400, proper message handling tends to come with experience. In Java, when a coder uses a function that throws (generates) an exception, he or she must explicitly handle the error in the code or it will not compile. That's another big plus: Java strictly enforces error handling.

How does a Java programmer know that an error has to be handled? That question has two answers. First, the compiler error explicitly states the name of the exception. Second, the class function that throws the exception has the exception as a part of its function's *signature* (the combination of the function name, parameters, return type, and exceptions thrown by that function). The API of a class is its list of functions and their signatures. You can find out how to use a Java class in one of two ways. You could use a Java utility called JAVAP, which lists the function signatures of a class, or you could review the HTML Java documentation of a class using your favorite Web browser. The following function signature is that of IBM's Java Toolbox for the AS/400 (jt400) KEYEDFILE READ function:

```
public Record read(Object key[])
throws AS400Exception, AS400SecurityException,
InterruptedException, IOException
```

Notice the explicit identification of Java exceptions. Java Toolbox for the AS/400's HTML listing further elaborates on the object definition for each of the four exceptions that you must handle if you use its READ function. You could, if you're the sloppy sort, simply catch the generic EXCEPTION object as the code in Figure 11.4 does. That coding style, however, is as pointless as the CL style of adding MONMSG CPF0000 with no DO clause; you are effectively ignoring the error. This generic Java error handling is possible because all four of the exceptions thrown by the KEYEDFILE object's READ function inherit from JAVA.LANG. EXCEPTION; you can catch the generic exception object rather than the specific objects. Although you will often see this poor coding style, realize that it's as if the coder has said, "I know I should catch and handle explicit errors here, but I just don't care." I suggest you dole out the same punishment to such Java violators as you give to CL programmers who use MONMSGS without the EXEC clause.

```
try {
    Record record = file.read(keyField);
} catch (Exception error) {}
// this catch is no better than MONMSGs with no DO
```

Figure 11.4: Although Java forces programmers to handle errors, it does not force us to handle them well.

Figure 11.5 presents a better example for handling jt400's READ function exceptions. Two of the CATCH clauses monitor explicitly for AS400EXCEPTION and AS400SECURITYEXCEPTION; if INTERRUPTEDEXCEPTION or IOEXCEPTION is thrown, the third clause will catch it and handle it as a generic message. You might take a moment to look further at the code in Figure 11.5. Because IBM has implemented some sophisticated AS/400-specific Java exception classes, the code can handle those exceptions by using the functions provided with IBM's custom AS/400 exception classes.

```
try {
  Record as400record = as400File.read(keyField);
} catch(AS400Exception except) {
  AS400Message msg = except.getAS400Message();
  System.out.println("ID: " + msg.getID() + "\n" +
            "Severity: " + msg.getSeverity() + "\n" +
              "Type: " + msg.getType() + "\n" +
              "Text: " + msg.getText());
} catch(AS400SecurityException except) {
    System.out.println(except.getMessage() +
        " return code: " + except.getReturnCode());
} catch(Exception except) {
    // print any other errors
    System.out.println(except.getMessage());
}
```

Figure 11.5: IBM's Java Toolbox for the AS/400 comes with AS/400-specific exception classes.

THROWING ERRORS AROUND

In addition to forcing users of class functions that throw exceptions to handle those exceptions, the Java compiler also makes sure that any functions that throw errors have a THROWS clause in the signature. That way, the compiler can also enforce exception handling for any users of that class's function. Actually, to be more precise, users of functions that throw an error don't have to handle that error; they can simple state a THROWS clause in the function's signature. Java will automatically propagate that exception up the call stack, just as OS/400 error messages are bubbled up. The process differs in that Java requires you to explicitly pass that exception baton, whereas OS/400 error messages do it implicitly.

Figure 11.6 shows a concise example of Java exception creation and exception handling. The print function of the INVOICE class instantiates one of my CPFUSRAUTHOUTQ objects and throws it to signal an error. Because the print function generates a CPFUSRAUTHOUTQ exception, that exception must be identified in the THROWS clause of the PRINT function's signature. The WEEKLYPROCAPP application class (which obviously handles weekly processing) uses the INVOICE class and its PRINT function. The PRINT function is enclosed in a try/catch block. The code for the catch is not very intelligent since it only prints the exception. The code would be significantly improved if it presented a GUI or otherwise allowed someone or something to fix the problem. The try/catch block also includes a FINALLY clause that merely prints a *job completed* message. Again, perhaps an e-mail or a GUI dialog would be better, but the idea is that the FINALLY clause executes code whether or not an error occurs.

```
class Invoice {
  void print () throws CPFUsrAuthOutq {
    // initial application code removed
    ...
    // unauthorized attempt to use an output queue
    if (authorized == false) {
      throw new CPFUsrAuthOutq(user, outqNam, outqLib);
    }
    // subsequent application code removed
    ...
  }
}
class WeeklyProcApp {
  void printAllInvoices () {
    try {
      invoice.print();
    } catch (CPFUsrAuthOutq msg) {
      System.out.println(msg.toString() +
          msg.user + " " + msg.lib + "/" msg.outq);
    } finally {
      System.out.println("Weekly processing completed");
    }
  }
}
```

Figure 11.6: Java enforces error handling; any code that uses a function that throws an exception must have a try/catch block around that function call or it will not compile.

FINALLY {JAVA ERROR HANDLING SUMMARIZED}

Have you *caught* most of the concepts explained in this chapter? First, remember that a Java error is an object, whereas in OS/400 errors are messages. Second, you can use existing exception classes or you can design your own exceptions by deriving custom classes from Java's EXCEPTION class. Third, Java exceptions are thrown in a manner similar to CL's SNDPGMMSG. Fourth, Java exceptions are handled within try/catch blocks. Java goes beyond CL's MONMSG, however, because its compiler strictly enforces error handling. Fifth, the FINALLY clause of a try/catch block allows you to specify code that must execute regardless of whether an error occurred. Finally, to ensure that exception messages thrown by the functions of a class are handled by users of that class, THROWS clauses are included in the signature of those functions.

Java exception handling is a vital part of robust applications. The designers of the Java language did a great job of making it both mandatory and easy to handle exceptions. We programmers should follow suit and do a great job of using the exception infrastructure in the design of our business applications.

SECTION III

~

ACCESSING YOUR AS/400

12

INTRODUCTION TO IBM's JAVA TOOLBOX FOR THE AS/400

To enable Java access to the AS/400, IBM created a package of Java classes bundled as a product called the Java Toolbox for the AS/400 (jt400). Java packages are delivered in either a standard zip compressed file or a Java archive file; IBM's Java Toolbox is delivered as both a JT400.JAR and a JT400.ZIP. The classes contained in those compression files encapsulate a wide variety of AS/400 accessibility:

- DB2/400 record-level access
- Java Database Connectivity (JDBC) driver for DB2/400
- Program call
- Command call
- Data queue support
- Integrated File System (IFS) file I/O
- Spool file support
- Data conversion utilities classes

The package name for these Java classes, combined under the package name of com.ibm.as400.access, have been available since OS/400 V3R7. JT400.JAR comes free with OS/400 V4R2 or higher but can be purchased as a separate program product for earlier versions of OS/400. V4R3 adds a new package of classes: com.ibm.as400.vaccess. The extra V in front of the word *access* represents the word *visual*, as those classes are all Java components that make the creation of AS/400 GUIs ridiculously easy.

IBM's Java package of visual components includes an SQL-based table, which provides a subfile-like interface as it displays rows of records and columns of fields in a gridlike or table structure. Also included is another component that presents DB2/400 data in the same manner except that the records are retrieved using record-level access rather than SQL access. The visual access components also contain button components that are easily tied to the invocation of AS/400 commands or programs. Yet another component that presents the display of various AS/400 objects is a tree structure much like Windows Explorer.

PRODUCT INSTALLATION

You don't install the Java Toolbox for the AS/400, per se; you merely copy the JAR file to a directory on either your AS/400's IFS or your PC. Note that the license program installation of the AS/400's Java Toolbox product (5763-JC1) loads the JT400.ZIP file in the IFS in the following directory:

```
/QIBM/ProdData/HTTP/Public/jt400/lib
```

The path to that JAR file's location is then added as a part of your job's Java CLASSPATH environment VARIABLE. On the PC this is done with the DOS SET command in a batch file:

```
SET CLASSPATH=C:\YourJavaDir\jt400.jar;
```

Or, if your class path ENVIRONMENT is already set, the following SET command is used:

```
SET CLASSPATH=%CLASSPATH%;C:\YourJavaDir\jt400.jar;
```

On the AS/400, the CLASSPATH environment variable is set with the Add Environment Variable command:

```
ADDENVVAR ENVVAR(CLASSPATH) +
VALUE('/QIBM/ProdData/HTTP/Public/jt400/lib/jt400.zip')
```

Or, if your class path environment is already set, you can use the Work with Environment Variables panel as invocated with the WRKENVVAR command.

You can add multiple paths to your class path environment. On the PC, you separate those paths with a semicolon; but, strangely, on the AS/400 you separate paths with a colon. For instance, suppose you have a package for your inventory application called INVENTORY.JAR. On the PC, your class path might be set as follows:

```
SET CLASSPATH C:\YourJavaDir\jt400.jar;C:\Applicatons\inventory.jar
```

On the AS/400, you would use:

```
ADDENVVAR ENVVAR(CLASSPATH) +
VALUE('/QIBM/ProdData/HTTP/Public/jt400/lib/jt400.zip:/Applications
/inventory.zip')
```

On the AS/400, when you execute a Java application with the Run Java (RUNJVA) command, it defaults to using the job's CLASSPATH environment variable:

```
RUNJVA CLASS('/JavaApps/MyJavaApp.class') +
            CLASSPATH(*ENVVAR)
```

Of course, you could set the class path for that Java application's execution manually:

```
RUNJVA CLASS('/JavaApps/MyJavaApp.class') +
        CLASSPATH(/QIBM/ProdData/HTTP/Public/jt400/lib/jt400.zip')
```

OS/400's Submit Job (SBMJOB) command also has a useful parameter for the execution of Java applications: Copy Environment Variables or CPYENVVAR. This parameter to the SBMJOB command defaults to *NO, but you can set it to *YES if you want the submitted job to use the submitting job's CLASSPATH environment variable.

ENHANCING PERFORMANCE

One point that deserves mention here relates to IBM's Java Toolbox for the AS/400 and performance: Java classes that are contained in AS/400-based ZIP files do not take advantage of the AS/400's automatic compilation of Java classes. To enhance the performance of Java classes, which, by design, are interpreted, the AS/400 automatically compiles them into native AS/400 ILE service programs. Those service programs are hidden, so don't go looking for them.

The first time a Java class executes, OS/400 does its native compile and makes the class part of a service program with the same name as that Java class's package. Subsequent uses of that Java class do not require the native compilation, because the service program that was previously compiled into a native AS/400 service program is used.

The problem with Java ZIP files is that OS/400 continues to re-create that service program on every invocation of any of the classes in that file—not very efficient. However, you can manually create those service programs for all the classes in that ZIP file with the Create Java Program command:

```
CRTJVAPGM +
CLSF('/QIBM/ProdData/HTTP/Public/jt400/lib/jt400.zip') +
OPTIMIZE(30)
```

You should submit that command as a batch job because it takes several hours to run. Realize that, if you do not run this command, a small, but nontrivial, portion of that compilation time will take place every time you instantiate one of the classes in that ZIP file.

SUMMARY

IBM's Java Toolbox for the AS/400 provides almost all the classes necessary to write AS/400 Java applications. IBM's jt400 is cool for two reasons: it's free, and it's 100 percent pure Java. You get jt400 free with V4R2 of OS/400 or later and your Java applications that you develop with jt400 will run on any JVM-compliant platform. The next two chapters cover the use of jt400 for DB2/400 access, either with the familiar record-level access or with the SQL access of

Java Database Connectivity (JDBC). Chapter 14 then provides a tutorial that explains the use of jt400's AS/400 program call, command call, and data queue support.

13

DB2/400 RECORD-LEVEL ACCESS FOR JAVA

Java's standard method for accessing data from a relational database is Java Database Connectivity (JDBC). Yet, legacy AS/400 programmers are more comfortable with the dynamic access that RPG and COBOL directly support. And it turns out that this record-level access, as it is often called, works faster than SQL anyway.

The AS/400's predecessor, the S/38, was one of the first platforms that provided a relational database and it did so by bundling it as an integral part of the operating system. The architects of the S/38 understood the strengths of a relational database. They also understood that many business applications do not require full normalization. In fact, transactional applications often run much more slowly when constrained by a fully normalized database. So, as the access methodology for most other relational databases is the set-based processing of SQL and its ODBC and JDBC derivatives, the AS/400 allows you to dynamically access DB2/400 at the record level. IBM's Java Toolbox for the AS/400 (jt400) provides both a JDBC driver and record-level access Java classes. For reasons of speed and familiarity, you might choose to use record-level access over JDBC.

The use of jt400's record-level access is straightforward, although it does involve a few more steps than a COBOL or RPG program would require. The major classes associated with record-level access are listed in Table 13.1.

Table 13.1: jt400 Classes Used for DB2/400 Record-Level Access.	
Class Name	**Description**
AS400	Manages connection to an AS/400.
QSYSObjPathName	Provides a path through the integrated file system to an object in the QSYS library file system.
KeyedFile	Provides dynamic access to an AS/400 physical or logical file.
SequentialFile	Provides sequential access to an AS/400 physical or logical file.
AS400FileRecordDescription	Represents the record descriptions of an AS/400 physical or logical file.
Record	Represents the data described by a RecordFormat object.
RecordFormat	Represents the format of data returned from an AS/400 physical or logical file.

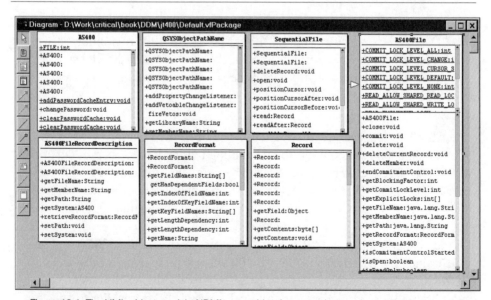

Figure 13.1: The UML object model of IBM's record-level access classes shows the classes required to access DB2/400.

Figure 13.1 displays a Unified Modeling Language (UML) object model for those same classes. At first look, they seem a little daunting. After you see how they collaborate, however, you'll find them fairly simple to use.

SIX STEPS TO JAVA RECORD-LEVEL ACCESS

The six steps to record-level access are as follows.

DB2/400 Record-Level Access for Java

1. Connect to an AS/400.
2. Specify file location.
3. Get and set the record format.
4. Open the file.
5. Read a record.
6. Retrieve field values.

STEP 1: CONNECT TO AN AS/400

The first step, connecting to an AS/400, is easily handled by instancing an AS400 object:

```
AS400 as400 = new AS400();
```

The AS400 object created above is instanced by invoking the default constructor of the AS400 class. Reverting to chapter 7's discussion of function overloading, the AS400 class has no less than five overloaded constructor functions. One is the default constructor shown above. Another one takes one parameter– a string representation of the IP address or domain name of the AS/400 to which you wish to connect. And a third takes that plus the user name. If you use any one of those three constructors, jt400 presents you with the dialog in Figure 13.2—that is, unless your

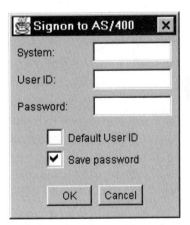

Figure 13.2: A sign-on dialog is presented if the system, user ID, or password is not specified in the construction of the As400 connection object.

169

Java class is running on a platform that doesn't have a graphical interface (e.g., an AS/400).

Of the two other constructor functions of the AS400 class, one takes another AS400 object instance as a parameter and the other takes the IP address or domain name, user profile, and password so the sign-on dialog is not required.

If your Java application executes on the AS/400 rather than remotely to that AS/400, you should take note of a couple simple but important points about the AS400 connection class. First, you must specify the IP, profile name, and password. You can, however, take advantage of some special values that specify the local machine and the current job's user profile and password:

```
AS400 local = new AS/400("localhost", "*current", "*current");
```

The special value of *CURRENT can also be used when connecting from one AS/400 to another. Using the special value of LOCALHOST for the URL deserves attention here, as it creates a performance advantage. When jt400 sees LOCALHOST for the URL, it uses native AS/400 code—which performs better than the cross-platform Java code—to access DB2/400.

STEP 2: SPECIFY THE FILE LOCATION

You specify your AS/400 file location using two classes: QSYSOBJECTPATH NAME and SEQUENTIALFILE (or KEYEDFILE, as the case may be). Realize that all Java access to the AS/400 takes place through the Integrated File System (IFS) of the AS/400. It is the job of the QSYSOBJECTPATHNAME class to provide a path from the IFS system to the good old library system of QSYS where your user libraries and DB2/400 files reside. The QSYSOBJECTPATHNAME's constructor takes the user library name, the object name, and the object type. You have to understand that QSYSOBJECTPATHNAME is used for more than just database files; it can be used to point to any object type in the QSYS library system such as data queues, programs, and commands. The following statement creates an interface through the IFS to a file called CUSTMAST in a library of my last name:

```
QSYSObjectPathName fileName =
    new QSYSObjectPathName("DENONCOURT",  "CUSTMAST", "FILE");
```

After this IFS-to-QSYS path name object is constructed, you use its GETPATH function as a parameter along with an AS/400 connection object in the instantiation of a SEQUENTIALFILE object:

```
SequentialFile file =
    new SequentialFile(as400,  fileName.getPath());
```

If your Java class requires keyed access, you construct a KEYEDFILE object with the same two parameters.

STEP 3: GET AND SET THE RECORD FORMAT

Your Java application now has access through the IFS system of the connected AS/400 to a DB2/400 file. Now your application must specify the record format for the data to be retrieved and perhaps updated. With RPG that's done automatically, but Java makes you do it yourself with the help of two more jt400 classes: AS400FILERECORDDESCRIPTION and RECORDFORMAT. The AS400FILE-RECORDDESCRIPTION's constructor takes an AS/400 connection object followed by the strange looking DOS-like qualifier for your DB2/400 file:

```
AS400FileRecordDescription recDesc =
new AS400FileRecordDescription(
as400,"/QSYS.LIB/DENONCOURT.LIB/CUSTMAST.FILE");
```

Let me break down the syntax for that second parameter. The /QSYS is followed by .LIB, which qualifies the file as being in the QSYS library system. The /DENON-COURT.LIB section says to look in the user library called DENONCOURT. The /CUSTMAST.FILE portion points to an explicit file and redundantly says that the file is a file.

The DENONCOURT.LIB portion can be replaced with the special value of %LIBL% to support the proper use of AS/400 library lists. Also, if you are working with multiple-membered files, you can insert /MEMBERNAME.MBR at the end of that qualifier string. This second parameter supplies the path through the IFS system to the QSYS library system; so, as you did in the construction of the SEQUENTIAL-FILE object, you could simply specify FILENAME.GETPATH() rather than explic-itly spelling it out:

```
AS400FileRecordDescription recDesc =
    new AS400FileRecordDescription(as400, fileName.getPath());
```

With the AS400FILERECORDDESCRIPTION object, you can finally retrieve the record format of the DB2/400 file you intend to process. You use the AS400FILE RECORDDESCRIPTION object's RETRIEVERECORDFORMAT function to get a list of all the record formats for that file's record description. (Who uses multiformat files anyway? Well, companies that have converted S/36 or mainframe files do, for one.) The RETRIEVERECORDFORMAT function returns an array of RECORD FORMAT objects—even if the file that you specified has only one format. (It seems IBM should have put an S at the end of RETRIEVERECORDFORMAT to show plurality.)

Ultimately, you want to set a record format in the SEQUENTIALFILE or KEYEDFILE object that you created earlier. You can do this in a variety of ways. You could use RETRIEVERECORDFORMAT to get that array of record formats, stuffing it into a local array of RECORDFORMAT objects. Then, using the first element of that array, you can set the file's record format:

```
RecordFormat recordFormats[] = recDesc.retrieveRecordFormat();
file.setRecordFormat(recordFormats[0]);
```

With another, shorter method, you get the array and immediately stuff it into the file, without storing it in a local array variable:

```
file.setRecordFormat(recDesc.retrieveRecordFormat()[0]);
```

In this example, the first element of the returned array of record formats is specified with [0]. You will see this kind of code quite often, as it gives programmers a handy way to cut down the number of statements in the Java class. It works exactly the same way as the first method shown because the Java Virtual Machine still creates a local object to hold the array of record formats. That local object just has no variable—why should it? It is only used as a parameter to the file's SETRECORDFORMAT function.

STEP 4: OPEN THE FILE

Finally, you can open the file. Yes, this step is just a little bit easier with RPG since you don't even have to open the file in an RPG program. But, even with Java, opening the file requires only one statement:

```
file.open(AS400File.READ_ONLY,
     BlockFactor,
     AS400File.COMMIT_LOCK_LEVEL_NONE);
```

Take a look at this statement for a moment. The OPEN function is from the SEQUENTIALFILE (or KEYEDFILE, as the case may be) object. The READ_ONLY specification in the OPEN function's first parameter represents just one of three options available; the other two include READ_WRITE and WRITE_ONLY. The second parameter requires an integer value for the blocking factor. Here, I've used a variable that I had earlier set to maybe 10 or something. A better standard is to use the value of zero because the AS/400 then calculates the blocking factor for you. The fourth parameter allows you to specify whether or not you want commitment control. (Now you know that jt400's record-level access supports commitment control.)

To change the subject for a moment, let me point out the use of AS400FILE. READ_ONLY. Perhaps you've guessed, by simply looking at this code, that READ_ONLY is a static final field of the AS400File class (which is the base class of SEQUENTIALFILE). You can rule out READ_ONLY as a function because, for one thing, no parentheses immediately follow it; so READ_ONLY must be a field. Also, the AS400FILE qualifier starts with an uppercase character. You should know that the coding convention for classes calls for the use of uppercase for the first character and the coding convention for an object instance of a class calls for a lowercase character. When you use a class qualifier, like AS400FILE. (note the dot separator), you explicitly specify to Java that you are referring to a static final field of that class. When you use an object variable name as a field qualifier, such as ANOBJECT.FIELD, you are referencing the field of that object's specific instance of its class and not the shared values of the class's static and final fields. In Java coding convention, you use all uppercase letters for static final fields.

STEP 5: READ A RECORD

With the file open, you can finally read records. That's the easy part. You simply use, for sequential access, the READ function. The READNEXT function returns a RECORD object that contains the data from the DB2/400 file or a null value:

```
Record record = file.readNext();
```

The SEQUENTIALFILE class has a variety of functions that provide the capabilities you would expect of a sequential file. Table 13.2 provides a complete list those functions while Table 13.3 provides a complete list of KEYEDFILE's specific functions. But don't forget that this is object-oriented programming; both SEQUENTIALFILE and KEYEDFILE have a common parent, AS400FILE. This base class contains a large set of general file functions that are neither sequential nor keyed in nature. Table 13.4 provides a partial list of those functions. Please remember that anytime you want to fully understand the API of a class, you must look at not only the functions that it provides but also the functions of its base class and then perhaps its base class's superclass.

Table 13.2: Sequential Access Functions Specific to the SEQUENTIALFILE Class.

Function	Description
deleteRecord(int)	Deletes the record specified by record number.
Open(int, int, int)	Opens the file.
positionCursor(int)	Positions the file cursor to the first record whose record number matches the specified record number.
positionCursorAfter(int)	Positions the file cursor to the record after the record specified by the record number.
positionCursorBefore(int)	Positions the file cursor to the record preceding the record specified by the record number.
read(int)	Reads the record with the specified record number.
readAfter(int)	Reads the record after the record with the specified record number.
readAll()	Reads all the records in the file.
readBefore(int)	Reads the record preceding the record with the specified record number.
Update(int, Record)	Updates the record at the position specified by the record number.

Table 13.3: Keyed Access Functions Specific to the KEYEDFILE Class.

Function	Description
deleteRecord(Object[ ])	Deletes the record specified by key.
Open(int, int, int)	Opens the file.
positionCursor(Object[ ])	Positions the file cursor to the first record matching the specified key.
PositionCursor(Object[ ], int)	Positions the file cursor to the first record meeting the specified search criteria based on key.
positionCursorAfter(Object[ ])	Positions the file cursor to the record after the record specified by key.
positionCursorBefore(Object[ ])	Positions the file cursor to the record preceding the record specified by key.
read(Object[ ])	Reads the first record with the specified key.
Read(Object[ ], int)	Reads the first record meeting the specified search criteria based on key.
readAfter(Object[ ])	Reads the record after the record with the specified key.
readAll()	Reads all the records in the file.
readBefore(Object[ ])	Reads the record preceding the record with the specified key.
readNextEqual()	Reads the next record whose key matches the full key of the current record.
readNextEqual(Object[ ])	Reads the next record whose key matches the specified key.
readPreviousEqual()	Reads the previous record whose key matches the key of the current record.
readPreviousEqual(Object[ ])	Reads the previous record whose key matches the specified key.
update(Object[ ], Record)	Updates the record specified by key.
update(Object[ ], Record, int)	Updates the first record meeting the specified search criteria based on key.

Table 13.4: Partial List of Functions of the AS400File Base Class. (Part 1 of 3)

Function	Description
close()	Closes the file on the AS/400.
commit()	Commits all transactions since the last commit boundary.
Create(RecordFormat, String)	Creates a physical file using the specified record format.
Create(String, String)	Creates a physical file using the specified DDS source file.
delete()	Deletes the file.
deleteCurrentRecord()	Deletes the record at the current cursor position.
deleteMember()	Deletes the member associated with this object from the file.
endCommitmentControl()	Ends commitment control for this connection.
finalize()	Closes the file when this object is garbage-collected.
getBlockingFactor()	Returns the blocking factor being used for this file.
getCommitLockLevel()	Returns the commit lock level for this file as specified on open.
getExplicitLocks()	Returns any explicit locks that have been obtained for this file.
getFileName()	Returns the file name.
getMemberName()	Returns the member name.
getPath()	Returns the IFS path name for the file as specified on the constructor or the setPath () method.
getRecordFormat()	Returns the record format of this file.
getSystem()	Returns the AS400 system object for this object.
isCommitmentControlStarted()	Indicates if commitment control is started for the connection.
isOpen()	Indicates if the file is open.
isReadOnly()	Indicates if this object is open for read only.
isReadWrite()	Indicates if this object is open for read/write.
isWriteOnly()	Indicates if this object is open for write only.

Table 13.4: Partial List of Functions of the AS400File Base Class. (Part 2 of 3)

Function	Description
lock(int)	Obtains a lock on the file.
Open(int, int, int)	Opens the file.
OpenFile(int, int, int, String)	Opens the file.
positionCursorAfterLast()	Positions the file cursor to after the last record.
positionCursorBeforeFirst()	Positions the file cursor to before the first record.
positionCursorToFirst()	Positions the file cursor to the first record.
positionCursorToLast()	Positions the file cursor to the last record.
positionCursorToNext()	Positions the file cursor to the next record.
positionCursorToPrevious()	Positions the file cursor to the previous record.
read()	Reads the record at the current cursor position.
readAll()	Reads all the records in the file.
readFirst()	Reads the first record in the file.
readLast()	Reads the last record in the file.
readNext()	Reads the next record in the file from the current cursor position.
readPrevious()	Reads the previous record in the file from the current cursor position.
refreshRecordCache()	Refreshes the record cache for this file.
releaseExplicitLocks()	Releases all locks acquired via the lock () method.
RemovePropertyChangeListener (PropertyChangeListener)	Removes a listener from the change list.
RemoveVetoableChangeListener (VetoableChangeListener)	Removes a listener from the veto change listeners list.
rollback()	Rolls back any transactions since the last commit/rollback boundary.

Table 13.4: Partial List of Functions of the AS400File Base Class. (Part 3 of 3)

Function	Description
setPath(String)	Sets the IFS path name for the file.
setRecordFormat(RecordFormat)	Sets the record format to be used for this file.
setSystem(AS400)	Sets the system to which to connect.
startCommitmentControl(int)	Starts commitment control on this file (for this connection).
update(Record)	Updates the record at the current cursor position.
write(Record)	Writes a record to the file.
write(Record[ ])	Writes an array of records to the file.

STEP 6: RETRIEVE FIELD VALUES

After completing step five, you probably think you're done because, after all, with RPG, the fields of a retrieved database record are immediately available to the program. Not so with jt400's record-level access. To access the fields of that retrieved record, you have to use the RECORD class's GETFIELD() function. This function takes a string parameter that contains the name of the field of which you wish to retrieve the value. Although this sounds easy enough, the data types of Java do not map directly to our favorite data types from the AS/400. Because the GETFIELD function does not know at compile time what the data type of the AS/400 field will be at runtime, it returns the ambiguous object type of the OBJECT class. That means if you invoke the GETFIELD function, passing a field name of a zoned number, it returns an OBJECT object instance:

```
Object ambiguousObject = record.getField("SALARY");
```

Now, what can you do with that AMBIGUOUSOBJECT variable? Certainly you can't get the numerical value of that record's SALARY field's value. Or can you? Internally, the GETFIELD function at runtime knows the data type of the salary field from the record format you retrieved earlier. It creates a Java object that correlates to the AS/400 data type as shown in Table 13.5. Then, darn it, GETFIELD returns it as the ambiguous OBJECT object. You can, however, use a

Java feature called *casting* to upcast that OBJECT to the object type specified between parentheses:

```
BigDecimal salary = (BigDecimal)ambiguousObject;
```

This operation generates a runtime exception if the class of the object stored in the AMBIGUOUSOBJECT variable is not originally instantiated as a BIGDECIMAL inside the GETFIELD function.

The following is the suggested method of retrieving the value of your DB2/400 fields:

```
String str = (String) record.getField("CHARFLD");
BigDecimal money = record.getField("DECFLD");
```

Or, in other words, you cast that generic OBJECT object returned from GETFIELD to be of the proper specific object class, as shown in Table 13.5.

Table 13.5: AS/400 Data Types Get Converted to Corresponding Java Classes.	
AS/400 Data Type	**Java Class**
Signed binary 2 bytes	Short
Signed binary 4 bytes	Integer
Unsigned binary 2 bytes	Integer
Unsigned binary 4 bytes	Long
Float 4 bytes	Float
Float 8 bytes	Double
Packed	BigDecimal
Zoned	BigDecimal
Character	String

A COMPLETE EXAMPLE

Figure 13.3 contains a complete but concise example of accessing an AS/400 database file. You should be able to run this example as-is from your PC to access the data file on your AS/400 because the example uses file QCUSTCDT, found on all AS/400s that have the QIWS library.

```
package jt400;

import java.io.*;
import java.util.*;
import java.math.*;
import com.ibm.as400.access.*;

public class ListRecords {

  public ListRecords() {
    // Step 1:
    // Connect to an AS/400
    AS400 system = new AS400();

    // Step 2:
    // Specify file location
    QSYSObjectPathName filePathName =
      new QSYSObjectPathName("QIWS","QCUSTCDT","FILE");
    SequentialFile theFile =
        new SequentialFile(system,
                        filePathName.getPath());

    // Step 3:
    // Retrieve a record format
    AS400FileRecordDescription recDesc =
      new AS400FileRecordDescription(system,
                        filePathName.getPath());
    try
    {

theFile.setRecordFormat(recDesc.retrieveRecordFormat()[0]);
```

Figure 13.3: The LISTRECORDS class uses record-level access to read all the records in the QCUSTCDT file. (Part 1 of 2)

```
        // Step 4:
        // 1pen the file
        theFile.open(AS400File.READ_ONLY,
                0,
                AS400File.COMMIT_LOCK_LEVEL_NONE);
        // Step 5:
        // Read a record
        for (Record record = theFile.readNext();
            record != null;
            record = theFile.readNext()) {
        // Step 6:
        // Retrieve the field values of that record
        BigDecimal CustnoField =
                (BigDecimal) record.getField( "CUSNUM" );
        String NameField =
                (String) record.getField( "LSTNAM" );
        System.out.println(NameField + CustnoField);
        }

        // Close the file
        theFile.close();

    } catch (Exception e) {
        System.out.println(
            "Error occurred listing the file.");
        try
        {
            theFile.close();
        } catch(Exception x) {
            System.out.println(
                "Error occurred closing the file.");
        }
        System.exit(0);
    }
    System.exit(0);
    }

    public static void main(String[] args) {
        ListRecords listRecords = new ListRecords();
    }
}
```

Figure 13.3: The LISTRECORDS class uses record-level access to read all the records in the QCUSTCDT file. (Part 2 of 2)

Figure 13.4 shows a UML sequence diagram for jt400's record-level access.

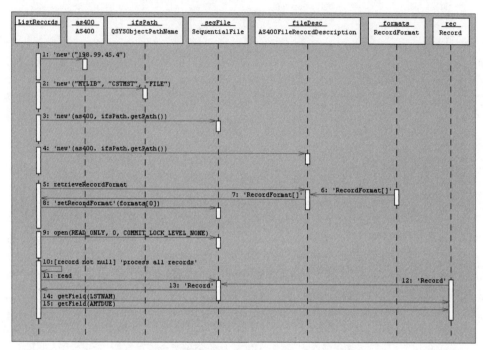

Figure 13.4: The nested invocation of object function calls is represented in a time sequence diagram.

ADD, UPDATE, AND DELETE

You can add records to DB2/400, if the file is open for update, with the WRITE function. WRITE takes as its only argument a RECORD object, which it then uses to create a new DB2/400 record. You'll notice, however, if you look at IBM's Java documentation that the WRITE function may throw an AS400EXCEPTION exception. That makes sense; perhaps the user profile of someone running your Java application does not have add authorization, or maybe the record contains a unique key that already exists in the file. Because the write function contains a THROWS clause, your code must handle the AS400EXCEPTION explicitly or generically. You would handle it explicitly with a try block that contained a CATCH clause for AS400EXCEPTION, as shown in Figure 13.5.

```
try {
write(aNewRecord);
} catch (AS400Exception error) {
    System.out.println(error.toString());
} catch (Exception error) {
    System.out.println(error.toString());
}
```

Figure 13.5: A CATCH clause for AS400EXCEPTION illustrates explicit handling of the AS400EXCEPTION error.

You could, however, handle the error by catching merely the generic EXCEPTION:

```
try {
write(aNewRecord);
} catch (Exception error) {
    System.out.println(error.toString());
}
```

Figure 13.6: An alternative to explicitly handling AS400EXCEPTION is to catch generic EXCEPTION errors.

Updates to DB2/400 records can be performed using one of a variety of update functions. You can update the record that is at the current file cursor's position with UPDATE(RECORD MODIFIEDRECORD); you can update a record by key with the KEYEDFILE class's UPDATE(OBJECT[] KEY, RECORD MODIFIEDRECORD), or you can update a record by relative record number using the SEQUENTIALFILE class's UPDATE(INT RRN, RECORD MODIFIEDRECORD). Again, as with the WRITE function, the UPDATE functions also throw AS400EXCEPTION errors.

Deletion of records can be accomplished with the DELETECURRENTRECORD function, which requires no arguments; the DELETERECORD(INT RRN), to delete by relative record number; or the DELETERECORD(OBJECT[] KEY) function, to delete by the full key of the record.

The set of record-level access classes in IBM's AS/400 Toolbox for Java supports much of the same dynamic file access that you have come to expect. You'll find full support for commitment control and file locking; you can even create new DB2/400 files and formats using Java and the jt400 record-level access classes. For a good source of general information on the use of jt400's record-level access, you can view the RLA.HTM document that comes with jt400's JavaDoc files.

SUMMARY

These steps seem like a lot of work when you consider that in RPG you need only create an F-spec and then READ a record. Realize, however, that when you build a Java application using these classes, that application will execute from any platform that has a Java Virtual Machine and is TCP/IP enabled. Applications that I have written using jt400's record-level access have run on Windows, UNIX, Linux, and even Apple platforms. Try *that* with your RPG program.

You must always keep in mind that this is object-oriented programming. In practice, this means that each of your business entities should be represented by one class. That class will encapsulate the steps shown in this chapter. Whenever a programmer needs to access the data represented in a Java class, that programmer should not perform these six steps and process the DB2/400 file. Rather, he or she should instance a CUSTOMER object from the CUSTOMER class, or an INVOICE object, or an ITEM, and so on.

Chapter 16 of Section IV illustrates a strategy for encapsulating DB2/400 entities into a Java class. The three chapters of Section III show a complete strategy that makes the creation and use of these Java business entity classes easy with the help of the full power of object-oriented programming. With well-encapsulated Java business classes, application programming will be easier, more productive, and much more fun with Java than it ever was with RPG.

14

SQL ACCESS TO DB2/400 WITH JAVA DATABASE CONNECTIVITY

Many people speak of Java as the language of the Internet. Even though I am a Java advocate, I say that the language of the Internet is SQL. Java is also purported to be the world's most successful cross-platform language. Again, I say it's SQL. COBOL was originally touted as a cross-platform language, then it was C, and now Java. No one ever says that SQL is the ubiquitous language of the Internet—except me.

Why do I claim such omnipresence for SQL? The preponderance of the world's electronically stored data is kept in relational databases (RDBs). The standard method of designing, manipulating, and retrieving relational data is—you guessed it—SQL. (DDS is an AS/400-specific incarnation.)

DB2/400 is one of the few relational databases that allow record-level access to data. Almost all other databases, to be as RDB-compliant as possible, only allow data manipulation through SQL. I've worked with Oracle and Ingres programmers who manipulated their data with SQL. I also know a number of AS/400 sites that use SQL exclusively for DB2/400 manipulation, mostly because they develop applications for cross-platform use. You might not consider SQL a language, in which case you need to ponder why the L follows the S and the Q. Yes, SQL is a language, and a powerful one at that.

Almost everyone has learned of Open Database Connectivity (ODBC). Microsoft designed ODBC as a standard communications protocol to allow multiple languages to access relational data from any database that had an ODBC driver. Microsoft's ODBC developers wanted everyone to access the RDBs of midrange and mainframe servers, as well as of Microsoft SQL servers, from a Microsoft workstation. They were pretty darn successful. Today, all the major RDBs have ODBC drivers and most PC-based languages have APIs to those ODBC drivers.

The Java designers at Sun Microsystems looked at ODBC and decided, rather than providing a Java API to ODBC, to improve and simplify ODBC. The result is JDBC, or Java Database Connectivity. The fellows at Sun did a great job—JDBC is powerful, yet easy to learn and use.

THE FOUR COMPONENTS OF JDBC

JDBC has four components: the driver manager, the host connection, an SQL statement, and a result set. Components in Java, as you know, are classes. Obviously, four classes encapsulate the features of those four components:

- DRIVERMANAGER
- CONNECTION
- STATEMENT
- RESULTSET

Realize that, as yet, discussion has not turned to IBM's Java Toolbox for the AS/400. These four, and the associated JDBC utility classes, are standard JDBC classes and conform to the JDBC standard published by Sun—conceivably. Your JDBC Java code could access DB2/400 one day, and the next day, after one of those nasty mergers, that same application might be accessing Oracle or Ingres.

AN EXAMPLE JDBC APPLICATION

The steps to using JDBC are quite simple. To illustrate, the example application in Figure 14.1 and the explanation that follows, step through the use of the four components.

```java
import java.sql.*;
import java.math.BigDecimal;

public class JDBCExample01 {

   public static void main(String[] args) {
   Connection con = null;
   try {
     // Load the JDBC driver
     DriverManager.registerDriver(
            new com.ibm.as400.access.AS400JDBCDriver());
     // Connect to the database
     con = DriverManager.getConnection("jdbc:as400://my400Domain",
                                   "Profile", "Password");
     // Run an SQL SELECT statement
     Statement stmt = con.createStatement();
     ResultSet rs = stmt.executeQuery(
               "SELECT CUSNUM, LSTNAM, INIT, STREET, CITY, STATE, " +
               "        ZIPCOD, CDTLMT, CHGCOD, BALDUE, CDTDUE " +
               " FROM QIWS.QCUSTCDT ORDER BY LSTNAM");
     // Display each row(record) retrieved by the SQL statement
     while (rs.next()) {
            String cusnum = rs.getString(1);
            String cusnam = rs.getString("LSTNAM ");
            BigDecimal baldue = rs.getBigDecimal(10, 2);
            System.out.println(cusnum + " " + cusnam + " " + baldue);
     }
     rs.close();
     stmt.close();
   }
   catch (Exception e) {
       System.out.println("\nERROR: " + e.getMessage());
   }
   finally {
      try {
      con.close();
```

Figure 14.1: The four components of a JDBC example are easy to use. (Part 1 of 2)

```
    }
    catch (SQLException e) {
    }
  }
  System.exit(0);
  }
}
```

Figure 14.1: The four components of a JDBC example are easy to use. (Part 2 of 2)

First, note the absence of the import statement for the com.ibm.as400.access package that you saw in the last chapter. The MAIN function starts out by loading the JDBC driver:

```
DriverManager.registerDriver(
new com.ibm.as400.access.AS400JDBCDriver());
```

Yes, here you refer to IBM's implementation of a JDBC driver, but that's the only place. When you register the JDBC driver, you have to refer to an explicit JDBC driver. If you wish to switch your relational database, you'd have to change this line to specify a JDBC driver that works with the new RDB.

The next step, after registering the driver, involves setting up a connection to the RDB's host. To do this, you specify a URL with the protocol of JDBC and a subprotocol, for the AS/400, of as400 followed by the IP address or domain name of your AS/400 and the user profile and password:

```
Connection con = DriverManager.getConnection(
"jdbc:as400://my400Domain", "Profile", "Password");
```

Setting the protocol of JDBC is similar to setting the protocol of HTTP when you surf the Internet. To access Midrange Computing's Web site, for instance, you enter the following URL on your browser: www.midrangecomputing.com. No, no subprotocol for Hypertext Transfer Protocol (HTTP), as yet. With the connection enabled, the example application is ready to specify the SQL statement by creating a STATEMENT object:

```
Statement stmt = con.createStatement();
```

This STATEMENT object is an interface class whose EXECUTEQUERY function enables SQL statements to funnel through the JDBC driver to your host RDB:

```
ResultSet rs = stmt.executeQuery(
"SELECT * FROM QIWS.QCUSTCDT ORDER BY LSTNAM");
```

When that SQL query function completes, it returns a set of records in the form of a RESULTSET object. Table 14.1 shows all the functions of the JDBC STATEMENT class. One particularly noteworthy function, EXECUTEUPDATE, is used for executing an SQL INSERT, UPDATE, or DELETE statement.

Table 14.1: The Statement Class Has a Variety of Useful Functions. (Part 1 of 2)

Function	Description
cancel()	Enables one thread to cancel a statement being executed by another thread.
clearWarnings()	After this call, returns null until a new warning is reported for this Statement object.
close()	Immediately releases a Statement's database and JDBC resources instead of waiting for this to happen when it is automatically closed; desirable in many cases.
execute(String)	Executes an SQL statement that may return multiple results.
executeQuery(String)	Executes an SQL statement that returns a single ResultSet.
executeUpdate(String)	Executes an SQL insert, update, or delete statement.
getMaxFieldSize()	Specifies (in bytes) the maximum amount of data returned for any column value; applies only to BINARY, VARBINARY, LONGVARBINARY, CHAR, VARCHAR, and LONGVARCHAR columns.
getMaxRows()	Specifies the maximum number of rows a ResultSet can contain.
getMoreResults()	Moves to a Statement's next result.
getQueryTimeout()	Limits the number of seconds the driver will wait for a Statement to execute.
getResultSet()	Returns the current result as a ResultSet.
getUpdateCount()	Returns the current result as an update count; if the result is a ResultSet or there are no more results, -1 is returned.

Table 14.1: The Statement Class Has a Variety of Useful Functions. (Part 2 of 2)

Function	Description
getWarnings()	Returns the first warning reported by calls on this Statement.
setCursorName(String)	Defines the SQL cursor name for use by subsequent Statement execute methods.
SetEscapeProcessing (boolean)	Tells the driver to perform escape substitution before sending the SQL to the database, if escape scanning is on (the default).
setMaxFieldSize(int)	Limits the size of data (in bytes) that can be returned for any column value; applies only to BINARY, VARBINARY, LONGVARBINARY, CHAR, VARCHAR, and LONGVARCHAR fields.
setMaxRows(int)	Limits the number of rows that any ResultSet can contain.
setQueryTimeout(int)	Specifies the number of seconds the driver will wait for a Statement to execute.

To retrieve the records from the RESULTSET object returned from the EXECUTE-QUERY function, you simply use the NEXT function of that object. The example application invokes the NEXT function within the clause of a while loop. That way, the application continues retrieving records until the NEXT function returns a Boolean value of false:

```
while (rs.next())
```

The NEXT function simply positions the pointer to a subsequent record in the RESULTSET. To retrieve the values of that record, you have a little work to do; you must use one of the RESULTSET's get functions to pull those values out of the record. Table 14.2 lists all of the get functions of the RESULTSET class.

They can be categorized into two groups: one in which you specify the ordinal number of the SQL statement's column position and another in which you specify the field name (much like you would with the GETFIELD function used for record-level access):

```
String cusnum = rs.getString(1);
String lstnam = rs.getString("LSTNAM");
String baldue = rs.getString(10);
```

**Table 14.2: ResultSet Class Functions Used to Retrieve
Data from the Set of Records that ResultSet Contains. (Part 1 of 2)**

Function	Description
GetBigDecimal(int, int)	Gets the value of a column in the current row as a java.lang.BigDecimal object.
GetBigDecimal(String, int)	Gets the value of a column in the current row as a java.lang.BigDecimal object.
getBinaryStream(int)	Retrieves a column value as a stream of uninterpreted bytes and then reads chunks from the stream.
getBinaryStream(String)	Retrieves a column value as a stream of uninterpreted bytes and then reads chunks from the stream.
getBoolean(int)	Gets the value of a column in the current row as a Java boolean.
getBoolean(String)	Gets the value of a column in the current row as a Java boolean.
getByte(int)	Gets the value of a column in the current row as a Java byte.
getByte(String)	Gets the value of a column in the current row as a Java byte.
getBytes(int)	Gets the value of a column in the current row as a Java byte array.
getBytes(String)	Gets the value of a column in the current row as a Java byte array.
getCursorName()	Gets the name of the SQL cursor used by this ResultSet.
getDate(int)	Gets the value of a column in the current row as a java.sql.Date object.
getDate(String)	Gets the value of a column in the current row as a java.sql.Date object.
getDouble(int)	Gets the value of a column in the current row as a Java double.

Function	Description
getDouble(String)	Gets the value of a column in the current row as a Java double.
getFloat(int)	Gets the value of a column in the current row as a Java float.
getFloat(String)	Gets the value of a column in the current row as a Java float.
getInt(int)	Gets the value of a column in the current row as a Java int.
getInt(String)	Gets the value of a column in the current row as a Java int.
getLong(int)	Gets the value of a column in the current row as a Java long.
getLong(String)	Gets the value of a column in the current row as a Java long.
getMetaData()	Provides the number, types, and properties of a ResultSet's columns.
getObject(int)	Gets the value of a column in the current row as a Java object.
getObject(String)	Gets the value of a column in the current row as a Java object.
getShort(int)	Gets the value of a column in the current row as a Java short.
getShort(String)	Gets the value of a column in the current row as a Java short.
getString(int)	Gets the value of a column in the current row as a Java String.
getString(String)	Gets the value of a column in the current row as a Java String.
getTime(int)	Gets the value of a column in the current row as a java.sql.Time object.
getTime(String)	Gets the value of a column in the current row as a java.sql.Time object.
getTimestamp(int)	Gets the value of a column in the current row as a java.sql.Timestamp object.

Because the example uses the string GET functions, all of the values—even the numeric values—are retrieved as strings. To get the zoned, six-digit, two-decimal values for BALDUE, you'd use one of the GETBIGDECIMAL functions:

```
BigDecimal baldue01 = rs.getBigDecimal(10, 2);
BigDecimal baldue02 = rs.getBigDecimal("BALDUE", 2);
```

The second argument for both of the GETBIGDECIMAL function calls contains the count of decimals to be set in the retrieved value. If you run the example JDBC application, you will obtain a simple list of customer number, name, and balance due, as shown in Figure 14.2.

```
846283 Alison   10.00
475938 Doe      250.00
938472 Henning  37.00
938485 Johnson  3987.50
839283 Jones    100.00
192837 Lee      489.50
389572 Stevens  58.75
693829 Thomas   0.00
397267 Tyron    0.00
392859 Vine     439.00
593029 Williams 25.00
```

Figure 14.2: The execution of the JDBCEXAMPLE01 application lists the customer number, name, and balance due of records in the QCUSTCDT file.

BE PREPARED AND CALL ME

JDBC, or rather, SQL, has three ways of accessing data: SQL statements, prepared SQL statements, and callable statements. The above example used the basic SQL statement (via the STATEMENT class). SQL statements work great for ad hoc queries; but if you find that same statement being executed over and over again, you should use prepared statements. The callable statement allows you to invoke a stored procedure using SQL. Stored procedures on the AS/400 can be written in any language, which, of course, encompasses RPG and COBOL. This important feature gives JDBC the ability to interoperate with legacy RPG programs.

PREPARED STATEMENTS

With JDBC's SQL statement class (STATEMENT), the JDBC driver checks and pseudocompiles the SQL syntax in the STATEMENT object every time it is executed. With JDBC's SQL prepared statement class (PREPAREDSTATEMENT), on the other hand, the syntax check and pseudocompile happen only once. Subsequent executions of that statement then run much faster. Additionally, the prepared statement can accept variable data on each subsequent invocation. The prepared statement uses a parameter marker (for SQL, a question mark) where the values will be supplied at execution time:

```
PreparedStatement prepSQL = con.prepareStatement(
"SELECT * QIWS.QCUSTCDT WHERE LSTNAM = ?");
```

Before you can execute that statement, you need to tell JDBC what the value of the variable data will be. You do that using the proper SET function of the PREPAREDSTATEMENT class, as shown in Table 14.3.

Table 14.3: The PREPAREDSTATEMENT Class's SET Functions Correspond to Specific Data Types of Placeholder Parameters.

Function	Description
SetBigDecimal(int, BigDecimal)	Sets a parameter to a java.lang.BigDecimal value.
SetBoolean(int, boolean)	Sets a parameter to a Java boolean value.
SetByte(int, byte)	Sets a parameter to a Java byte value.
SetBytes(int, byte[ ])	Sets a parameter to a Java array of bytes.
SetDate(int, Date)	Sets a parameter to a java.sql.Date value.
SetDouble(int, double)	Sets a parameter to a Java double value.
SetFloat(int, float)	Sets a parameter to a Java float value.
SetInt(int, int)	Sets a parameter to a Java int value.
SetLong(int, long)	Sets a parameter to a Java long value.
SetShort(int, short)	Sets a parameter to a Java short value.
SetString(int, String)	Sets a parameter to a Java String value.
SetTime(int, Time)	Sets a parameter to a java.sql.Time value.
SetTimestamp(int, Timestamp)	Sets a parameter to a java.sql.Timestamp value.

The first integral argument to each of those functions relates to the ordinal position of the variable parameter marker (the question mark) in your prepared SQL statement:

```
prepSQL.setString(1, gui.LastNamePrompt.getText());
```

You might have been tempted to build the above statement dynamically by inserting the variable customer name from a GUI text field:

```
Statement sql =
"SELECT * QIWS.QCUSTCDT WHERE LSTNAM = " +
gui.LastNamePrompt.getText());
```

Resist that temptation. As pointed out earlier, this statement must be syntax-checked and pseudocompiled each time it executes. The prepared SQL statement does not and, as a result, executes far more quickly. Just remember to use the JDBC prepared statements when the SQL statement is to execute iteratively.

CALLABLE STATEMENTS

JDBC (more correctly, SQL) has a third type of statement: a callable statement. As its name implies, a callable statement allows you to call a legacy applications program from SQL. Callable statements, like prepared statements, sound complicated; but just like prepared statements, these callable statements are easy to set up and use. There are six simple steps to using a callable statement.

1. Create a callable statement object:

```
CallableStatement sqlCall;
```

2. Specify to that JDBC CALLABLESTATEMENT object the name of your RPG (or COBOL or C or whatever) program along with those question mark parameter markers for the program's arguments:

```
sqlCall = con.prepareCall("CALL INVLIB/INV001(?, ?, ?");
```

3. Specify which program arguments to use for output. You do that with the register output parameter statement:

```
sqlCall.registerOutParameter(3, java.sql.Types.INTEGER);
```

4. Set the values of the input arguments using those same functions that you used for the prepared statement:

```
sqlCall.setInt(1, 456);
sqlCall.setInt(2, 972);
```

5. Call the program:

```
sqlCall.execute();
```

6. Retrieve the program's return values from its arguments using a GET function:

```
int returnedInte™gerValue = sqlCall.getInt(3);
```

Note that the GET function's argument relates to the ordinal position of the callable statement's output argument.

DATA ABOUT DATA

JDBC gives you access to the *metadata* (information about data) of your DB2/400 database including the attributes of files, formats, and fields. Both the CONNECTION class and the RESULTSET class of JDBC have GETMETADATA functions. The CONNECTION class's GETMETADATA function returns information about the files available on the machine to which you have established a connection. The RESULTSET class's GETMETADATA function returns information about the record format such as its fields and their attributes.

JDBC 2.0

OS/400 V4R4's enhancements to IBM's Java Toolbox for the AS/400 include a JDBC 2.0 driver. JDBC 2.0 is Sun Microsystems' new standard for Java Database Connectivity. The most significant features of JDBC 2.0 add the following capabilities:

- Reading backward as well as forward in a result set.
- Dynamic positioning of the result set cursor.
- Database updates using Java function calls rather than SQL commands.
- Batch processing of SQL statements.
- Direct support for Binary Large Objects (BLOBs) and Character Large Objects (CLOBs) made available with V4R4.

The JDBC 2.0 driver that comes with IBM's Java Toolbox for the AS/400 modification 2 is one of the first 2.0 drivers available in the industry. JDBC 2.0 is a part of Java 2 (Sun's new name for Java 1.2), so to use JDBC 2.0 you'll also have to use JDK 1.2 or a Java Integrated Development Environment that supports JDK 1.2. Figure 14.3 contains a sample Java application called JDBC2POINT0 that uses many of the features of JDBC 2.0. This section of the chapter provides an overview of the JDBC 2.0 features used in the example application.

```
import java.sql.*;
import java.math.*;
import com.ibm.as400.access.*;

class JDBC2Point0 {
  static final String URL = "199.999.99.9";
  static final String USER = "profile";
  static final String PASS = "password";
  Connection con = null;
  AS400 as400 = null;
  CommandCall cmdCall = null;

  JDBC2Point0() {
    try {
      DriverManager.registerDriver(new
              com.ibm.as400.access.AS400JDBCDriver());
      con = DriverManager.getConnection("jdbc:as400://"+URL, USER, PASS);
    } catch (SQLException e) {
      System.out.println("Connection failed: " + e);
    }
```

Figure 14.3: The JDBC2POINT0 class uses many of the new features of JDBC 2.0. (Part 1 of 5)

```
  if (isNumbersFileReady()) {
    insert1n2asBatchTransactions();
    insert3to10asPreparedStatements();
    scrollForwardAndBack();
    watchTheBouncingCursor();
    methodUpdates();
  }
}

void listCustomersBackwards() {
  try {
    Statement stmt = con.createStatement(ResultSet.TYPE_SCROLL_INSENSITIVE,
                                    ResultSet.CONCUR_READ_ONLY);
   ResultSet srs =
    stmt.executeQuery("SELECT * FROM qiws.qcustcdt ORDER BY cusnum");
    srs.afterLast();
    while (srs.previous()) {
      String cusnum = srs.getString(1);
      String cusnam = srs.getString("LSTNAM");
      BigDecimal baldue = srs.getBigDecimal(10, 2);
      System.out.println(cusnum + " " + cusnam + " " + baldue);
    }
  } catch (SQLException e) {}
}
boolean isNumbersFileReady() {
  try {
    as400 = new AS400(URL, USER, PASS);
    cmdCall = new CommandCall( as400 );
    cmdCall.run("ENDJRNPF DENONCOURT/NUMBERS");
    cmdCall.run("DLTJRN DENONCOURT/NUMBERS");
    cmdCall.run("DLTJRNRCV DENONCOURT/NUMBERS " +
                "DLTOPT(*IGNINQMSG *IGNTGTRCV)");
    Statement stmt = con.createStatement();
    stmt.executeUpdate("DROP TABLE DENONCOURT.NUMBERS");
  } catch (Exception e) {
    System.out.println("table not dropped " + e);
  }
  try {
    Statement stmt = con.createStatement();
    stmt.executeUpdate("CREATE TABLE denoncourt.numbers " +
                    "(number INT, word CHAR (20))");
    String crtjrnrcv = "CRTJRNRCV JRNRCV(DENONCOURT/NUMBERS)";
    if (cmdCall.run(crtjrnrcv) == true) {
```

Figure 14.3: The JDBC2Point0 class uses many of the new features of JDBC 2.0. (Part 2 of 5)

```
      String crtjrn = "CRTJRN JRN(DENONCOURT/NUMBERS) " +
                      "JRNRCV(DENONCOURT/NUMBERS)";
      if (cmdCall.run(crtjrn) == false) {
        System.out.println("create journal failed");
        return false;
      } else {
        String strjrn = "STRJRNPF FILE(DENONCOURT/NUMBERS) " +
                        "JRN(DENONCOURT/NUMBERS) IMAGES(*BOTH)";
        if (cmdCall.run(strjrn) == false) {
          System.out.println("start journal physical file failed");
          return false;
        }
      }
    } else {
      System.out.println("create journal receiver failed");
      return false;
    }
  } catch (Exception e) {
    System.out.println("starting journaling failed " + e);
    return false;
  }
  return true;
}
void insert1n2asBatchTransactions() {
  try {
    con.setAutoCommit(false);
    Statement stmt = con.createStatement(ResultSet.TYPE_SCROLL_INSENSITIVE,
                                    ResultSet.CONCUR_UPDATABLE);
    stmt.addBatch("INSERT INTO denoncourt.numbers (number, word) " +
                                    "VALUES(1, 'one')");
    stmt.addBatch("INSERT INTO denoncourt.numbers (number, word) " +
                                    "VALUES(2, 'two')");
    int [] updateCounts = stmt.executeBatch();
  } catch (SQLException e) {
    System.out.println("insert failed " + e);
  }
}

void insert3to10asPreparedStatements() {
  try {
    con.setAutoCommit(true);
    PreparedStatement insert = con.prepareStatement(
        "INSERT INTO denoncourt.numbers " +
```

Figure 14.3: The JDBC2POINT0 class uses many of the new features of JDBC 2.0. (Part 3 of 5)

```
                    "(number, word) VALUES (?, ?)");
    String[] words = new String[] {"zero", "one", "two", "three", "four",
                        "five", "six", "seven", "eight", "nine", "ten"};
    for (int i = 3; i <= 10; ++i) {
      insert.setInt(1, i);
      insert.setString(2, words[i]);
      insert.executeUpdate();
    }
  } catch (SQLException e) {
    System.out.println("executeUpdate for inserts failed " + e);
  }
}
void scrollForwardAndBack() {
  try {
    Statement stmt = con.createStatement(ResultSet.TYPE_SCROLL_SENSITIVE,
                                ResultSet.CONCUR_READ_ONLY);
    ResultSet rs = stmt.executeQuery("SELECT * FROM denoncourt.numbers");
    for (int i = 0; rs.next() && i < 5; i++) {
      System.out.println("Number: " + rs.getInt("number")+ ": " +
                        rs.getString("word"));
    }
    while (rs.previous()) {
      System.out.println("Number: " + rs.getInt("number")+ ": " +
                        rs.getString("word"));
    }
  } catch (SQLException e) {
    System.out.println("scrollForwardAndBack() failed " + e);
  }
}
void watchTheBouncingCursor() {
  try {
    Statement stmt = con.createStatement(ResultSet.TYPE_SCROLL_INSENSITIVE,
                                ResultSet.CONCUR_READ_ONLY);
    ResultSet rs = stmt.executeQuery(
          "SELECT * FROM denoncourt.numbers ORDER BY number");
    rs.absolute(4);
    System.out.println("Number: " + rs.getInt("number")+ ": " +
                        rs.getString("word"));
    rs.relative(-3);
    System.out.println("Number: " + rs.getInt("number")+ ": " +
                        rs.getString("word"));
    rs.relative(2);
    System.out.println("Number: " + rs.getInt("number")+ ": " +
```

Figure 14.3: The JDBC2POINTO class uses many of the new features of JDBC 2.0. (Part 4 of 5)

```
                         rs.getString("word"));
    } catch (SQLException e) {
      System.out.println("executeUpdate for inserts failed " + e);
    }
  }
  void methodUpdates() {
    try {
      Statement stmt = con.createStatement(ResultSet.TYPE_SCROLL_SENSITIVE,
                                    ResultSet.CONCUR_UPDATABLE);
      ResultSet rs = stmt.executeQuery(
            "SELECT * FROM denoncourt.numbers FOR UPDATE of number, word");
      rs.last();
      rs.updateString("word", "X");
      rs.updateRow();
      rs.absolute(3);
      rs.updateString("word", "III");
      rs.cancelRowUpdates();
      rs.absolute(9);
      rs.deleteRow();

      rs.moveToInsertRow();
      rs.updateInt("number", 11);
      rs.updateString("word", "XI");
      rs.insertRow();

      rs.beforeFirst();
      while (rs.next()) {
        System.out.println("Number: " + rs.getInt("number")+ ": " +
                          rs.getString("word"));
      }

    } catch (SQLException e) {
      System.out.println("updateRow failed " + e);
    }
  }
  public static void main (String[] pList) {
    new JDBC2Point0();
    System.exit(0);
  }
}
```

Figure 14.3: The JDBC2POINT0 class uses many of the new features of JDBC 2.0. (Part 5 of 5)

JDBC2POINT0's constructor registers IBM's AS/400 JDBC driver and then executes a series of functions that create and manipulate a DB2/400 file called NUMBERS. The NUMBERS file has two fields: NUMBER (an integer) and WORD (a character string). The ISNUMBERSFILEREADY function creates the file using an SQL CREATE TABLE statement and then, because some of the new JDBC 2.0 features require commitment control, ISNUMBERSFILEREADY starts journaling the DB2/400 file. For ease of use, this function has been coded with the COMMANDCALL class (which chapter 14 covers in detail) so each execution of the application starts with a fresh file.

BATCH PROCESSING OF SQL STATEMENTS

Once the NUMBERS file is created with the ISNUMBERSFILEREADY function, the JDBC2POINT0 class needs to populate the file. Rather than using the strategies of JDBC 1.0, the JDBC2POINT0 application uses JDBC 2.0's new capability of processing SQL transactions in batch. The INSERT1N2ASBATCHTRANSACTIONS function creates a batch of two SQL INSERT statements and then submits the batch with the STATEMENT object's EXECUTEBATCH function, as Figure 14.4 shows.

```
stmt.addBatch("INSERT INTO denoncourt.numbers (number, word) " +
              "VALUES(1, 'one')");
stmt.addBatch("INSERT INTO denoncourt.numbers (number, word) " +
              "VALUES(2, 'two')");
int [] updateCounts = stmt.executeBatch();
```

Figure 14.4: The two INSERT statements are batched and submitted within the INSERT1N2ASBATCHTRANSACTIONS function.

For batch processing to work, JDBC 2.0 uses commitment control. That's why the NUMBERS file must be journaled and that's why the CONNECTION object must have its auto-commit attribute set to false:

```
con.setAutoCommit(false);
```

The STATEMENT object also needs to be created with a call to the CONNECTION object's CREATESTATEMENT object, with the second parameter specifying concurrent updates:

```
Statement stmt =
con.createStatement(ResultSet.TYPE_SCROLL_INSENSITIVE,
                                    ResultSet.CONCUR_UPDATABLE);
```

Within the INSERT3TO10ASPREPAREDSTATEMENTS function, the EXE-CUTEUPDATE function of the PREPAREDSTATEMENT class adds the rest of the 10 records to the NUMBERS file, as shown in Figure 14.5.

```
con.setAutoCommit(true);
PreparedStatement insert = con.prepareStatement(
                "INSERT INTO denoncourt.numbers " +
                "(number, word) VALUES (?, ?)");
String[] words = new String[] {"zero", "one", "two", "three",
"four", "five",
                            "six", "seven", "eight", "nine",
"ten"};
for (int i = 3; i <= 10; ++i) {
    insert.setInt(1, i);
    insert.setString(2, words[i]);
    insert.executeUpdate();
}
```

Figure 14.5: JDBC's EXECUTEUPDATE method of the PREPAREDSTATEMENT class is often used in a loop to iteratively add records.

READING BACKWARD

The most elementary of the JDBC 2.0 enhancements is the ability to read backwards. Prior to JBBC 2.0, you only had the NEXT function to process the records of an SQL result set. JDBC 2.0, however, has the additional functions shown in Table 14.4 to process SQL result sets.

Table 14.4: JDBC 2.0 Provides Several New Functions for Processing an SQL Result Set.

Returned object type	Function	Description
Boolean	Absolute(int row)	Moves the cursor to the given row number in the result set.
Void	afterLast()	Moves the cursor to the end of the result set, just after the last row.
Void	beforeFirst()	Moves the cursor to the front of the result set, just before the first row.
Boolean	last()	Moves the cursor to the last row in the result set.
Void	MoveToCurrentRow()	Moves the cursor to the remembered cursor position, usually the current row.
Boolean	Next()	Moves the cursor down one row from its current position.
Boolean	Previous()	Moves the cursor up one row from its current position.
Void	RefreshRow()	Refreshes the current row with its most recent value in the database.
Boolean	Relative(int rows)	Moves the cursor a relative number of rows, either positive or negative.

The SCROLLFORWARDANDBACK function of the JDBC2POINT0 Java application reads five records with the NEXT function and then reads those same five records in reverse with the PREVIOUS function, as shown in Figure 14.6.

```
for (int i = 0; rs.next() && i < 5; i++)
    System.out.println("Number: " + rs.getInt("number")+ ": " +
                       rs.getString("word"));
while (rs.previous())
    System.out.println("Number: " + rs.getInt("number")+ ": " +
                       rs.getString("word"));
```

Figure 14.6: A NEXT function in the FOR loop reads five records before the PREVIOUS function in the WHILE loop reads the same records in reverse order.

Figure 14.7 shows the resulting list of records.

```
Number: 1: one
Number: 2: two
Number: 3: three
Number: 4: four
Number: 5: five
Number: 5: five
Number: 4: four
Number: 3: three
Number: 2: two
Number: 1: one
```

Figure 14.7: The PREVIOUS and NEXT functions within SCROLLFORWARDANDBACK generate this list of records.

To be able to read the prior record in a result set, the CONNECTION object's CREATESTATEMENT function must instantiate the JDBC STATEMENT object, with TYPE_SCROLL_SENSITIVE specified as CREATESTATEMENT's first parameter. (This example uses CONCUR_READ_ONLY as it does not perform any updates.) The sensitive scroll option allows you to read a result set backward and also to randomly position the cursor:

```
Statement stmt =
con.createStatement(ResultSet.TYPE_SCROLL_SENSITIVE,
                    ResultSet.CONCUR_READ_ONLY);
```

THE DYNAMIC CURSOR

AS/400 programmers have grown accustomed to dynamically setting a file cursor with RPG op codes such as Set Lower Limits (SETLL) and Set Greater Than (SETGT). Now with JDBC 2.0, programmers can dynamically position the cursor of an SQL result set with the ABSOLUTE and RELATIVE functions. The ABSOLUTE function requires an unsigned integer value that it uses to position the cursor within the result set. The RELATIVE function, on the other hand, can accept a signed integer value. If the integer is negative, the RELATIVE function repositions the cursor backward relative to the current cursor position. If the integer is positive, the RELATIVE function repositions the cursor forward relative to the current cursor position.

The WATCHTHEBOUNCINGCURSOR function of the JDBC2POINT0 class uses the
ABSOLUTE function to list the values for the fourth record; then it uses the RELA-
TIVE function to list the first and third records of the set, producing the output
shown:

```
Number: 4: four
Number: 1: one
Number: 3: three
```

RDB UPDATE FUNCTIONS VERSUS SQL STATEMENTS

The last new feature of JDBC 2.0 that JDBC2POINT0 uses is the ability to update
DB2/400 through Java function calls rather than SQL UPDATE statements. The
JDBC2POINT application uses a function called METHODUPDATES to modify the
values of several records in the NUMBERS file. Because METHODUPDATES modifies data, the JDBC STATEMENT object requires the CONCUR_UPDATABLE
option to be specified in the CREATESTATEMENT function and the SQL SELECT
statement requires the FOR UPDATE clause. Figure 14.8 shows the coding to
fulfill these requirements.

```
Statement stmt =
con.createStatement(ResultSet.TYPE_SCROLL_SENSITIVE,

ResultSet.CONCUR_UPDATABLE);
ResultSet rs =
    stmt.executeQuery("SELECT * FROM denoncourt.numbers " +
                      "FOR UPDATE of number, word");
```

Figure 14.8: To be able to update the values of a RESULTSET, the FOR UPDATE clause
must be specified listing the fields that may be updated.

To test the update facilities of JDBC 2.0, the METHODUPDATES function sets the
value of the WORD field in the last record of the NUMBERS file to have a roman
numeral representation for the number 10. The METHODUPDATES function uses a
feature of JDBC 2.0 that allows you to update DB2/400 through Java function
calls rather than through SQL UPDATE statements like the following:

```
UPDATE numbers SET word = "X" WHERE number = 10;
```

The METHODUPDATES function sets the value of the WORD field of the last DB2/400 record in the result set by positioning the set with the LAST function, invoking the UPDATESTRING function, and then invoking the UPDATEROW function to commit the modification to DB2/400:

```
rs.last();
rs.updateString("word", "X");
rs.updateRow();
```

The METHODUPDATES function updates record number three to also have a roman numeral value by explicitly positioning the cursor and invoking the UPDATESTRING function:

```
rs.absolute(3);
rs.updateString("word", "III");
```

Then METHODUPDATES acquiesces and cancels the record update:

```
rs.cancelRowUpdates();
```

The CANCELROWUPDATES function will come in handy in coding error-handling routines. The METHODUPDATES function then deletes record number nine:

```
rs.absolute(9);
rs.deleteRow();
```

Prior to JDBC 2.0, this kind of deletion would have meant resorting to an SQL DELETE statement like the following embedded within a call to the EXECUTEUPDATE function:

```
Stmt.executeUpdate("DELETE FROM numbers WHERE number = 9;");
```

JDBC 2.0 function update also supports the insertion of records. To insert records into a result set, you must first reposition the cursor to what JDBC 2.0 calls the INSERT ROW:

```
rs.moveToInsertRow();
```

Then you can update the record (which is still in transient memory) with the update functions before making the record persistent with the INSERT ROW function:

```
rs.updateInt("number", 11);
rs.updateString("word", "XI");
rs.insertRow();
```

To list the results of the METHODUPDATES function's database modifications, the function spins through the entire result set by positioning the cursor before the first record and iteratively calling the NEXT function, as Figure 14.9 illustrates.

```
rs.beforeFirst();
while (rs.next())
    System.out.println("Number: " +
                       rs.getInt("number")+ ": " +
                       rs.getString("word"));
```

Figure 14.9: The METHODUPDATES function spins through the result set to list the results of the database modifications.

The resulting list in Figure 14.10 shows all of the records, including the added record, but with the notable exception of the deleted record number nine.

```
Number: 1: one
Number: 2: two
Number: 3: three
Number: 4: four
Number: 5: five
Number: 6: six
Number: 7: seven
Number: 8: eight
Number: 11: XI
Number: 10: X
```

Figure 14.10: The list generated by the METHODUPDATES function reflects the added and deleted records.

SELECT SUM(JDBC) FROM CHAPTER

This chapter has quickly covered Java Database Connectivity. You have learned that SQL supports three types of statements: basic dynamic SQL statements (STATEMENT class), prepared statements (PREPAREDSTATEMENT class), and callable statements (CALLABLESTATEMENT class). You have also received an overview of the enhancements that come with JDBC 2.0.

The STATEMENT class works well for ad hoc SQL queries that are invoked once; the PREPAREDSTATEMENT class should be used for SQL statements executed iteratively; and the CALLABLESTATEMENT should be used to interoperate with your legacy HLL programs.

It is my opinion that JDBC works best for set-based processing and record-level access works best for dynamic processing. Record-level access is covered in chapter 14. You should use JDBC when your applications truly perform dynamic data access and speed is critical. IBM states that record-level access with IBM's Java Toolbox for the AS/400 is 20 percent faster than JDBC. The problem, however, with using the record-level access provided with IBM's Java Toolbox for the AS/400 is that you tie your application to DB2/400. With JDBC, you could conceivably switch relational databases and the only modification required to your Java code would be to change the registration of the JDBC driver and the URL of the host.

Programmers on the AS/400 have been so pleased with RPG's and COBOL's dynamic record-level access that when they look at other programming strategies they discount SQL. Don't. Take a long, hard look at it. Realize that applications that use JDBC can run on any JVM (including the AS/400's JVM) to any RDB. And, remember, if you develop applications with Java and JDBC, not only will your applications be cross-platform but you too will be cross-platform.

15

INTEGRATING JAVA
WITH AS/400 APPLICATIONS

The AS/400 Toolbox for Java's (jt400) implementations of program call and command invocation work fairly similarly. Both of them use the AS400 connection class; both of them use the QSYSOBJECTPATHNAME class; they each use a jt400 class— PROGRAMCALL and COMMANDCALL, respectively—that encapsulates the call; and they both return a message list of AS/400 errors in an array of AS400MESSAGE objects, should the call fail.

Jt400's program call facility necessarily requires a few extra steps to handle program arguments. This chapter first covers the six steps to calling a legacy program from Java and then covers the five steps to calling an AS/400 command.

SIX STEPS TO REMOTE PROGRAM CALL

Calling an AS/400 program from Java entails six basic steps:

1. Create an AS400 object for the system that contains the program.
2. Create an array to hold the parameter list.
3. Create the path to the program.

4. Create the program call object.
5. Execute the program.
6. Handle any errors if the program call failed; otherwise, convert the data type of return parameters to Java.

STEP ONE: ESTABLISH AN AS/400 CONNECTION

In step one, you create an As400 object for the system that contains the program, which is easily done by invoking one of the constructors of the AS400 connection class:

```
AS400 as400 = new AS400(systemName);
```

Chapter 12 on record-level access covered the use of the As400 class and its constructor functions in detail.

STEP TWO: *ENTRY PLIST

Step two instructs you to create an array to hold the parameter list. A jt400 class called PROGRAMPARAMETER encapsulates the functions required to set up an AS/400 program parameter. You create an array of objects of that class simply by using the bracket operator and instancing the number of parameters that your AS/400 program requires:

```
ProgramParameter[] pList = new ProgramParameter[3];
```

The above method reflects standard procedure for creating a Java array. Realize, however, that the PLIST array merely serves as a placeholder for references to objects of the class type PROGRAMPARAMETER—no PROGRAMPARAMETER objects are created yet. You need to create three PROGRAMPARAMETER objects and assign their references to the elements of the PROGRAMPARAMETER array.

PROGRAM PARAMETERS

The first three constructors for the PROGRAMPARAMETER class, shown in Table 15.1, allow you to build parameter objects for input, output, or both input and output; with the fourth constructor, you can build a parameter object even if you're not really sure what it's for. (As you can guess, I do not suggest you use that fourth constructor.)

Table 15.1: The PROGRAMPARAMETER Object's Constructors.

Constructor	Description
ProgramParameter(byte data[])	Constructs a ProgramParameter object as an input parameter.
ProgramParameter(int size)	Constructs a ProgramParameter object as an output parameter where size is the amount of data to be returned from the program.
ProgramParameter(byte data[],int size)	Constructs a ProgramParameter object as both an input and an output parameter object. The byte data is the input and size is the amount of data to be returned from the program.
ProgramParameter()	Constructs a generic ProgramParameter object.

An input-only PROGRAMPARAMETER object's constructor takes the single parameter of the raw data in the form of Java's primitive data type of byte. An output-only PROGRAMPARAMETER's constructor takes an integer value to specify the size of the value that is to be returned from the called AS/400 program. A program parameter that is both input and output takes a byte data value and an integer value for the length of the returned value.

OUTPUT PARAMETERS

This chapter's example RPG program shown in Figure 15.1 takes three parameters: a zoned number, a packed number, and a character string.

```
*************** Beginning of data *********************
D Char20          S            20A
D Packed          S             9P 2
D Zoned           S             6S 0
D TimeNow         S              T

C     *ENTRY       PLIST
```

Figure 15.1: RPG program parameters can be input, output, or both. (Part 1 of 2)

```
C                 PARM                    Zoned
C                 PARM                    Packed
C                 PARM                    Char20

C                 Z-ADD    Packed         Zoned
C                 add      1              Packed
C                 Move     *BLANKS        Char20
C                 Time                    TimeNow
C                 eval     Char20 = %CHAR(TimeNow)

C                 Return
****************** End of data ************************
```

Figure 15.1: RPG program parameters can be input, output, or both. (Part 2 of 2)

Of course you know that AS/400 parameters can be used as both input and output. A parameter used for output only makes construction of the PROGRAMPARAMETER object easy—you just specify the length of the returned value as the argument to a PROGRAMPARAMETER object constructor. INV001's first parameter (a six-byte, zoned number) is output only, so Figure 15.1 creates a PROGRAMPARAMETER object using the constructor that takes the integer size of returned data:

```
pList[0] = new ProgramParameter(6);
```

INPUT PARAMETERS

The second parameter to the INV001 program—a packed decimal number with a length of nine and two decimal positions—is both an input and an output parameter. Things get a little nasty here. The binary representations for the data of the parameters of an AS/400 program differ quite a bit from those of the basic data types and objects of a Java program. The biggest task of using jt400's program call mechanism is converting Java data types to AS/400 data types before the call and then converting returned AS/400 values back to Java after the call. To help meet this end, jt400 has a number of AS/400 conversion classes, as shown in Table 15.2.

For INV001's second parameter, the Java code must create a PROGRAM PARAMETER object, passing two arguments to its constructor. The first argument must contain the packed decimal data required for parameter one of the INV001 RPG program. The second argument of the ProgramParameter object contains the length of the value that the INV001 program is to return.

Table 15.2: jt400 Data Conversion Classes.	
AS400Text	Java String object and AS/400 text.
AS400Bin2	Java Short object and AS/400 signed two-byte binary number.
AS400Bin4	Java Integer object and AS/400 signed four-byte binary number.
AS400ByteArray	Java byte array and AS/400 fixed-length byte array.
AS400Float4	Java Float object and AS/400 four-byte floating point number.
AS400Float8	Java Double object and AS/400 eight-byte floating point number.
AS400UnsignedBin2	Java Integer object and AS/400 unsigned two-byte binary number.
AS400UnsignedBin4	Java Long object and AS/400 unsigned four-byte binary number.
AS400PackedDecimal	Java BigDecimal object and AS/400 packed decimal number.
AS400ZonedDecimal	Java BigDecimal object and AS/400 zoned decimal number.

The returned length is easy; a packed decimal number with nine digits would be five bytes long. (It might be easier to always use 15, however, for the longest number of bytes supported in a packed decimal number.) It's that byte value that causes a problem. You have to use the AS400PACKEDDECIMAL utility object from Table 15.2 to convert a decimal number to the raw data expected in your AS/400 RPG program.

You can do this in one of two ways: The long form that's easy to understand or the short form that's a bit more difficult to understand. To set up the second parameter for the INV001 call using the easy-to-understand form, start by creating a Java BIGDECIMAL object:

```
BigDecimal decimalValue = new BigDecimal(1.25);
```

That object could perhaps already exist in your Java application, but I simply constructed one to hold the value of a buck and a quarter. Next, you construct one of those converter classes—AS400PACKEDDECIMAL, in this case. With the constructor function, you initialize the AS400PACKEDDECIMAL object to a length of nine and two decimal positions:

```
AS400PackedDecimal packConv = new AS400PackedDecimal(9, 2);
```

You can then use that converted class to convert the value of a BIGDECIMAL object to the raw bytes of data required for your AS/400 RPG program:

```
byte[] packedInput = packConv.toBytes(decimalValue);
```

Finally, you have the two arguments required to construct a PROGRAMPARAMETER object for both input and output—that is, the raw data containing the EBCDIC value of a packed number and the length required for the value to be returned from the RPG program:

```
pList[1] = new ProgramParameter( packedInput, 5);
```

The hard-to-understand short form consists of just one line:

```
pList[1] = new ProgramParameter(new AS400PackedDecimal(9, 2)
.toBytes(decimalValue), 5);
```

It's hard to understand because one line of code does so much. This single Java statement accomplishes the same four steps as the easy-to-understand form:

1. Creates a converter object of the proper length for the RPG program's parameter.

2. Uses that converter object to convert a Java object or basic data type to a raw byte value.

3. Passes that raw byte value as the first argument to the PROGRAMPARAMETER constructor.

4. Specifies the output length, if the AS/400 program parameter is used for input and output, as the second argument to the PROGRAMPARAMETER object constructor.

The setup for the third parameter to the INV001 RPG program, a character value, follows these same steps, differing only in the use of the AS400TEXT conversion object, the character input, and the length of the parameter.

```
AS400Text textConv = new AS400Text(20);
byte[] charInput = textConv.toBytes("input value");
pList[2] = new ProgramParameter( charInput, 20 );
```

STEP THREE: WHERE'S THE PROGRAM?

Where's the program? To answer that question, you need to create a path to the program using the QSYSOBJECTPATHNAME class. This same class appears in chapter 12's explanation of record-level access; an object of the QSYSOBJECTPATHNAME class is used to direct the standard AS/400 IFS Java I/O through to a more familiar library system where your legacy programs reside:

```
QSYSObjectPathName programName =
new QSYSObjectPathName("INVLIB", "INV001","PGM");
```

The first parameter to QSYSOBJECTPATHNAME's constructor function is the name of the library that contains the program. The second parameter contains the program name and the third parameter specifies the AS/400 object type.

STEP FOUR: THE PROGRAM CALL OBJECT

In step four, you create the program call object. Jt400's PROGRAMCALL class has several constructors—the one I suggest you use takes three arguments: the As400 connection object, the path to the program, and the parameter list:

```
ProgramCall inv001 = new ProgramCall(as400, programName.getPath(),
pList);
```

If your AS/400 program has no parameters, you would use the PROGRAMCALL constructor that accepts only the AS400 object and program path:

```
ProgramCall noParmsPgm = new ProgramCall(as400,
noParmsPgmName.getPath());
```

STEP FIVE: GO

You're all set. With the parameter list built, the AS/400 connection enabled, and the program found on the AS/400, it's time to execute the RPG program:

```
inv001.run()
```

STEP SIX: HOW'D IT GO?

Running the program is simple enough; the program call's RUN function, however, might fail and you'll have to find out what went wrong. On the other hand, if the call works, you still have to convert the returned output parameters back into Java objects or data types.

You've heard the old adage, "If something can go wrong, it will." You must provide handling for unexpected errors that can occur when you run that program call object. PROGRAMCALL's RUN function can throw a number of Java exceptions so you'll have to wrap a try block around the function call. While you *could* simply catch the generic exception message, you should at least monitor for the object-does-not-exist exception and then use CATCH for the generic EXCEPTION exception as shown in Figure 14.2.

```
try {
  inv001.run();
} catch (ObjectDoesNotExistException dnf) {…}
} catch (Exception error) {…}
```

Figure 15.2: Catch specific errors first; then catch more general errors.

This code snippet, however, does not handle the Boolean return value from the RUN function. A return value of false signals that a problem occurred, and a value of true indicates that the call worked. If the run function returns a value of false, you can retrieve the list of errors from the PROGRAMCALL object with its GETMESSAGELIST function:

```
if (inv001.run() == false)
        AS400Message[] messageList = inv001.getMessageList();
```

That array of AS/400 messages contains the OS/400 CPF, RPG, and other familiar messages. You can list them in a log or perhaps even display them to the user in a Windows dialog box.

If everything goes smoothly and the AS/400 program executes successfully, you then need to convert any return values from output parameters back into Java data types. To do this, you use the conversion objects shown in Table 15.1. This time, however, instead of using the TOBYTES function, which converts data from Java objects to AS/400 format, you'll be using the TOOBJECT function, which converts data from AS/400 format to Java objects.

Remembering that the zoned parameter of the INV001 RPG program is stored as the first element of the PROGRAMPARAMETER array called PLIST, you use PROGRAMPARAMETER's GETOUTPUTDATA function to retrieve the return value:

```
byte[] rawAs400Data = pList[0].getOutputData();
```

The resulting value still retains the EBCDIC format of OS/400, so you must convert that raw data back into a Java BIGDECIMAL object. This process entails two steps because the conversion class's TOOBJECT function always return the ambiguous OBJECT object:

```
Object anObject = new AS400ZonedDecimal(6, 0).toObject(
rawAs400Data);
BigDecimal zonedReturn = (BigDecimal)anObject;
```

That second step uses Java's casting mechanism to promote the OBJECT object back into its true form—a BIGDECIMAL object. Again, these steps can be incorporated into one Java statement:

```
BigDecimal zonedReturn =
   (BigDecimal) new
AS400ZonedDecimal(6,0).toObject(pList[0].getOutputData());
```

Again, the short form is harder to understand until you get used to it. Yet, its advantages extend beyond requiring just one Java statement; it also removes the requirement for several temporary objects. Every additional statement or variable makes a program harder to read and understand. When you review someone else's code and notice that a variable is created, you assume that the variable is used many times in the program, thus increasing its complexity. Eventually, you will prefer this short form because you'll find that it truly is easier to understand. Using the short form (as shown in Figure 15.3), you can easily retrieve the return values of the packed and character parameters:

```
BigDecimal packedReturn =
    (BigDecimal)new
AS400PackedDecimal(9, 2).toObject(pList[1].getOutputData() );
String charReturn =
        (String) new
AS400Text(20).toObject(pList[2].getOutputData() );
```

Figure 15.3: The short form of retrieving return values can reduce overall complexity of the code.

Figure 15.4 shows the example Java program in its entirety.

```
import java.math.*;
import com.ibm.as400.access.*;

public class Inv001PgmCall {

  public Inv001PgmCall() {

    // Create an AS400 object for the system that contains the
program
    AS400 as400 = new AS400(Profile.MC, Profile.USER,
Profile.PASS);

    // Create an array to hold the parameter list
    ProgramParameter[] pList = new ProgramParameter[3];
    // the first parameter is output only zoned 6/0
    pList[0] = new ProgramParameter(6);
    // the second parameter is input and output packed 9/2
    BigDecimal decimalValue = new BigDecimal(1.25);
    AS400PackedDecimal packConv = new AS400PackedDecimal(9, 2);
    byte[] packedInput = packConv.toBytes(decimalValue);
    pList[1] = new ProgramParameter( packedInput, 5);
```

Figure 15.4: Calling an AS/400 program requires conversion between the EBCDIC data of the AS/400 and Java objects. (Part 1 of 3)

```
// short form, although redundant:
pList[1] = new ProgramParameter(
    new AS400PackedDecimal(9, 2).toBytes(decimalValue), 5);
// the third parameter is input and output character 20
AS400Text textConv = new AS400Text(20);
byte[] charInput = textConv.toBytes("input value");
pList[2] = new ProgramParameter( charInput, 20 );
// short form, although redundant:
pList[2] =
  new ProgramParameter(
         new AS400Text(20).toBytes("input value"), 20);


// Create the path to the program
QSYSObjectPathName programName =
    new QSYSObjectPathName("DENONCOURT", "INV001","PGM");
// Create the program call object
ProgramCall inv001 =
    new ProgramCall(as400, programName.getPath(), pList);
// Execute the program
try {
  if (inv001.run() == false){
     // Handle any errors if the program call failed
     AS400Message[] msgList = inv001.getMessageList();
     for (int i=0; i<msgList.length; i++) {
       System.out.println(msgList[i].getText());
     }
     return;
  }
} catch (ObjectDoesNotExistException dnf) {
    System.out.println("Program not found");
    return;
} catch (Exception error) {
    System.out.println("Exception: " + error);
    return;
}


// Convert the value of output parameters to Java

// convert parameter one back to Java
byte[] rawAs400Data = pList[0].getOutputData();
Object anObject =
  new AS400ZonedDecimal(6, 0).toObject( rawAs400Data);
BigDecimal zonedReturn  = (BigDecimal)anObject;
// convert parameter two back to Java
```

Figure 15.4: Calling an AS/400 program requires conversion between the EBCDIC data of the AS/400 and Java objects. (Part 2 of 3)

```
    BigDecimal packedReturn =
      (BigDecimal)
      new AS400PackedDecimal(9, 2).toObject(
pList[1].getOutputData() );
    // convert parameter three back to Java
    String charReturn =
      (String) new AS400Text(20).toObject(
pList[2].getOutputData() );

    // list the returned values
    System.out.println("pList[0]: " + zonedReturn.toString() +
                 "\npList[1]: " + packedReturn.toString() +
                 "\npList[2]: " + charReturn);
  }


  public static void main(String[] args) {
    Inv001PgmCall Inv001PgmCall = new Inv001PgmCall();
    System.exit(0);
  }
}
```

Figure 15.4: Calling an AS/400 program requires conversion between the EBCDIC data of the AS/400 and Java objects. (Part 3 of 3)

A STRATEGY FOR ENCAPSULATING AS/400 PROGRAM CALLS

Now that you have a full understanding of the steps required to invoke an AS/400 program, let me point out that the example class, INV001PGMCALL, is not very object-oriented. The call to an AS/400 program should be encapsulated into a class. A simple strategy for doing this involves creating a class that has the name and maybe even the purpose of the AS/400 program.

For example, you might encapsulate an inventory update program bearing the AS/400 name of INV023 in a program class called UPDATEINVENTORYINV023. Let's say that program takes part number, aisle, row, bin, and quantity values as input parameters and has output parameters of an error message and the new quantity on hand. One of the overloaded constructors for that class could take the required input parameters, whereas the other could simply take the PARTNO:

```
UpdateInventoryINV023 (int partNo)
UpdateInventoryINV023 (int partNo, BigDecimal quantityChange,
                int aisle, int row, int bin)
```

If a user of the UPDATEINVENTORYINV023 class constructs an object using the PARTNO constructor, the other input parameters can be set with a default value in that constructor or the user could make an explicit call to the required parameter's SET function, as shown in Figure 15.5.

```
void setQuantityChange()
void setBin (int bin)
void setAisle (int aisle)
void setRow(int row)
```

Figure 15.5: A function is declared for each program parameter.

The program call class should also override the RUN function of the PROGRAMCALL class, as shown in Figure 15.6.

```
void run() throws
PartNumberNotFoundException,
NoAvailableInventoryException,
InvalidParmException
```

Figure 15.6: Program-specific exceptions should be declared in a RUN function.

The RUN function of the UPDATEINVENTORYINV023 class does not return a Boolean value as does the PROGRAMCALL object's RUN function. That's because UPDATEINVENTORYINV023's version of the RUN function is coded to handle exceptions and to pull out the returned values of INV023's program parameters.

Finally, each output parameter of the INV023 AS/400 program should have an associated GET function:

```
int getNewQuantityOnHand()
```

Note the absence of a GET function for the message parameter of INV023; that message was used to generate the PARTNUMBERNOTFOUNDEXCEPTION, NOAVAILABLEINVENTORYEXCEPTION, and INVALIDPARMEXCEPTION exceptions. The user of the UPDATEINVENTORYINV023 class should not have to figure out all the possible errors that might be returned—that job goes to the person who codes the UPDATEINVENTORYINV023 class.

Encapsulating the AS/400 program call in a class allows for more intuitive use of the AS/400 program. Java programmers will not be duplicating the code to call that AS/400 program, and the error handling exists in one place. In fact, a properly encapsulated AS/400 program call class makes it very easy for non-AS/400 programmers to call legacy application programs.

OS/400 COMMAND INVOCATION

IBM's AS/400 Toolbox for Java also comes with the COMMANDCALL object to allow you to execute OS/400 commands. Use of the COMMANDCALL object is very similar to the PROGRAMCALL but does not entail dealing with parameters. AS/400 command invocation involves five basic steps:

1. Create an As400 connection object.
2. Create a command call object.
3. Create a command string object.
4. Run the command.
5. Review error messages, if the command fails.

The first step, as with PROGRAMCALL, involves creating an As400 connection object. If you've already created one, obviously you can use it for your command invocation also. In the second step, you create a COMMANDCALL object, passing an As400 connection object:

```
CommandCall cmd = new CommandCall (as400);
```

The third step is to create an AS/400 command string:

```
String cmdStr = "ADDLIBLE DENONCOURT";
```

In step four, you simply run the command COMMANDCALL's RUN function, passing the command string:

```
cmd.run(cmdStr);
```

You could combine steps three and four and remove the requirement for the string variable:

```
cmd.run("DLTLIB *ALL ");
```

As stated earlier in the ProgramCall section of this chapter, if something can go wrong, it will. The RUN function of CommandCall, just like the RUN function of ProgramCall, will return a Boolean value, a false value of which shows a problem. When an error occurs, you can retrieve the list of AS/400 error messages (step five of the command invocation), as shown in the code snippet of Figure 15.7.

```
if (cmd.run("ADDLIBLE DENONCOURT") == false) {
  AS400Message[] msgs = command.getMessageList();
  for (int i=0; i < msgs.length; i++)
    String cpfMsg = msgs[i].getID()+":"+msgs[i].getText();
}
```

Figure 15.7: The command call invocation of the RUN function should spin through the list of errors if the command invocation fails.

JAVA NATIVE INTERFACE

You do have means other than the PROGRAMCALL class of jt400 to leverage AS/400 host programs. The C programming language is the easiest way to take advantage of the full breadth of OS/400's system APIs. As you might expect, this holds true for many other operating systems also; after all, C has historically been the language of systems programmers. For this reason, the Java programming language has a feature, the Java Native Interface (JNI), that allows you to easily integrate C (and C++) code with your Java applications.

As of V4R3, OS/400 only has direct JNI support for ILE C and C++. (Yes, the AS/400 has had C++ for a number of years!) As of V4R4, OS/400 supports the use of ILE RPG modules with your Java applications. To understand the potential power of integrating ILE RPG modules with your Java class, you'll learn in the following paragraphs how JNI works with ILE C as of V4R3.

A Java class has a list of functions that describe the behaviors of the entity that the Java class represents. For those functions that you would like to implement with C, you simply add Java's reserved word NATIVE as a modifier preceding the function declaration. Figure 15.8 shows an example.

```
public class JNIExample  {
  private int value;
  native void callCFunction();
  int getValue() {
    return value;
  }
  static {
    System.loadLibrary("C_CODE.SRVPGM");
  }
}
```

Figure 15.8: The AS/400's Java Native Interface allows you to specify an ILE service program with ILE module implementations for functions of a Java class.

Functions that do *not* have the native modifier provide Java code implementations between the functions' enclosing curly braces. Java functions with the native modifier have no code implementation; you code the implementation in C and then compile that C code into an ILE module. That ILE module is bound into a service program that is then associated with the Java class through a call to Java's LOADLIBRARY function. A good place to insert that LOADLIBRARY call is in your Java class's static pseudofunction. (Java guarantees that the pseudofunction is called the first time that class is instantiated.) On an AS/400, the LOADLIBRARY function must be passed a string that contains the .SRVPGM qualifier. On a Microsoft platform, the LOADLIBRARY qualifier would be .DLL for a Dynamic Link Library.

You compile your Java JNI class as you would any other class, with Java's JAVAC command. However, with a Java class that uses JNI, you then run Java's JAVAH command, specifying your Java class as a parameter. The JAVAH utility then generates a C header file in a language native to your operating system. That file contains the C prototypes for the Java functions you said you would use. The C function prototypes contain not only any parameters that correspond to the Java class functions but also a C pointer (JNIENV*) to the JNI environment and a special C structure called JOBJECT. Through that pointer and the JOBJECT structure, your C function can access the fields of the Java class as well as the other functions of that Java class.

In effect, the C function (and, later, the RPG function) is just like its sister Java function in that it has access to all of the fields and functions of its class. However, the use of the JNIENV Java environment pointer and the JOBJECT Java object structure does get fairly complex.

OS/400 V4R4 supports the use of RPG modules with JNI, which means you can develop ILE RPG modules that implement the interfaces of a Java class. There is a caveat, however, in that you'll have to manually convert the C header files generated with the JAVAH utility to RPG D-specifications. Rather than the Java header files that the JAVAH utility provides for the C generator, I expect IBM (or a third-party software vendor) to develop an RPG incarnation of the JAVAH utility, probably called JAVAD for Java D-specification, for the RPG generator. Such a utility could create D-specifications that have the D-spec prototypes for ILE RPG functions. You could include those generated D-specs in your RPG module source with a /COPY statement. Then your RPG legacy application programmer could implement Java functions with RPG. The performance of JNI is superior to the external program call of jt400's PROGRAMCALL class because each external program call requires program startup and initialization.

DATA QUEUES

Another viable alternative for integrating Java with your AS/400 applications comes in the form of data queues. Data queues, which have been employed in AS/400 applications for some time, allow asynchronous communication from one program to another or perhaps to several other programs. IBM's Java Toolbox for the AS/400 supports both keyed and sequential data queues with its DATAQUEUE and KEYEDDATAQUEUE classes. The DATAQUEUE class's constructor, just like PROGRAMCALL, requires an AS400 connection object and a path:

```
DataQueue dataq = new DataQueue(as400,
qsysObjectPathNameToDataQueue.getPath())
```

You can then read from that AS/400 data queue with the DATAQUEUE's READ function and you can write to that data queue with the WRITE function. Figure 15.9 shows the prototypes for these functions.

```
void write(byte data[]) throws
AS400SecurityException, ErrorCompletingRequestException
DataQueueEntry read()throws
AS400SecurityException, ErrorCompletingRequestException
```

Figure 15.9: The READ and WRITE functions of jt400's data queue class allow you to put and get data queue entries.

The WRITE function takes the raw data in the form of Java's primitive byte data type, just as a PROGRAMPARAMETER object requires in order to use the PROGRAMCALL class. The READ function of DATAQUEUE returns a DATAQUEUEENTRY object, whose GETDATA function returns the raw data as an array of bytes. So, if your Java application communicates with an RPG program by way of a data queue, the raw data of the data queue entries must be in EBCDIC.

You can use any of the converter classes shown in Table 15.2 to convert Java objects to an AS/400 data type. IBM's documentation, however, suggests an alternative. It suggests that you develop a record format that describes the data to be transmitted in the data queue as shown in Figure 15.10. Your Java application can retrieve that record format as a RECORDFORMAT object, as described in chapter 13.

```
AS400FileRecordDescription recDesc =
new AS400FileRecordDescription(
as400, pathNameToFile.getPath());
RecordFormat dataqFormat = recDesc.retrieveRecordFormat()[0];
```

Figure 15.10: The RECORDFORMAT is a handy class to use for Java data queue programming because of its automatic conversion of Java to AS/400 data types.

The application then uses the RECORDFORMAT's GETNEWRECORD function that takes the data queue entry's byte array to construct a new record, the values of which come from the data queue entry. Those field values are retrievable with the RECORDFORMAT's GETFIELD function, which automatically performs the necessary data conversion:

```
DataQueueEntry dataqEntry = dataq.read();
Record dataqRecordEntry =
dataqFormat.getNewRecord(dataqEntry.getData());
BigDecimal = (BigDecimal)dataqRecordEntry.getField("PCKFLD");
```

To put data queue entries, the Java application first creates a new RECORD object whose format comes from the RECORDFORMAT object retrieved earlier. The values of the fields within that RECORD object are then filled with calls to RECORD's SETFIELD function. Finally, the GETCONTENTS function retrieves a byte array that contains the contents of the RECORD object, and the array is then passed as the parameter to the data queue object's WRITE function:

```
Record dataqRecordEntry = new Record(dataqFormat);
dataqRecordEntry.setField("PCKFLD", someBigDecimalValue);
dataq.write(dataqRecordEntry.getContents());
```

RPG PROGRAM CALL WITH PCML

The Java Toolbox for the AS/400, as of OS/400 V4R4, comes with a new facility for calling AS/400 programs. This facility is enabled with an Extensible Markup Language (XML) called Program Call Markup Language (PCML). PCML was created to ease the difficulty of calling legacy AS/400 programs from Java. Calling legacy programs using the method shown earlier in this chapter is difficult mostly due to the fact that Java's data types are not kept in EBCDIC. When you use the PROGRAMCALL class, you must set up an array of PROGRAMPARAMETER objects and then use the various utility conversion classes to convert Java objects to and from the associated RPG field type before and after the program call.

With PCML, you don't have to worry about data conversions. And don't be concerned about learning what sounds like a whole new language, because PCML is easy. Compare the complexity of the INV001PGMCALL class shown in Figure 15.4 with the INV001 class shown in Figure 15.11. Both of those Java classes call the same INV001 RPG program shown in Figure 15.1; surely you'll agree that the INV001PGMCALL version is far easier to understand.

```
import com.ibm.as400.data.*;
import com.ibm.as400.access.*;
import java.math.*;

public class Inv001 {
  ProgramCallDocument pcml;
    AS400 as400;

    BigDecimal zonedField;
    BigDecimal packedField;
    String charField;

    public static void main(String[] pList) {
      Inv001 inv001 = new Inv001();
      System.exit(0);
    }

    Inv001 () {
     as400 = new AS400("localhost");
     try {
      // construct a program call doc from the PCML XML file
      pcml = new ProgramCallDocument(as400, "inv001");
      // set the values of input parameters
      pcml.setValue("inv001.packedField", new BigDecimal("1.25"));
      pcml.setValue("inv001.charField", new String("char input value"));
      // call the program and handle errors, if any
      if (pcml.callProgram("inv001") == false) {
        AS400Message[] msgs = pcml.getMessageList("inv001");
        String msgId, msgText;
        for (int m = 0; m < msgs.length; m++) {
         msgId = msgs[m].getID();
          msgText = msgs[m].getText();
          System.out.println("        " + msgId + " - " + msgText);
          }
          System.exit(0);
       }
       // OK, call successful
       // retrieve data values from the program call object
       // and cast them to their associated Java class
       zonedField = (BigDecimal)pcml.getValue("inv001.zonedField");
       packedField = (BigDecimal)pcml.getValue("inv001.packedField");
       charField = (String)pcml.getValue("inv001.charField");

     System.out.println("zonedField: " + zonedField.toString() + "\n");
```

Figure 15.11: The use of the jt400's Program Call Markup Language makes it easier to interoperate Java and legacy RPG and COBOL applications. (Part 1 of 2)

```
    System.out.println("packedField: " + packedField.toString() + "\n");
    System.out.println("charField: " + charField + "\n");
  } catch (PcmlException e) {
    System.out.println(e.getLocalizedMessage());
    e.printStackTrace();
  System.exit(0);
  }
 }
}
```

Figure 15.11: The use of the jt400's Program Call Markup Language makes it easier to interoperate Java and legacy RPG and COBOL applications. (Part 2 of 2)

PCML COMPLETE

The INV001 class takes just half the lines of code that its older brother, the INV001PGMCALL class, needs. The reason for its simplicity is PCML. The PCML syntax is fairly straightforward, especially when the parameters are all atomic data types. Take a look at Figure 15.12, which contains the PCML used to describe the INV001 RPG program complete with its list of parameters and their associated data types.

```
<pcml version="1.0">
<program name="inv001"
path="/QSYS.lib/DENONCOURT.lib/INV001.pgm">
  <data name="zonedField"  type="zoned"  length="6"
                           precision="0" usage="output"/>
  <data name="packedField" type="packed" length="9"
                           precision="2" usage="inputoutput"/>
  <data name="charField"   type="char"   length="20"

                           usage="inputoutput"/>
</program>
</pcml>
```

Figure 15.12: Program Call Markup Language is an XML language that allows for the simple qualification of an AS/400 program, its parameters, and their data types.

Those of you familiar with hypertext markup language (HTML) have probably noticed PCML's similarity in that it is comprised of sets of tags. That's because PCML, XML, and HTML are all examples of a markup language. The <PCML>

and </PCML> tag pair delimits the entire PCML source. The VERSION option qualifies this source as the initial version of PCML:

```
<pcml version="1.0">
```

The <PROGRAM> tag qualifies the AS/400 program. Notice the IFS route from the QSYS library to a library of my name to the INV001 program:

```
<program name="inv001" path="/QSYS.lib/DENONCOURT.lib/INV001.pgm">
```

The program tag is followed by three <DATA> tags before the program tag is closed with the </PROGRAM> tag. The data tags are used to specify the data types of each parameter of the called program. Figure 15.13 illustrates the use of one of those three data tags.

```
<data name="zonedField"
      type="zoned"
      length="6"
      precision="0"
      usage="output"/>
```

Figure 15.13: The data tag specifies the data type for each parameter of the called program.

As an aside, one trick that helps me decipher a complex markup (be it HTML, PCML, or any other XML-derived language) is to view markup tags as a comparable AS/400 Control Language (CL) command. Figure 15.14 shows a CL command that correlates with the preceding figure's data tag.

```
DATA NAME(packedField) +
     TYPE(packed) +
     LENGTH(9) +
     PRECISION(2) +
     USAGE(inputoutput)
```

Figure 15.14: To facilitate understanding, approach a complex markup by viewing it in CL terms.

With that aside, the NAME option identifies the name of the program parameter that you intend to use in your Java applications. You should name that parameter carefully and follow standard Java naming conventions. (My own field name of ZONEDFIELD is not a very good example, but because the INV001 RPG program doesn't do anything worthwhile, it was the best I could come up with. So, do as I say, not as I do.)

The TYPE option sets the AS/400 data type. For the most part, existing legacy programs require ZONED, PACKED, and CHAR, but other data types are supported such as INTEGERS, FLOAT, and DOUBLE. The LENGTH option specifies the length of the field. For a packed field of nine digits with two decimal positions, the length option should be set to 9—don't bother calculating the actual number of bytes used, because the jt400 class will figure that out for you.

The PRECISION option specifies the number of decimals for zoned and packed fields. For integers, the specification of precision becomes more complex and warrants a look at the documentation that comes with modification 2 of jt400. With the USAGE option, you specify whether the parameter is INPUT, OUTPUT, or INPUTOUTPUT. Take care to set the usage parameter appropriately. If you specify INPUT or INPUTOUTPUT, you must set initial values for the parameter; if you don't specify OUTPUT, you will not be able to retrieve returned values.

USING PCML IN JAVA

You can call the AS/400 program specified in the PCML document with relative ease (especially when you consider the old method). First, construct a ProgramCallDocument object, specifying an As400 connection object and the file name of the PCML associated with the legacy program. (Your PCML files must have a suffix of .pcml.) Here the PCML file is named after the INV001 RPG program, so the instantiation of the ProgramCallDocument object goes as follows:

```
ProgramCallDocument  pcml = new ProgramCallDocument(as400,
"inv001");
```

With the program call document object created, you can set the values of the INV001 program's input parameters. To do so, you use PROGRAMCALLDOCUMENT's SETVALUE function. The SETVALUE function requires the name of the legacy program's parameter in argument one and the Java object in argument two:

```
pcml.setValue("inv001.packedField", new BigDecimal("1.25"));
pcml.setValue("inv001.charField", new String("char input value"));
```

The qualification of field names corresponds exactly to the data names described in the DATA tag of the INV001.PCML PCML file, with the "INV001" qualifying the field with the PROGRAM tag.

With the input values all set, the INV001 class can call the INV001 AS/400 program:

```
pcml.callProgram("inv001")
```

Note that the call program function returns a Boolean value to tell you whether or not the call worked. If the CALLPROGRAM function returns a false value, you can retrieve the list of AS/400 error messages with the PROGRAMCALLDOCUMENT's GETMESSAGELIST function:

```
AS400Message[] msgs = pcml.getMessageList("inv001");
```

You can spin through the array of messages and list them in a screen of error logs or perhaps even correct the problem at runtime with your Java code.

But if the CALLPROGRAM function returns a value of true, you want to retrieve data values from the PROGRAMCALLDOCUMENT object by using its GETVALUE function:

```
Object returnValue = pcml.getValue("inv001.zonedField");
```

However, the GETVALUE function presents a problem in that it returns the ambiguous OBJECT object. As required with values returned by the older program call method, the returned object must be cast to the Java class associated with the legacy program parameter's data type:

```
BigDecimal zonedField = (BigDecimal)returnValue;
```

You can concatenate those two lines into one, thus removing the requirement for a temporary OBJECT variable, as Figure 15.15 does with the packed and character values returned from the INV001 RPG program.

```
BigDecimal packedField =
    (BigDecimal)pcml.getValue("inv001.packedField");
String charField =
    (String)pcml.getValue("inv001.charField");
```

Figure 15.15: The GETVALUE function handles the conversion of EBCDIC parameter values to a Java object of the appropriate class.

JAR REQUIREMENTS

Modification 2 of jt400 consists of several Java archive files (JARs). Your Java CLASSPATH will need to specify JT400.JAR, as it always did, but your CLASSPATH also needs two other JARs: X4J400.JAR and DATA400.JAR. The first archive, X4J400.JAR, contains the Java XML processor code (it's 220 KB in size). The DATA400.JAR archive file contains the PROGRAMCALLDOCUMENT class and its associated classes (it runs about 57 KB in size).

HONEY, CAN WE TALK?

PCML improves the marriage of legacy AS/400 applications and Java applications by enabling those applications to more easily "talk about it." The union of legacy and Java applications will strengthen because of the ease with which PCML allows program communication. For most of your AS/400 programs, you can copy this book's INV001.PCML PCML source and INV001.JAVA Java source and easily modify it to work with your various RPG programs. Some AS/400 programs, however, such as OS/400's system APIs, require complex structures for parameters. The PCML documentation that comes with IBM's Java Toolbox for the AS/400 covers the use of complex data types with PCML in detail.

SUMMARY

IBM's Java Toolbox for the AS/400 provides full support for all your legacy application programs. For instance, jt400's PROGRAMCALL class enables calls to existing programs, and its COMMANDCALL class allows you to invoke commands. You can use data queues to enable high-speed asynchronous communications between your Java applications and your RPG applications. OS/400 V4R4 makes it easier to marry Java and RPG applications with jt400's Program Call Markup Language (PCML). As you develop your Java applications to integrate with legacy applications, just remember to ensure that interoperability through encapsulated, object-oriented classes.

SECTION IV

~

OBJECT-ORIENTED STRATEGIES FOR MAPPING DB2/400 TO JAVA

16

ENCAPSULATING DB2/400 DATA ACCESS INTO JAVA CLASSES

Sections I and II of this book went into copious detail about object-oriented programming. Section III discussed DB2/400 access using IBM's Java Toolbox for the AS/400 (jt400). Now that you've reached Section IV, you have an advanced object-oriented language with which to write AS/400 applications.

Yet, the jt400 examples in the chapters on record-level access and Java Database Connectivity (JDBC) serve as poor examples of object-oriented programming. Written in the same structured style prevalent in your legacy application programs, the examples do not truly utilize an object-oriented approach. They open a file and then read and process that file in a big loop.

Contributing to the examples' poor illustration of object-oriented principles is the burden of extra code that seems to accompany every Java program that accesses the business entities you store in DB2/400. Each of those example programs serves a specific purpose, which could lead you to believe that every Java application program should do the same file open and structured processing. But where would that leave us? We'd just proliferate the same problems that we had with legacy application programs. Problems like having a multitude of programs updating the same file. Problems like having code that serves the same purpose in an innumerable set of programs. Problems like nonconformance to business rules because you haven't followed the standard encapsulation techniques that chapter 6 tells you are the first level of object-oriented programming.

This chapter is the first of several to cover object-oriented design techniques for AS/400 Java classes. This chapter covers encapsulation procedures for writing a Java class that represents a business entity stored in DB2/400: a customer. The basic idea is to encapsulate DB2/400 access, using the record-level access of Distributed Data Management (DDM), the SQL access of JDBC, or both, into a single Java class, the CUSTOMER class. Other programmers then use this class rather than opening and processing the customer master file directly. Users of the CUSTOMER class, therefore, are no longer required to have any knowledge of AS/400-specific processing, be it DB2, DDM, JDBC, or otherwise.

ENTITY ENCAPSULATION

You follow eight basic steps to encapsulate one of your AS/400 business entities:

1. Design one Java class for each business entity stored in DB2/400.

2. Define as private class fields that correspond to fields in the DB2/400 record format.

3. Define getter functions for private fields.

4. Define setter functions for private fields with validation.

5. Define CREATE, READ, UPDATE, and DELETE (CRUD) functions.

6. Add functions that return associated objects.

7. Add function interfaces as required for the manipulation of the business entity.

8. Produce Java HTML documentation for the class.

As covered in chapter 6, you design Java business classes to encapsulate the manipulation of business entities through the API of that class. The class API encapsulates your company's business rules, which implicitly enforces compliance because the only way a programmer should be able to access that business entity is through the Java class that represents it.

Step one instructs you to define a Java class for the DB2/400 business entity. The name of that class should be the same name that users use when they refer to the entity. That Java business class normally corresponds directly to a single DB2/400 record format, although you may have to create a JOIN logical if the attributes of a single business entity are spread over multiple files.

In step two, you define a group of private Java class fields that correlate to the fields of the DB/400 record format. Steps three and four call for you to define public getter and setter functions for retrieving and modifying the attributes of the business entity. Step five, with its unappealing name of CRUD, relates to the design of function interfaces for object creation, DB2/400 READ operations, and UPDATE and DELETE functions.

In step six, you add functions specific to the manipulation of that business object. The last step, seven, directs you to produce Java documentation. You should follow the standard given by Sun and IBM: When you use their classes, you always have Java documentation available. Your own classes should do the same—and, besides, it's easy to do anyway.

CLASS ATTRIBUTES

The CUSTOMER class is designed to encapsulate the business entities that every AS/400 (with Client Access installed) stores in the QCUSTCDT file in library QIWS. A look at Figure 16.1 reveals that I have defined class fields by using standard Java objects that relate to the specific field types of the QCUSTCDT DB2/400 file. (Table 16.1 shows the Java objects that correspond to DB2/400 data types.) Those field names follow my own naming convention, in which the Java field names have the same spelling and case as they have on the AS/400. This naming standard makes it easier for DB2/400 programmers to understand the Java code because they spot familiar field names. Perhaps spelling the names out more fully (e.g., CUSTOMERNUMBER and BALANCEDUE) would improve clarity, but I opted instead for the clarity associated with familiar field names.

```
public class Customer {
  // class data members should be private
  private BigDecimal CUSNUM; // ZONED 6/0
  private String LSTNAM;// CHAR 8
  private String INIT;// CHAR 3
  private String STREET;// CHAR 13
  private String CITY;// CHAR 6
  private String STATE;// CHAR 2
  private BigDecimal ZIPCOD;// ZONED 5/0
  private BigDecimal CDTLMT;// ZONED 4/0
  private BigDecimal CHGCOD;// ZONED 1/0
  private BigDecimal BALDUE;// ZONED 6/2
  private BigDecimal CDTDUE;// ZONED 6/2
```

Figure 16.1: All the fields of the CUSTOMER class are private.

Table 16.1: AS/400 Data Types and Corresponding Java Classes.

AS/400 Data Type	Java Class
Signed binary 2 bytes	Short
Signed binary 4 bytes	Integer
Unsigned binary 2 bytes	Integer
Unsigned binary 4 bytes	Long
Float 4 bytes	Float
Float 8 bytes	Double
Packed	BigDecimal
Zoned	BigDecimal
Character	String

Step three involves defining public getter functions so that users of the Java class can retrieve the values of class attributes. In chapter 6, you learned that declaring class attributes as private protects them from inadvertent modification. Remember that the class encapsulates the control of the entity; if users have direct access to the fields, they bypass the controls imposed on the setter functions.

The implementation of getter functions is simple; Figure 16.2 shows that you define a function that returns the same object type as the field. Notice the standard Java naming convention, in which the names of getter functions are preceded by the word *get* and followed by the field name of the attribute whose value is returned with that function.

```
public String getLSTNAM() { return LSTNAM; }
public String getINIT() { return INIT; }
public String getSTREET() { return STREET; }
public String getCITY() { return CITY; }
public String getSTATE() { return STATE; }
public BigDecimal getZIPCOD() { return ZIPCOD; }
public BigDecimal getCDTLMT() { return CDTLMT; }
public BigDecimal getCHGCOD() { return CHGCOD; }
public BigDecimal getBALDUE() { return BALDUE; }
public BigDecimal getCDTDUE() { return CDTDUE; }
```

Figure 16.2 Define getter functions for each of the private fields of the class.

Step four calls for the definition of public setter functions. You should define setter functions only for those attributes you want the class's user to modify. These functions should have at least some basic validation, and they should also conform to business rules. If the value is in error, your function should throw some type of exception. For example, the SETSTATE function shown in Figure 16.3 checks the validity of the state string argument before updating the value of the STATE class field. Because SETSTATE throws an exception, the function signature must include the THROWS clause that specifies the explicit exception. The SETLSTNAM function also shown in Figure 16.3 works similarly except that it throws an INVALIDLENGTHEXCEPTION error.

```
public void setSTATE (String state) throws InvalidStateException
{
    String states[] = {"AL","AL","AZ","AR","CA","CO","CT",
    "CE","FL","GA","HI","ID","IL","IN","IA","KS","KY","LA",
    "ME","MD","MA","MI","MN","MS","MO","MT","NE","NV","NH",
    "NJ","NM","NY","NC","ND","OH","OK","OR","PA","RI","SC",
    "SD","TN","TX","UT","VT","VA","WA","DC","WV","WI","WY"};
    for (int i=0; i<states.length;i++) {
        if (state.equals(states[i])) {
```

Figure 16.3: If a function throws an exception, its function signature must contain a THROWS clause. (Part 1 of 2)

```
            STATE = state;
            return;
        }
    }
    throw new InvalidStateException(state);
    }
public void setLSTNAM(String str) throws InvalidLengthException {
    if (str.length() > 8)
        throw new InvalidLengthException("LSTNAM", str.length(), 8);
    LSTNAM = str;
    }
```

Figure 16.3: If a function throws an exception, its function signature must contain a THROWS clause. (Part 2 of 2)

The SETSTATE function appropriately uses an INVALIDSTATEEXCEPTION error class to explicitly signal a specific error. The implementation of an exception class need not be overly complex; it can simply extend the EXCEPTION class and then pass the initial value for the message to its parent with Java's SUPER keyword, as shown in Figure 16.4.

```
public class InvalidStateException extends Exception {
    public InvalidStateException(String stateCode) {
        super("Invalid state code: " + stateCode);
    }
}
```

Figure 16.4: Exception classes can be defined for the explicit qualification of an error.

The INVALIDLENGTHEXCEPTION class does basically the same thing but with a different message and constructor arguments, as shown in Figure 16.5.

```
public class InvalidLengthException extends Exception {
    public InvalidLengthException(String fieldName,
int given, int allowed) {
        super("Entry length for " + fieldName +
            " of " + given +
            " is greater than the maximum allowed of " +
            allowed + ".");
    }
}
```

Figure 16.5: The INVALIDLENGTHEXCEPTION simply passes its arguments to the constructor of its parent.

You might think this approach too trivial to warrant a completely new exception class, but this fine-grained approach to error handling allows programmers to handle specific errors. More importantly, it *forces* programmers to do so. A programmer who uses this class function can "monitor" for the INVALIDSTATE EXCEPTION and then initiate a dialog so the user can correct the state code, as shown in Figure 16.6.

```
while (true) {
  appPanel.show();
  String state = appPanel.stateTextField.getText();
  try {
    currentCustomer.setState(state);
  } catch (InvalidStateException err) {
    appPanel.add(new Label(err.toString()));
    continue;
  }
  break;
}
```

Figure 16.6: Programmers should monitor for application-specific exceptions in a try/catch block.

DESIGN THE CLASS API

With the CUSTOMER class's getter and setter functions created, you can begin to design the API of the class. Chapter 6 defines a class's API as its list of public functions. CUSTOMER's getter and setter functions, therefore, are considered part of the API because you've specified public access and therefore made them available for use outside the class. However, Java database fields such as CUSNUM and LSTNAM are not part of the API because their access specifiers are private.

Other than the getter and setter functions, what other functional interfaces would a programmer need when developing a Java application that retrieves and manipulates customer entities (that just so happen to be stored in DB2/400)? Step five, the CRUD step, tells you to add methods to create, read, update, and delete; you implement those functions using jt400 DB2/400 access objects.

A well-designed Java object should have not only state and behavior but also a unique identity. Therefore, the CUSTOMER class—and all business entity classes—must represent a specific identity. A specific entity in DB2/400 is identified with the unique key of the primary access path of its file. At invocation time for a CUSTOMER object, you know the identity of that object; it's the key of the DB2/400 customer record. You know the identity because the user has keyed it in on a dialog or your code has accessed another object that contains a reference to a specific customer number. So, at construction time, you can specify the attributes of the unique key for that entity.

With a customer, that unique identity is the customer number. You can design a CUSTOMER constructor that accepts the numeric value for a customer number:

```
public Customer(BigDecimal custNum)
```

This example uses BIGDECIMAL. It might have been more appropriate to use Java's basic integer data type. I chose not to, however, because the customer number value in DB2/400 is a zoned number that corresponds to BIGDECIMAL in Java. Because that zoned customer number has no decimal positions, the integer would work fine but you still would have to convert that integer to a BIGDECIMAL when accessing DB2/400.

Now the CUSTOMER class API consists of a CUSTOMER constructor that accepts a customer number value. With that value, the constructor can retrieve from DB2/400 the attributes of that specific customer. The user of that class then has the ability to retrieve the values of that customer with the getter functions and can also modify those values with the setter function.

What other interfaces would the CUSTOMER class need? Obviously, since the CUSTOMER class has setter functions that enable users to change the class's attributes, it should have an UPDATE function. And, if it has an UPDATE, it should also have a DELETE function and a means of adding a new customer to DB2/400. So the example CUSTOMER class now needs several new public functions: UPDATE, WRITE, and DELETE. The explanation of how to implement those classes comes later in this chapter, but the API, as it stands now, has a hole.

With the CUSTOMER API, you can instantiate a CUSTOMER object for an existing customer. You can then use the setter functions to change that customer's attributes and the UPDATE function to commit those changes back into DB2/400 (or *make them persistent,* in object-oriented terminology). If you'd like, you can even instantiate a specific customer and then use the DELETE function to remove that instance of a customer from DB2/400. Now, here's the hole: Suppose you want to add a customer. You can't invoke the WRITE function without having a CUSTOMER object, and you can't invoke a CUSTOMER object without having the number for an existing customer.

The solution to this problem lies in adding a default constructor (a constructor with no arguments) to the CUSTOMER class.

```
public Customer()
```

That constructor does not look to DB2/400 to retrieve the specific customer—the customer doesn't exist yet. An object's constructor is responsible for setting the initial state of the object. The customer number constructor, for instance, uses values retrieved from DB2/400 to set the initial state. With the default constructor, however, those initial values remain blank until they are set with the setter functions. So you simply construct a default customer, set the state of its attributes with the setter functions, and then use the write function to update DB2/400, as shown in Figure 16.7.

```
Customer newCust = new Customer();
newCust.setCUSNUM(new
BigDecimal(appPanel.custNumber.getText()));
newCust.setLSTNAM(appPanel.lastName.getText());
// code omitted
newCust.write();
```

Figure 16.7: The CUSTOMER class's setter functions are used to set the attributes of the CUSTOMER object.

PROCESSING SETS

Now Java programmers can easily use the CUSTOMER class's API to code business applications. Yet, as you begin to use the CUSTOMER class, you realize a few additional situations that you need to address. First of all, customers don't live in a vacuum; they collaborate with invoices and purchase orders. Second, it is normal in application programming to process sets of entities. The CUSTOMER class needs to provide the ability to work with sets of customers and should also enable users to retrieve information about such things as a customer's existing purchase orders and outstanding invoices.

To meet the requirement for processing sets of customers, the CUSTOMER class has a function that returns an array of CUSTOMER objects:

```
public static Vector search(String SqlWhereClause)
```

This function differs from the other public functions of the CUSTOMER class in that a static qualifier follows the public access specifier. A static function is known as a class function because it can be invoked by qualifying it with a class name rather than the name of the variable that holds a reference to an object instance of class. This means that you don't need to create a CUSTOMER object to be able to retrieve a set of customers. It wouldn't make sense to create an object since you don't want to work with a specific customer; rather, you want to work with a set of customers. Static functions, consequently, are not invoked with an object qualification:

```
someCustomer.search("CDTLMT > 1000"); // invalid qualifier
```

Static functions are invoked by qualifying the function with the name of its class:

```
Customer.search("CDTLMT > 1000");
```

This static function gives you a very handy method for processing a set of customers: You simply spin through the returned VECTOR of customers (a VECTOR is a dynamically sizable array) as shown in Figure 16.8.

```
Vector custs = Customer.search("CDTLMT > 1000");
for (int i = 0; i < custs.size(); i++) {
  Customer aCust = (Customer)custs.elementAt(i));
    System.out.println(aCust.getINIT() + " " +
aCust.getLSTNAM());
}
```

Figure 15.8: A vector of customer objects can be retrieved from the SEARCH function.

Now that you have the ability to process sets of customers, your next step (step six) is to enable the retrieval of other business entities associated with a customer, such as purchase orders or invoices. Your relational database maintains these associations with *foreign keys*. For instance, the record format of a purchase order would include a field for customer number. That customer number is the foreign key that enables relational access to the associated customer master record. The record of an invoice header would also contain a customer number field.

An entity relational chart would show the relations among files; your Unified Modeling Language (UML) object model should also graphically portray the relationships among objects. Because the objects in the UML chart show associations to other objects, you know to add functions to classes that represent those associated objects so that they return object references to their collaborating objects. For instance, the CUSTOMER class might add two functions to return VECTORS of purchase orders and invoices:

```
Vector getPurchaseOrders();
Vector getInvoices();
```

The implementation of those functions is to simply turn around and call the SEARCH function of the associated class:

```
Vector getPurchaseOrders() {
    return PurchaseOrder.search("CUSNUM = " + CUSNUM);
}
```

The API for the CUSTOMER class shown in Figure 16.9 now seems to be relatively complete, but you have not yet addressed two of the eight steps. Step seven tells you to add function interfaces as required for the manipulation of the business entity. This step encompasses the addition of application-specific functions to perform tasks such as checking credit ratings and printing customer invoices. Remember that any modification to the customer entity should occur through this class.

```
public synchronized class Customer.Customer extends
java.lang.Object
{
    public Customer.Customer();
    public Customer.Customer(BigDecimal custNo);
    protected Record putFields(Record record);
    public static Vector search(String sqlWhereClause);
    public String getLSTNAM();
    public String getINIT();
    public String getSTREET();
    public String getCITY();
    public String getSTATE();
    public BigDecimal getCUSNUM();
    public BigDecimal getZIPCOD();
    public BigDecimal getCDTLMT();
    public BigDecimal getCHGCOD();
    public BigDecimal getBALDUE();
    public BigDecimal getCDTDUE();
    public Vector getPurchaseOrders();
    public Vector getInvoices();
    public void setSTATE(String state);
    public void setLSTNAM(String lastName);
    public void setINIT(String firstMiddleInit);
    public void setSTREET(String street);
    public void setCITY(String city);
    public void setCUSNUM(BigDecimal custNo);
    public void setZIPCOD(BigDecimal zipCode);
    public void setCDTLMT(BigDecimal creditLimit);
    public void setCHGCOD(BigDecimal chargeCode);
    public void setBALDUE(BigDecimal balanceDue);
    public void setCDTDUE(BigDecimal creditDue);
    public void delete();
    public void update();
    public void write();
    public void print();
    public static void main(String[] pList);
}
```

Figure 16.9: The JAVAP listing of the CUSTOMER class shows an intuitive API.

IMPLEMENTATION OF CRUD

The API of the CUSTOMER class is fairly straightforward, but the code implementation of that class gets a little more complex. The constructor function that takes the customer number uses it to access the specific customer using jt400's record-level access to the unique access path of the primary file. Record-level access requires a number of jt400 objects, including an As400 connection object, a KEYEDFILE object, and a RECORDFORMAT. In the initial implementation of this class, the CUSTOMER constructor created new instances of each of these three objects, which presents a big problem. If you instance a number of CUSTOMER objects, perhaps to fill a table of customers, each of those objects would trigger a file open on the AS/400. File opens on the AS/400 are among the slowest tasks an application job ever performs.

To circumvent this problem, the CUSTOMER class now has *class fields* for these three jt400 objects. Class fields, like class functions, have a qualifier of static. The value of the static field of a class is shared among all instances of that class. In fact, it's the same storage location that is referenced for all object instances of that class for the static field. With nonstatic fields, each object instance is relegated to separate storage. The point is that the three jt400 objects (KEYEDFILE, AS400, and RECORDFORMAT) are shared among all object instances of the CUSTOMER class. As a result, you'll only have one file open on the AS/400, which conserves resources and improves performance.

With the discussion of static fields aside, the CUSTOMER constructor starts by checking to see whether the As400 connection object, called *system*, has been instantiated. If it hasn't (i.e., if its value is null), the INIT function is called to establish a connection, open the file, and set up the record format. The INIT function's access specifier of private makes INIT available only for internal use within the CUSTOMER class. Following the call to the INIT function, the constructor then uses the KEYEDFILE's READ function to retrieve the specific record. Upon record retrieval, the private GETFIELDS function is called. The GETFIELDS function simply retrieves each of the record's field values and inserts them into the Java objects that are CUSTOMER attributes. At that point, the CUSTOMER object is available for application use.

The other method of retrieving CUSTOMER objects employs the SEARCH function, which uses JDBC (rather than record-level access) to access DB2/400. In general, SQL is faster when you retrieve a set of records. The SEARCH function spawns CUSTOMER objects for each element of the set of records returned from the SQL SELECT statement.

You might have noticed that there are two GETFIELDS functions. The first takes a RECORD object, which is part of jt400's record access; the second takes a RESULTSET object, which is part of JDBC. They both provide the same feature, hence the same function name. The SEARCH function uses the RESULTSET version of GETFIELDS to populate the field attributes for each new CUSTOMER instance from the elements of the JDBC RESULTSET.

WRITE, UPDATE, AND DELETE

The WRITE, UPDATE, and DELETE functions are relatively similar. All three functions begin by checking whether the static As400 connection object with the class field name of *system* is set up yet (see Figure 16.10). All three functions perform this check because the CUSTOMER object could have been instanced with the SEARCH function or CUSTOMER's default constructor, which means that the record-level access static class fields might not have been instanced yet. There is no need to set them up until they are required (a coding procrastination concept that even has a name—*lazy initialization*). If the static object field check (SYSTEM == NULL) is true, then the INIT function is called to initialize those jt400 record-level access objects, now that their existence is required.

```
public void delete() throws Exception, AS400Exception {
    if (system == null)
        init();
    String key[] = new String[1];
    key[0] = CUSNUM;
    file.deleteRecord(key);
}
  public void update() throws Exception, AS400Exception {
    if (system == null)
        init();
    Record record = format.getNewRecord();
    record = putFields(record);
    String key[] = new String[1];
    key[0] = CUSNUM;
    file.update(key ,record);
}
  public void write () throws Exception, AS400Exception {
    if (system == null)
```

Figure 16.10: The DELETE, UPDATE, and WRITE functions. (Part 1 of 2)

```
    init();
    Record record = format.getNewRecord();
    putFields(record);
    file.write(record);
}
```

Figure 16.10: The DELETE, UPDATE, and WRITE functions. (Part 2 of 2)

The CUSTOMER's UPDATE and DELETE functions both require an array of key values. This requirement might seem kind of silly for the CUSTOMER class because the array of keys ends up holding only one element: the customer number. But the KEYEDFILE class's DELETERECORD and UPDATE functions of jt400 require an array of keys to delete or update a specific record. KEYEDFILE's DELETERECORD function uses the key to get a lock on the specific record so that it can delete it.

Notice that the signature for the CUSTOMER class's DELETE, UPDATE, and WRITE functions says that they may throw AS400EXCEPTION exceptions. That's because KEYEDFILE's DELETERECORD function may throw the AS400EXCEPTION message and the CUSTOMER class is delegating the responsibility of handling AS400EXCEPTION errors to users of its DELETE function. An application GUI, for instance, might simply present any AS/400 errors in a dialog, or it might go a little further and check for explicit AS/400 error messages (e.g., a record lock) and correct the problem.

UNIT TESTING

One handy feature of Java is the capability it gives programmers to code a MAIN function for every class. The MAIN function is how Java applications execute. When the Java command is invoked specifying a Java class name, the MAIN function of the class executes. Very few of the classes that you create will be designed as the application driver class, so they won't require a MAIN function.

However, a rule of thumb—using the MAIN function for unit testing—makes for a very clean method of testing all your classes. You just design a MAIN function for the purpose of testing all the functions of that class. The CUSTOMER class's MAIN does just that; you can run it from the command line and it goes through a number of manipulations to test the validity of the CUSTOMER class's functions.

Another function commonly created for testing purposes is the PRINT function. For instance, the PRINT function of the CUSTOMER class is not designed for production; it is designed merely as a utility function to list the values of an object instance of the CUSTOMER class during testing.

JavaDoc

Step eight instructs you to produce JavaDoc documentation for the class. It specifies that you *produce* the documentation, not *write* it, because written documentation should have been generated as you developed each function.

When you use any of the Java classes developed by Sun, IBM, or a third-party vendor, you have Java documentation in the form of HTML. You can read this documentation in your browser and, because it takes full advantage of the hypertext capabilities of HTML, you can quickly gain an understanding of a class and the classes associated with it. Your Java classes should also have the same style of documentation.

The Java language was developed to enable proper documentation. When you follow a standard commenting style in your Java code, those comments can be gleaned out of the code with the use of Java's JavaDoc tool. Further, if you adhere to a few simple conventions, the HTML documentation that the JavaDoc tool generates will include full hypertext capabilities.

To execute the JavaDoc tool, from a DOS command line you specify the JavaDoc tool name followed by the name of the JAVA class source file:

```
javadoc Customer.java
```

All JavaDoc comments start with a slash and a double asterisk and close with the sequence of asterisk slash. The comment, because it will ultimately become an HTML file, can include HTML tags:

```
/**
 * The comment, because it will ultimately become an <b>HTML</b>
 file, can include HTML tags.
 */
```

JavaDoc comments fall into three categories: field, function, and class (or interface). The difference between these three comment types lies in their placement: A field comment is placed before a class field, a function comment precedes a function declaration, and a class or interface comment comes just before the class or interface declaration. The class-level JavaDoc comments for the CUSTOMER class (listed in Figure 16.11) are converted into HTML (Figure 16.12) when the following command executes over the CUSTOMER.JAVA source file:

```
javadoc -author -version -noindex -notree Customer.java
```

When viewed in a browser, the resulting JavaDoc HTML looks like that of Figure 16.14. Note the use of the @AUTHOR and @VERSION tags. The default use of the JavaDoc utility omits generation of author and version information in the HTML; but for internal company use, this information is important. The JavaDoc utility has command line options of -AUTHOR and -VERSION to request the author and version information to be included. The -NOINDEX and -NOTREE options tell JavaDoc not to generate an alphabetic index of all classes and functions of a package and not to generate a tree of the classes associated with the class.

```
/** The Customer class is an example of encapsulation
 * techniques. It holds the state, behavior, and
 * identity of customers whose persistence is
 * maintained by DB2/400. The database file
 * is a copy of the QCUSTCDT that is shipped
 * with all AS/400s in the QIWS library. The
 * copy was put in a user library, with a logical
 * file added to contain a unique
 * index on the CUSNUM field. That primary
 * access path is QCUSTCDT01.
 *
 * @author Don Denoncourt
 * @version 1.02, 17 October 1998
 */
public class Customer {
```

Figure 16.11: If you follow a standard Java commenting style, the JavaDoc utility can turn your comments into HTML.

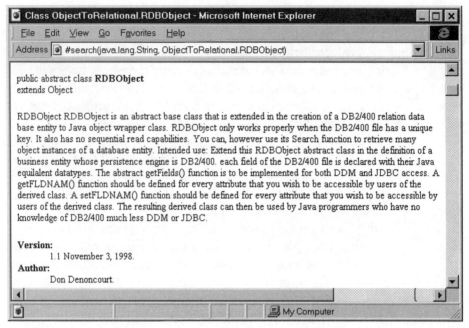

Figure 16.12: There should always be JavaDoc HTML for each of your business entity classes.

Field-level comments are added just before field definitions in a Java class. Normally, you would add field-level JavaDoc comments for public fields only. And, since standard encapsulation technique says to hide mutable class fields from users with the private access specifier, you should have to provide field-level comments only for the immutable static final fields that your class uses as constants.

Function-level comments should contain information about how to use the function beyond what can be inferred by the function name and arguments. If the function returns a value, the comment should contain an @RETURN tag. If the function throws errors, you should have @EXCEPTION comments for those as well. For a function that accepts arguments, you should include @PARAM comments. Figure 16.13 shows the JavaDoc comment for the CUSTOMER class's SEARCH and UPDATE functions, and Figure 16.14 shows the browser view of the HTML listing for the SEARCH function.

```
/**  gets all the DB2/400 entities based on an SQL where clause.
  * JDBC is then used to retrieve a set of records. Each record
is
  * used to instance an object derived from this class.
  * @param whereClause the SQL where clause statement. Null is
  * acceptable.
  * @return a Vector of Customer objects whose state equaled
the
  * search criterion.
  */
public static Vector search(String SqlWhereClause) {..}
/**  deletes the DB2/400 entity that corresponds to this object.
  * @exception com.ibm.as400.access.AS400Exception
  * AS400 exception which contains
  * an array of AS/400 message strings.
  * @exception java.lang.Exception    standard Java exception.
  */
public void delete() throws Exception, AS400Exception {…}
```

Figure 16.13: Field-level JavaDoc comments may include @PARAM, @RETURN, and @EXCEP-TION special tags.

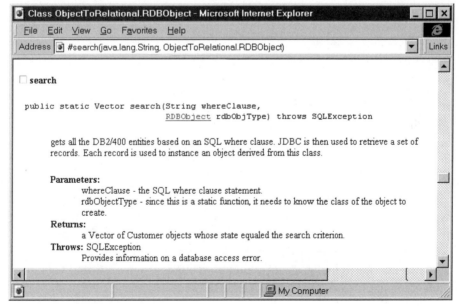

Figure 16.14: The JavaDoc utility generates HTML documentation from the comments in your Java classes.

MORE COMMENTS

The ability to automatically generate JavaDoc from the comments within your code can be a very powerful application programming tool—*if* you use it. Probably the neatest feature of JavaDoc is that even if you don't comment your code at all, JavaDoc still generates a nice HTML listing from the class and function declarations. Table 16.2 displays all the special tags that can be added to your JavaDoc comments. And don't forget that you can add standard HTML tags to enhance the generated HTML as you like. Often, for instance, the <PRE> and </PRE> tags are used to insert example Java code.

Table 16.2: JavaDoc Tags to Describe Class.	
@Author name-text	Comment may contain multiple @author tags.
@Version version-text	Comment may contain at most one @version tag.
@See classname	Comment adds a hyperlink to another HTML file.
@Since since-text	Comment usually refers to JDK (e.g., the function has "since" been supported).
@Deprecated depre-cated-text	Comment suggests you no longer use this function and refer to re-placement function.
@Param parameter-name	Comment describes the parameter.
@Return description	Comment describes the return value.
@Exception fully-qualified-class-name	Comment describes exception.

DESIGN FLAWS

This chapter has provided a tutorial on the eight design steps required to create a Java class to encapsulate the state and behavior of an entity stored in DB2/400. The example CUSTOMER class shown in Figure 16.15 follows all eight steps. While the example does work well, you'll recognize a problem when you apply the same pattern to another business entity– redundancy. You'll find yourself reimplementing record-level access and JDBC code over and over again.

Remember, Java is supposed to be an object-oriented language. When you find yourself repeatedly writing similar sections of code, you factor that code out into a base class. The next chapter does just that. Chapter 16 introduces you to a framework for creating Java classes that encapsulate the fields and functions of business entities kept in DB2/400.

```java
package Customer;
import java.math.*;
import java.sql.*;
import java.util.*;
import com.ibm.as400.access.*;

/** The Customer class is an example of encapsulation
 * techniques. It holds the state, behavior, and
 * identity of customers whose persistence is
 * maintained by DB2/400. The database file
 * is a copy of the QCUSTCDT that is shipped
 * with all AS/400s in the QIWS library. The
 * copy was put in a user library, with a logical
 * file added to contain a unique
 * index on the CUSNUM field. That primary
 * access path is QCUSTCDT01.
 *
 * @author Don Denoncourt
 * @version 1.02, 17 October 1998
 */
public class Customer {
    // class data members should be private
    private BigDecimal CUSNUM; // ZONED 6/0
    private String LSTNAM;// CHAR 8
    private String INIT;// CHAR 3
    private String STREET;// CHAR 13
    private String CITY;// CHAR 6
    private String STATE;// CHAR 2
    private BigDecimal ZIPCOD;// ZONED 5/0
    private BigDecimal CDTLMT;// ZONED 4/0
    private BigDecimal CHGCOD;// ZONED 1/0
    private BigDecimal BALDUE;// ZONED 6/2
    private BigDecimal CDTDUE;// ZONED 6/2

    private static KeyedFile file;
    private static AS400 system;
```

Figure 16.15: The CUSTOMER class encapsulates the state, behavior, and identity of a single customer. (Part 1 of 7)

```
   private static RecordFormat format;
   public Customer() {
   }

   public Customer(BigDecimal custNum) {
     if (system == null)
       init();
     // Read records
     Object key[] = new Object[1];
     key[0] = custNum;
     // Read the record for customer number keyValues[i]
     try {
       Record record = file.read(key);
       if (record != null) {
         getFields(record);
       }
     } catch(Exception x) {}
   }
   private void init() {
     // Create AS400 object and connect for the
     // record-level access service.
     system = new AS400(Profile.MC, Profile.USER, Profile.PASS);

     // Specify file location
     QSYSObjectPathName filePathName =
       new
QSYSObjectPathName("DENONCOURT","QCUSTCDT01","*FIRST","MBR");
     try {
       file = new KeyedFile(system, filePathName.getPath());
     } catch(Exception x) {}
     // Retrieve a record format
     AS400FileRecordDescription recordDescription =
       new AS400FileRecordDescription(system,
filePathName.getPath());
     try {
       RecordFormat[] formats =
recordDescription.retrieveRecordFormat();
       format = formats[0];
       file.setRecordFormat(format);
       file.open(AS400File.READ_ONLY, 1,
AS400File.COMMIT_LOCK_LEVEL_NONE);
     } catch (Exception e) {
       System.out.println(
"Error occurred attempting to display the file.");
```

Figure 16.15: The CUSTOMER class encapsulates the state, behavior, and identity of a single customer. (Part 2 of 7)

```
    }
  }

  // function members that are for internal use only are private
  private void getFields(Record record) {
    try {
      CUSNUM = (BigDecimal)record.getField("CUSNUM");
      LSTNAM = (String)record.getField("LSTNAM");
      INIT = (String)record.getField("INIT");
      STREET = (String)record.getField("STREET");
      CITY = (String)record.getField("CITY");
      STATE = (String)record.getField("STATE");
      ZIPCOD = (BigDecimal)record.getField("ZIPCOD");
      CDTLMT = (BigDecimal)record.getField("CDTLMT");
      CHGCOD = (BigDecimal)record.getField("CHGCOD");
      BALDUE = (BigDecimal)record.getField("BALDUE");
      CDTDUE = (BigDecimal)record.getField("CDTDUE");
    } catch(Exception x) {}
  }
  private void getFields(ResultSet rs) {
    try {
      CUSNUM = (BigDecimal)rs.getBigDecimal("CUSNUM",0);
      LSTNAM = (String)rs.getString("LSTNAM");
      INIT = (String)rs.getString("INIT");
      STREET = (String)rs.getString("STREET");
      CITY = (String)rs.getString("CITY");
      STATE = (String)rs.getString("STATE");
      ZIPCOD = (BigDecimal)rs.getBigDecimal("ZIPCOD",0);
      CDTLMT = (BigDecimal)rs.getBigDecimal("CDTLMT",0);
      CHGCOD = (BigDecimal)rs.getBigDecimal("CHGCOD",0);
      BALDUE = (BigDecimal)rs.getBigDecimal("BALDUE",2);
      CDTDUE = (BigDecimal)rs.getBigDecimal("CDTDUE",2);
    } catch(Exception x) {
      System.out.println ("\n Problem in getFields(ResultSet rs)");
    }
  }
  protected Record putFields(Record record) {
    record.setField("CUSNUM", CUSNUM);
    record.setField("LSTNAM", LSTNAM);
    record.setField("INIT", INIT);
    record.setField("STREET", STREET);
    record.setField("CITY", CITY);
    record.setField("STATE", STATE);
    record.setField("ZIPCOD", ZIPCOD);
```

Figure 16.15: The CUSTOMER class encapsulates the state, behavior, and identity of a single customer. (Part 3 of 7)

```
      record.setField("CDTLMT", CDTLMT);
      record.setField("CHGCOD", CHGCOD);
      record.setField("BALDUE", BALDUE);
      record.setField("CDTDUE", CDTDUE);
      return record;
   }
   /**  gets all the DB2/400 entities based on an SQL where clause.
    * JDBC is then used to retrieve a set of records. Each record is
    * used to instance an object derived from this class.
    * @param whereClause the SQL where clause statement. Null is
    * acceptable.
    * @return a Vector of Customer objects whose state equaled the
    * search criterion.
    */
   public static Vector search(String SqlWhereClause) {
      Connection con = null;
      Vector vector = new Vector();
      try {
         // Load the JDBC driver
         DriverManager.registerDriver(
new com.ibm.as400.access.AS400JDBCDriver());
         // Connect to the database
         String sourceURL = "jdbc:as400://"+Profile.MC;
         con = DriverManager.getConnection (
sourceURL,Profile.USER, Profile.PASS);
         // Run an SQL SELECT statement
         Statement stmt = con.createStatement ();
         String SQLStmt =
"SELECT CUSNUM,LSTNAM,INIT,STREET,CITY,STATE, " +
"ZIPCOD,CDTLMT,CHGCOD,BALDUE,CDTDUE "+
"FROM DENONCOURT.QCUSTCDT01 WHERE " +
SqlWhereClause;
         ResultSet rs = stmt.executeQuery (SQLStmt);
         // Display each row (record) retrieved by the SQL statement
         while (rs.next ()) {
            Customer customer = new Customer();
            customer.getFields(rs);
            vector.addElement(customer);
         }
         rs.close ();
         stmt.close ();
      } catch (Exception e) {
         System.out.println ("\nERROR: " + e.getMessage());
      }
```

Figure 16.15: The CUSTOMER *class encapsulates the state, behavior, and identity of a single customer. (Part 4 of 7)*

```
    int numCustomers = vector.size();
    return vector;

  }

// create getter functions for private data members so
// users cannot directly update values
public String getLSTNAM() { return LSTNAM; }
public String getINIT() { return INIT; }
public String getSTREET() { return STREET; }
public String getCITY() { return CITY; }
public String getSTATE() { return STATE; }
public BigDecimal getCUSNUM() { return CUSNUM; }
public BigDecimal getZIPCOD() { return ZIPCOD; }
public BigDecimal getCDTLMT() { return CDTLMT; }
public BigDecimal getCHGCOD() { return CHGCOD; }
public BigDecimal getBALDUE() { return BALDUE; }
public BigDecimal getCDTDUE() { return CDTDUE; }

public Vector getPurchaseOrders() {
  // return PurchaseOrders.getPOsWhere("CUSNUM = " + CUSNUM);
  return null;
}
public Vector getInvoices(){
  // return Invoices.getPOsWhere("CUSNUM = " + CUSNUM);
  return null;
}

// create setter function members for those data members
// that require update. These functions should
// at least have basic validation but should also include
// conformance to business rules.

public void setSTATE (String state) throws InvalidStateException {
  String states[] = {"AL","AL","AZ","AR","CA","CO","CT",
  "CE","FL","GA","HI","ID","IL","IN","IA","KS","KY","LA",
  "ME","MD","MA","MI","MN","MS","MO","MT","NE","NV","NH",
  "NJ","NM","NY","NC","ND","OH","OK","OR","PA","RI","SC",
  "SD","TN","TX","UT","VT","VA","WA","DC","WV","WI","WY"};
  if (state.length() != 2)
    throw new InvalidStateException(state);
  for (int i=0; i<states.length;i++) {
    if (state.equals(states[i])) {
      STATE = state;
```

Figure 16.15: The CUSTOMER class encapsulates the state, behavior, and identity of a single customer. (Part 5 of 7)

```
        return;
      }
    }
    throw new InvalidStateException(state);
  }
  public void setLSTNAM(String str) { LSTNAM = str;}
  public void setINIT(String str)   { INIT = str; }
  public void setSTREET(String str) { STREET = str; }
  public void setCITY(String str)   { CITY = str; }
  public void setCUSNUM(BigDecimal num) { CUSNUM = num; }
  public void setZIPCOD(BigDecimal num) { ZIPCOD = num; }
  public void setCDTLMT(BigDecimal num) { CDTLMT = num; }
  public void setCHGCOD(BigDecimal num) { CHGCOD = num; }
  public void setBALDUE(BigDecimal num) { BALDUE = num; }
  public void setCDTDUE(BigDecimal num) { CDTDUE = num; }

  /** deletes the DB2/400 entity that corresponds to this object.
   * @exception com.ibm.as400.access.AS400Exception
   * AS400 exception which contains
   * an array of AS/400 message strings.
   * @exception java.lang.Exception   standard Java exception.
   */
  public void delete() throws Exception, AS400Exception {
    if (system == null)
      init();
    Object key[] = new Object[1];
    key[0] = CUSNUM;
    file.deleteRecord(key);
  }
  public void update() throws Exception, AS400Exception {
    if (system == null)
      init();
    Record record = format.getNewRecord();
    record = putFields(record);
    Object key[] = new Object[1];
    key[0] = CUSNUM;
    file.update(key ,record);
  }
  public void write () throws Exception, AS400Exception {
    if (system == null)
      init();
    Record record = format.getNewRecord();
    putFields(record);
    file.write(record);
```

Figure 16.15: The CUSTOMER class encapsulates the state, behavior, and identity of a single customer. (Part 6 of 7)

```
    }

public void print() {
  System.out.println ("\n" +
    INIT + " " + LSTNAM + "      " + CUSNUM + " " +
    STREET + " " + CITY + ", " + STATE + " " + ZIPCOD +
    "\n Credit: " + CDTLMT + " Charge Code: " + CHGCOD +
    " Balance Due: " + BALDUE + " Credit Due: " + CDTDUE);
}

// always create a main function for unit testing
public static void main (String[] args) {
  Customer cust = new   Customer(new BigDecimal("2"));
  cust.print();
  try {
    cust.setSTATE("ZL");
  } catch (InvalidStateException err) {}
  try {
    cust.setSTATE("MA");
  } catch (InvalidStateException err) {}
  try {
    cust.update();
  } catch (AS400Exception asError) {
    AS400Message[] msgs = asError.getAS400MessageList();
    for (int iMsg = 0; iMsg < msgs.length; iMsg++)
      System.out.println(msgs[iMsg]);
  } catch (Exception error) {
    System.out.println(error);
  }
  // Customer[] custs = search("CDTLMT > 1000");
  Vector custs = search("CDTLMT > 1000");
  for (int i = 0; i < custs.size(); i++) {
    ((Customer)custs.elementAt(i)).print();
  }
  System.exit(0);
  }
}
```

Figure 16.15: The CUSTOMER class encapsulates the state, behavior, and identity of a single customer. (Part 7 of 7)

17

AN ADVANCED STRATEGY FOR ENCAPSULATING DB2/400 ACCESS

The encapsulation techniques covered in the preceding chapter represent an improvement over the DB2/400 access examples shown in the section on IBM's Java Toolbox for the AS/400 (jt400). Still, chapter 16's techniques to embed record-level access are too painful to be duplicated in every Java class that is to access DB2/400. When you find yourself duplicating code, you should factor that code out into a base class. Then, using standard object-oriented inheritance, design your classes to extend that base class.

This chapter serves as a tutorial on creating object-oriented frameworks of classes to provide mapping of relational database fields to Java classes. The example class of this chapter is the same CUSTOMER class designed in chapter 16. The CUSTOMER class of this chapter exposes the same encapsulated API of the last chapter. However, in the pages that follow, you'll learn to factor out much of the implementation of the new CUSTOMER class's interface into a base class. Figure 17.1 shows a Unified Modeling Language (UML) object model with the RDBOBJECT base class.

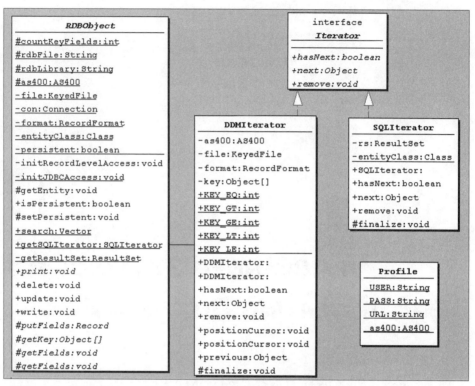

Figure 17.1: The RDBOBJECT class is an abstract base class.

The easiest way to learn what code to factor out into a base class is to design another business class following the same methods shown in chapter 17. Once you realize what is repeated, you can pull the duplicate code out into the base class. Of course, it takes time to reimplement code that already works, and management might not give you that time. Yet, if you don't take the time to reimplement common code into a base class, you'll end up reimplementing the same code for every new class. Until you become an object-oriented programming expert, this *do-over* strategy may be the only way you can spot common code. You (and your boss) must have enough discipline to pull out the common code into a base class and then reimplement that common code into your existing classes.

SPECIFIC CODE

Your plan of action involves building frameworks for use in creating Java classes for all the business entities represented in your DB2/400 database. With the CUSTOMER class of chapter 15 as an example, you have an idea that sections of code are specific to the business entity. Let's look at the eight basic steps used in the preceding chapter to encapsulate a DB2/400 business entity into a Java class, and see which steps could be put into a base class.

1. Design one Java class for each business entity stored in DB2/400.

2. Define as private class fields that correspond to fields in the DB2/400 record format.

3. Define getter functions for private fields.

4. Define setter functions for private fields with validation.

5. Define CREATE, READ, UPDATE, and DELETE (CRUD) functions.

6. Add functions that return associated objects.

7. Add function interfaces as required for the manipulation of the business entity.

8. Produce Java HTML documentation for the class.

Step one encompasses the reason for creating a class framework—you want to use that framework to take full advantage of the object-oriented nature of Java in the creation of your business classes. Step two tells you to define the class fields that correspond to the database fields. Surely that code can't be factored to a base class; the base class would have no knowledge about the fields of the specific database file. (That's another point, you need a database file name of the primary index on the file.)

The getter and setter functions defined in steps three and four also cannot become part of the base class. Step five calls for creating, reading, updating, or deleting the DB2/400 records associated with the objects; aren't those also specific to one database file? So then, what steps can you factor out? The creation of the AS/400 connection class (AS400), which would be the same in all entities; the file open, using a file name value specified by the derived class; and the logic to read, update, and delete records, using key and record values that are to be kept in the derived class.

DESIGNING TO AN INTERFACE

It's not enough to simply factor out the common code; you also should design to a common interface. The base class for your frameworks, therefore, will also specify a standard interface for those functions that must be implemented by derived classes. Do you remember what kind of function has no implementation and is added to a class simply in the design of a standard interface? It's an abstract function. Those functions will have a modifier of ABSTRACT and, as a result, the base class will be declared as an abstract base class, as shown in Figure 17.2.

```
public abstract void print();
protected abstract Record putFields(Record record);
protected abstract Object[] getKey();
protected abstract void getFields(Record record);
protected abstract void getFields(ResultSet rs);
```

Figure 17.2: Functions that are designed to create a common interface are added to the base class with the ABSTRACT modifier.

Notice that the access specifier of protected precedes all but the PRINT function of the base class. That base class, called RDBOBJECT, by the way, is designed to coordinate relational database maintenance of the business entities represented in classes that are derived from this base class.

At any rate, if you recall from chapter 6 on encapsulation, the protected functions of a class are usable only by implementation of their declaring class and any classes derived from that class. That sounds fairly complex, but think about it: A class derived from RDBOBJECT would have to define the PUTFIELDS function because only the derived class would know how to get the fields from a particular database file. The new version of the CUSTOMER class, for example, after it is changed to extend RDBOBJECT, knows how to get the CUSNUM, LSTNAM, and other fields of the QCUSTCDT file. RDBOBJECT is delegating to the CUSTOMER class the responsibility of getting DB2/400 fields into the Java object fields.

Now think about the users of the CUSTOMER class: Do you want them to be able to get a RECORD object with the PUTFIELDS function? No, otherwise the user would have access to the DB2/400 field values contained within a jt400 RECORD object. Thus, by making those four functions abstract and protected, RDBOBJECT forces the derived class (e.g., CUSTOMER) to implement those functions and also ensures against inadvertent access. The derived class must also implement the PRINT function; but PRINT, a part of the interface, is explicitly designed so that users of the derived class can print. Here the framework actually separates the interface of a Java object representation of a business entity from its implementation. Remember the admonition from the chapter on encapsulation: Tell users only what they need to know; if they can't touch it, they can't break it.

RDBOBJECT not only declares protected functions; it also declares protected fields as shown in Figure 17.3.

```
protected static int countKeyFields;
protected static String rdbFile;
protected static String rdbLibrary;
protected static AS400 as400;
```

Figure 17.3: Fields whose values are to be shared among all instances of a class are declared with the static modifier.

These four fields also take the STATIC modifier. Chapter 15 introduced the use of a static qualifier for the As400 connection object so that only one connection to the AS/400 is established. When a field is static, its value is shared among all object instances of that field's class. Obviously, you would only ever have one value for the names of the library and file, and the same holds true for the count of key fields of that file. These four fields are declared as protected so that derived classes may access them.

Further, the values for the first three fields (COUNTKEYFIELDS, RDBFILE, and RDBLIBRARY) are set by the derived class. You'll learn how that's done later. For now, the focus remains on the implementation of the RDBOBJECT base class. Somewhat parenthetical but still worthy of note here, Figure 17.4 shows JavaDoc comments contained within the RDBOBJECT class to provide information to RDBOBJECT's users, such as programmers who extend the class when designing another class like CUSTOMER.

```
/** this should be set in the static function of all
 * derived classes */
protected static int countKeyFields;
/** this should be set by the static function
 * of all derived classes to be the name of the
 * AS/400 file
<PRE> static {
  rdbFile = "QCUSTCDT01";
  rdbLibrary = "DENONCOURT";
  countKeyFields = 1;
} </PRE> */
protected static String rdbFile;
/** this should be set by the static function
 * of all derived classes to be the name of the
 * AS/400 Library. A subsequent version will
 * support library lists. */
protected static String rdbLibrary;
/** this is the DDM connection object. */
protected static AS400 as400;
```

Figure 17.4: RDBOBJECT requires the use of fields whose values the derived class must fill.

The RDBOBJECT class also declares several other static fields, but they have an access specifier of PRIVATE rather than protected, as shown in Figure 17.5.

```
private static KeyedFile file;
private static Connection con;
private static RecordFormat format;
```

Figure 17.5: The record-level access file open, the SQL connection, and the record format objects are stored as private fields in a base class.

The derived class needs no knowledge of—much less access to—these fields; they are implementation-specific. The KEYEDFILE and RECORDFORMAT objects are required for record-level access and the CONNECTION object is for Java Database Connectivity (JDBC) access. All three of these objects need only one value; the KEYEDFILE is the file open whose associated RECORDFORMAT is not subject to change.

Only one class field has not yet been described:

```
boolean persistent = false; // Is this entity in DB2/400 yet?
```

The PERSISTENT field is used to maintain knowledge of whether or not the specific object instance is currently in DB2/400. Because the Boolean value PERSISTENT is not static, it is said to be an *object field* because every object instance contains a different persistent value. A static field is considered a *class field* because it can have only one value per class and that value is shared among all object instances of that class.

RDBOBJECT IMPLEMENTATION

Now that you know what responsibilities the RDBOBJECT base class delegates to its derived classes, you might wonder what the base class does. This base class does quite a bit even if it contains just a small amount of code in a few functions (see Figure 17.6). It establishes one, and only one, connection to the AS/400. It opens the file (that's specified in the derived class) only once. It does all the busy work of getting the record format for the file and it handles the addition, deletion, and update to DB2/400 for the database values of that record.

```
public RDBObject ()
public boolean isPersistent()
public static Vector  search(String whereClause, Object rdbObjType)
throws SQLException
public static SQLIterator
getSQLIterator(String whereClause, RDBObject rdbObjType)
throws SQLException
public void delete() throws Exception, AS400Exception
public void update() throws Exception, AS400Exception
public void write () throws Exception, AS400Exception
protected void  getEntity() throws AS400Exception,
AS400SecurityException
protected void setPersistent(boolean persistent)
private void initRecordLevelAccess()
```

Figure 17.6: RDBOBJECT implements all the common and low-level DB2/400 database access.

AN ADVANCED STRATEGY FOR ENCAPSULATING DB2/400 ACCESS

CONSTRUCTION

RDBOBJECT's constructor includes only two statements:

```
if (file == null)
    initRecordLevelAccess();
```

The FILE field, you'll remember, is one of those static fields. In particular, FILE is the field designated to hold a reference to a KEYEDFILE object. Until instantiation of that KEYEDFILE object, the FILE field's value is null, meaning it does not yet hold a reference to a KEYEDFILE object. If the FILE field is null, the constructor function knows that the AS/400 database file has not yet been opened. The result is that the first time RDBOBJECT's constructor is invoked, the INITRECORDLEVELACCESS function will be invoked.

The INITRECORDLEVELACCESS function (shown in Figure 17.7) is designed to execute once, the first time a class derived from RDBOBJECT is constructed. This function's specification as private makes it available for use only by the RDBOBJECT class. The As400 connection object is created by a utility class called PROFILE, which will be explained in a moment. The rest of the code should look familiar to you because chapter 15 covered it in depth. Before moving on, turn your attention briefly to the RDBLIBRARY and the RDBFILE variables. The value of those static fields is to be set by the derived class (the CUSTOMER class, in this example).

```
private void initRecordLevelAccess() {
    as400 = Profile.as400;
    // Specify file location
    QSYSObjectPathName filePathName =
      new QSYSObjectPathName(rdbLibrary,rdbFile,
"*FIRST","MBR");
    try {
      file = new KeyedFile(as400, filePathName.getPath());
    } catch(Exception x) {
      System.out.println(
          "Error occurred attempting to create a KeyedFile.");
    }
    // Retrieve a record format
    AS400FileRecordDescription recordDescription =
```

Figure 17.7: The INITRECORDLEVELACCESS function initializes all the DDM connection objects required for the DB2/400 file associated with the RDBOBJECT's derived class. (Part 1 of 2)

```
     new AS400FileRecordDescription(as400,
filePathName.getPath());
   try {
      format = recordDescription.retrieveRecordFormat()[0];
      file.setRecordFormat(format);
      file.open(AS400File.READ_WRITE, 1,
             AS400File.COMMIT_LOCK_LEVEL_NONE);
   } catch (Exception e) {
      System.out.println(
            "Error occurred attempting to display the file.");
   }
 }
```

Figure 17.7: The INITRECORDLEVELACCESS function initializes all the DDM connection objects required for the DB2/400 file associated with the RDBOBJECT's derived class. (Part 2 of 2)

SINGLETON PROFILE

The utility class called PROFILE, initially shown in the UML of Figure 17.1, is used in Figure 17.7 to set the value of the static As400 connection object field. This type of utility class even has a name: singleton. You use *singleton classes* when you want to ensure only a single object instance of a particular class. In this case, that object is an As400 class. Figure 17.8 shows the source for the PROFILE class.

The source defines all the fields of the PROFILE class as static. Perhaps you noticed another rather strange-looking use of the word STATIC followed by the construction of an As400 object within curly braces. It looks like a function, but no function name is given. This special function, called the *static initializer function,*

```
class Profile {
  static String USER =  "user profile ";
  static String PASS =   "password";
  static String URL =     "IP or domain name";
  static AS400   as400;
  static {
    as400 = new AS400(Profile.URL, Profile.USER, Profile.PASS);
  }
}
```

Figure 17.8: You can use the singleton strategy to define a class if you want to ensure that only one connection to the AS/400 is made.

is automatically called the first time its class is referenced in a Java application. Further, Java guarantees that static initializer functions are called only once. Thus, the PROFILE class, with its static initializer function, automatically initializes the As400 connection object once per application. Even if numerous classes use the PROFILE class, you still have a guarantee that the As400 connection object will be created only once.

This sample implementation of the PROFILE class lacks robustness because it contains a hardcoded profile name, password, and URL. Your version of the PROFILE class might present a GUI to prompt the user, or it could simply use the default As400 class constructor which, as you know from chapter 15, automatically prompts for the profile, password, and domain.

The next implementation-specific function of interest is the GETENTITY function shown in Figure 17.9. This function has an access specifier of protected because derived classes will use it. GETENTITY is not public, however, because you do not want to give users of the derived class the chance to invoke it.

```
protected void  getEntity()
    throws AS400Exception, AS400SecurityException,
            IOException, InterruptedException {
    // Read the record for customer number keyValues[i]
    Record record = file.read(getKey());
    if (record == null) {
      persistent = false;
    } else {
      getFields(record);
      persistent = true;
    }
}
```

Figure 17.9: RDBOBJECT'S GETENTITY function uses the GETFIELDS function that is to be implemented by a derived class.

The GETENTITY signature says the function potentially throws several exceptions. Yet, a look at the code reveals that the function does not, in fact, throw any exceptions. Although the GETENTITY function might not throw any exceptions, the functions used by GETENTITY do—specifically KEYEDFILE's READ function. The

THROWS clause of the GETENTITY function effectively delegates the responsibility for handling those exceptions to the caller. And, if you've ever written a CL command-processing program and had to catch and resend error messages, you know how handy this feature is.

The GETENTITY function retrieves the DB2/400 record that is associated with this CUSTOMER object's key value. The single argument to the READ function consists of a value returned from the GETKEY function. GETKEY, one of the abstract functions covered earlier in this chapter, is implemented by the derived class with code to return an array of key fields. The READ function uses those key values to get a jt400 RECORD object that contains the current data for that DB2/400 record.

If the record does not exist, the Boolean value for the persistent field is set to false; otherwise, its value is set to true and the GETFIELDS function is called. GETFIELDS, another of those abstract classes, is implemented in the derived call with a series of calls to jt400's RECORD object's GETFIELD function to populate the values of the Java fields that represent the attributes for this business entity.

So what's that PERSISTENT field all about? RDBOBJECT needs to know when the value of an entity represented by the derived class is already in DB2/400. The GETENTITY function, for instance, might not be able to retrieve a DB2/400 record that is associated with the key values of the CUSTOMER object. In that circumstance, the value of PERSISTENT is false. Users of the derived class may query the value of PERSISTENT with the ISPERSISTENT function. That way they would know, for instance, whether or not a CUSTOMER object were in DB2/400 storage. Perhaps a better name for ISPERSISTENT would have been ISACTIVE.

SET PROCESSING

Groups of RDBOBJECTS can be retrieved from the static function called SEARCH. The SEARCH function (shown in Figure 17.10, along with the private GETRESULTSET utility function) returns a Java VECTOR of objects of the derived class that are retrieved from DB2/400 via JDBC. The SEARCH function takes two arguments: the SQL WHERE clause, and a handle to an RDBOBJECT object.

Now wait a minute, you say, how can you pass an RDBOBJECT to this function when the RDBOBJECT class is an abstract class and you can't instantiate an abstract class? You're witnessing a little bit of Java magic here. Any class derived from the RDBOBJECT class, such as CUSTOMER, becomes an RDBOBJECT by order of inheritance. The SEARCH function of RDBOBJECT must, at runtime, create objects of the same type as the derived class. Yet, at compile time, RDBOBJECT has no idea what the class type will be at runtime. The trick is to pass to the SEARCH function an object of the derived class:

```
Vector ohioCustomers = Customer.search("STATE = 'OH'", new
Customer());
Vector allAttendees = Attendee.search("1 = 1", new Attendee());
```

Because both the ATTENDEE and CUSTOMER objects are derived from RDBOBJECT, the SEARCH function accepts them as RDBOBJECT objects. Then, after the SQL statement returns the RESULTSET object, each element of that set is used to create the object of the derived class's type. The SEARCH function enlists the help of the Java OBJECT class's GETCLASS function to obtain the name of the class that the passed RDBOBJTYPE object was originally created as. Then the NEWINSTANCE function is used to create the proper object type, which, in the above examples, would be a CUSTOMER or an ATTENDEE object. The SEARCH function in Figure 17.10 gets a little complex, but remember that it only gets implemented once. All Java business classes inherit the SEARCH function, and you'll never have to recode it. You might improve the code, but you won't duplicate it over and over.

```
public static Vector   search(String whereClause, RDBObject
rdbObjType)
        throws SQLException {
   Vector vector = new Vector();
   ResultSet rs = getResultSet (whereClause);
   while (rs.next ()) {
     RDBObject rdbObj = null;
     try {
       rdbObj = (RDBObject)rdbObjType.getClass().newInstance();
```

Figure 17.10: The public SEARCH function is a part of the API for the RDBOBJECT class; it uses the private GETRESULTSET function that is internal to the implementation of RDBOBJECT. (Part 1 of 2)

```
        } catch (IllegalAccessException e) {
          System.out.println("RDBObject.search: " + e);
          return null;
        } catch (InstantiationException e) {
          System.out.println("RDBObject.search: " + e);
          return null;
        }
        rdbObj.getFields(rs);
        vector.addElement(rdbObj);
        rdbObj.persistent = true;
      }
      rs.close ();
      return vector;
    }
    private static ResultSet getResultSet (String whereClause)
          throws SQLException {
      if (con == null) {
        initJDBCAccess();
      }
      Statement stmt = con.createStatement ();
      String SQLStmt = "SELECT * FROM " + rdbLibrary + "." +
rdbFile;
      if (whereClause.length() > 0)
        SQLStmt += " WHERE " + whereClause;
      return stmt.executeQuery (SQLStmt);
    }
```

Figure 17.10: The public SEARCH function is a part of the API for the RDBOBJECT class; it uses the private GETRESULTSET function that is internal to the implementation of RDBOBJECT. (Part 2 of 2)

You might have noticed the GETSQLITERATOR function listed in Figure 17.6 and viewed graphically in Figure 17.1. The GETSQLITERATOR function returns an SQLITERATOR object that allows you to efficiently traverse a large set of RDBOBJECTS. The SEARCH function is limited in that it returns the whole set of RDBOBJECTS as an array. If you have hundreds or thousands of objects that might match the WHERE clause of the SEARCH function, then SEARCH is not a good choice.

The SQLITERATOR allows you to fetch one element at a time from JDBC. The DDMITERATOR teams up with the RDBOBJECT class to allow you to iterate through business entities that are stored in various indexes while still using the classes derived from the RDBOBJECT class. This avoids the trap that legacy programmers fall into when they simply code a new program to process the database in the different sequence of the alternate index. Those extra programs create a problem because they duplicate code. The DDMITERATOR class works around this problem by accepting the alternate index name; then it has operations to iterate through that index, returning to you one of those derived RDBOBJECT classes. (Chapter 18 covers the design and implementation of the SQLITERATOR along with its sister class, the DDMITERATOR, in detail.)

Note that you can improve performance of the SQL processing implemented in the GETRESULTSET function by replacing the STATEMENT object with a PREPAREDSTATEMENT object. PREPAREDSTATEMENT's placeholder variables, however, require application-specific code, so the current example instead makes use of the generic WHERE clause.

CRUD: CREATE, READ, UPDATE, DELETE

So far you've learned how the RDBOBJECT base class creates instances of a set of objects for the various classes derived from RDBOBJECT. The chapter has not yet covered how RDBOBJECT creates a single instance of a class derived from RDBOBJECT. Although you have been introduced to RDBOBJECT's constructor, which sets up the record-level access objects required to read DB2/400 records by key, and to the GETENTITY function, which reads a record by key, you haven't heard the whole story.

The derived class is responsible for implementing a constructor that accepts arguments for the key values. The CUSTOMER class, for instance, accepts a customer number value, assigns it to the class attribute that holds that key value, and then invokes the GETENTITY function. (GETENTITY, by the way, is implemented by the RDBOBJECT class.) RDBOBJECT's GETENTITY function, as you already know, uses the key from the derived class and reads a DB2/400 record as shown in Figure 17.11.

```
public Customer(BigDecimal custNum)  {
CUSNUM = custNum;
getEntity();
}
```

Figure 17.11: One of the overloaded constructors for your business entity class uses the unique key of an entity to be able to retrieve that entity from DB2/400.

So, you can create RDBOBJECT classes in one of three ways:

1. Using the default constructor, for entities not yet in DB2/400.

2. Using a derived class's constructor that accepts the entity's key values to build the object from values retrieved from DB2/400.

3. Using the SEARCH function, to retrieve a set of objects from DB2/400 with the SQL of JDBC.

The addition, updating, and deletion of the DB2/400 records associated with object instances of RDBOBJECT-derived classes is handled totally by the RDBOBJECT class. The DELETE function, shown in Figure 17.12, first checks the value of that PERSISTENT field. If it is false, the DELETE function has no work to do because the DB2/400 object does not exist yet. You might want to change the DELETE function to throw an exception that signals a potential problem with the calling program. At any rate, if PERSISTENT is true, DELETE then double-checks to see if record-level access must be initialized before it deletes the DB2/400 record using KEYEDFILE's DELETERECORD and the key value of the object.

```
public void delete() throws Exception, AS400Exception {
    if (persistent == false)
      return;
    if (file == null)
      initRecordLevelAccess();
    file.deleteRecord(getKey());
    persistent = false;
}
public void update() throws Exception, AS400Exception {
    // if it isn't persistent yet, write it instead
    if (persistent == false) {
      write();
      return;
    }
    if (as400 == null)
      initRecordLevelAccess();
```

Figure 17.12: The DELETE, UPDATE, and WRITE functions use lazy initialization to initialize AS/400 record-level access. (Part 1 of 2)

```
        Record record = format.getNewRecord();
        record = putFields(record);
        file.update(getKey(),record);
    }
public void write () throws Exception, AS400Exception {
    // if it's already persistent, update it instead
    if (persistent == true) {
        update();
        return;

    }
    if (file == null)
        initRecordLevelAccess();
    Record record = format.getNewRecord();
    record = putFields(record);
    file.write(record);
    persistent = true;
}
```

Figure 17.12: The DELETE, UPDATE, and WRITE functions use lazy initialization to initialize AS/400 record-level access. (Part 2 of 2)

The UPDATE function does the opposite of the DELETE function. If the PERSISTENT field has a value of false, UPDATE simply turns around and calls the WRITE function. Otherwise, UPDATE uses KEYEDFILE's update function to put the field values of the current object back into DB2/400 based on the key.

Notice that RDBOBJECT's UPDATE function builds a RECORD object from the FORMAT object's GETNEWRECORD function. This temporary RECORD object is passed to the PUTFIELDS function defined in an RDBOBJECT-derived class. The purpose of the PUTFIELDS function is to set the values of the AS/400 fields that are a part of the RECORDFORMAT that is kept in the RECORD object. The PUTFIELDS function returns a RECORD object that contains all the new copy of the record, which KEYEDFILE's UPDATE function then uses to update DB2/400. Note that the UPDATE function could throw AS400EXCEPTION errors (e.g., a record lock).

The WRITE function, again, checks PERSISTENT to see if UPDATE should be called instead. Otherwise, WRITE uses the same RECORD object creation and UPDATE logic as UPDATE except it then calls KEYEDFILE's WRITE function. With

DB2/400 now holding the value of the current object, RDBOBJECT's WRITE function sets the value of PERSISTENT to true (see Figure 17.12).

THE DERIVED CLASS

If the contents of this chapter seem conceptual, they should; after all, RDBOBJECT is an abstract class. The concepts don't come together until you extend the RDBOBJECT abstract class in the implementation of a Java class that is to represent a real-world business entity. You should, however, have a pretty good idea how to implement that derived class.

First, you know that RDBOBJECT has not implemented steps three and four or six and seven of the eight basic steps (presented early in this chapter) to encapsulate AS/400 business entities. RDBOBJECT does implement steps one and five and, although this chapter doesn't go into it, the complete code listing for RDBOBJECT (see appendix) contains the JavaDoc comment that fully documents the use of RDBOBJECT functions. Further, the RDBOBJECT class contains JavaDoc comments that explain how to implement the abstract functions and how the protected static fields should be set.

Now you will reimplement the CUSTOMER class from the preceding chapter. The interface for the CUSTOMER class will remain the same, but much of the previous CUSTOMER class's implementation has already been coded in this CUSTOMER's RDBOBJECT base class.

As you can see, the CUSTOMER class extends the RDBOBJECT class and then declares the Java class attributes that correspond to the DB2/400 QCUSTCDT file, as shown in Figure 17.13.

```
public class Customer extends RDBObject {
    private BigDecimal CUSNUM; // ZONED 6/0
    private String LSTNAM;     // CHAR 8
    private String INIT;       // CHAR 3
    private String STREET;     // CHAR 13
    private String CITY;       // CHAR 6
```

Figure 17.13: A business class that encapsulates access to an entity stored in a DB2/400 file extends RDBOBJECT and adds the entity's attributes. (Part 1 of 2)

```
private String STATE;       // CHAR 2
private BigDecimal ZIPCOD;  // ZONED 5/0
private BigDecimal CDTLMT;  // ZONED 4/0
private BigDecimal CHGCOD;  // ZONED 1/0
private BigDecimal BALDUE;  // ZONED 6/2
private BigDecimal CDTDUE;  // ZONED 6/2
```

Figure 17.13: A business class that encapsulates access to an entity stored in a DB2/400 file extends RDBOBJECT and adds the entity's attributes. (Part 2 of 2)

The CUSTOMER class then has code to statically initialize the file, library name, and key count using that strange-looking static initializer function, as shown in Figure 17.14.

```
static {
  rdbFile = "QCUSTCDT01";
  rdbLibrary = "DENONCOURT";
  countKeyFields = 1;
}
```

Figure 17.14: The static initializer function sets the value for the file and library and the count of key fields for the full key of that file.

If you recall from the last chapter, I have copied the QIWS library's version of the QCUSTCDT file into my library and created a unique index over the customer number. The CUSTOMER class then declares a default constructor as shown in Figure 17.16.

```
public Customer()
  {
    CUSNUM = new BigDecimal("0");
    LSTNAM = new String("        ");
    INIT = new String("   ");
    STREET = new String("            ");
    CITY = new String("       ");
    STATE = new String("  ");
    ZIPCOD = new BigDecimal("0");
    CDTLMT = new BigDecimal("0");
    CHGCOD = new BigDecimal("0");
```

Figure 17.15: The default constructor function should initialize all of its attributes. (Part 1 of 2)

```
    BALDUE = new BigDecimal("0");
    CDTDUE = new BigDecimal("0");
}
```

Figure 17.15: The default constructor function should initialize all of its attributes. (Part 2 of 2)

This constructor sets the initial value of all the attributes of its class. It is used when you need to create a customer that does not yet exist in DB2/400. A second constructor is designed to build a CUSTOMER object from an existing relational database entity, using the constructor's argument as the full key (Figure 17.16). You gained exposure to this constructor earlier because the GETENTITY function was implemented in the RDBOBJECT base class.

```
public Customer(BigDecimal custNum)
    throws AS400Exception, AS400SecurityException,
           IOException, InterruptedException {
    CUSNUM = custNum;
    getEntity();
}
```

Figure 17.16: The CUSTOMER constructor uses the GETENTITY function to retrieve the attributes for a customer from DB2/400.

RDBOBJECT's GETENTITY function, by the way, requires that its derived class implements the abstract GETKEY function, which CUSTOMER obligingly does (actually it has to implement all the abstract functions of RDBOBJECT) with the code in Figure 17.17.

```
protected Object[] getKey() {
    Object key[] = new Object[countKeyFields];
    key[0] = CUSNUM;
    return key;
}
```

Figure 17.17: The GETKEY function returns an array of objects that is a list of values that are the key for this object's customer.

Following standard encapsulation procedures, the CUSTOMER class then defines getter functions for all its private attributes, as shown in Figure 17.18.

```
public String getLSTNAM() { return LSTNAM; }
public String getINIT() { return INIT; }
public String getSTREET() { return STREET; }
public String getCITY() { return CITY; }
public String getSTATE() { return STATE; }
public BigDecimal getZIPCOD() { return ZIPCOD; }
public BigDecimal getCDTLMT() { return CDTLMT; }
public BigDecimal getCHGCOD() { return CHGCOD; }
public BigDecimal getBALDUE() { return BALDUE; }
public BigDecimal getCDTDUE() { return CDTDUE; }
```

Figure 17.18: Each of the attributes of the business class requires getter functions.

Then the CUSTOMER class defines setter functions for those attributes that users of the class can modify. Notice that the SETSTATE function checks for validity and throws the invalid state exception. Proper encapsulation requires you to check not only the validity of the value but also conformance to business rules, as shown in Figure 17.19.

```
public void setSTATE (String state) throws InvalidStateException
{
    String states[] = {"AL","AL","AZ","AR","CA","CO","CT",
    "CE","FL","GA","HI","ID","IL","IN","IA","KS","KY","LA",
    "ME","MD","MA","MI","MN","MS","MO","MT","NE","NV","NH",
    "NJ","NM","NY","NC","ND","OH","OK","OR","PA","RI","SC",
    "SD","TN","TX","UT","VT","VA","WA","DC","WV","WI","WY"};
    if (state.length() != 2)
      throw new InvalidStateException(state);
    for (int i=0; i<states.length;i++) {
      if (state.equals(states[i])) {
        STATE = state;
        return;
      }
    }
    throw new InvalidStateException(state);
}
```

Figure 17.19: All user-modifiable attributes of the business class require setter functions; those setter functions should throw exceptions where appropriate for invalid values. (Part 1 of 2)

```
  public void setLSTNAM(String str) throws
InvalidLengthException {
    if (str.length() > 8)
      throw new InvalidLengthException("LSTNAM", str.length(),
8);
    LSTNAM = str;
  }
  public void setINIT(String str)  throws InvalidLengthException
{
    if (str.length() > 3)
      throw new InvalidLengthException("INIT", str.length(), 3);
    INIT = str;
  }
  public void setSTREET(String str)  throws
InvalidLengthException {
    if (str.length() > 13)
      throw new InvalidLengthException("STREET", str.length(),
8);
    STREET = str;
  }
  public void setCITY(String str)  throws InvalidLengthException
{
    if (str.length() > 6)
      throw new InvalidLengthException("CITY", str.length(), 6);
    CITY = str;
  }
  public void setCUSNUM(BigDecimal num) { CUSNUM = num; }
  public void setZIPCOD(BigDecimal num) { ZIPCOD = num; }
  public void setCDTLMT(BigDecimal num) { CDTLMT = num; }
  public void setCHGCOD(BigDecimal num) { CHGCOD = num; }
  public void setBALDUE(BigDecimal num) { BALDUE = num; }
  public void setCDTDUE(BigDecimal num) { CDTDUE = num; }
```

Figure 17.19: All user-modifiable attributes of the business class require setter functions;
those setter functions should throw exceptions where appropriate for invalid values.
(Part 2 of 2)

Notice that the CUSTOMER example's GETLSTNAM function checks (as do some
of the other functions) for the length of the passed string. Because the fields of
the QCUSTCT customer master file on the AS/400 have length constraints, the setter functions must ensure the proper length. The exceptions thrown from the setter functions shown in Figure 17.19 use the fine-grained error-handling approach
of describing the particular error. Figure 17.20 shows how easily you can imple-

ment these explicit exception classes to gain the advantages of application-specific exceptions (covered in chapter 11).

```
public class InvalidStateException extends Exception {
  public InvalidStateException(String stateCode) {
    super("Invalid state code: " + stateCode);
  }
}
public class InvalidLengthException extends Exception {
  public InvalidLengthException(String fieldName, int given, int
allowed) {
    super("Entry length for " + fieldName +
        " of " + given +
        " is greater than maximum of " +
        allowed + ".");
  }
}
```

Figure 17.20: Exceptions thrown from setter functions should approach error handling with the fine-grained tactic of describing the particular error.

ENFORCED FUNCTION IMPLEMENTATION

At this point, the Gestapo steps in. The CUSTOMER class must provide implementations for the five abstract functions of RDBOBJECT or risk compilation failure. Those five abstract functions are PRINT, PUTFIELDS, GETKEY, GETFIELDS, and GETFIELDS. Hey, did I write GETFIELDS twice? Sure did.

The GETFIELDS function is an example of an overloaded function, and the CUSTOMER class must, in fact, implement two GETFIELDS functions. One of those overloaded functions accepts a jt400 RECORD object as a parameter used with record-level access; the other accepts a JDBC RESULTSET object as a parameter, used with SQL access. The GETFIELDS overloaded function that accepts a jt400 RECORD object uses that object to retrieve each of CUSTOMER's class attributes from the DB2/400 values stored in the RECORD object. The other GETFIELDS function uses the getter functions from the RESULTSET class also to set the values of the CUSTOMER class's fields, as Figure 17.21 shows.

```
protected void getFields(Record record) {
    try {
      CUSNUM = (BigDecimal)record.getField("CUSNUM");
      LSTNAM = (String)record.getField("LSTNAM");
      INIT = (String)record.getField("INIT");
      STREET = (String)record.getField("STREET");
      CITY = (String)record.getField("CITY");
      STATE = (String)record.getField("STATE");
      ZIPCOD = (BigDecimal)record.getField("ZIPCOD");
      CDTLMT = (BigDecimal)record.getField("CDTLMT");
      CHGCOD = (BigDecimal)record.getField("CHGCOD");
      BALDUE = (BigDecimal)record.getField("BALDUE");
      CDTDUE = (BigDecimal)record.getField("CDTDUE");
    } catch(Exception x) {}
}
protected void getFields(ResultSet rs) {
    try {
      CUSNUM = (BigDecimal)rs.getBigDecimal("CUSNUM",0);
      LSTNAM = (String)rs.getString("LSTNAM");
      INIT = (String)rs.getString("INIT");
      STREET = (String)rs.getString("STREET");
      CITY = (String)rs.getString("CITY");
      STATE = (String)rs.getString("STATE");
      ZIPCOD = (BigDecimal)rs.getBigDecimal("ZIPCOD",0);
      CDTLMT = (BigDecimal)rs.getBigDecimal("CDTLMT",0);
      CHGCOD = (BigDecimal)rs.getBigDecimal("CHGCOD",0);
      BALDUE = (BigDecimal)rs.getBigDecimal("BALDUE",2);
      CDTDUE = (BigDecimal)rs.getBigDecimal("CDTDUE",2);
    } catch(Exception x) {
      System.out.println ("\n Problem in getFields(ResultSet rs)");
    }
}
```

Figure 17.21: The business class needs to implement the two abstract GETFIELDS functions declared in RDBOBJECT; one sets the attributes based on a RECORD object and the other sets the attributes based on a RESULTSET object.

The PUTFIELDS function puts the values of the attributes of a customer class object into a jt400 RECORD object, as shown in Figure 17.22.

```
protected Record putFields(Record record) {
    record.setField("CUSNUM", CUSNUM);
    record.setField("LSTNAM", LSTNAM);
    record.setField("INIT", INIT);
    record.setField("STREET", STREET);
    record.setField("CITY", CITY);
    record.setField("STATE", STATE);
    record.setField("ZIPCOD", ZIPCOD);
    record.setField("CDTLMT", CDTLMT);
    record.setField("CHGCOD", CHGCOD);
    record.setField("BALDUE", BALDUE);
    record.setField("CDTDUE", CDTDUE);
    return record;
}
```

Figure 17.22: The RDBOBJECT base class requires the business class to implement the SETFIELDS function as RDBOBJECT uses it in its implementation of its UPDATE and WRITE functions.

The UPDATE and WRITE functions of RDBOBJECT then use the RECORD object returned from the PUTFIELDS function for DB2/400 updates.

The PRINT function is simply used as a method of printing the current values of the attributes of a CUSTOMER. You can implement the PRINT function in as fancy a manner as you'd like, but I just slapped the values together in a string and printed it as shown in Figure 17.23.

```
public void print() {
    System.out.println ("\n" +
    INIT + " " + LSTNAM + "     " + CUSNUM + " " +
    STREET + " " + CITY + ", " + STATE + " " + ZIPCOD +
    "\n Credit: " + CDTLMT + " Charge Code: " + CHGCOD +
    " Balance Due: " + BALDUE + " Credit Due: " + CDTDUE);
}
```

Figure 17.23: The CUSTOMER class's implementation of the PRINT function simply concatenates the values of its attribute and prints it as a single line with the SYSTEM.OUT.PRINTLN function.

ADDITIONAL INTERFACES

Steps six and seven call for you to add functions that return associated objects and any additional interfaces as required for the manipulation of the business entity. The CUSTOMER class example provides two: one for purchase orders and one for invoices. The implementation of these functions uses the SEARCH function of two more classes that extend the RDBOBJECT base class, as Figure 17.24 illustrates.

```
public Vector getPurchaseOrders() {
    return PurchaseOrders.search(
        "CUSNUM = " + CUSNUM, new PurchaseOrder());
}
public Vector getInvoices(){
    return Invoices.search(
        "CUSNUM = " + CUSNUM, new Invoices());
}
```

Figure 17.24: Business classes should have functions that return object instances of associated business classes.

USE OF THE CUSTOMER CLASS

The last step to implementing the CUSTOMER class involves generating the JavaDoc from the comments that you keyed as you coded the CUSTOMER class. Users of the CUSTOMER class—that is, you and the rest of your applications staff—can then refer to the HTML Java documentation to learn how to use the class. After working with one or two of the classes that extend RDBOBJECT, the programming users will become quite comfortable with the interface because it is standard across all the Java business classes. If you find some performance-enhancing techniques, you need only to change the RDBOBJECT base class and all the derived objects immediately take advantage of that improvement, with no recompilation required.

Even if the use of the CUSTOMER class is easy, the implementation of the frameworks covered in this chapter might seem relatively complex, especially for newcomers to object-oriented programming. Yet, the methods prescribed use some of the standard features of object-oriented programming.

For instance, you used inheritance to factor out common behavior to a base class. That base class was implemented as an abstract class to force its derived classes to comply with a standard interface. You used static fields so that the same value could be shared across object invocations. You used static functions so that you could implement functions that could operate outside the context of an object instance. You followed standard encapsulation techniques by using the private access specifier for class fields and public specifiers for getter and setter functions. You even used the protected access specifier for the base class's fields and functions so that its derived classes could use them even though they remained protected from alteration by users.

POTENTIAL ENHANCEMENTS

The code for my relational-to-object framework of classes is rather lean, with only a couple hundred lines. That's pretty good when you consider you never have to open a file again. You might find, however, that you want to improve and enhance the framework presented here.

In fact, one area of potential improvement comes to mind right away. Remember how the UPDATE function used the key of the record to be updated? That practice suggests that jt400 must reread the record before it can be updated. Further, that means someone else could have updated the record. Your change would then wipe out his or her changes. In legacy RPG code, records of files that are open for update are locked as they are read. No one else can read that record for update. That presents a problem as well in that your applications then have to update the record as soon as possible.

One standard way to handle this involves reading records with no lock specified. Then, when the user changes a value, you read for update. That's exactly the strategy that IBM employed with jt400's READ operations. With my frameworks, you instance as many objects as you want (for example, to fill a subfile) and, on request for modification, you use the UPDATE function, which essentially reads from and then updates to DB2/400. How do you see if someone has modified the record since that time? You could store a copy of the original record as a RECORD object, no less, and then do a read before the update and compare the two RECORD object values.

That logic is not implemented in the frameworks presented here because it involves an extra read. If you feel that double-check is required, you can simply add it to the RDBOBJECT class. The beauty of Java's implementation of object-oriented programming is that when you modify the RDBOBJECT class, those modifications are immediately available to all derived classes—no recompilation necessary.

18

USING JAVA ITERATORS

The relational-to-object frameworks introduced in chapter 16 included two utility classes, DDMITERATOR and SQLITERATOR. I've designed both classes to allow you to efficiently traverse the elements of a relational database file. That's what application programmers do—process groups of entities. An RPG subfile program, for instance, prompts the user for a customer number, which you then use to present a subfile of all the open orders for that customer. Programmers also might use a batch procedure to spin through some or perhaps all of the records of a DB2/400 file.

Yet, many AS/400 legacy applications present a problem in that often they have tens or even hundreds of programs that open and then update the same files. When that happens, you begin to lose control of your application. Still, since this approach to processing data represents the norm, it is all too tempting when you first begin programming in Java to open an AS/400 file and start to code update logic, thus violating the intent of object-oriented programming.

The DDMITERATOR and SQLITERATOR classes help you address this problem. They make it easy for you to process sets of AS/400 business entities using those same alternate indexes, access paths, and various SQL ORDER BY and WHERE clauses that you used in your RPG applications—while still conforming to the standards of object-oriented programming. Figure 18.1 contains the functional interfaces for these two classes.

```
public class SQLIterator implements Iterator
{
    SQLIterator(ResultSet rs,Class derivedRdbObjectClass);
    public boolean hasNext();
    public Object next();
    public void remove();
    protected void finalize();
}
public class DDMIterator implements Iterator
{
    public static final int KEY_EQ;
    public static final int KEY_GT;
    public static final int KEY_GE;
    public static final int KEY_LT;
    public static final int KEY_LE;
    public DDMIterator(String file, String lib,
                       RDBObject derivedRdbObject);
    public DDMIterator(String file, String lib,
                       RDBObject derivedRdbObject, Object[]
key);
    public boolean hasNext();
    public Object next();
    public void remove();
    public void positionCursor(Object[] key);
    public void positionCursor(Object[] key, int searchType);
    public Object previous();
    protected void finalize();
}
```

Figure 18.1: Listings generated from the JAVAP utility show the function interface of the SQLITERATOR and DDMITERATOR classes.

Both the DDMITERATOR and the SQLITERATOR classes implement the Java interface called ITERATOR, shown in Figure 18.2. That ITERATOR interface is not of my design; Sun has added it as a part of the JAVA.UTIL package in Java 1.2. Java already had an interface called ENUMERATION that served a similar purpose to that of the more recent ITERATOR interface. The ENUMERATION interface, however, clashed with C++'s use of the word *enumeration*; and *iterator* has long been an accepted term for C++ and Smalltalk for traversing sets of objects. So, to follow that strategy, I provided my own version of the Iterator interface that is exactly like Java 1.2's ITERATOR. When you start to use Java 1.2, simply remove my version and Sun's ITERATOR interface will be used instead.

```
import java.util.*;
public abstract interface Iterator  {
  public boolean hasNext();
  public Object next() throws NoSuchElementException;
  public void remove();
}
```

Figure 18.2: The RDBOBJECT frameworks' ITERATOR interface is exactly the same as Java 1.2's ITERATOR interface.

Why use the ITERATOR interface at all? Wouldn't it have been better to develop an interface that had function names that are familiar to AS/400 programmers, such as READNEXT? Think back to chapter 8's explanation of designing to an interface. When you program Java classes to use common functions implemented in various ways and in numerous classes, you reduce the amount of overall code because you've developed generic classes.

Sun designed the ITERATOR interface to allow the traversal of any group of objects, whether they are stored in DB2/400, a hash table, an array, a binary tree, or any old bag of objects. Conceivably, a function of some hard-core UNIX programmer's Java classes could receive objects instanced from my DDMITERATOR or SQLITERATOR classes. That generic function, because it takes an ITERATOR object, can traverse objects stored in DB2/400 without having any prior knowledge of the AS/400, much less DB2/400. Because the DDMITERATOR and SQLITERATOR classes conform to the standard Java interface of ITERATOR, they are usable by any class designed to handle that interface.

THE SQLITERATOR IMPLEMENTATION

The ITERATOR interface is, to say the least, trivial, consisting of just three functions: NEXT, HASNEXT, and REMOVE. And, like all interfaces, ITERATOR has no implementation. Classes that implement the ITERATOR interface must provide code for those three functions. The JAVAP listing for the SQLITERATOR class's functions (shown in Figure 18.1) contains the three functions inherited from the ITERATOR interface, a constructor function, and an overridden form of the OBJECT class's FINALIZE function.

When you look at the constructor function for the SQLITERATOR class, you might think I forgot to qualify it with an access specifier. Not so—the use of the default access specifier (no public, private, or protected keyword specified) is intended. From chapter 6, you've learned that the default access specifier (also called *friendly* or *package*) makes a field or function accessible only to classes contained in the same package. Here the default specifier limits the scope of the SQLITERATOR constructor for use only by other classes of the OBJECTTORELATIONAL package. Thus, you gain control over when and how SQLITERATOR objects are instanced. The first parameter to the SQLITERATOR's constructor, a Java Database Connectivity (JDBC) RESULTSET object, must be created appropriately, so access to this constructor is kept within the package.

You'll notice later that DDMITERATOR does not have this restriction; classes that use the RELATIONALTOOBJECT package, but are outside the package, may instance a DDMITERATOR. At any rate, to get an SQLITERATOR object, users of the RELATIONALTOOBJECT package will have to use the getSQLITERATOR function of the RDBOBJECT base class.

The implementation of RDBOBJECT's GETSQLITERATOR function requires only two statements, as Figure 18.3 shows.

```
public static SQLIterator
getSQLIterator(String whereClause, RDBObject rdbObjType)
        throws SQLException {
    ResultSet rs = getResultSet (whereClause);
    return new SQLIterator(rs, rdbObjType.getClass());
}
```

Figure 18.3: The implementation of the GETSQLITERATOR function requires two simple statements: a call to the GETRESULTSET function and then the invocation of the SQLITERATOR constructor.

The first statement retrieves a JDBC RESULTSET object using the private GETRESULTSET function. That RESULTSET object is then passed as a parameter along with the RDBOBJECT's derived class's CLASS (retrieved from the OBJECT class's GETCLASS function) to SQLITERATOR's constructor. The CLASS object is required by SQLITERATOR's NEXT function so that it knows which RDBOBJECT derived class to instance.

This little bit of Java magic might warrant explanation in more detail. As covered in chapter 16, you extend the RDBOBJECT class to define a Java class that serves as an object-oriented wrapper for business entities stored in DB2/400. The example created in chapter 16 is a CUSTOMER class. A programmer who wants to traverse a set of those customers can use the GETSQLIterator function that the CUSTOMER class inherits from the RDBOBJECT. That GETSQLITERATOR function requires an SQL where clause (which may be null) and a CUSTOMER object. Because the GETSQLITERATOR function is implemented in the RDBOBJECT base class, it does not have prior knowledge, at compile time, of the class derived from RDBOBJECT that is using the GETSQLITERATOR function. So, the GETSQLITERATOR function of the RDBOBJECT class uses the OBJECT's GETCLASS function to retrieve, at runtime, that RDBOBJECT-derived class's CLASS.

Returning to SQLITERATOR (shown in Figure 18.4), the constructor accepts a RESULTSET object and a CLASS object as parameters, which it stores in the private class fields called RS and ENTITYCLASS. At runtime, SQLITERATOR's NEXT function turns around and uses the RESULTSET object's own NEXT function to fetch the successive row of the SQL set. SQLITERATOR then uses its ENTITYCLASS object's NEWINSTANCE function to create a new instance of the appropriate class.

```
package com.midrangecomputing.ObjectToRelational;

import java.io.*;
import java.util.*;
import java.sql.*;
```

Figure 18.4: The SQLITERATOR class allows you to generically traverse a set of RDBOBJECT objects. (Part 1 of 2)

```
public class SQLIterator implements Iterator {
  private ResultSet rs = null;
  private Class entityClass = null;
SQLIterator(ResultSet rs, Class entityClass) {
    this.rs = rs;
    this.entityClass = entityClass;
  }
public boolean hasNext()
    throws RuntimeException {
    throw new RuntimeException("hasNext()is an unsupported
operation");
  }
public Object next() throws NoSuchElementException {
    RDBObject rdbObj = null;
    try {
      if (rs.next ()) {
        rdbObj = (RDBObject)entityClass.newInstance();
        rdbObj.getFields(rs);
        rdbObj.setPersistent(true);
        return rdbObj;
      }
    } catch (Exception e) {
        System.out.println(e);
    }
    return null;
  }
  public void remove() throws RuntimeException {
    throw new RuntimeException("remove()is an unsupported
operation");
  }
  protected void finalize() throws Throwable {
    rs.close();
  }
}
```

Figure 18.4: The SQLITERATOR class allows you to generically traverse a set of RDBOBJECT objects. (Part 2 of 2)

That new object instance of an RDBOBJECT-derived class then invokes its custom implementation of the GETFIELDS function. (Remember that the GETFIELDS function is always implemented in the RDBOBJECT-derived class to set the initial state of the attributes of the Java class from the column values of the current row of the RESULTSET.) SQLITERATOR's NEXT function then returns that newly constructed object of the proper RDBOBJECT-derived class. That's pretty cool when you consider that at compile time the SQLITERATOR class has no idea what the class of the object using SQLITERATOR will ultimately be. It's also fairly impressive that the SQLITERATOR class was able to do that with only a few lines of code.

So why doesn't the NEXT function simply return an RDBOBJECT object? Yes, that would have made things clearer; but remember that SQLITERATOR implements the ITERATOR interface and the ITERATOR's NEXT function returns the ambiguous OBJECT object. To use an OBJECT object that is returned from the NEXT function, you'll have to cast it to the appropriate RDBOBJECT-derived class.

The implementations of the HASNEXT and REMOVE functions do not involve nearly as much complexity as the NEXT function. In fact, they really don't even get implemented. Both functions are merely used to throw a RUNTIME-EXCEPTION, for two reasons. First, with the HASNEXT function, JDBC 1.0 does not have the facility to easily see if more rows are available in the RESULTSET. Second, I don't want to deliver delete capabilities through the REMOVE function of the iterator. Still, the HASNEXT and REMOVE functions require some sort of implementation (because they are in the ITERATOR interface) so I have them simply throw a RUNTIMEEXCEPTION object. This style of programming is fairly standard. Often, you will not want to support specific functions of an interface, so you simply code them to throw a RUNTIMEEXCEPTION exception.

The FINALIZE function simply closes the SQL connection. The FINALIZE function of any object will be called by the Java Virtual Machine (JVM) when it is garbage-collected. An object becomes tagged for garbage collection when it is no longer referenced and hence is wasting memory (and, in this case, an SQL connection). At one Java seminar, I told the attendees that when an object becomes orphaned it is tagged for garbage collection. One attendee said, "So Sun's solution to orphans is to kill them?" I replied in a Dickens' theme, "That's right and thus decrease the surplus population of unwanted objects."

SQLITERATOR USE

Figure 18.5 shows a sample code snippet that uses an SQLITERATOR object. First, from within the context of a try/catch block, the sample code retrieves an

SQLITERATOR instance from RDBOBJECT's GETSQLITERATOR function. It qualifies the call to the GETSQLITERATOR function with CUSTOMER, a class derived from RDBOBJECT. The GETSQLITERATOR function requires two arguments: the where clause for the SQL statement that retrieves the result set, and instance of an RDBOBJECT-derived class.

```
SQLIterator sqlIter = null;
try {
  sqlIter = Customer.getSQLIterator("", new Customer());
} catch (SQLException e) {
  System.out.println(e);
}
for (Customer aCust = (Customer)sqlIter.next();
  aCust != null;
  aCust = (Customer)sqlIter.next()) {
  aCust.print();
}
```

Figure 18.5: Use of an SQLITERATOR object is a simple matter of getting an instance of that object from the GETSQLITERATOR function and then looping until the NEXT function returns a null.

The example then uses the NEXT function of the returned SQLITERATOR object to iterate through the set until NEXT returns a null. The sample code casts the OBJECT object returned from NEXT to be of the CUSTOMER class just before it assigns that object to the ACUST variable. The example then uses that ACUST variable (a handle to a CUSTOMER object) to qualify the invocation of the PRINT function, which simply dumps the attributes of the current customer to a default output.

LOGICAL FILE SUPPORT

A majority of AS/400 legacy applications are comprised of data files, many of which have a variety of logical views built over them. These logical views often simply specify alternate keyed paths by which your RPG program could process the records of the associated physical file. Other logical views might include SELECT and OMIT clauses so that your RPG application program can process a subset of the records based on some selection criterion. My relational-to-object framework provides the DDMITERATOR so that your Java applications can use your favorite access paths (logical files) to iterate through the entities stored in your DB2/400 database.

This implementation of the ITERATOR interface uses the acronym *DDM* as a prefix because RECORDLEVELACCESSITERATOR is too long; and, because record-level access is implemented through Distributed Data Management, DDM works well as a synonym for record-level access.

A look at the list of DDMITERATOR's functions shown in Figure 18.1 reveals a few more functions than SQLITERATOR. DDMITERATOR does have the same NEXT function—a requirement of using the ITERATOR interface—but it also has some fairly interesting advantages over SQLITERATOR. First, in the JAVAP listing of Figure 18.1, you can see that it has something similar to RPG's SETLL operation with its POSITIONCURSOR functions. Second, DDMITERATOR, unlike SQLITERATOR, has the ability to read in reverse sequence with its PREVIOUS function. And third, the public constructors for DDMITERATOR mean you can instantiate DDMITERATOR objects yourself, whereas you have to ask RDBOBJECT to build an instance of an SQLITERATOR for you.

DDMITERATOR has two constructors: one accepts the file name, a library name, and an object instance of an RDBOBJECT-derived class; and the other accepts those same three parameters as well as a key list. DDMITERATOR is designed to allow the sequential processing of all relational database entities in a logical view or of a subset of entities by key.

The key list version of the DDMITERATOR constructor allows you to set the initial cursor position of the file. If you look at the code for the DDMITERATOR class shown in Figure 18.6, you can see that it uses the file and library parameters to instance a jt400 KEYEDFile, set the record format, open the file, and position the file cursor. The first constructor uses a typical Java programming technique (often used to reduce the duplication of code) of turning around and invoking some other constructor function. This nonkeyed version of the constructor function sets the default value for the keyed version of the constructor to null and invokes the other constructor using the THIS keyword:

```
this(rdbFile, rdbLib, rdbObjType, null);
```

The THIS keyword always means *me* or *mine* and, in this context (with the parenthetical parameters that follow the THIS keyword), it causes the constructor function to accept two strings, an RDBOBJECT, and one other object for which the calling function doesn't have an object instance. The compiler figures, since only one constructor function takes two strings, an RDBOBJECT, and something else, that you must mean the keyed version of the constructor function. That keyed DDMITERATOR constructor checks to see if the passed array of OBJECTS (the key list) is equal to null. If that key list is null, the constructor knows to position the file cursor to the beginning of the file; but if key list is not null, the constructor positions the file cursor just before the value of the key list.

The NEXT function works much the same as SQLITERATOR's NEXT in that it returns an RDBOBJECT, the attributes of which are retrieved from DB2/400. The difference, of course, lies in DDMITERATOR's use of jt400's KEYEDFILE object to access records sequentially by key. The important thing is that DDM-ITERATOR, just like SQLITERATOR, does not allow direct access to the data; rather, it instances an object of the appropriate RDBOBJECT-derived class. If the DDMITERATOR has been constructed with a key list, the NEXT function returns only those objects whose DB2/400 records have a key value that equals the key value passed to the DDMITERATOR constructor. If the DDMITERATOR is constructed without a key list, the NEXT function iteratively returns all the records of the file sequentially.

The PREVIOUS function operates in a manner similar to NEXT except it reads records from DB2/400 in reverse order. The HASNEXT function returns a Boolean value of true if the iteration has more elements. If you remember, SQLITERATOR does not implement the HASNEXT function. DDMITERATOR does implement HASNEXT but I (and the JavaDoc that accompanies the package) caution you against using it because it is not very efficient. HASNEXT reads ahead for more records and then repositions the file with a READPREVIOUS. It is more efficient to simply query the object returned from a call to the NEXT function to find out if more elements are available for processing.

The two overloaded POSITIONCURSOR functions both position the DB2/400 file cursor by key; they differ in that one of them allows you to specify the search criteria of equal to, greater than or equal to, less than, or less than or equal to. If you construct the DDMITERATOR object with a key, subsequent use of the NEXT function after invoking the POSITIONCURSOR function would retrieve only those RDBOBJECTS that have the same key value, essentially like an RPG SETLL and READE. If you instead construct the DDMITERATOR object without a key, subsequent use of the NEXT function following invocation of the POSITIONCURSOR function would continue to return RDBOBJECTS until an end-of-file condition, essentially like an RPG SETLL and READ (rather than READE).

Just as SQLITERATOR's FINALIZE function closes the SQL connection, here FINALIZE is used to close the file when the DDMITERATOR object is no longer associated with any Java classes currently executing in the JVM. To reduce the number of file opens and to improve performance, you can force the file to close by setting the variable handle to null. In fact, it's a good practice to set any value of all objects that you are done using to null—just make sure that you really are done with that object.

```
package com.midrangecomputing.ObjectToRelational;

import com.ibm.as400.access.*;
import java.util.*;
import java.io.*;

public class DDMIterator implements Iterator {
  private AS400 as400;
  private KeyedFile file;
  private RecordFormat format;
  private Object[] key;
  private RDBObject rdbObjType;
  public static final int KEY_EQ = KeyedFile.KEY_EQ;
  public static final int KEY_GT  = KeyedFile.KEY_GT;
  public static final int KEY_GE  = KeyedFile.KEY_GE;
  public static final int KEY_LT  = KeyedFile.KEY_LT;
  public static final int KEY_LE  = KeyedFile.KEY_LE;

  public DDMIterator(String rdbFile, String rdbLib,
                     RDBObject rdbObjType)
                throws AS400Exception, AS400SecurityException {
    this(rdbFile, rdbLib,rdbObjType, null);
```

Figure 18.6: The DDMITERATOR class allows you to process objects of classes derived from the RDBOBJECT base class based on the access path of a logical file. (Part 1 of 4)

```
    }
  public DDMIterator(String rdbFile, String rdbLib,
                    RDBObject rdbObjType, Object[] key)
                    throws AS400Exception, AS400SecurityException {
    this.key = key;
    this.as400 = Profile.as400;
    this.rdbObjType = rdbObjType;
    // Specify file location
    QSYSObjectPathName filePathName =
      new QSYSObjectPathName(rdbLib,rdbFile,"*FIRST","MBR");
    try {
      file = new KeyedFile(as400, filePathName.getPath());
    } catch(Exception x) {
      System.out.println(
            "Error occurred attempting to create a KeyFile." + x);
    }
    // Retrieve a record format
    AS400FileRecordDescription recordDescription =
      new AS400FileRecordDescription(as400, filePathName.getPath());
    try {
      format = recordDescription.retrieveRecordFormat()[0];
      file.setRecordFormat(format);
      file.open(AS400File.READ_ONLY,
              0,
              AS400File.COMMIT_LOCK_LEVEL_NONE);
    } catch (Exception e) {
      System.out.println(
            "Error occurred attempting to open a file." + e);
    }
    try {
      if (key == null)
        file.positionCursorBeforeFirst();
      else
        file.positionCursor(key);
    } catch (Exception except) {
      System.out.println(except);
    }
  }
public boolean hasNext() {
    try {
      Record record = null;
      if (key == null)
        record = file.readNext();
      else
```

Figure 18.6: The DDMITERATOR class allows you to process objects of classes derived from the RDBOBJECT base class based on the access path of a logical file. (Part 2 of 4)

```
         record = file.readNextEqual();
      if (record == null) {
        return false;
      }
      if (key == null)
        file.readPrevious();
      else
        file.readPreviousEqual();
    } catch (Exception except) {
      System.out.println(except);
      return false;
    }
    return true;
  }
public Object next() throws NoSuchElementException {
    Record record = null;
    try {
      if (key == null)
        record = file.readNext();
      else
        record = file.readNextEqual();
      if (record == null) {
        throw new NoSuchElementException();
      }
    } catch (Exception except) {
      System.out.println(except);
      return null;
    }
    try {
      RDBObject rdbObj = (RDBObject)rdbObjType.getClass().newInstance();
      rdbObj.setPersistent(true);
      rdbObj.getFields(record);
      return rdbObj;
    } catch (Exception except) {
      System.out.println(except);
    }
    return null;
  }
public void remove() throws RuntimeException {
    throw new RuntimeException("remove()is an unsupported operation");
  }
public void positionCursor(Object key[]) throws AS400Exception,
AS400SecurityException, InterruptedException, IOException {
    file.positionCursor(key);
```

Figure 18.6: The DDMITERATOR class allows you to process objects of classes derived from the RDBOBJECT base class based on the access path of a logical file. (Part 3 of 4)

```
    }
public void positionCursor(Object key[], int searchType)
        throws AS400Exception, AS400SecurityException,
               InterruptedException, IOException {
    file.positionCursor(key, searchType);
  }

public Object previous() throws NoSuchElementException {
    Record record = null;
    try {
      if (key == null)
        record = file.readPrevious();
      else
        record = file.readPreviousEqual();
      if (record == null) {
        throw new NoSuchElementException();
      }
    } catch (Exception except) {
      System.out.println(except);
      return null;
    }
    try {
      RDBObject rdbObj =
          (RDBObject)rdbObjType.getClass().newInstance();
      rdbObj.setPersistent(true);
      rdbObj.getFields(record);
      return rdbObj;
    } catch (Exception except) {
      System.out.println(except);
    }
    return null;
  }
protected void finalize() throws Throwable {
    file.close();
  }
}
```

Figure 18.6: The DDMITERATOR class allows you to process objects of classes derived from the RDBOBJECT base class based on the access path of a logical file. (Part 4 of 4)

DDMITERATOR USE

You can use DDMITERATOR in two ways. One use involves processing all of the business entities as accessed through a logical view. The other way is to process a subset of the business entities that match the key of the logical view. If you use the DDMITERATOR that accepts a key list, you in essence tell DDMITERATOR that you want to iterate through only those entities associated with DB2/400 records that are equal to that key list. On the other hand, if you don't construct DDMITERATOR with a key, you tell it that you want to iterate through all of the entities associated with the specified logical view.

The TESTITERATORS class of Figure 18.7 shows an example Java application that tests both DDMITERATOR and SQLITERATOR. It uses two RDBOBJECT-derived classes called ATTENDEE and CUSTOMER to provide an object wrapper around DB2/400 files called ATTENDEE and QCUSTCDT. The ATTENDEE database file has two indexes: one, appropriately called ATTENDEE, is the primary index by attendee number and the other, ATTENDEE01, is by last name. The TESTITERATORS class tests the SQLITERATOR using the CUSTOMER class and then tests the DDMITERATOR using the ATTENDEE class.

```
import com.midrangecomputing.ObjectToRelational.*;
import com.ibm.as400.access.*;
import java.sql.*;

public class TestIterators {
  private void testSQLIterator() {
    SQLIterator sqlIter = null;
    try {
      sqlIter =
          Customer.getSQLIterator("BALDUE > 100", new Customer());
    } catch (SQLException e) {
      System.out.println(e);
    }
    for (Customer aCust = (Customer)sqlIter.next();
         aCust != null;
         aCust = (Customer)sqlIter.next()) {
      aCust.print();
    }
  }
  private void testDDMIterator() {
    DDMIterator iter = null;
    Object key[] = new Object[1];
    key[0] = new String("Denoncourt          ");
    try {
```

Figure 18.7: The TESTITERATORS application tests the SQLITERATOR and DDMITERATOR classes using the CUSTOMER and ATTENDEE business classes, respectively. (Part 1 of 3)

```
    iter =
      new DDMIterator("ATTENDEE01", "DENONCOURT", new Attendee(),
key);
  } catch (AS400Exception excp) {
    AS400Message msg = excp.getAS400Message();
    System.out.println(msg.getID() + " " + msg.getText());
    return;
  } catch (AS400SecurityException excp) {
    System.out.println(excp.getMessage());
    return;
  }
  // First for loop
  for (Attendee atn = (Attendee)iter.next();
       atn != null;
       atn = (Attendee)iter.next()) {
    atn.print();
  }
  key[0] = new String("Smith                    ");
  try {
    iter.positionCursor(key, DDMIterator.KEY_EQ);
  } catch (Exception e) {
    System.out.println(e.getMessage());
    return;
  }
  // Second for loop
  for (Attendee atn = (Attendee)iter.next();
       atn != null;
       atn = (Attendee)iter.next()) {
    atn.print();
  }
  iter = null;
  try {
    iter =
      new DDMIterator("ATTENDEE", "DENONCOURT", new Attendee());
  } catch (Exception excp) {
    System.out.println(excp);
    return;
  }
  // Third for loop
  for (Attendee atn = (Attendee)iter.next();
       atn != null;
       atn = (Attendee)iter.next()) {
    atn.print();
```

Figure 18.7: The TESTITERATORS application tests the SQLITERATOR and DDMITERATOR classes using the CUSTOMER and ATTENDEE business classes, respectively. (Part 2 of 3)

```
    }
    for (Attendee atn = (Attendee)iter.previous();
         atn != null;
         atn = (Attendee)iter.previous()) {
      atn.print();
    }
  }

  public static void main(String[] args) {
    TestIterators x = new TestIterators ();
    x.testDDMIterator();
    x.testSQLIterator();
    System.exit(0);
  }
}
```

Figure 18.7: The TESTITERATORS application tests the SQLITERATOR and DDMITERATOR classes using the CUSTOMER and ATTENDEE business classes, respectively. (Part 3 of 3)

The TESTDDMITERATOR function creates the first DDMITERATOR by invoking the constructor function that accepts file name, library name, a derived RDB-OBJECT object, and a key list. The file name parameter is set to the alternate index of attendee and the library name is set to my personal library. The key list parameter is an array of OBJECT objects and the first and only element of that array is set to equal a STRING object that consists of my last name concatenated with enough blanks to equal 25 characters. For DB2/400 character fields that are key values, you must pad the Java String objects with blanks for jt400's keyed lookup to work. The first FOR loop of the TESTDDMITERATOR function iterates through all the records in the attendee file that have a last-name value of Denoncourt. Because the Attendee test file contains one record for each of five members of my family, the for loop iterates through those five elements and then exits. Figure 18.8 shows the resulting output.

```
Denoncourt              . Don        G Company No: 1111 Attendee No: 1111
Denoncourt              . Suzanne    R Company No: 22222 Attendee No: 22222
Denoncourt              . Joshua     A Company No: 3333 Attendee No: 3333
Denoncourt              . Jacob      A Company No: 4444 Attendee No: 4444
Denoncourt              . Tyler      S Company No: 5555 Attendee No: 5555
```

Figure 18.8: Output from the first for loop of TESTITERATORS' TESTDDMITERATOR function.

Before the next FOR loop, the TEST function invokes DDMITERATOR's POSI-
TIONCURSOR function to set the file cursor to the first of two records that contain
a last name of SMITH. That second FOR loop then iterates twice before the NEXT
function returns a null to indicate that DDMITERATOR has finished processing
the set of attendees equal to Smith. Figure 18.9 shows the resulting output.

```
Smith                  . John          A Company No: 1212 Attendee No: 1212
Smith                  . Dave          A Company No: 99999 Attendee No: 9999
```

Figure 18.9: Output from the second FOR loop of TESTITERATORS' TESTDDMITERATOR function.

Just prior to the third FOR loop, the test function creates a new DDMITERATOR
object using the constructor that accepts a file name and library but no key. That
FOR loop then iterates through all the records in the file. Figure 18.10 shows the
resulting output.

```
Denoncourt             . Don           G Company No: 1111 Attendee No: 1111
Smith                  . John          A Company No: 1212 Attendee No: 1212
Jones                  . Paul          A Company No: 3232 Attendee No: 3232
Denoncourt             . Joshua        A Company No: 3333 Attendee No: 3333
Denoncourt             . Jacob         A Company No: 4444 Attendee No: 4444
Denoncourt             . Tyler         S Company No: 5555 Attendee No: 5555
Smith                  . Dave          A Company No: 99999 Attendee No: 9999
Denoncourt             . Suzanne       R Company No: 22222 Attendee No: 22222
```

Figure 18.10: Output from the third FOR loop of TESTITERATORS' TESTDDMITERATOR function.

When the FOR loop terminates because the NEXT function has returned a null to
signify the end of the group, the last FOR loop then spins through the ATTENDEE
objects in reverse order using the DDMITERATOR's previous function. Figure
18.11 shows the resulting output.

```
Denoncourt          , Suzanne      R Company No: 22222 Attendee No: 22222
Smith               , Dave         A Company No: 99999 Attendee No: 9999
Denoncourt          , Tyler        S Company No: 5555 Attendee No: 5555
Denoncourt          , Jacob        A Company No: 4444 Attendee No: 4444
Denoncourt          , Joshua       A Company No: 3333 Attendee No: 3333
Jones               , Paul         A Company No: 3232 Attendee No: 3232
Smith               , John         A Company No: 1212 Attendee No: 1212
Denoncourt          , Don          G Company No: 1111 Attendee No: 1111
```

Figure 18.11: Output from the final FOR loop of TESTITERATORS' TESTDDMITERATOR function.

The TESTSQLITERATOR function of the TESTITERATORS class uses the
CUSTOMER class's GETSQLITERATOR function to retrieve all the customers
whose balance exceeds $100. The records are retrieved iteratively from the re-
turned SQLITERATOR object. Figure 18.12 shows the resulting output.

```
S S Vine       3 PO Box 79      Broton, VT 5046
  Credit: 700 Charge Code: 1 Balance Due: 439.00 Credit Due: 0.00

J A Johnson    12 3 Alpine Way  Helen , GA 30545
  Credit: 9999 Charge Code: 2 Balance Due: 3987.50 Credit Due: 33.50

J W Doe        5 59 Archer Rd   Sutter, CA 95685
  Credit: 700 Charge Code: 2 Balance Due: 250.00 Credit Due: 100.00

F L Lee        1 5963 Oak St    Hector, NY 14841
  Credit: 700 Charge Code: 2 Balance Due: 489.50 Credit Due: 0.50

M T Abraham    6 392 Mill St    Isle  , MN 56342
  Credit: 9999 Charge Code: 3 Balance Due: 500.00 Credit Due: 0.00
```

Figure 18.12: Output from records retrieved from an SQLITERATOR.

SUMMARY

Java 1.2's ITERATOR interface and its ENUMERATOR predecessor are designed for
use as a standard strategy for the traversal of a set of objects. The DDM-
ITERATOR and SQLITERATOR implementations of the ITERATOR interface allow
the efficient traversal of objects stored in a DB2/400 database file.

It would seem, at first, that perhaps these two iterators should have been implemented using function names analogous to DB2/400 file access. DDMITERATOR could have used function names like READNEXT and SETLOWERLIMITS. However, SQLITERATOR, because it is implemented with SQL, would have used a different set of function names than DDMITERATOR.

Because the DDMITERATOR and SQLITERATOR classes both conform to the same interface, objects constructed from either of these classes can be processed by any class whose function is coded to use the standard ITERATOR interface.

SECTION V

~

GRAPHICAL USER INTERFACE

19

LEARN JAVA GUI PROGRAMMING IN 21 MINUTES

Do you know why users want a GUI? A graphical user interface puts *them* in the driver's seat. For decades, the logic of programmers has driven user applications. Finally, with a GUI, users seize control! They can place application windows wherever they please, open as many windows as they want, and even cut and paste data between applications. In short, a GUI empowers a user. Users want a graphical interface, and Java is a great language for GUI development.

Java's base GUI classes are called the Abstract Windowing Toolkit (AWT). Through AWT, Java offers a package of well-designed, object-oriented classes that provides APIs for graphical programming. This chapter provides a concise tutorial of how to program with the AWT classes. The advantages of studying the AWT classes is two-fold:

1. You learn how to create graphical Java applications.

2. You acquire object-oriented programming skills.

AWT Classes as Foundation Classes

The AWT classes, known as *foundation classes*, provide the foundation on which you build a custom GUI. Foundation object classes first became widely known in the form of C++ classes, specifically Microsoft's Foundation Classes (MFC) and the Object Windows Library (OWL) from Inprise (the company formerly known as Borland).

AWT has one feature that makes it superior to MFC or OWL: AWT is platform independent. The MFC and OWL classes, on the other hand, provide an object-oriented interface to the complex and low-level Microsoft Windows API. AWT was not written to directly interface with a specific operating system. Consequently, any Java GUI application you write that uses the AWT classes should run on any platform that has a Java Virtual Machine (JVM) and supports a graphical interface (such as Windows 95, Apple, or a network computer). The AS/400 does have a JVM but lacks a graphical interface so it does not directly support the execution of a Java AWT GUI application.

The AWT Component Classes

I once heard an IBMer incorrectly refer to the AWT classes as the Advanced Windows Classes. You already know that the A in AWT means *abstract* and, besides, the AWT classes are not all that advanced. For one thing, the AWT classes lack components such as trees, tables, and tabbed dialogs. Robust GUI applications need such components. Windows 95, for instance, uses a tabbed dialog in its DISPLAY PROPERTIES window, as shown in Figure 19.1. Tables, also known as grids, are essential to business applications for presenting multiple rows of database records, which AS/400 programmers have done for years via subfiles.

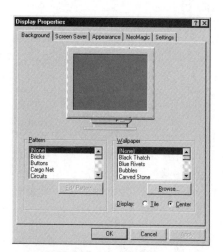

Figure 19.1: Windows 95 makes great use of tabbed dialogs to improve its user interface.

For these advanced components, you have to use another package of Java classes such as Java 1.2's Java Foundation Classes (JFC), Microsoft's Windows Foundation Classes (WFC), or a package supplied by a vendor of third-party JavaBeans. (Chapter 20 provides an introduction to JFC with specific emphasis on its table component as a replacement paradigm for subfiles.)

You might wonder why this book devotes a whole chapter to the use of the AWT classes. The central topic, of course, is object-oriented programming, and the advanced GUI classes are built on top of the AWT classes. Sun's JFC package should become the dominant Java GUI package. The JFC classes, because they extend the AWT classes, inherit all of their parent's fields and functions. This means that while the JFC classes add functionality, they have the same interface as the AWT classes. So all of the knowledge you acquire about AWT classes is transferable to programming with the JFC classes. Additionally, until the JFC classes are readily available in the millions of installed JVMs, the use of the AWT classes means that your Java application will run on more machines.

THE FOUR STEPS TO A JAVA GUI

You can break down the development of any Java GUI into four basic steps:

1. Create the components.
2. Add the components to a container.
3. Arrange, or lay out, the components within their containers.
4. Handle the events generated by the components.

First, you create an AWT component. You already know that's easy: Simply define a variable typed by the component's class name and assign an instantiated object of that variable's class type to the variable. Table 19.1 lists the most commonly used graphical components from the AWT package of GUI classes.

The following statement uses AWT's BUTTON class to create a button by invoking the BUTTON class's constructor with Java's NEW operator:

```
Button start = new Button("Start");
```

Notice that the single parameter is the string to be placed as a label identifying the button's use.

Table 19.1: The Abstract Windowing Toolkit for Developing a GUI.

AWT Component	Analogous DDS Behavior	Description
Label	Constant	A single-line text display
Button	Function key	A graphical push button that the user can click
TextField	Input/output text with no length constraint	A single-line text input area
TextArea	Input/output text mini-word processor	A multiline text area for displaying and editing text
Frame	Record format for the placement of other components	A top-level window with a title and border
Panel	Record format for the placement of other components	Provides space in which an application can attach any other component, including other panels
List	Subfile with one output-only field	A list of selectable items
Choice	No analogous DDS behavior	A drop-down list or option menu
Scrollbar	Roll keys	A slider for scrolling
Checkbox	VALUES('Y', 'N')	A toggle button that can be selected and deselected
CheckboxMenuItem, Menu, MenuBar, MenuComponent, MenuItem, PopupMenu	Menus	Application menus

Step two says to add that newly created component to a container, which is simply a window that holds components. The APPLET class itself is a container and AWT's FRAME class is also a container. An AWT FRAME, by the way, is a top-level window with decorated border that can contain a menu bar. All container classes, including APPLETS and FRAMES, have a function called ADD for adding a component that appears within that container's window. The Java applet shown in Figure 19.2 adds a button to itself.

```
import java.applet.*;
import java.awt.*;
class MiniApplet extends Applet {
        init() {
                Button start = new Button ("Start");
                add(start);
        }
}
```

Figure 19.2: The INIT function of the APPLET class is usually overridden to add components to the applet's panel.

A Java application, on the other hand, might add a button to its window using code similar to that of Figure 19.3.

```
import java.awt.*;
class MiniFrame extends Frame {
        MiniFrame (String title) {
                super(title);
                Button start = new Button ("Start");
                add(start);
        }
        public static void main(String[] args) {
                MiniFrame myFrame = new MiniFrame("TestFrame");
                myFrame.show();
        }
}
```

Figure 19.3: A Java application often extends AWT's FRAME class, bootstraps itself in its MAIN function, and then adds a component to the application's FRAME in its constructor.

The implementation is simple enough, but the two Java examples for an applet and an application do little besides present a button.

Step three specifies that you arrange, or lay out, the components within their containers. If you compile and then execute the MINIFRAME application, your start button will expand to fill the entire window frame. This wouldn't work so well because you would have failed to lay out the button component within its container. Java's AWT GUI environment differs significantly from any other GUI programming language. Most of the other languages that support a GUI have you arrange components within containers by explicitly setting the pixel position of each component's upper left-hand corner relative to its containing window. Component size is also specified with explicit pixel height and width. Although you can also use that approach with AWT, it is neither the default nor preferred behavior.

AWT's strategy for arranging components in a container allows your applets and applications to adapt to a variety of screen sizes, fonts, and operating systems. Java's AWT strategy is implemented in *layout managers*. Layout managers dynamically rearrange component placement when users resize application windows, change fonts, or do anything to affect the presentation of your GUI.

Layout managers take a while to become comfortable with, so first you'll learn the easy way—that is to say, the wrong way—to hardcode the placement of your components. The first step to hardcoding your component alignment is to say, "Okay, I'm switching to autopilot by setting the layout manager for the container to null."

```
setLayout(null);
```

Next you set the coordinates and size of the component with the SETBOUNDS function:

```
start.setBounds(20, 30, 100, 30);
```

This code snippet would set the start button's list box at pixel row 20 column 30 relative to its container. It also sets the button's width at 100 pixels and its height at 30.

The right way of designing a GUI application makes use of layout managers. Five layout managers come as a part of AWT: BORDERLAYOUT, FLOWLAYOUT, GRIDLAYOUT, CARDLAYOUT, and GRIDBAGLAYOUT.

AWT's BORDERLAYOUT allows you to align your components relative to a container's northern, southern, eastern, or western boundaries as well as place components into the window's center. The code shown in Figure 19.4 can replace the MINIFRAME class's constructor of Figure 19.3; it illustrates the use of the BORDERLAYOUT.

```
MiniFrame (String title) {
    super(title);
    setLayout(new BorderLayout());
    add(new Button("North"), BorderLayout.NORTH);
    add(new Button("South"), BorderLayout.SOUTH);
    add(new Button("East"), BorderLayout.EAST);
    add(new Button("West"), BorderLayout.WEST);
    add(new Button("Center"), BorderLayout.CENTER);
}
```

Figure 19.4: Java's preferred strategy for component placement utilizes an AWT layout manager such as the BORDERLAYOUT.

The ADD function works in a slightly different manner for the BORDERLAYOUT because it takes a second parameter to specify the alignment. Figure 19.5 shows the GUI presented from the code in Figure 19.4.

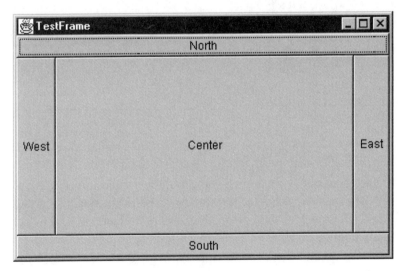

Figure 19.5: The BORDERLAYOUT arranges components within a window's northern, southern, eastern, and western boundaries as well as at the center of the window.

AWT's FLOWLAYOUT, the easiest layout manager to use, simply slaps your components into the container left to right, top to bottom as you add them to the window. Figure 19.6's replacement for MINIFRAME's constructor sets the layout to FLOWLAYOUT, uses a loop to create 10 buttons, and then adds them to FRAME.

```
MiniFrame (String title) {
    super(title);
    setLayout(new FlowLayout());
    for (int i = 0; i < 10; i++) {
        add(new Button(""+i));
    }
}
```

Figure 19.6: AWT's FLOWLAYOUT places components left to right, top to bottom in the sequence that they are added to the window panel.

Figures 19.7 and 19.8 show how the buttons are arranged by AWT's layout manager when a user manually resizes the application's window frame.

AWT's GRIDLAYOUT allows you to place your application's components within its container in orderly rows and columns. GRIDLAYOUT's constructor takes two param-

Figure 19.7: Ten Buttons auto-arranged by the FLOWLAYOUT layout manager class.

Figure 19.8: Ten buttons rearranged by the FLOWLAYOUT layout manager class in reaction to a user resizing the application window.

eters, in which you specify the desired number of rows and columns. The code in Figure 19.9 once again replaces the MINIFRAME class's constructor shown in Figure 19.3, this time illustrating the use of the GRIDLAYOUT. Figure 19.10 shows the resulting application frame.

```
MiniFrame (String title) {
    super(title);
    setLayout(new GridLayout(3,2));
    for (int i = 0; i < 6; i++)
        add(new Button(""+i));
}
```

Figure 19.9: AWT's GRIDLAYOUT layout manager allows you to place your application's components within its container in orderly rows and columns.

I'm not going to provide any examples for AWT's CARDLAYOUT or GRIDBAGLAYOUT. The CARDLAYOUT functions like a rolodex by displaying only one component in the container at a time. It is sort of like a tabbed dialog without the tabs. The GRIDBAGLAYOUT provides what I call "advanced tabular" design because it gives you ways to improve the default layout of the GRIDLAYOUT.

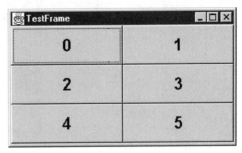

Figure 19.10: AWT's GRIDLAYOUT arranges components by columns and rows.

TETRIS

One last point remains to be made about the arranging or laying out the components within their containers: Containers themselves are components and, as such, they too can be arranged within a container. In other words, containers are often nested within other containers. You might, for instance, use the BORDERLAYOUT because of its clean placement of components and put a panel container in its center. Then you might set the layout manager for that panel container to GRIDLAYOUT and place components within it as the TESTAPPLICATION constructor does in Figure 19.11 to present the GUI shown in Figure 19.12.

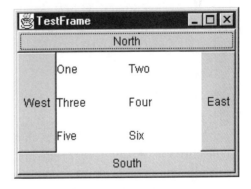

Figure 19.12: Often the application's frame uses one layout manager and then stacks other panels on top of itself.

```
TestApplication (String title) {
    super(title);
    setLayout(new BorderLayout());
    add(new Button("North"), BorderLayout.NORTH);
    add(new Button("South"), BorderLayout.SOUTH);
```

Figure 19.11: The TESTAPPLICATION constructor sets its application frame to use the BORDERLAYOUT and then places a panel in its center; the panel's layout manager is then set to GRIDLAYOUT. (Part 1 of 2)

```
        add(new Button("East"), BorderLayout.EAST);
        add(new Button("West"), BorderLayout.WEST);
        Panel panelCenter = new Panel();
        add(panelCenter, BorderLayout.CENTER);
        panelCenter.setLayout(new GridLayout(3,2));
        panelCenter.add(new Label("One"));
        panelCenter.add(new Label("Two"));
        panelCenter.add(new Label("Three"));
        panelCenter.add(new Label("Four"));
        panelCenter.add(new Label("Five"));
        panelCenter.add(new Label("Six"));
}
```

Figure 19.11: The TESTAPPLICATION constructor sets its application frame to use the BORDERLAYOUT and then places a panel in its center; the panel's layout manager is then set to GRIDLAYOUT. (Part 2 of 2)

The important point to remember about AWT's layout managers is that multiple AWT panels are often used in a containment hierarchy, sort of like the game of Tetris where you start stacking panels within the application's frame in the design of a sophisticated GUI.

EVENT HANDLING

With the three steps covered thus far, you now know how to develop cool-looking GUIs but, again, they don't do anything. To enable your Java GUI applications to do anything worthwhile, you have to code your Java application to handle events that your application's components fire off as a result of user action—events such as keying text into a text field, clicking on a button, or selecting an item from a list box.

All AWT components generate *events*, which are objects that encapsulate information about the user's activity in a given component. Table 19.2 shows the basic AWT components and the events objects they generate. Note that the COMPONENT base class is the parent of all the other components. By order of inheritance, those other components also have the ability to generate sizing, focus, and keystroke events.

Table 19.2: AWT Components and Event Objects Generated.

Component	Events Generated	Event Description
Button	ActionEvent	User clicked on the button.
Checkbox	ItemEvent	User selected or deselected an item.
CheckboxMenuItem	ItemEvent	User selected or deselected an item.
Choice	ItemEvent	User selected or deselected an item.
Component	ComponentEvent	Component moved, resized, hidden, or shown.
	FocusEvent	Component gained or lost focus.
	MouseEvent	User pressed or released mouse button, mouse entered or exited component, or user moved or dragged mouse.
List	ActionEvent	User double-clicked on list item.
	ItemEvent	User selected or deselected an item.
MenuItem	ActionEvent	User selected a menu item.
TextComponent	TextEvent	User changed text.
TextField	ActionEvent	User finished editing text.
Window	WindowEvent	Window opened, closed, iconified, deiconified, or requested close.
Scrollbar	AdjustmentEvent	User moved the scrollbar.

On the AS/400, your 5250's user interface has one event. That event takes place when an active record format is sent to your program with the Enter key, Help key, Rollup key, Rolldown key, or one of the 24 function keys. Your RPG program sits in the driver's seat while a big loop processes that information and then slaps another dull 5250 record format onto the display. With Java, the user takes the driver's seat; he or she can generate any number of events from components on potentially a variety of panels. Java GUI programming involves more difficulty than good old 5250 DDS, but users often are happier and potentially are more productive with a GUI.

AWT event handling revolves around three objects: the source object, the event object, and the listener object. The source object can be any AWT component, and the event is an object created by that component to encapsulate user action. That event object is then sent (or *broadcast*, as the AWT designers call it) to any objects whose class is coded to respond to the event and has already been registered with the source object as an interested party.

The source objects are any of the AWT components listed in Table 19.1. Your job entails coding a Java class to handle the events objects generated by the components. Perhaps you want to handle a click of a button by calling an AS/400 program. Or maybe you want to delete a record from a DB2/400 data file when a user double-clicks an item in a list box. Or maybe you just want to add a value from a text field to a list box when a user clicks on an add button. Figure 19.13 graphically shows how the source generates an event object and passes it to the listener object coded to handle it.

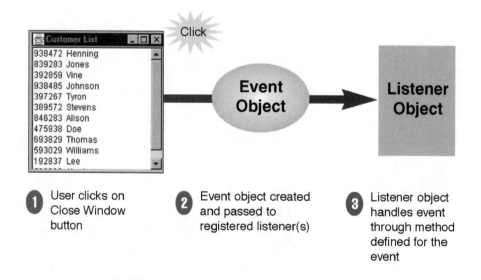

Figure 19.13: Java's event-handling model revolves around three objects: source, event, and listener objects.

INSIDER INFORMATION

To use an analogy to the Java event-driven model, let's say you hear about this guy who has the inside scoop on sports. You know– recent injuries, illnesses, perhaps morale problems—anything that could have some effect on a game. So you send this guy, this source, a note. On this note, you ask him to put your fax number on his list and to let you know when something interesting happens. You might be the only person on that list but, more than likely, there are many. When something happens, your source sends you and all the other people on his list a fax with information relating to the event.

When you get this fax, you might respond by calling your bookie. The other people on the list might respond similarly, but they can do whatever they want with that same piece of information. For instance, your own bookie might also be on the list and revise the odds for the game. The source himself could also respond to the event by placing his own bet.

The Java 1.1 event-handling model works similarly. Each AWT component has an internal list of listeners. You can register interested parties (classes) with a component so that those classes receive notification when an event occurs within that component. Registration takes place by invoking the ADDXYZLISTENER() function of the component (where XYZ refers to the event type specific to the AWT component). For instance, the LIST class defines the ADDACTION LISTENER() and ADDITEMLISTENER() functions so users of the LIST class can register LISTENER classes to be notified in case of an ACTIONEVENT or ITEMEVENT.

Java 1.1's event-handling model is commonly referred to as the *source-event-listener model*. The source in the sports analogy is the unscrupulous insider; the event might have been a sports injury; and the listener is anyone interested enough to register with the source (and pay him). With an AWT component placed in a Java applet or application's container, the source is the AWT component. The event is specific to that component and also the events inherited from the COMPONENT superclass. The listener is any class prepared to react to an event notification that has registered with the component by invoking that component's ADDXYZLISTENER() function.

LISTENER INTERFACES

You can't just add any old class as an interested party to a component. The listener class must be prepared to receive notifications from the event source; and such classes prepare themselves by implementing a standard AWT listener interface. (If you skipped the chapter on interfaces—chapter 8—now's the time to go back and read it). Table 19.3 lists 10 listener interfaces along with their functions and the events with which the listener is associated.

Table 19.3: Listener Interfaces, Functions, and Events. (Part 1 of 2)

Component	Listener interface	Listener function
ActionEvent	ActionListener	actionPerformed()
AdjustmentEvent	AdjustmentListener	adjustmentValueChanged()
ComponentEvent	ComponentListener	componentHidden()
		componentMoved()
		componentResized()
		componentShown()
FocusEvent	FocusListener	focusGained()
ItemEvent	ItemListener	itemStateChanged()
KeyEvent	KeyListener	keyPressed()
		keyReleased()
		keyTyped()
MouseEvent	MouseListener	mouseClicked()
		mouseEntered()
		mouseExited()
		mousePressed()
		mouseReleased()
	MouseMotionListener	mouseDragged()
		mouseMoved()

Table 19.3: Listener Interfaces, Functions, and Events. (Part 2 of 2)

Component	Listener interface	Listener function
TextEvent	TextListener	textValueChanged()
WindowEvent	WindowListener	windowActivated()
		windowClosed()
		windowClosing()
		windowDeactivated()
		windowDeiconified()
		windowIconified()
		windowOpened()

A good example of an event that should always be handled is the main application window-closing event. With Java, if you do not explicitly code an application (not an applet) to handle the window close event, the application cannot be closed. Figure 19.14 shows the Java code for an application that presents only a window frame with no components. The application's constructor, DULLAPPLICATION(), adds a listener that is coded to shut down the application when a user selects CLOSE from the WINDOW FRAME menu. The DULLAPPLISTENER class implements the WINDOWLISTENER Interface.

```
import java.awt.*;import java.awt.event.*;
public class DullApplication extends Frame {
  public static void main(String args[]) {
    DullApplication app = new DullApplication("Dull App");
    app.show();
  }
  public DullApplication (String frameTitle) {
    super(frameTitle);
      // helper class is the listener
    DullAppListener appListener = new DullAppListener();
    addWindowListener(appListener);
```

Figure 19.14: The DULLAPPLICATION class implements the WINDOWLISTENER interface so that it can handle the window-closing event. (Part 1 of 2)

```
    }
  }
  class DullAppListener implements WindowListener {
    public void windowClosing(WindowEvent event) {
      Window window = (Window)event.getSource();
      window.dispose();
      System.exit(0);
    }
    // null implementations for events that we don't care about:
   public void windowActivated(WindowEvent event) {}
    public void windowClosed(WindowEvent event) {}
    public void windowDeactivated(WindowEvent event) {}
    public void windowDeiconified(WindowEvent event) {}
    public void windowIconified(WindowEvent event) {}
    public void windowOpened(WindowEvent event) {}
  }
```

Figure 19.14: The DULLAPPLICATION class implements the WINDOWLISTENER interface so that it can handle the window-closing event. (Part 2 of 2)

The WINDOWLISTENER interface has seven functions to handle a variety of events (Figure 19.15), but the current example focuses only on the WINDOWCLOSE event. The WINDOWCLOSING() function, therefore, is the only one for which I provide real code. The others I simply designate as null functions with empty curly braces since I must provide implementations for all functions inherited from an interface. The DULLAPPLICATION() constructor function instantiates a DULLAPPLISTENER object and then adds it as a window listener with the ADDWINDOWLISTENER() function. Now when the user selects CLOSE, the application reacts as the user would expect.

```
interface WindowListener {
  public void windowClosing(WindowEvent event);
  public void windowActivated(WindowEvent event);
  public void windowClosed(WindowEvent event);
  public void windowDeactivated(WindowEvent event);
  public void windowDeiconified(WindowEvent event);
  public void windowIconified(WindowEvent event);
  public void windowOpened(WindowEvent event);
}
```

Figure 19.15: The WINDOWLISTENER interface has seven functions that will be called for a variety of events.

THREE WAYS TO SKIN A CAT

The old saying "there is more than one way to skin a cat" works just as well with Java event handling. Earlier I skinned that cat by creating a helper class that implements an interface. Figure 19.14 defines the helper class, DullAppListener, that implements the WindowListener interface.

That leaves two other ways to skin this particular cat. The second way is to have the component source class itself implement the listener interface—in effect, the source listens to itself. In the example Java application of Figure 19.16, the DULLAPPLICATION class extends the AWT Frame class but it also implements the WINDOWLISTENER Interface.

```
public class DullApplication extends Frame implements
WindowListener {
  public static void main(String args[]) {
      new DullApplication("Dull App").show();
  }
  public DullApplication (String frameTitle) {
    super(frameTitle);
      addWindowListener(this); // Source may be the Listener
  }
  public void windowClosing(WindowEvent event) {
    ((Window)event.getSource()).dispose();
    System.exit(0);
  }
  public void windowActivated(WindowEvent event) {}
  public void windowClosed(WindowEvent event) {}
  public void windowDeactivated(WindowEvent event) {}
  public void windowDeiconified(WindowEvent event) {}
  public void windowIconified(WindowEvent event) {}
  public void windowOpened(WindowEvent event) {}
}
```

Figure 19.16: The source of an AWT event may also register itself as a listener, provided it implements the proper listener interface.

Notice how this version of the DULLAPPLICATION class has to implement all the listener interfaces as the DULLAPPLISTENER helper class did in Figure 19.14. Then the DULLAPPLICATION class registers itself with the ADDWINDOW LISTENER function. It uses the Java keyword THIS to refer to itself. Then, when DULLAPPLICATION's frame generates an event (the window-closing event), the

DULLAPPLICATION notifies itself so that it can respond by closing the window and shutting down the application.

An application handling its own window-closing event serves as one example of a source listening to itself, but let me give you another. Suppose you have a button that, when pressed, sets the state of an application. Perhaps it is a CONNECT button for attaching to the AS/400. When the user clicks on that button, another class stands ready to handle that event and establish AS/400 connectivity; but you want the button itself to respond to the click by changing its appearance to look as if someone has pressed it. When the button remains depressed, the users have a graphical indication that CONNECT was already selected. You might also code that same button to respond to the mouse event (inherited from the COMPONENT AWT class). Your button responds by presenting a tool tip that explains the purpose and use of that button when the user's mouse enters the button area. Your button then drops the tool tip when the user's mouse pointer leaves the button.

That's only two cat-skinning strategies. The third approach calls for the source to create an *inner class.* Once you feel comfortable with the advanced concept of inner classes, you'll find they make the handling of events easy. In Figure 19.17, notice that the ADDWINDOWLISTENER function creates a WINDOWADAPTER object as the object that is registered to handle window events. Okay, you say, I know that you can create an object on the fly, but what is a WINDOWADAPTER and why does the definition for the WINDOWCLOSING function fall within the ADDWINDOWLISTENER function's parentheses? You'll get the answers, but one question at a time, please.

```
public class DullApplication extends Frame {
  public static void main(String args[])
  {new DullApplication("Dull App").show();}
  public DullApplication (String frameTitle) {
    super(frameTitle);
      //  inner class handles event
    addWindowListener(new WindowAdapter() {
      public void windowClosing(WindowEvent e) {
        ((Window)e.getSource()).dispose();
```

Figure 19.17: Inner classes can also be defined to handle an event; they are complex to understand but easy to code. (Part 1 of 2)

```
            System.exit(0);
        }});
    }
}
```

Figure 19.17: Inner classes can also be defined to handle an event; they are complex to understand but easy to code. (Part 2 of 2)

The inner class of Figure 19.17 instantiates a WINDOWADAPTER, one of a number of helper classes that AWT makes available (such as KEYADAPTER and MOUSEADAPTER). These helper classes implement each of the LISTENER interfaces. Their implementations, however, are all null (i.e., their implementations have no code). You could, for instance, add a WINDOWADAPTER as the window listener with the following code:

```
addWindowListener(new WindowAdapter());
```

However, a problem arises when the window-closing event occurs: The WINDOWADAPTER's window-closing function is invoked and does what the AWT designers told it to do—nothing. These various listener adapter classes are, by themselves, worthless.

Why does the definition for the WINDOWCLOSING function occur within the ADDWINDOWLISTENER function's parentheses? To make that WINDOWADAPTER class worthwhile, Java allows you to define a new Java class on the fly. These Java classes, known as inner classes, get defined inside of another class.

The WINDOWADAPTER class has functions that correspond to each of those in the WINDOWLISTENER interface. What you want to do is extend the WINDOWADAPTER class by redefining the WINDOWCLOSING function. You do so with the following steps (illustrated in Figure 19.18):

1. Immediately following the WINDOWADAPTER constructor function's right parenthesis, open up a new class definition's curly brace.

2. Redefine the function (within its own set of curly braces).

3. Close the new class definition with a curly brace.

4. Close ADDWINDOWLISTENER's function call with a right parenthesis.

```
addWindowListener(new WindowAdapter() {
      public void windowClosing(WindowEvent e) {
        ((Window)e.getSource()).dispose();
          System.exit(0);
}});
```

Figure 19.18: Many Java GUI applications define an inner class to handle the WIN-DOWCLOSING event by invoking the System class's EXIT function.

Of course, you don't have to use inner classes if you haven't gained a comfortable grasp of this advanced concept. But once you understand inner classes, you'll find they make the coding of Java event-handling routines much easier. You'll see this same example of inner-class usage over and over again in other people's code because it so elegantly handles the window-closing event.

HANDLING THE GUI SUMMARY EVENT

The final paragraphs of this chapter must of course handle the chapter-closing event. They handle this event by reiterating the four steps for creating a GUI and then summarizing event handling.

Step one for creating a Java GUI involves creating the desired components. In step two, you add the components into a container before arranging them within the container in step three. You can accomplish this third step with the help of layout managers (a good choice) or by hardcoding the alignment of components (a poor choice). Step four directs you to handle the events generated by those components.

Alas, step four is not so easy. First you must decide which of many component-generated events you need your applications to handle. Then you design listener classes by implementing the listener interface that corresponds to the event you wish to handle. Your custom listener class is coded to react to the event notification. You can then create an object of that class and register it with the component by invoking the ADDXYZLISTENER() function (where XYZ is the event name).

The rest is up to the user.

NOTHING WORTHWHILE IS EVER EASY

My father always answered my complaints about how difficult something was with "Nothing worthwhile is ever easy." Then, after I'd grumble, Dad would say, "If it's not worth doing, don't do it." Coding Java GUIs is *not* easy but it brings substantial benefits. Users love a GUI and they'll love you for giving them one. Java GUIs—any GUIs written in any language, for that matter—are hard to write because of the event-handling model of a graphical user interface. Consider the alternatives.

You can use an HTML front-end to your DB2/400 database applications with AS/400 host Java servlets. The HTML front-end then operates almost like 5250 coding. You present an HTML form which the user fills in before pressing the submit button. That form is sent to the AS/400 host server, and a Java servlet processes and dynamically builds an HTML form that responds to the user query. Another option entails the use of Domino as a sophisticated front-end with Domino Agents written in Java. The combination of Domino and Java will enable Internet access to DB2/400.

But if you want users to love you, create that GUI and don't discount the power of the various visual programming environments such as IBM's VisualAge for Java, Inprise's JBuilder, and Symantec's Visual Café.

20

USING
ENCAPSULATED BUSINESS
OBJECTS TO DEVELOP A GUI

Section IV introduced you to a strategy on mapping your relational database to Java objects. In that section, you learned to create Java classes that encapsulate the attributes and behaviors of business entities stored in DB2/400. This chapter provides a tutorial on how to use the example CUSTOMER class from chapter 15 in the development of two simple Java GUI applications. The first GUI presents individual customers and the second presents a list of customers.

Sometimes you don't understand the power of object-oriented programming until you start to use classes that you've developed. You expect classes that come standard with Java, such as the Abstract Windowing Toolkit (AWT) or Java Database Connectivity (JDBC) classes, to be well crafted. You might think of the AWT classes as part of the Java language, but actually they are *extensions* to the language. When you develop your own Java classes, they also become extensions to the Java language. Perhaps those extensions of Java pertain only to your company, but those classes are nevertheless a part of your application programming language. Further, because those classes model the real world, the names of those classes are also the language of the users.

DISPLAYCUSTOMER OVERVIEW

The DISPLAYCUSTOMER Java application initially presents an AWT TEXTFIELD component, so the user can enter a customer number, and an AWT BUTTON, so the user can say it's okay to get the customer associated with the number entered in the text field (Figure 20.1). When the OK button is clicked, the application instantiates a CUSTOMER object using the customer number that was entered in the AWT

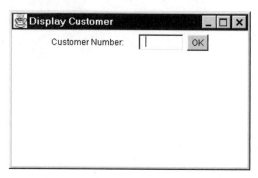

Figure 20.1: The Display Customer GUI prompts the user for the customer number.

TEXTFIELD component as a parameter to the CUSTOMER's constructor function. If a customer of that number exists, the application creates an AWT LABEL for each of the attributes of the CUSTOMER object. The text for those labels is the value of the attributes of the CUSTOMER object.

The DisplayCustomer class is itself an AWT frame so it extends the AWT FRAME class:

```
public class DisplayCustomer extends Frame
    implements ActionListener {
```

To enable the use of classes provided in the AWT package, the application imports the JAVA.AWT PACKAGE. So that it can handle AWT event classes, the application imports the JAVA.AWT.EVENT package. To have BIGDECIMAL objects to hold those fixed-point decimals for the packed and zoned fields of the customer master file, the application imports the JAVA.MATH class that contains the BIGDECIMAL class. It also imports the OBJECTTORELATIONAL package that performs AS/400 DB2/400 access. And, to catch and handle AS/400-specific exceptions, the application imports IBM's AS/400 access package as shown in Figure 20.2.

```
import java.awt.*;
import java.awt.event.*;
import java.math.*;
import com.ibm.as400.access.*;
import com.midrangecomputing.ObjectToRelational.*;
```

Figure 20.2: The DISPLAYCUSTOMER class imports standard Java packages, IBM's AS/400 access package, and my object-to-relational frameworks package.

The DISPLAYCUSTOMER class performs all four steps presented in chapter 18:

1. Create the components.
2. Add the components to a container.
3. Arrange, or lay out, the components within their containers.
4. Handle the events generated by the components.

The AWT components to be presented in the window frame of the DISPLAYCUSTOMER application are all declared as class-level fields so as not to limit the scope of those components to one function. If declared inside a function, the components go out of scope when the function completes execution. You can think of these AWT components as fields that are global to a class and, as a result, usable by all the functions of the class. The following three statements show how the text, add button, and one of the label fields are declared:

```
private Label lastName;
private TextField custNum;
private Button okButton;
```

The DISPLAYCUSTOMER application creates the OK BUTTON and TEXTFIELD components in its constructor:

```
custNum = new TextField(6);
okButton = new Button("OK");
```

DISPLAYCUSTOMER waits to create the labels that display the attributes of a customer until a CUSTOMER object is instanced in the ACTIONPERFORMED function (shown in its entirety in Figure 20.8). The DISPLAYCUSTOMER constructor function uses it parent's ADD function to add the TEXTFIELD and BUTTON components to the container, the application FRAME:

```
add(custNum);
add(okButton);
```

DISPLAYCUSTOMER arranges the components within their container (again, the frame) by creating a FLOWLAYOUT layout manager and setting the frame's layout manager with the FRAME class's SETLAYOUT function. Because DISPLAY CUSTOMER extends the FRAME class and therefore is a frame, it can invoke the public and private functions of its parent class– SETLAYOUT being one of them:

```
setLayout(new FlowLayout());
```

UPCOMING EVENTS

The only event handling that the DISPLAYCUSTOMER class does, other than the obligatory handling of the WINDOWCLOSING event, is the click of the OK button. Chapter 19 enumerates three ways to handle events, with one of those methods involving the use of an inner class. DISPLAYCUSTOMER adopts this inner-class method to handle the WINDOWCLOSING event, as shown in Figure 20.3.

```
addWindowListener( new WindowAdapter () {
    public void windowClosing(WindowEvent event) {
      Window window = (Window)event.getSource();
      window.dispose();
      System.exit(0);
}});
```

Figure 20.3: The DISPLAYCUSTOMER class handles the WINDOWCLOSING event with an inner class.

A second method of handling events enlists a helper class whose purpose is to handle events. The DISPLAYCUSTOMER class handles the click of its OK button with the third event-handling method: The class itself handles the events generated by the components that it contains by implementing the interface associated with that event. A look at DISPLAYCUSTOMER's class declaration statement reveals that, besides extending the AWT FRAME class, the statement also implements the ACTIONLISTENER interface:

```
public class DisplayCustomer extends Frame
    implements ActionListener {
```

The ACTIONLISTENER interface defines the ACTIONPERFORMED function, which the DISPLAYCUSTOMER class implements with code that responds to the user's click of the application's OK button:

```
public void actionPerformed(ActionEvent e) {…}
```

The DISPLAYCUSTOMER class registers itself to be notified when a user clicks on the OK button with the ADDACTIONLISTENER function:

```
okButton.addActionListener(this);
```

Here the ADDACTIONLISTENER function takes as a parameter the Java reserved word THIS, as if the application is saying, "If the user clicks my OK button, let me know and I'll handle it."

The DISPLAYCUSTOMER application handles a double-click of the OK button in its ACTIONPERFORMED function by attempting to instantiate a CUSTOMER object using the CUSTOMER's constructor function, which accepts a customer number as a parameter:

```
customer = new Customer(new BigDecimal(custNum.getText()));
```

The value of that customer number is retrieved with the GETTEXT function of DISPLAYCUSTOMER's customer number TEXTFIELD. That value is used to create the BIGDECIMAL object that is required as the parameter to the CUSTOMER constructor. If all goes well—that is, a corresponding customer record exists in the customer master file—a reference to a CUSTOMER object is returned to the customer variable. If something goes wrong, one of the catch clauses of the try block handles the exception. If an AS400EXCEPTION is thrown, the application handles it by adding a LABEL to the application's FRAME, with the text of the label bearing the AS/400 message:

```
AS400Message[] msgs = x.getAS400MessageList();
add(new Label((msgs[0]).toString()), BorderLayout.SOUTH);
```

But if everything goes smoothly and no exceptions are thrown or caught, the AC-TIONPERFORMED function checks for a customer who has a key value equal to the number the user entered in the TEXTFIELD component. To do so, AC-TIONPERFORMED queries the ISPERSISTENT function of the CUSTOMER class, as shown in Figure 20.4.

```
if (customer.isPersistent() == false) {
    new NoRecordDialog(this, custNum.getText());
    return;
}
```

Figure 20.4: DISPLAYCUSTOMER checks to see if the customer object is in DB2/400 using the ISPERSISTENT function.

The CUSTOMER class doesn't actually implement that ISPERSISTENT function; its implementation is coded in the RDBOBJECT base class. Regardless, the IS-PERSISTENT function simply indicates whether or not the CUSTOMER object is persistent in DB2/400. In other words, does the customer exist in the customer master file?

If the ISPERSISTENT function returns a false Boolean value, the ACTION-PERFORMED function creates a custom dialog class called NORECORD-DIALOG to inform the user that the customer was not found. Figure 20.5 displays the complete code for the NORECORDDIALOG class.

```
class NoRecordDialog extends Dialog {
  NoRecordDialog(Frame parent, String custNum) {
    super(parent, "Customer not found", true);
```

Figure 20.5: The NORECORDDIALOG class is used to present a dialog much like a Send Break Message (SNDBRKMSG) command does, except with a superior interface. (Part 1 of 2)

```
    addWindowListener( new WindowAdapter () {
      public void windowClosing(WindowEvent event) {
        Window window = (Window)event.getSource();
        window.dispose();
      }});
    setLayout(new FlowLayout());
    add(new Label(custNum));
    setSize(200,75);
    show();
  }
}
```

Figure 20.5: The NORECORDDIALOG class is used to present a dialog much like a Send Break Message (SNDBRKMSG) command does, except with a superior interface. (Part 2 of 2)

NORECORDDIALOG extends, as you might have guessed, AWT's DIALOG class. Its constructor passes to its DIALOG parent class, with a call to the SUPER function, the application FRAME object, a descriptive error string, and the Boolean true. The DIALOG class uses that information to construct a standard error dialog. NORECORDDIALOG's constructor function then adds the obligatory code to handle the window-closing event with a call to the ADDWINDOWLISTENER function and an inner class. NORECORDFOUND then sets the layout manager to FLOWLAYOUT, adds a LABEL that contains the customer number (that was not found in the customer master file), sets the size of the DIALOG, and then invokes the show function to present the dialog shown in Figure 20.6.

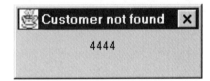

Figure 20.6: The error dialog informs the user that no customer matched the number entered.

From the information displayed in the NORECORDDIALOG dialog, the user knows that the customer was not found and can enter another customer number.

If the customer object is persistent in DB2/400, the DISPLAYCUSTOMER's AC-TIONPERFORMED function can obtain the values of the customer's attributes. The first time a customer is found, the ACTIONPERFORMED function must create the AWT labels to hold those values. The function uses another of the DISPLAY CUSTOMER class's global fields, the Boolean FIRSTPASS variable, to trigger this task. If FIRSTPASS is equal to true, the ACTIONPERFORMED function creates each of the required labels.

At the bottom of the if FIRSTPASS conditional block, you'll notice a call to a function named REPAINT. You call this a low-level AWT function to force the application frame to refresh its screen, sort of like an F5=REFRESH on the AS/400. Following the call to REPAINT, the ACTIONPERFORMED function sets the Boolean value of FIRSTPASS to false so the labels will not be re-created the next time the user clicks the OK button and a customer is found.

THE LABELS

Why does this application use labels? It seems like the use of AWT's TEXTFIELD component would work better, but the default behavior for a TEXTFIELD component allows modification of the value displayed in that text component. Users cannot change the value displayed in AWT's LABEL component. See Figure 20.7.

The text value for those labels is set with the CUSTOMER's GET functions. One final point to highlight in this application is that some of the CUSTOMER class's get functions return BIGDECIMAL objects. DISPLAYCUSTOMER's ACTIONPERFORMED function invokes the TOSTRING function over the returned BIGDECIMAL object. TOSTRING converts BIGDECIMAL to a STRING object that can then be inserted into the LABEL.

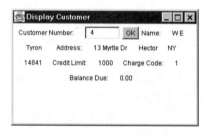

Figure 20.7: The DISPLAY CUSTOMER GUI simply lists the attributes of a customer as AWT LABEL components.

Figure 20.7 shows how the DISPLAYCUSTOMER application GUI looks after a customer is found, and Figure 20.8 shows the complete code for the DISPLAYCUSTOMER application.

```
import java.awt.*;
import java.awt.event.*;
import java.math.*;
import com.ibm.as400.access.*;
```

Figure 20.8: The programmer of the DISPLAYCUSTOMER application does not have to know anything about the AS/400 to develop a GUI because the DB2/400 access is encapsulated in the CUSTOMER class. (Part 1 of 4)

```
public class DisplayCustomer extends Frame
    implements ActionListener {
  private TextField custNum;
  private Label lastName;
  private Label firstMiddleInitials;
  private Label street;
  private Label city;
  private Label state;
  private Label zip;
  private Label creditLimit;
  private Label chargeCode;
  private Label balDue;
  private Label creditDue;

  private Button okButton;
  private boolean firstPass = true;
  private Customer customer;

  public DisplayCustomer() {
    super("Display Customer");

    // create components
    custNum = new TextField(6);
    okButton = new Button("OK");
    // add components to container
    add(new Label("Customer Number: "));;
    add(custNum);
    add(okButton);
    // arrange components within their containers
    setLayout(new FlowLayout());
    // handle component events
    okButton.addActionListener(this);
    addWindowListener(new WindowAdapter () {
      public void windowClosing(WindowEvent event) {
        ((Window)event.getSource()).dispose();
        System.exit(0);
    }});
  }
  public void actionPerformed(ActionEvent e) {
    try {
      customer = new Customer(new
BigDecimal(custNum.getText()));
```

Figure 20.8: The programmer of the DISPLAYCUSTOMER application does not have to know anything about the AS/400 to develop a GUI because the DB2/400 access is encapsulated in the CUSTOMER class. (Part 2 of 4)

```
    } catch (AS400Exception x) {
      AS400Message[] msgs = x.getAS400MessageList();
      add(new Label((msgs[0]).toString()), BorderLayout.SOUTH);
      return;
    } catch (Exception x) {
      System.out.println(x);
    }

    if (customer.isPersistent() == false) {
      new NoRecordDialog(this, custNum.getText());
      return;
    }

    if (firstPass == true) {
      lastName = new Label();
      firstMiddleInitials = new Label();
      street = new Label();
      city = new Label();
      state = new Label();
      zip = new Label();
      creditLimit = new Label();
      chargeCode = new Label();
      balDue = new Label();
      creditDue = new Label();
      add(new Label("Name: "));
      add(firstMiddleInitials);
      add(lastName);
      add(new Label("Address: "));
      add(street);
      add(city);
      add(state);
      add(zip);
      add(new Label("Credit Limit: "));
      add(creditLimit);
      add(new Label("Charge Code: "));
      add(chargeCode);
      add(new Label("Balance Due: "));
      add(balDue);
      repaint();
      firstPass = false;
    }
    lastName.setText(customer.getLSTNAM());
    firstMiddleInitials.setText(customer.getINIT());
```

Figure 20.8: The programmer of the DISPLAYCUSTOMER application does not have to know anything about the AS/400 to develop a GUI because the DB2/400 access is encapsulated in the CUSTOMER class. (Part 3 of 4)

```
      street.setText(customer.getSTREET());
      city.setText(customer.getCITY());
      state.setText(customer.getSTATE());
      zip.setText(customer.getZIPCOD().toString());
      creditLimit.setText(customer.getCDTLMT().toString());
      chargeCode.setText(customer.getCHGCOD().toString());
      balDue.setText(customer.getBALDUE().toString());
      creditDue.setText(customer.getCDTDUE().toString());
   }
   public static void main (String[] args) {
      DisplayCustomer cust = new DisplayCustomer();
      cust.show();
   }

}
```

Figure 20.8: The programmer of the DISPLAYCUSTOMER application does not have to know anything about the AS/400 to develop a GUI because the DB2/400 access is encapsulated in the CUSTOMER class. (Part 4 of 4)

THE LISTCUSTOMERS APPLICATION

The second example application, LISTCUSTOMERS, uses an AWT LIST box to present the names of customers that match an SQL selection criterion. The LISTCUSTOMERS class extends the AWT FRAME class. LISTCUSTOMERS sets its layout manager to a BORDERLAYOUT, adds a descriptive LABEL in the northern border, an AWT LIST box in its center, and a LABEL centered at the southern border of the FRAME as a note to the user. That note tells the user that a single click on a customer element of the list will present that customer's address.

The LISTCUSTOMERS class contains code to handle just one event: a single-click of an item of the LIST box. The AWT event associated with that event is the ITEMEVENT, which has a listener interface of ITEMLISTENER. Thus, the LISTCUSTOMERS class implements that interface:

```
public class ListCustomers
      extends Frame implements ItemListener
```

The LISTCUSTOMERS class then declares three class-level fields: a LIST, a LABEL, and a VECTOR. The VECTOR is later used to hold the list of CUSTOMER objects returned from a call to the CUSTOMER class's SEARCH function. The LISTCUSTOMERS' constructor function asks its parent to set the frame's title and then does the obligatory window-closing event handling. Then it sets the layout manager to AWT's BORDERLAYOUT. The constructor function adds a label to the frame before LABEL's overloaded constructor function centers the label in its container:

```
add(new Label(query, Label.CENTER), BorderLayout.NORTH);
```

The label called ADDRESS is then created and added to the frame:

```
address = new Label("Click on Customer for address", Label.CENTER);
add(address, BorderLayout.SOUTH);
```

The LIST is created next and added to the frame; then the LISTCUSTOMERS class is added as the LISTENER object for any ITEMEVENTS emitting from that list box:

```
list = new List();
add(list, BorderLayout.CENTER);
list.addItemListener(this);
```

The CUSTOMER class's SEARCH function retrieves customers into the CUSTS VECTOR object. A FOR loop spins through the vector, adding the initials and last names of all CUSTOMER objects in that vector to the list box as elements. The elements of the CUSTS vector are retrieved with the VECTOR class's ELEMENTAT function, as shown in Figure 20.9.

```
try {
  custs = Customer.search(query, new Customer());
  for (int i = 0; i < custs.size(); i++) {
    list.add(((Customer)custs.elementAt(i)).getINIT() + " " +
        ((Customer)custs.elementAt(i)).getLSTNAM());
  }
} catch (Exception e) {System.out.println(e);}
```

Figure 20.9: Elements of a Java vector can be retrieved with the VECTOR class's ELEMENTAT function.

This section of code does not handle exceptions well; LISTCUSTOMER just dumps the errors to the default output. Also, it would have been more efficient to pull the CUSTOMER object out of the CUSTS vector only once, as shown in Figure 20.10.

```
for (int i = 0; i < custs.size(); i++) {
  Customer aCust = (Customer)custs.elementAt(i);
  list.add(aCust.getINIT() + " " + aCust.getLSTNAM());
}
```

Figure 20.10: Each CUSTOMER element of the CUSTS vector is added to the list box.

Finally, the LISTCUSTOMERS constructor completes by setting the initial size of the frame:

```
setSize(400,300);
```

The LISTCUSTOMERS class must provide some implementation of the ITEMSTATECHANGED function—the only function of the ITEMLISTENER interface—because LISTCUSTOMERS uses the ITEMLISTENER interface. The ITEMSTATECHANGED function first removes the currently displayed address label with a call to the REMOVE function:

```
remove(address);
```

Then the ITEMSTATECHANGED function gets the index of the user-selected item with the ITEMEVENT object's GETITEM function. The GETITEM function returns an ambiguous OBJECT object so ITEMSTATECHANGED casts it to an Integer object and stores it in a variable called IDX:

```
Integer idx = (Integer)e.getItem();
```

The next line uses the INTEGER class's INTVALUE Function to retrieve the basic INT data value from the IDX INTEGER object. That INT value is used to get the CUSTOMER object in the CUSTS vector of customers (which was returned from the CUSTOMER class's search function in LISTCUSTOMERS' constructor):

```
Customer cust = (Customer)custs.elementAt(idx.intValue());
```

With the user-selected customer set, the ITEMSTATECHANGED function then creates a STRING object consisting of a concatenation of the customer's city, state, and zip code. That address STRING object is then used as a parameter to the LABEL object constructor. The new LABEL is then added to the frame as shown in Figure 20.11.

```
String addr = cust.getCITY() + ", " +
              cust.getSTATE() + " " +
              cust.getZIPCOD();
address = new Label(addr, Label.CENTER);
add(address, BorderLayout.SOUTH);
```

Figure 20.11: The city, state, and zip code are added to the southern border of the application panel as a label.

Because the components of the LISTCUSTOMERS GUI have changed, the VALIDATE function call asks the Java Virtual Machine to repaint the display:

```
validate();
```

The graphical user interface of the LISTCUSTOMERS application is shown in Figure 20.12. When a user selects a name from the customer list (with a single mouse click), that customer's address is displayed at the southern portion of the application's window frame. The complete code for the application is shown in Figure 20.13.

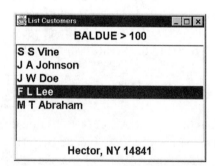

Figure 20.12: The LISTCUSTOMER application presents all customers with a balance due greater than 100.

```
import java.awt.*;
import java.awt.event.*;
import java.util.*;
import com.midrangecomputing.ObjectToRelational.*;
```

Figure 20.13: The LISTCUSTOMER application uses a set of CUSTOMER objects to present all customers with a balance due greater than 100. (Part 1 of 3)

```
public class ListCustomers
       extends Frame implements ItemListener
{
  private List list;
  private Label address;
  private Vector custs;

  public ListCustomers(String query) {
    super("List Customers");
    addWindowListener( new WindowAdapter () {
      public void windowClosing(WindowEvent event) {
        System.exit(0);
    }});
    setLayout(new BorderLayout());

    add(new Label(query, Label.CENTER), BorderLayout.NORTH);
    address = new Label("Click on Customer for address", Label.CENTER);
    add(address, BorderLayout.SOUTH);

    list = new List();
    add(list, BorderLayout.CENTER);
    list.addItemListener(this);

    try {
      custs = Customer.search(query, new Customer());
      for (int i = 0; i < custs.size(); i++) {
        list.add(((Customer)custs.elementAt(i)).getINIT() + " " +
                 ((Customer)custs.elementAt(i)).getLSTNAM());
      }
    } catch (Exception e) {System.out.println(e);}

    setSize(400,300);
  }
  public void itemStateChanged(ItemEvent e) {
    remove(address);
    Integer idx = (Integer)e.getItem();
    Customer cust = (Customer)custs.elementAt(idx.intValue());
    String addr = cust.getCITY() + ", " +
                  cust.getSTATE() + " " +
                  cust.getZIPCOD();
    address = new Label(addr, Label.CENTER);
    add(address, BorderLayout.SOUTH);
    validate();
```

Figure 20.13: The LISTCUSTOMER application uses a set of CUSTOMER objects to present all customers with a balance due greater than 100. (Part 2 of 3)

```
  }
  public static void main (String[] args) {
    ListCustomers custs = new ListCustomers("BALDUE > 100");
    custs.show();
  }

}
```

Figure 20.13: The LISTCUSTOMER application uses a set of CUSTOMER objects to present all customers with a balance due greater than 100. (Part 3 of 3)

SUMMARY

These two sample GUIs might seem overly trivial when compared to the robust GUIs required for real business applications. I've kept them simple so the AWT code remains easy to understand and learn.

One important point that underlies this chapter is the ease with which these applications interface with DB2/400. Nowhere do you see any code to attach to an AS/400, open a file, or access fields—that is all encapsulated in the CUSTOMER class.

The examples in this book use record-level access classes; but you can develop your own business classes to encapsulate DB2/400 business entities using one of the variety of relational database class wrapper tools, such as those that come bundled with Inprise's JBuilder and VisualAge for Java's Enterprise Editions. The important point is that you should separate the code that manages your business entities from your GUI applications. No longer should your user interface open files for update and directly modify your data.

21

DESIGNING PROFESSIONAL GUIs

For interactive application programming on the AS/400, nothing beats a subfile. Subfiles are so important to the AS/400 that the first question asked of job applicants who boast of their programming strengths is "Can you code subfiles?"

Through subfiles, interactive applications programmers can easily present multiple and related records on a 5250 terminal. Subfiles present a visual subset of a database file that can be written to, updated, and retrieved. Subfile records can contain the complete spectrum of AS/400 data types with sophisticated, built-in editing capabilities.

So what will the next generation of AS/400 programmers do with their Java applications to give users similar functionality? Having read this far into this book, you might now be wondering what will replace subfiles. The standard components that Java 1.1 supplies in its Abstract Windowing Toolkit (AWT) fall far short of providing anything that replaces a subfile. The AWT components do include a list box, but it only presents a simple list of unformatted strings, with no dynamic entry facilities and no support for various data types.

Like most of you, I have programmed more subfiles than I can remember. But I have also programmed Java graphical applications using a medium very similar to a subfile: the grid. A grid such as the one shown in Figure 21.1 resembles a spreadsheet with its two-dimensional table of rows and columns.

A grid, like a subfile, presents a set of related records in a tabular format. But a grid also provides significant advantages over subfiles. A grid supports undo and redo, its rows can be dynamically sorted, and each of its cells can contain visual editors like checkboxes, choice lists, and date calendars. And, because a grid is graphical, it can support images and window resizing and respond to typical windows events like keystrokes and mouse clicks. This chapter presents grids as the replacement paradigm for subfiles.

Customer Master Maintenance JTable Example			
Last Name	Customer No.	Uses Charge Card	Balance Due
Henning	11	☐	37.00
Jones	9	☑	100.00
Vine	3	☑	439.00
Johnson	12	☐	3987.50
Stevens	2	☑	58.75
Alison	10	☐	10.00
Doeskin	5	☐	250.00

Update

Figure 21.1: JFC's JTABLE can be used as a replacement strategy for subfiles.

GRIDS VERSUS SUBFILES

Grids are powerful software components; for years, C and C++ programmers have used the rows and columns that make up grids to present the records and fields of database files. Software components such as grids are reusable pieces of code that can be easily assembled to create applications. Using software components for development is much more efficient than developing the software yourself.

You can place a grid component on a window panel, and each cell within that grid contains a software component. Usually, all the elements for a particular grid column are assigned the same component. For instance, the third column in Figure 21.1 has a checkbox component assigned to it to allow the intuitive indication of a customer's charge card use. The component assigned to the other columns consists of a simple text string editor. The rows of a grid typically contain database records except for the first row, which is usually reserved for column headers. The header row normally contains simple labels, but often the labels are set as buttons to enable features such as a dynamic sort by a user-selected column.

The similarities between grids and subfiles are obvious. Both constructs present a subset of a database in tabular format, and you can browse through multiple pages of those records with scroll keys. Grids are also enhanced with scroll bars. The thumb button's position on the scroll bar gives the viewed record's relative position in the grid. The height of the thumb also gives some visual representation of the number of records in the grid based on its size relative to the window. But try to find something comparable to subfile record formats or subfile control record formats in Java grid classes and the analogy appears to break down.

What you are dealing with is a paradigm shift from subfiles to grids. This shift seems overwhelming, but keep in mind what it was like when you first began to learn DDS. Also, keep in mind that, by learning and understanding grids, you will acquire the full benefits of the broad capabilities of both grids and object-oriented programming.

GRID CHOICES

A perplexing problem with grids is that you have so many to choose from. With subfiles, as with almost everything in your AS/400 programming arsenal, you have one choice—IBM. However, with grids come alternatives. I have used grids from four different vendors: Stingray, Rogue Wave, Microsoft, and SunSoft. Another grid worth mentioning, Taligent's MULTICOLUMNLISTBOX, is used in the Java examples found in IBM's Redbook, *Accessing the AS/400 System with Java*. Taligent's grid, while extremely simple to use, does not provide the breadth of capabilities that other grid vendors provide in their products. Both Stingray and Rogue Wave deliver industrial-strength grids—but at a price. SunSoft's grid, JTable, as a standard part of the base Java 1.2 Java Virtual Machine (JVM), is free. Microsoft's grid component is also free.

MICROSOFT'S AFC VERSUS SUNSOFT'S JFC

SunSoft's JTable grid is one of the main components of its Java Foundation Classes (JFC), just as Microsoft's grid is a part of its Application Foundation Classes (AFC).

You might have been following the feud between Microsoft and SunSoft; one of their skirmishes concerns JFC and AFC. SunSoft decided to make JFC a standard part of Java 1.2, so JFC classes need not be dynamically downloaded for Web applications that use JFC components—as long as the Web browser running the applet is SunSoft-compliant. Microsoft's browser, Internet Explorer (IE), does not and will not include JFC. Rather, it will include AFC. Microsoft claims to have no intention of supporting SunSoft's JFC because the Microsoft technology is better. Microsoft also does not support standard Java's Remote Method Invocation (RMI) or Java Native Interface (JNI), both of which are vital to AS/400 Java Web or client/server applications.

You can get Microsoft's AFC-based applets to work with Netscape, but it is not simple or straightforward. On the other hand, SunSoft's JFC will work in IE, although you have to dynamically download the classes because they are not in the IE JVM. If you intend to limit your Java applications to platforms based on Microsoft's operating system, AFC is probably a reasonable choice. However, I suggest that you start application development with JTABLE and review third-party grids for features that may be important for your application. The JFC components have been widely accepted. The JFC beta program was a rampant success, and I am confident that JFC will prevail as the Java package used for programming Java GUIs.

THE JTABLE GRID

I developed the example Java grid application displayed in Figure 21.1 using JFC's JTable. JTable, like all the JFC components and JFC's AWT ancestors as well, conforms to the JavaBean specification. Sun's JavaBean specification is now the industry standard interface for Java components (although Microsoft might not agree). Once you use and learn one component written to the JavaBean standard, you'll find it easier to pick up and use other components that also follow this standard. JFC use should be widespread because it is powerful, well designed, easily extensible, and free. For example, IBM's Java Toolbox for the AS/400 visual access JavaBeans were developed using the JFC package.

Implementing an application that employs a JTable grid requires the use of a group of Java classes, only one of which is named JTable. This makes it rather confusing when you first begin to use JFC's JTable grid. But JTable and its supporting classes are designed so that each class encapsulates functionality specific to one conceptual area.

These JTable classes are implemented with an architecture known as *Document/View*. This architecture separates the code for data manipulation (the document) from the code for data display (the view) into different classes. The JTABLE class handles the graphical presentation (the view of the data). The document class is your application's implementation of the associated JTABLE class—ABSTRACTDATAMODEL. In the example application, the class derivation of ABSTRACTDATAMODEL is called CUSTOMERDATAMODEL. (The complete code for this example application appears at the end of this chapter in Figures 21.29 and 21.30.)

The main function of the CUSTOMERSUBFILE Java application contains only the two statements shown in Figure 21.2.

```
public static void main(String[] parms) {
    CustomerSubfile sfl = new CustomerSubfile();
    sfl.setVisible(true);
}
```

Figure 21.2: The MAIN function of the CUSTOMERSUBFILE class invokes its constructor and then sets its graphical state to visible.

This MAIN function is invoked when you specify CUSTOMERSUBFILE as a parameter to the JAVA.EXE program:

```
JAVA.EXE CustomerSubfile
```

The Java Virtual Machine automatically calls CUSTOMERSUBFILE's MAIN function, which is coded to bootstrap the application by invoking Java's NEW operator on the CUSTOMERSUBFILE constructor function. Then the Java application's

MAIN function makes the "subfile" component visible on the screen with the SETVISIBLE function.

The CUSTOMERSUBFILE extends JFRAME to present the top-level application window; to this CUSTOMERSUBFILE derivation of the JFRAME, I will add the JTABLE "subfile." The CUSTOMERSUBFILE's constructor function begins by asking its JFRAME parent class's constructor to set the frame's title with a call to the SUPER function. The SETSIZE function then sets the size of the frame. Then, to handle the window-closing event, an inner class simply performs the system EXIT function as shown in Figure 21.3.

```
public CustomerSubfile() {
  super("Customer Master Maintenance JTable Example");
  setSize (500, 200);
  addWindowListener( new WindowAdapter () {
    public void windowClosing(WindowEvent event)
{System.exit(0);
  }});
```

Figure 21.3: The constructor function sets the frame's title and size and then uses an inner class to handle the WINDOWCLOSING event.

So far everything sounds similar to an AWT application, and, for the most part, applications that use the JFC components *are* similar to AWT applications. The next few statements, however, fulfill a requirement for JFC applications.

For some odd reason, you can't add components directly to the JFRAME object. All JFC applications have what's known as the topmost panel. Following the ADDWINDOWLISTENER function, the CUSTOMERSUBFILE constructor creates a JPANEL object called TOPPANEL and invokes a strange function called GET-CONTENTPANE. The GETCONTENTPANE function retrieves a JFRAME component that the Sun designers call a root pane and allows you to add a panel to that root component. To that panel, you add the other components of the application, which is why I called mine TOPPANEL.

CUSTOMERSUBFILE's constructor then sets the layout manager of that topmost panel to BORDERLAYOUT as shown in Figure 21.4.

```
JPanel topPanel = new JPanel();
getContentPane().add( topPanel );
topPanel.setLayout(new BorderLayout());
```

Figure 21.4: The topmost panel is set as the content pane for the application.

THE VIEW

The CUSTOMERSUBFILE class constructor function creates the document object that contains and manages the data to be presented in the JTABLE view object with the following statement:

```
custDataModel = new CustomerDataModel(topPanel, "BALDUE > 0");
```

In the document/view architecture of a JTable grid, the CUSTOMERDATAMODEL object represents the document and the JTABLE object creates the view. The document is associated with the view by passing it as the parameter of JTABLE's constructor:

```
JTable sfl = new JTable (custDataModel);
```

Notice the use of a custom data model class called CUSTOMERDATAMODEL in conjunction with the use of the default JTABLE class. The JTABLE class visually presents a two-dimensional table but delegates the acquisition and processing of the data displayed within its grid to the document object.

THE DOCUMENT

To clarify this association between the instance variable and the JTABLE, I prefer to jump ahead to a description of the CUSTOMERDATAMODEL class (the API listing of which is shown in Figure 21.5). As the document handler, the CUSTOMERDATAMODEL object has the job of retrieving data and passing it on to the view (the JTABLE). It also performs the job of managing any changes that may be made to the data from within the view object (JTABLE).

The JTABLE view object collaborates with the CUSTOMERDATAMODEL document object by invoking the functions of CUSTOMERDATAMODEL. JTABLE

retrieves the data headers, for instance, from CUSTOMERDATAMODEL's GET-
COLUMNNAME function. It retrieves the values of the data from the GET-
VALUEAT function. JTABLE finds out how many rows and columns to present
with the GETROWCOUNT and GETCOLUMNCOUNT functions. JTABLE can tell if
one of the data elements presented in its grid is modifiable by calling CUSTOMER-
DATAMODEL's ISCELLEDITABLE function. And, if a user does change data in a
grid element's data, the JTABLE delegates the responsibility of modifying the database by calling CUSTOMERDATAMODEL's SETVALUEAT function.

All of the functions just mentioned are defined in a standard JFC class called
ABSTRACTDATAMODEL. All but the last three functions shown in Figure 21.5
have default implementations in the ABSTRACTTABLEMODEL. The ISCELL-
EDITABLE function, for instance, which returns a Boolean value, is implemented
in ABSTRACTTABLEMODEL to always return a false (effectively disabling modification of the data presented in the grid).

For most of your JTABLE applications, you'll need to override ABSTRACT-
TABLEMODEL's implementation of these functions in a derived class. But you
must define functions for those last three functions shown in Figure 21.5. That's
because GETCOLUMNCOUNT, GETROWCOUNT, and GETVALUEAT are all defined
as abstract functions in the ABSTRACTTABLEMODEL class, which may be how
ABSTRACTTABLEMODEL got part of its name. The UPDATE function? Well, okay,
I added that one so that the application could specify when to put the data
changes to DB2/400.

```
class CustomerDataModel extends AbstractTableModel {
   public CustomerDataModel(JPanel container, String
whereClause);
   public void update();
   // functions inherited from the AbstractTableModel class:
   public String getColumnName(int column);
   public Class getColumnClass(int col);
   public boolean isCellEditable(int row, int col);
   public void setValueAt(Object aValue, int aRow, int aColumn);
   // AbstractTableModel functions that must be implemented:
   public int getColumnCount();
```

Figure 21.5: The CUSTOMERDATAMODEL class overrides many of the functions inherited
from its ABSTRACTTABLEMODEL superclass. (Part 1 of 2)

```
    public int getRowCount();
    public Object getValueAt(int aRow, int aCol);
}
```

Figure 21.5: The CUSTOMERDATAMODEL class overrides many of the functions inherited from its ABSTRACTTABLEMODEL superclass. (Part 2 of 2)

POPULATE THE GRID

Now with that introduction to the CUSTOMERDATAMODEL aside, it's time to describe its implementation. The CUSTOMERDATAMODEL's constructor builds the data model's internal storage of data in the RECORDS vector (see Figure 21.6). It does not, as you might expect, jump right in and populate the data to be shown in the JTABLE grid. Remember that the JTABLE is a view. The actual data buffer resides in the data model—the CUSTOMERDATAMODEL.

The RECORDS vector is essentially a two-dimensional array, and another name for a two-dimensional array is a grid or table. That vector is filled from CUSTOMER objects that have been retrieved with the SEARCH function. Note that the vector could be built in any manner from any type of data. For the purpose of this example, the data is retrieved with the example business class developed in Section IV of this book.

CUSTOMERDATAMODEL's constructor function loops through all the elements in the vector of customers returned from the CUSTOMER class's SEARCH function. For each of those CUSTOMER objects, the last name, customer number, and charge code values are added as a new row of the RECORDS vector. Note too that because I will allow data to be modified within the grid, the CUSTOMERDATAMODEL has an array of Boolean values that keeps track of whether or not the user has modified one of the rows of the RECORDS vector. You can think of the elements of that array as modified data tags. Anyway, the constructor's loop sets each element of the MODIFIEDRECORD array to the initial value of false.

```
class CustomerDataModel extends AbstractTableModel {
   final String[] headers =
     {"Last Name","Customer No.","Uses Charge Card", "Balance
Due"};
```

Figure 21.6: The CUSTOMERDATAMODEL builds a VECTOR of customer records in its constructor. (Part 1 of 2)

```
private Vector records = new Vector();
private boolean modifiedRecord[];
private Vector custs = null;
private JPanel container = null;

public CustomerDataModel(JPanel container, String whereClause)
{
  this.container = container;
  try {
    custs = Customer.search(whereClause, new Customer());
  } catch (Exception e) {System.out.println(e);}
  modifiedRecord = new boolean[custs.size()];
  for (int i = 0; i < custs.size(); i++) {
    Customer cust = (Customer)custs.elementAt(i);
    Vector newRow = new Vector();
    newRow.addElement(cust.getLSTNAM());
    newRow.addElement(cust.getCUSNUM().toString());
    int chargeCode = (cust.getCHGCOD().intValue());
    newRow.addElement(new Boolean(chargeCode == 1));
    newRow.addElement(cust.getBALDUE().toString());
    records.addElement(newRow);
    modifiedRecord[i] = false;
  }
}
```

Figure 21.6: The CUSTOMERDATAMODEL builds a VECTOR of customer records in its constructor. (Part 2 of 2)

The CUSTOMERDATAMODEL's constructor function accepts two parameters: a JPANEL and a STRING that contains an SQL WHERE clause. The JPANEL is a handle to the container that houses the JTABLE (for this example, it is the application's topmost panel). The CUSTOMERDATAMODEL object needs a handle to that panel when it pops up an error dialog (error handling receives more detailed coverage later). The SQL STRING parameter is used in the call to the CUSTOMER class's SEARCH function to specify the selection criterion. Realize that this constructor and its parameters are application-specific; you implement your own version of an ABSTRACTTABLEMODEL-derived class's constructor as necessary for your application.

HEADERS

Presenting headers for the data of a table is easy. You just define a STRING array (see the top of Figure 21.3) and then override ABSTRACTDATAMODEL'S GETCOLUMNNAME function in the derived class:

```
public String getColumnName(int column) {
    return headers[column];
}
```

MINIMUM REQUIREMENTS

When you code your own DATAMODEL class (by extending ABSTRACTDATA-MODEL), you must provide code implementations for the GETROWCOUNT, GETCOLUMNCOUNT, and GETVALUEAT functions. CUSTOMERDATAMODEL'S implementation of these functions is minimal. For instance, in this example, GETCOLUMNCOUNT simply returns the length of the headers array; and GET-ROWCOUNT returns the number of elements in the RECORDS vector, which CUSTOMERDATAMODEL'S constructor retrieved from the CUSTOMER class's SEARCH function:

```
public int getColumnCount() { return headers.length; }
public int getRowCount() { return records.size();}
```

CUSTOMERDATAMODEL implements the GETVALUEAT function by returning the value of the element in vector RECORDS that corresponds to a grid cell, as shown in Figure 21.7.

```
public Object getValueAt(int aRow, int aCol) {
   Vector row = (Vector)records.elementAt(aRow);
   return row.elementAt(aCol);
}
```

Figure 21.7: The value of an element of the JTABLE is retrieved with the getValueAt function.

Through the custom implementation of these ABSTRACTDATAMODEL functions, a JTABLE knows how to paint a grid on the screen. JTABLE knows how many columns the grid should have from CUSTOMERDATAMODEL'S implementation of the GETCOLUMNCOUNT function, and it knows how many rows to place in the grid from CUSTOMERDATAMODEL'S GETROWCOUNT function.

JTABLE also knows which data values to place in each element of its grid because it calls the GETVALUEAT function iteratively for each element of its table. You do not code the calls to these functions; you merely provide the implementations for them. Sun's implementation of the JTABLE class calls your derived class's versions of the functions that were originally declared in the ABSTRACTDATAMODEL class.

COLUMN ATTRIBUTES

The JTABLE view object finds out the data type of the columns of its grid by invoking the document's GETCOLUMNCLASS function. The ABSTRACTDATAMODEL's version of this function is implemented to return the default class of JTEXTFIELD. If you intend to use a class other than JTEXTFIELD for any of your grid's columns, your derived class must override this GETCOLUMNCLASSFUNCTION.

Being inherently lazy, I code only what I have to in CUSTOMERDATAMODEL's overriding version of ABSTRACTDATAMODEL's GETCOLUMNCLASS. As depicted in Figure 21.1, the third field presented in the grid is a checkbox (indexed by the number 2), which represents a yes or no condition, a Boolean value. You'll see later that I take a value from DB2/400 and convert it to a Boolean. At any rate, because the third column is not a JTEXTFIELD, I override ABSTRACTDATA-MODEL's GETCOLUMNCLASS to specify Boolean for the third element of the JTABLE grid.

For the other columns of the grid, CUSTOMERDATAMODEL's version of GETCOLUMNCLASS turns around and uses its parent class's version (using the SUPER qualifier) to return the class of the requested column. My inherently lazy nature turns out to be good coding style because none of the code already in the base class has been duplicated, as Figure 21.8 shows.

```
public Class getColumnClass(int col) {
  if (col == 2)
    return Boolean.class;
  else
    return super.getColumnClass(col);
}
```

Figure 21.8: The GETCOLUMNCLASS function is overridden to explicitly specify the class of a column.

READ ONLY

ABSTRACTDATAMODEL's default behavior for all the columns of a grid is to make all of them read-only. The JTABLE view finds out if a column is modifiable through a call to the document object's ISCELLEDITABLE function. If my CUSTOMERDATAMODEL class had not overridden ISCELLEDITABLE, its parent class's version would return a false Boolean value for all rows of the table. Because I want my table to allow updates to the values in the first and third columns (last name and charge code), I code CUSTOMERDATAMODEL's ISCELLEDITABLE to return a value of true for column indexes zero and two and false for the other columns, as shown in Figure 21.9.

```
public boolean isCellEditable(int row, int col) {
  switch (col) {
    case 0:   return true;
    case 2:   return true;
    default:  return false;
  }
}
```

Figure 21.9: The ISCELLEDITABLE function is overridden when you want to allow modifications to a grid element.

Because the ISCELLEDITABLE function returns a true value for column zero, users are able to enter modifications, as Figure 21.10 illustrates.

The funny and yet powerful feature about the JTABLE component is that if you do override ABSTRACTDATAMODEL's ISCELLEDITABLE function without overriding the SETVALUEAT function, the user can modify values on the grid but the data will return to its original value once the user exits that value's cell. You see, once the user exits the cell, the JTABLE component passes those changes to the SETVALUEAT function. The SETVALUEAT function has the job of modifying the document object's internal value of the data. JTABLE then invokes CUSTOMER-DATAMODEL's GETVALUEAT function to get the new value for that cell and, if you don't code a SETVALUEAT function, the user modification cannot be passed back to JTABLE when JTABLE calls your GETVALUEAT function. As a result, the screen would not reflect the user's changes.

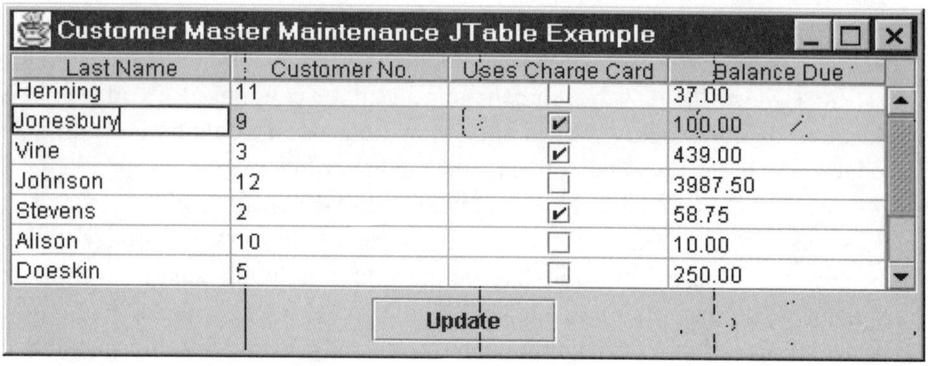

Figure 21.10: To allow a field to be modifiable, you have to code the ISCELLEDITABLE function to return a value of true for that field's column.

In the example CUSTOMERDATAMODEL, the values for the grid are stored in the RE-CORDS vector. It would not have been difficult to incorporate the user's modifications into the RECORDS vector, but I want to perform validations against those changes.

Remember that the CUSTOMERDATAMODEL's constructor keeps a vector of the CUSTOMER objects the attributes of which are presented in the grid. When CUSTOMERDATAMODEL's SETVALUEAT function is invoked (see Figure 21.11), the SETVALUEAT function uses the row number to access the specific CUSTOMER object represented in the grid for that row:

```
Customer cust = (Customer)custs.elementAt(aRow);
```

Validation then becomes a simple matter of using the CUSTOMER class's set functions. Figure 21.11 does not actually contain any code for validation; it simply invokes the SET functions, which, in turn, throw an exception if the value is invalid. In fact, when coding this routine, I didn't even remember which exceptions each SET function could throw. The compiler reminded me by sending compilation errors that told me to add try/catch blocks for specific exceptions.

```
public void setValueAt(Object aValue, int aRow, int aColumn) {
    Customer cust = (Customer)custs.elementAt(aRow);
    switch (aColumn) {
```

Figure 21.11: Validation of modified columns occurs through the SETVALUEAT function. (Part 1 of 2)

```
      case 0:
        try {
          cust.setLSTNAM((String)aValue);
        } catch (InvalidLengthException error) {
          JOptionPane errorDialog = new JOptionPane();
          errorDialog.showMessageDialog(container,
              error.toString(), "Error",
            JOptionPane.ERROR_MESSAGE);
          return;
        }
        break;
      case 2:
        if (((Boolean)aValue).booleanValue() == true)
          cust.setCHGCOD(new BigDecimal("1"));
        else
          cust.setCHGCOD(new BigDecimal("0"));
        break;
    }
    modifiedRecord[aRow] = true;

    // change the value of the internal table
    Vector row = (Vector)records.elementAt(aRow);
    row.setElementAt(aValue, aColumn);
  }
```

Figure 21.11: Validation of modified columns occurs through the SETVALUEAT function. (Part 2 of 2)

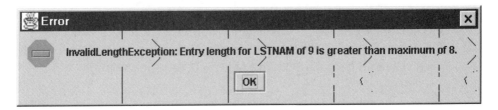

Figure 21.12: JFC's JOPTIONPANE can be used to present an informative dialog to the user.

If an application exception is thrown, the CATCH clause uses a handy JFC component called JOPTIONPANE to present an informative dialog to the user, as Figure 21.12 shows. Because the Boolean values of column three in the grid can only be true or false, no validation is needed. But if the call to the SET-LSTNAM function throws an exception, SETVALUEAT catches it, presents an error dialog to inform the user, and returns without modifying the document's data stored in the RECORDS vector.

(Note that the JOPTIONPANE dialog uses that container JPanel variable that was passed to CUSTOMERDATAMODEL's construction. When the user exits the dialog, JOPTIONPANE makes the window that is specified in the container the active window. That way control returns to the application's main window frame.)

No caught exceptions indicate that the SET function successfully modified the CUSTOMER object's attribute. The SETVALUEAT function uses the MODIFIED-RECORD Boolean array to tag the record as changed, retrieves the specific record from the RECORDS vector, and resets its value. Although the modified data is now in the CUSTOMERDATAMODEL and in the associated CUSTOMER object, the change still has not been updated to DB2/400.

DB2/400 UPDATE

The only CUSTOMERDATAMODEL function that has not yet been explained, the UPDATE function, is not derived from ABSTRACTDATAMODEL; it is of my own invention. This function updates DB2/400 with all the changes made to the business objects represented in JTABLE's grid.

CUSTOMERDATAMODEL's UPDATE function, shown in Figure 21.13, loops through all the elements of its vector of customers. For each element, it checks the MODIFIED-RECORD parallel array of Boolean values to see which CUSTOMER objects have been modified (sort of like a READN). Each modified CUSTOMER then tries to invoke its UPDATE function. (You should recall from chapter 15 that the UPDATE function of the CUSTOMER class calls jt400's KEYEDFILE object's UPDATE function.)

```
public void update() {
    Vector errors = new Vector();
    for (int i = 0; i < custs.size(); i++) {
        if (modifiedRecord[i] == true) {
            Customer cust = (Customer)custs.elementAt(i);
```

Figure 21.13: CUSTOMERDATAMODEL's UPDATE loops through the vector of CUSTOMER objects and invokes the UPDATE function associated with any modified CUSTOMER object. (Part 1 of 2)

```
        try {
         cust.update();
        } catch (Exception e) {
            errors.addElement("Cust No: " + cust.getCUSNUM() +
                              " " + e.getMessage());
        }
       }
      }
     }
    if (errors.size() > 0) {
       Object[] errorStrings = new Object[errors.size()];
       for (int i = 0; i < errors.size(); i++)
         errorStrings[i] = (Object)new
String((String)errors.elementAt(i));
       JOptionPane errorDialog = new JOptionPane();
       errorDialog.showInputDialog(container,
           "DB2/400 Update problems", "Errors",
           JOptionPane.ERROR_MESSAGE, null,
           errorStrings, errorStrings[0]);
     }
    }
```

Figure 21.13: CUSTOMERDATAMODEL'S update loops through the vector of CUSTOMER objects and invokes the UPDATE function associated with any modified CUSTOMER object. (Part 2 of 2)

If the UPDATE function throws any exceptions, the associated messages accumulate in an ERRORS vector. At the end of the FOR loop, you'll see code used to build and present a JFC JOPTIONPANE dialog that contains a list of all the errors, sort of like one of those 5250 program message subfiles.

Figure 21.14 shows the JOPTIONPANE generated following a test of the CUSTOMERSUBFILE application. The test consists of modifying information about two customers on the JTABLE grid while some poorly designed interactive 5250 application has a lock on those customer records.

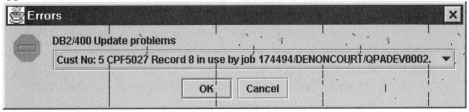

Figure 21.14: The JOPTIONPANE dialog can be constructed to present a list of error messages much like a program message subfile of an RPG subfile program (only better).

Figure 21.15 shows how the drop-down menu of errors works much like a program message subfile.

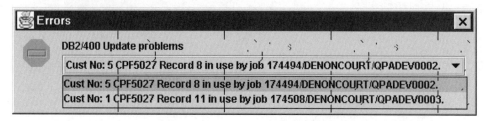

Figure 21.15: The user can scroll through the informative messages listed in a JOPTIONPANE.

THE GRID VIEW

With the document part of JTable's document/view architecture explained in full, it's time to finish explaining the implementation of the CUSTOMERSUBFILE application. You have already learned how the CUSTOMERDATAMODEL is created and associated with an instance of a JTABLE, but it can't hurt to quickly review the two statements that accomplish that:

```
custDataModel = new CustomerDataModel(topPanel, "BALDUE > 0");
JTable sfl = new JTable (custDataModel);
```

With the JTABLE constructed, the CUSTOMERSUBFILE application needs to enable scrolling. The standard visual interface for scrolling is a scroll bar. The JFC components include a scroll bar as well as a JSCROLLPANE. A JSCROLLPANE associates a panel along with a scroll bar. The panel, in this case, is the JTABLE object called SFL, so the addition of scrolling capabilities takes just one statement:

```
JScrollPane scrollpane = new JScrollPane(sfl);
```

At this point, the constructed JTABLE has a scroll pane associated with it but has not yet been added to the application window. As you read earlier, you should add your JFC GUI components to the topmost panel (here, the TOPPANEL component). The CUSTOMERSUBFILE application, therefore, adds the scroll panel (which itself contains the JTABLE) with a call to TOPPANEL's ADD function:

```
topPanel.add(scrollpane, BorderLayout.CENTER);
```

THE BOTTOM PANEL

The CUSTOMERSUBFILE application executes just fine even without the benefit of the last couple of inches of code found at the bottom of CUSTOMERSUBFILE's constructor. However, without those few lines of code, the application has no way of updating DB2/400 once a user modifies data. These last few statements of the CUSTOMERSUBFILE Java application, shown in Figure 21.16, add a button (a JFC JBUTTON, that is) so the user can say, "Okay, I'm done...you can update DB2/400 now."

I decided to place the update button on the bottom portion of the application's window frame, but adding the button directly to the bottom of the BORDER-LAYOUT makes the button the same width as the application window. So I created a JPANEL, set its layout manager to FLOWLAYOUT, and added that panel to the bottom of the topmost panel. Then I created a JBUTTON and added that to the bottom panel.

```
updButton = new JButton("Update");
updButton.setToolTipText(
"Updates QCUSTCDT using RDBObject's Update method");
updButton.setPreferredSize(new Dimension(100,25));
bottom.add(updButton, BorderLayout.SOUTH);
updButton.addActionListener(this);
```

Figure 21.16: JFC's JBUTTON class has a function that allows you to easily associate dynamic tool tip help for users.

This use of a FLOWLAYOUT panel at the bottom of an application is a standard strategy for laying out the buttons that allow users to control their application. JFC's JBUTTON class also lets you specify an icon in its constructor to be presented as a graphic in the button, which would improve the visual desktop paradigm of your application.

By now, you understand the purpose of the ADDACTIONLISTENER function; it allows you to specify a class coded to handle the ACTION event (e.g., a click of the UPDATE button). Here, ADDACTIONLISTENER adds the CUSTOMERSUBFILE application itself as the listener class. Note that CUSTOMERSUBFILE's class statement includes the implements ACTIONLISTENER clause, which forces the class to provide an implementation for the ACTIONPERFORMED function. Through the addition of this class as the listener, CUSTOMERSUBFILE's ACTIONPERFORMED function is automatically invoked when the user clicks the UPDATE button. The ACTIONPERFORMED function is coded to simply call the CUSTOMERDATAMODEL's UPDATE function:

```
public void actionPerformed(ActionEvent event) {
    if (event.getSource() == updButton) {custDataModel.update();}
}
```

You might have noticed that the discussion skipped over two of the UPDATE button's function calls: SETTOOLTIPTEXT and SETPREFERREDSIZE. These two functions are not necessary; they simply add a little pizzazz to the application. The SETTOOLTIPTEXT function, for instance, allows you to specify text for a tool tip to be presented whenever the mouse enters that component, as shown in Figure 21.17. Note the use of the word *component* and not *button*. Because SETTOOL-TIPTEXT is a function of the base JCOMPONENT class, any JFC COMPONENT may have a tool tip associated with it.

Last Name	Customer No.	Uses Charge Card	Balance Due
Henning	11	☐	37.00
Jones	9	☑	100.00
Vine	3	☑	439.00
Johnson	12	☐	3987.50
Stevens	2	☑	58.75
Alison	10	☐	10.00
Doeskin	5	☐	250.00

Customer Master Maintenance JTable Example

Updates QCUSTCDT using RDBObject's Update method

Figure 21.17: Tool tips make an application easier to use; and since JFC makes tool tips easy to add, you have little reason not to use them.

JFC's direct support for tool tips makes it easy to build user-friendly applications. The SETPREFERREDSIZE function allows you to specify the width and height for JBUTTON. Without this function included, the JBUTTON would have spanned the length of the bottom panel.

IBM's JT400 TABLES

IBM's Java Toolbox for the AS/400, as of OS/400 V4R3, contains several table components. IBM's VisualAge for Java AS/400 feature contains what IBM calls a Java subfile generator. Both of these products bear mention although, for robust applications, direct use of JFC's JTable will prove to be the more powerful and adaptive tool.

The jt400 version of a table is actually developed on top of Sun's JTable; in jt400, IBM just makes it easier for you to create a table from an AS/400 file. In the process of making it easier, IBM disallowed any update capabilities. Nevertheless, when you consider that you can create a table that presents DB2/400 data in the same JTable format shown earlier with just one statement, jt400's table components may prove useful for display-only grids. The following lines use JDBC and one of jt400's table grid components to create a table in one statement:

```
SQLResultSetTablePane pane =
      new SQLResultSetTablePane(
new SQLConnection("jdbc:as400://url"),
"SELECT * FROM QIWS.QCUSTCDT");
```

The SQLRESULTSETTABLEPANE makes up part of the package of visual classes called COM.IBM.AS400.VACCESS. The visual AS/400 components also contain a table pane constructed using record-level access. It performs quite well since it retrieves only those records required to paint one page. Both of the table panes—the JDBC and the record-level access versions—provide the quickest way to present multiple records from a DB2/400 file; just remember that update capabilities are not available.

If you want a Java GUI that presents updatable DB2/400 data, and if you are a proponent of computer-aided software engineering (CASE), then you might want to consider the AS/400 feature of VisualAge for Java (VAJ). VAJ's Enterprise Edition has a tool that generates a Java subfile program from information that you fill in on VAJ's SmartGuides (as VAJ wizards are called). The subfile generator tool, while easy to use, is a CASE tool. As all CASE tools do, VAJ's subfile builder creates ugly code, and lots of it. That creates two problems from my viewpoint.

First, the generated subfile program directly modifies DB2/400, which blatantly violates the principles of object-oriented programming. Nowhere did the JTable examples presented earlier in this chapter connect to an AS/400 or specify a file—that's the job of a Java class that represents the business entity stored in DB2/400. Your CASE-generated Java application also does not have any validation; you'll have to add that yourself. For each subfile that you create (or, more accurately, that VAJ creates), you'll again have to add validation.

A second problem with VAJ's subfile generator is that someone has to maintain all that ugly code. Enhancements will be difficult, which basically means you will not be able to adapt your application to changes in your business.

What we are really talking about here is structured applications and not object-oriented applications. My stance is that if you want to use a CASE tool, other programming languages and environments work better for computer-aided software engineering. Also, for the most part, object-oriented programming has already proven to be a superior development strategy over CASE.

TABBED DIALOGS

JFC's "Big Three" components, as I call them, are JTABLE, JTREE, and JTABBED PANE. As the replacement paradigm for subfiles, the JTABLE component has already received in-depth coverage here. JFC's JTREE and JTABBEDPANE components also deserve coverage, albeit brief.

JFC's JTABBEDPANE delivers sorely needed tabbed dialogs. Tabbed dialogs give you a powerful way of presenting a variety of related information in separate panels that are easily selected using the metaphor of a manila folder tab. The code required to present the tabbed dialog shown in Figures 21.18 and 21.19 is easy to implement.

Each tab of the JTABBEDPANE is a JPANEL that can contain whatever the application requires. The JPANEL shown in Figure 21.18, the first tab of the example application, contains a GRIDLAYOUT of JLABELS and TTEXTFIELDS. The JPANEL shown in Figure 21.19, associated with the third tab, contains a JTABLE that presents the CUSTOMERDATAMODEL featured earlier in this chapter.

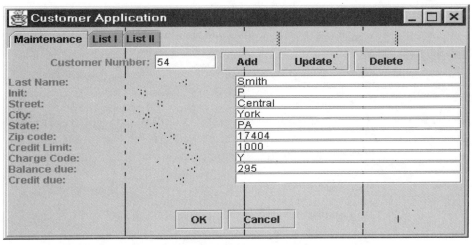

Figure 21.18: JFC's tabbed dialog component is very easy to use.

Last Name	No.	Charges	Balance Due
Henning	11	✔	37.00
Jones	9	✔	100.00
Vine	3	✔	439.00
Johnson	12	☐	3987.50
Tyron	4	✔	0.00
Stevens	2	✔	58.75
Alison	10	☐	10.00
Doe	5	☐	250.00
Thomas	8	☐	0.00
Williams	7	✔	25.00
Lee	1	☐	489.50
Abraham	6	☐	500.00

Figure 21.19: The JTABBEDPANE component automatically displays the panel associated with any tab that a user might click on.

It is not necessary to cover the code implementation for the three JPANEL containers; suffice it to say that those JPANELS are called MAINTCUSTPANE,

LISTCUSTPANE, and LIST2CUSTPANE. Anyway, the tabbed dialog is developed in three simple steps, the first of which involves creating a JTABBEDPANE with its default constructor:

```
JTabbedPane appCustPane = new JTabbedPane();
```

In the second step, you add the JPANELS to the JTABBEDPANE with its ADDTAB function. The ADDTAB function takes three parameters: the text for the tab, an optional icon for the tab, and the JPANEL to be associated with that tab:

```
appCustPane.addTab("Maintenance", null, maintCustPane);
appCustPane.addTab("List I", null, listCustPane);
appCustPane.addTab("List II", null, list2CustPane);
```

The third and final step is to add the JTABBEDPANE to the topmost panel (actually, for that matter, you can add the JTABBEDPANE to any JFC container):

```
topPanel.add(appCustPane, BorderLayout.CENTER);
```

You've just used five statements to develop a sophisticated GUI and you do not have to provide any of the code required to change the panels—that's all done for you by JFC.

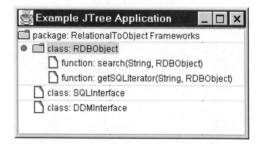

Figure 21.20: The JTREE class manages the expansion or compression of a node in the tree.

TREES

JFC's tree component offers the same ease of use as the JTABBEDPANE. All the source code necessary to present the GUI in Figure 21.20 appears within the example of the tree metaphor enabled with JFC's JTREE class in Figure 21.21.

To use JFC's JTREE, you create nodes and nest other nodes in them to form a hierarchy. The root node is passed as the single argument to the JTREE constructor. After you create a JSCROLLPANE to contain the tree, you add that JSCROLLPANE to the topmost JPANEL (or a JPANEL that is already attached to the topmost JPANEL).

```
import com.sun.java.swing.*;
import com.sun.java.swing.tree.*;
import java.awt.*;
import java.awt.event.*;

public class TreeExample extends JFrame {

  public TreeExample() {
    super("Example JTree Application");
    JPanel topPanel = new JPanel();
    topPanel.setLayout(new BorderLayout());
    getContentPane().add(topPanel);

    DefaultTreeModel treeModel = new
DefaultTreeModel(getRoot());

    JTree tree = new JTree(treeModel);
    JScrollPane scrollPane = new JScrollPane(tree);
    topPanel.add(scrollPane, BorderLayout.CENTER);
  }

  DefaultMutableTreeNode getRoot() {
    DefaultMutableTreeNode root  =
      new DefaultMutableTreeNode(
        "package: RelationalToObject Frameworks");
    DefaultMutableTreeNode level1a  =
      new DefaultMutableTreeNode(
        "class: RDBObject");
    DefaultMutableTreeNode level1b =
      new DefaultMutableTreeNode(
        "class: SQLInterface");
    DefaultMutableTreeNode level1c =
      new DefaultMutableTreeNode(
        "class: DDMInterface");
    root.add(level1a);
    root.add(level1b);
    root.add(level1c);
```

Figure 21.21: JFC's JTREE components are constructed with a hierarchy of nodes, and the DEFAULTMUTABLETREENODE node class should suffice for most business applications of JTREE. (Part 1 of 2)

```
    DefaultMutableTreeNode level2a =
      new DefaultMutableTreeNode(
        "function: search(String, RDBObject)");
    DefaultMutableTreeNode level2b =
      new DefaultMutableTreeNode(
        "function: getSQLIterator(String, RDBObject)");
    level1a.add(level2a);
    level1a.add(level2b);
    return root;
  }

  public static void main(String[] pList) {
    TreeExample frame = new TreeExample();
    frame.setVisible(true);
  }
}
```

Figure 21.21: JFC's JTREE components are constructed with a hierarchy of nodes, and the DEFAULTMUTABLETREENODE node class should suffice for most business applications of JTREE. (Part 2 of 2)

The TREEEXAMPLE in Figure 21.21 is designed to present a portion of this book's object-to-relational frameworks in a GUI. Because the frameworks are in a hierarchy—package, class, and functions—the tree metaphor works well to present the frameworks in a visual interface.

The TREEEXAMPLE constructor function creates the obligatory JFC topmost JPANEL, sets the layout manager, and sets TOPPANEL as the content pane for the application. Next, the constructor creates a DEFAULTTREEMODEL object to serve as the tree's root node. While you can develop a customized TREEMODEL class, the default JTREE node component supplied by JFC, DEFAULTTREEMODEL, works well for most applications.

The GETROOT function handles all the repetitive work of creating the different levels of nodes and returns the root DEFAULTTREEMODEL node. The root node is then passed as the argument to the JTREE component's constructor. Again, the document/view architecture applies, this time with the root DEFAULTTREEMODEL node as the document and the JTREE object representing the view. The TREEEXAMPLE class's constructor then creates a scroll pane by invoking the JSCROLLPANE constructor and using the JTREE component object as the parameter.

The GETROOT function gets a little tedious, but realize that your application will probably retrieve the nodes from your database. The GETROOT function, however, shows how easily you can create the tree hierarchy of data. The root DEFAULT-TREEMODEL node is created first. Then the Level 1 nodes are created and added to the root node with the root DEFAULTTREEMODEL object's ADD function. Finally, the Level 2 nodes are created and added to their respective Level 1 nodes (actually, the example shows a couple of nodes added to just one of the first-level nodes, but you get the point). Even this trivial example shows that the visual effect of a tree often works well for business applications such as a bill of materials.

EXPANDING SUBFILES

The JTable example shown earlier is analogous to an AS/400 *load-all subfile*. With load-all subfiles, the program fills the subfile with all the DB2/400 records that match a user's search criterion before presenting the subfile to the user. When the number of records retrieved is high, the user must wait for the program to finish filling the subfile before he or she can view the information. Often, with RPG and COBOL subfile programs, AS/400 programmers use one of two other design strategies for constructing the subfiles: *expanding* and *page-at-a-time*. These two strategies for displaying the information from multiple records of DB2/400 files can also be mimicked with JFC. Certainly you can add buttons that represent the roll keys of an AS/400 subfile, but a cleaner strategy is to use the JTable's scroll bar.

Figure 21.22 shows the initial JTABLE view of the data presented from Figure 21.31's EXPANDINGSUBFILEDATAMODEL class. Using two simple techniques, you

Expanding Subfile Example		
Table Index	Random Number 1	Random Number 2
1	-859363226	689823819
2	671939941	99003234
3	-1631138707	-1003193134
4	-640169368	572984258
5	-597108700	-1898178628
6	-1809932318	-620079755
7	-1752209841	1220023613
8	1966836625	-1703795017
9	1566633291	-882885489

Figure 21.22:This initial presentation of the expanding JTABLE example has a scroll bar whose thumb button visually represents that the set of records retrieved thus far was small.

can easily extend JFC's ABSTRACTDATAMODEL that dynamically expands the elements of the table as a user scrolls down the scroll bar.

Taking particular notice of the scroll bar, compare the thumb size in Figure 21.22 with that shown in Figure 21.23, after a user has scrolled. Then look at the thumb size in Figure 21.24 after the user has scrolled to the bottom of the table. On the initial screen, the number of rows in the grid was small; but after the user successively paged down the grid, the EXPANDINGSUBFILEDATAMODEL class dynamically sized the table.

Table Index	Random Number 1	Random Number 2
4	-640169368	572984258
5	-597108700	-1898178628
6	-1809932318	-620079755
7	-1752209841	1220023613
8	1966836625	-1703795017
9	1566633291	-882885489
10	230574277	923993150
11	1764226198	2120587560
12	114267674	-141821773

Figure 21.23: After scrolling once, the thumb button decreases in size to visually represent an increase in the number of records in the expanding subfile.

Table Index	Random Number 1	Random Number 2
337	162110885	-646962480
338	1873133523	-1093532654
339	502721955	1810064298
340	-631911087	835573297
341	711840672	-534549988
342	1372842918	-1544136692
343	-1604627869	-857778767
344	611551692	-283219516
345	-24423640	226875123

Figure 21.24: Once the last record of the set is retrieved, the thumb bar finally touches the bottom of the scroll bar, thus clearly representing the end of the data.

In the example, the number of records retrieved is 345. In fact, for the sake of simplicity, the example doesn't even use a database file; rather, it builds a

VECTOR of rows from information dynamically generated from Java's RANDOM utility class. The EXPANDINGSUBFILEDATAMODEL class looks much like the load-all example. For instance, it still has an array of STRINGS for the table headers and it still has a VECTOR of records:

```
final String[] headers =
      {"Table Index", "Random Number 1", "Random Number 2"};
private Vector records = null;
```

The EXPANDINGSUBFILEDATAMODEL class also has similar implementations for the GETCOLUMNNAME and GETCOLUMNCOUNT functions, shown in Figure 21.25.

```
public String getColumnName(int column) {
  return headers[column];
}
public int getColumnCount() {
  return headers.length;
}
```

Figure 21.25: EXPANDINGSUBFILEDATAMODEL implements the GETCOLUMNNAME and GETCOLUMNCOUNT functions in much the same way as the load-all example.

The EXPANDINGSUBFILEDATAMODEL class differs in how it implements the GETROWCOUNT and GETVALUEAT functions. The GETROWCOUNT function doesn't return the size of elements of the records retrieved from DB2/400 unless it is at an end-of-file condition. If the class has not yet read to the end of file, GETROWCOUNT returns the size of the RECORDS vector plus one. That "plus one" logic, illustrated in Figure 21.26, is one of two pieces of magic required to build an expanding subfile (JTABLE).

```
public int getRowCount() {
  if (endOfFile())
    return records.size();
  return records.size() + 1;
}
```

Figure 21.26: The EXPANDINGSUBFILEDATAMODEL class implements GETROWCOUNT by adding one to the size of the RECORDS vector.

The GETVALUEAT function no longer can simply return the values of data elements from the RECORDS vector, as did the load-all example presented at the beginning of this chapter; the next set of records might yet be retrieved from DB2/400. You could implement the GETVALUEAT function in one of many ways. The method used here, illustrated in Figure 21.27, involves reading the next page of records if the subfile data model class is not at an end-of-file condition and if the row being requested by JTABLE is past the current position of the file cursor.

```
public Object getValueAt(int row, int column) {
  if (endOfFile() == false && row >= fileCursor) {
    readNextPage(row);
  }
  String[] record = (String[])records.elementAt(row);
  return (String)record[column];
}
```

Figure 21.27: When the JTABLE object (the view) calls the GETVALUEAT function asking for the value of a row (for which a record hasn't yet been retrieved), the READNEXTPAGE function gets another set of records from DB2/400.

Assuring that the requested row does exist in the RECORDS vector, the GET-VALUEAT function then is able to return the value from the data element indexed by row.

Earlier you read of *two* pieces of magic required to dynamically grow the elements of data presented in a JTABLE grid. The second piece of magic comes into play when you retrieve the next set of records. The EXPANDINGSUBFILEDATA-MODEL class uses a function appropriately called READNEXTPAGE (shown in Figure 21.28) to expand the data elements of the RECORDS vector. The single parameter to that function represents the next largest row number requested from the JTABLE class.

The READNEXTPAGE function then uses a FOR loop to read another set of records, placing their values in the RECORDS vector with the ADDELEMENT function. (Note that this example uses dynamically generated data.)

```
private void readNextPage(int row) {
    Random rand = new Random();
    for (int newRow = 0;
        newRow <= row && records.size() < fakeEOF;
        newRow++, fileCursor++) {
      String threeFields[] = new String[3];
      threeFields[0] = new Integer(fileCursor+1).toString();
      threeFields[1] = new Integer(rand.nextInt()).toString();
      threeFields[2] = new Integer(rand.nextInt()).toString();
      records.addElement(threeFields);
    }
    fireTableStructureChanged();
  }
}
```

Figure 21.28: The second piece of magic required to dynamically build the data of a JTABLE is to fire a table structured change event whenever the data model is expanded.

That second piece of magic is found at the bottom of Figure 21.28. Immediately after expanding the elements of the RECORDS vector, the example fires off a table structured change event with the FIRETABLESTRUCTURECHANGED function. This function, provided by JFC, informs any JTABLE associated with this data model that it needs to refresh its display. See Figures 21.29 through 29.31.

Note that if the data model's internal table of data (in this example, the RECORDS vector) gets excessively large, you might consider lopping off the elements at the beginning of that table. Java's VECTOR class allows you to do that with its RE-MOVEELEMENTAT function.

The SUBFILE class shown in Figure 21.32 creates the EXPANDINGSUBFILEDATA-MODEL, associates it with a JTABLE object, and places them in a JSCROLLPANE on the topmost JPANEL of the application's JFRAME.

JFC AVAILABILITY

Sun's Java Foundation Classes come as a standard part of Java 1.2. That doesn't mean, however, that you have to wait for Java 1.2 to become readily available. The JFC package had a hugely popular beta program that went by the name of Swing. The example applications in this chapter use the Swing set of JFC. Perhaps you noticed the two IMPORT statements at the top of the source for the CUSTOMERSUBFILE application and the CUSTOMERDATAMODEL:

```
import com.sun.java.swing.*;
import com.sun.java.swing.table.*;
```

Note that the JTABLE classes belong to a separate Swing package called TABLE. Sun's Web site makes the Swing classes available for free as a downloadable Java JAR file called SWING.JAR.

Many Java Integrated Development Environments, including IBM's VisualAge for Java and Inprise's JBuilder, bundle the Swing components with their products. The requirement for industrial-strength components ran so high that many Java shops began to move Java applications that used the Swing beta components into production. For this reason, Sun has promised that all the enhancements it makes to JFC components in Java 1.2 will also be made available in the Swing components via a new SWING.JAR file. As a result, you can start using the JFC components today in Java 1.1 applications.

SWING VERSUS AWT

Every AWT component has a corresponding JFC (or Swing) component. For example, the JFC equivalent of AWT's BUTTON is the JBUTTON; for AWT's FRAME, it's JFRAME, and for AWT's LIST, it's JLIST. As you might have guessed, the naming convention for JFC components involves prefixing the name of the component with the letter J. The transition to JFC is not difficult at all (once you get past that strange GETCONTENTPANE function of JFRAME).

The only problem with using JFC, as yet, arises from most Web browsers' lack of support for Java 1.2. You can develop your applets to use the Swing set, but those Web browsers will have to download SWING.JAR along with your Java applets. Also, once you begin to use JFC components in a Java application, you'll avoid some bizarre problems if you refrain from mixing and matching AWT components with JFC components in the same application.

If you develop Java applets, for performance reasons you should wait to use JFC until the Web browsers predominantly used by visitors to your Web site support a

Java 1.2 JVM. But if you are developing Java applications, use of the JFC components (available as the Swing set until Java 1.2) is now considered standard. Incor-
porating the "Big Three" of JFC—JTABLE, JTREE, and JTABBEDPANE—into your
Java applications will make them more intuitive to use.

```
import com.midrangecomputing.ObjectToRelational.*;

import com.ibm.as400.access.*;
import com.sun.java.swing.table.*;
import com.sun.java.swing.*;
import java.util.*;
import java.awt.event.*;
import java.math.*;

class CustomerDataModel extends AbstractTableModel {
  final String[] headers =
  {"Last Name","No.","Charges", "Balance Due"};
  private Vector records = new Vector();
  private boolean modifiedRecord[];
  private Vector custs = null;
  private JPanel container = null;

  public CustomerDataModel(JPanel container, String whereClause)
{
    this.container = container;
    try {
      custs = Customer.search(whereClause, new Customer());
    } catch (Exception e) {System.out.println(e);}
    modifiedRecord = new boolean[custs.size()];
    for (int i = 0; i < custs.size(); i++) {
      Customer cust = (Customer)custs.elementAt(i);
      Vector newRow = new Vector();
      newRow.addElement(cust.getLSTNAM());
      newRow.addElement(cust.getCUSNUM().toString());
      int chargeCode = (cust.getCHGCOD().intValue());
      newRow.addElement(new Boolean(chargeCode == 1));
      newRow.addElement(cust.getBALDUE().toString());
      records.addElement(newRow);
      modifiedRecord[i] = false;
    }
  }
  public void update() {
```

Figure 21.29: The complete code for the CUSTOMERDATAMODEL. (Part 1 of 3)

```
Vector errors = new Vector();
for (int i = 0; i < custs.size(); i++) {
  if (modifiedRecord[i] == true) {
    Customer cust = (Customer)custs.elementAt(i);
    try {
     cust.update();
    } catch (Exception e) {
      errors.addElement("Cust No: " + cust.getCUSNUM() +
                        " " + e.getMessage());
    }
  }
}
if (errors.size() > 0) {
  Object[] errorStrings = new Object[errors.size()];
  for (int i = 0; i < errors.size(); i++)
    errorStrings[i] =
      (Object)new String((String)errors.elementAt(i));
  JOptionPane errorDialog = new JOptionPane();
  errorDialog.showInputDialog(container,
      "DB2/400 Update problems", "Errors",
      JOptionPane.ERROR_MESSAGE, null,
      errorStrings, errorStrings[0]);
}
}

// these methods do not have to be implemented
public String getColumnName(int column) {
  return headers[column];
}
// return Boolean for column two
// otherwise delegate the call to super
// which will simply return a JTextField class;
public Class getColumnClass(int col) {
  if (col == 2)
    return Boolean.class;
  else
    return super.getColumnClass(col);
}
public boolean isCellEditable(int row, int col) {
  switch (col) {
    case 0:  return true;
    case 2:  return true;
    default: return false;
```

Figure 21.29: The complete code for the CUSTOMERDATAMODEL. (Part 2 of 3)

```
    }
  }
  public void setValueAt(Object aValue, int aRow, int aColumn) {
    Customer cust = (Customer)custs.elementAt(aRow);
    switch (aColumn) {
      case 0:
        try {
          cust.setLSTNAM((String)aValue);
        } catch (InvalidLengthException error) {
          JOptionPane errorDialog = new JOptionPane();
          errorDialog.showMessageDialog(container,
              error.toString(), "Error",
            JOptionPane.ERROR_MESSAGE);
          return;
        }
        break;
      case 2:
        if (((Boolean)aValue).booleanValue() == true)
          cust.setCHGCOD(new BigDecimal("1"));
        else
          cust.setCHGCOD(new BigDecimal("0"));
        break;
    }
    modifiedRecord[aRow] = true;

    // change the value of the internal table
    Vector row = (Vector)records.elementAt(aRow);
    row.setElementAt(aValue, aColumn);
  }

  // these methods always need to be implemented
  public int getColumnCount() { return headers.length; }
  public int getRowCount() { return records.size();}

  // create a scroll pane and insert the JTable into it
  public Object getValueAt(int aRow, int aCol) {
    Vector row = (Vector)records.elementAt(aRow);
    return row.elementAt(aCol);
  }
}
```

Figure 21.29: The complete code for the CUSTOMERDATAMODEL. (Part 3 of 3)

```
import com.midrangecomputing.ObjectToRelational.*;

import com.sun.java.swing.table.*;
import com.sun.java.swing.*;
import java.awt.*;
import java.awt.event.*;
public class CustomerSubfile
        extends JFrame
        implements ActionListener
{
  JButton updButton = null;
  CustomerDataModel custDataModel = null;

  // bootstrap the application
  public static void main(String[] parms) {
    CustomerSubfile sfl = new CustomerSubfile();
    sfl.setVisible(true);
  }

  // constructor function
  public CustomerSubfile() {
    super("Customer Master Maintenance JTable Example");
    setSize (500, 200);
    addWindowListener( new WindowAdapter () {
      public void windowClosing(WindowEvent event) {
        System.exit(0);
    }});
    // create the topmost panel
    JPanel topPanel = new JPanel();
    getContentPane().add( topPanel);
    topPanel.setLayout(new BorderLayout());

    // create a model of the data
    custDataModel = new CustomerDataModel(topPanel, "BALDUE >
0");

    // create the table
    JTable sfl = new JTable (custDataModel);

    JScrollPane scrollpane = new JScrollPane(sfl);
    topPanel.add(scrollpane, BorderLayout.CENTER);

    // resize columns 1 and 2, leaving 0 and 3 at default
```

Figure 21.30: The complete code for the CUSTOMERSUBFILE Java application. (Part 1 of 2)

```
  /*
  TableColumn col1 = sfl.getColumnModel().getColumn(1);
  col1.setMaxWidth(50);
  // short form
  sfl.getColumnModel().getColumn(2).setMaxWidth(50);
  */

  // create button panel
  JPanel bottom = new JPanel();
  bottom.setLayout(new FlowLayout());
  topPanel.add(bottom, BorderLayout.SOUTH);

  // add update to button panel
  updButton = new JButton("Update");
  updButton.setToolTipText(
     "Updates QCUSTCDT using RDBObject\'s Update method");
  updButton.setPreferredSize(new Dimension(100,25));
  bottom.add(updButton, BorderLayout.SOUTH);
  updButton.addActionListener(this);
  }
  public void actionPerformed(ActionEvent event) {
    if (event.getSource() == updButton) {
      custDataModel.update();
    }
  }
}
```

Figure 21.30: The complete code for the CUSTOMERSUBFILE Java application. (Part 2 of 2)

```
import com.sun.java.swing.table.*;
import com.sun.java.swing.*;
import java.util.*;
import java.awt.event.*;

class ExpandingSubfileDataModel extends AbstractTableModel {
  final String[] headers = {"Table Index",
                            "Random Number 1",
                            "Random Number 2"};
  private Vector records = null;
```

Figure 21.31: The expanding subfile example uses two simple techniques to enable the dynamic extension of the data contained in the data model document. (Part 1 of 2)

```
final private int fakeEOF = 345;
private int fileCursor = 0;

public ExpandingSubfileDataModel() {
  records = new Vector();
  readNextPage(10);
}
public String getColumnName(int column) {
  return headers[column];
}
public int getColumnCount() {
  return headers.length;
}
public int getRowCount() {
  if (endOfFile())
    return records.size();
  return records.size() + 1;
}
public Object getValueAt(int row, int column) {
  if (endOfFile() == false && row >= fileCursor) {
    readNextPage(row);
  }
  String[] record = (String[])records.elementAt(row);
  return (String)record[column];
}
private boolean endOfFile() {
  return (fileCursor >= fakeEOF);
}
private void readNextPage(int row) {
  Random rand = new Random();
  for (int newRow = 0;
       newRow <= row && records.size() < fakeEOF;
       newRow++, fileCursor++) {
    String threeFields[] = new String[3];
    threeFields[0] = new Integer(fileCursor+1).toString();
    threeFields[1] = new Integer(rand.nextInt()).toString();
    threeFields[2] = new Integer(rand.nextInt()).toString();
    records.addElement(threeFields);
  }
  fireTableStructureChanged();
}
}
```

Figure 21.31: The expanding subfile example uses two simple techniques to enable the dynamic extension of the data contained in the data model document. (Part 2 of 2)

```
import com.sun.java.swing.table.*;
import com.sun.java.swing.*;
import java.awt.*;
import java.awt.event.*;

public class Subfile extends JFrame {
  JButton updButton = null;
  ExpandingSubfileDataModel dataModel = null;

  public static void main(String[] parms) {
    Subfile sfl = new Subfile();
    sfl.setVisible(true);
  }

  public Subfile() {
    super("Expanding Subfile Example");

    setSize (500, 200);
    addWindowListener( new WindowAdapter () {
      public void windowClosing(WindowEvent event) {
        System.exit(0);
    }});
    JPanel topPanel = new JPanel();
    getContentPane().add( topPanel);
    topPanel.setLayout(new BorderLayout());

    dataModel = new ExpandingSubfileDataModel();
    JTable sfl = new JTable (dataModel );

    JScrollPane scrollPane = new JScrollPane(sfl);
    topPanel.add(scrollPane, BorderLayout.CENTER);
  }
}
```

Figure 21.32: Using two simple techniques, you can easily extend JFC's
ABSTRACTDATAMODEL to create a JTABLE that functions like an expanding subfile.

APPENDIX: SOFTWARE LOADING INSTRUCTIONS

T he CD-ROM you receive with *Java® Application Strategies for the AS/400* contains all of the source code presented in the book. To install this code, you'll need a PC with Sun's Java Development Kit 1.1.7 (JDK1.1.7), Sun's Swing set of advanced GUI components, and IBM's Java Toolbox for the AS/400 (jt400). A Java Integrated Development Environment (IDE), however, such as IBM's VisualAge for Java, Inprise's JBuilder, or Symantec's Visual Café, would be a superior development environment to the JDK.

JAVA DEVELOPMENT KIT

You can download Sun's Java Development Kit from:

```
www.javasoft.com/products/jdk/1.1/download-jdk-windows.html
```

When the page is presented, select option 1 to specify the download of the JDK for Windows 95/98/NT. (For your convenience, the JDK installation file, JDK117B-WIN32.EXE, is available on the CD included with this book.) The downloaded file, which is a PC executable install program, prompts you for the drive and directory name to which you intend to install the JDK. For this purpose, consider creating a main directory called JAVA and a subdirectory called JDK1.1.7.

Later, if you opt to install the latest Java Development Kit (JDK1.2), you can install that JDK in a directory called JDK1.2.

Swing/JFC

The Swing/JFC package can be downloaded from Sun's Java Developer Connection site at http://developer.java.sun.com. The latest package of JFC components is called JAVAX.SWING (to be compatible with JDK 1.2's JFC package) whereas this book uses the package called COM.SUN.JAVA.SWING. The developers at Sun initially used the COM.SUN.JAVA prefix but recently that switched to the standard extensions name of JAVAX. The code samples in this book qualify the import as COM.SUN.JAVA.SWING, which means you either use the older version of the Swing classes (which the CD contains) or you modify the import statement that specifies the Swing/JFC package. The book's examples use the following statement:

```
import com.sun.java.swing.*;
```

If you choose to modify the import statement, you would make it read as follows:

```
import javax.swing.*;
```

The version of Swing required for the code examples in this book, Swing1.0.3, is delivered as a compressed ZIP file. (The CD includes the ZIP file that contains Swing1.0.3.) Open up the SWING103.ZIP file with WinZip (available at WWW.WINZIP.COM) and click on the EXTRACT icon. Try extracting Swing1.0.3 to a directory called SWING underneath your JAVA main directory; that way, if you also want to use Swing1.1, you can load that package to another directory within the /JAVA/SWING directory path.

AS/400 Toolbox for Java

You can download the latest IBM Java Toolbox for the AS/400 to your PC from one of two places: the Integrated File System (IFS) of your AS/400 (if it's V4R2 or later) or IBM's Java Toolbox for the AS/400 page. The IFS directory that contains the jt400.jar file is /QIBM/ProdData/HTTP/Public/jt400/lib, and you'll find IBM's Java Toolbox for the AS/400 page at www.as400.ibm.com/toolbox/downloads.htm. This book's companion CD contains the six JAR files from jt400 Modification 2 beta that are listed in Table A.1. Of these six files, the JT400.JAR file contains the bulk of the AS/400 access classes.

Table A.1: IBM's jt400 Modification 2 Contains Six JAR Files.

Name	Contents
Jt400.jar	AS/400 access classes
Uitools.jar	AS/400-specific GUI tools
Jui400.jar	AS/400-specific GUI classes
X4j400.jar	Extensible Markup Language parser
Data400.jar	Program Call Markup Language classes
Util400.jar	UI utility classes

The JT400.JAR file is required for DB2/400 record-level access, Java Database Connectivity (JDBC) SQL access, program call, and command call. The X4J400.JAR archive file contains the Java Extensible Markup Language (XML) processor code, and the DATA400.JAR archive file contains the PROGRAMCALLDOCUMENT class and its associated classes (it's about 57 KB in size). The X4J400.JAR and DATA400.JAR files are required along with JT400.JAR when you use the Program Call Markup Language technique prescribed in chapter 15.

IBM's jt400 Modification 2 classes are available for free with OS/400 V4R4. The JT400.JAR included on the CD, although a beta for OS/400 V4R4, will work fine with V4R2 and V4R3. I would suggest that you obtain the full set of downloads for Java Toolbox for the AS/400 so that you have the complete documentation available on your system.

COMPILATION INSTRUCTIONS

The Java source files contained on the CD are in directories that correspond to the sections and chapters of this book that contain code examples. You'll need to copy all of those directories to your PC's hard drive. Each directory has a DOS batch file called MAKE.BAT that will perform the Java compiles required for examples from that chapter. Each of these batch files, however, specifies directories in the Java CLASSPATH compile option specific to my machine. You'll have to change these to directories to locations specific to your machine. For instance, the following example simply qualifies the Java base classes:

```
javac *.java -classpath .;D:\java\jdk1.1.7\lib\classes.zip;
```

Your machine's DOS path environment variable, however, must include the path to the JDK so that the Windows operating system can find the JAVAC.EXE compile utility. To implement this, you can add the following statement in your AUTOEXEC.BAT file:

```
SET PATH=%PATH%;D:\JAVA\JDK1.1.7\BIN;
```

In this next example, the CLASSPATH contains a file reference to IBM's Java Toolbox for AS/400 (jt400.jar), a file reference to the JAR file that contains my relational-to-objects frameworks of classes, and the Java base classes:

```
javac *.java -classpath
.;D:\java\jt400\lib\jt400.jar;..\..\SECTIO~4\CHAP16~1\Rdb2Obj.jar;D
:\java\jdk1.1.7\lib\classes.zip;
```

That relational-to-objects frameworks JAR file (RDB2OBJ.JAR) can be created with the following statement that is contained in the MAKE.BAT batch file found in the chapter 17 FRAMEWORKS directory:

```
jar cvf Rdb2Obj.jar
com/midrangecomputing/ObjectToRelational/*.class
```

If you are using a Java Integrated Development Environment, be sure the CLASSPATH required for your Java compiles is specified with project options.

The –CLASSPATH option of the Java Development Kit's JAVAC compiler, by the way, would not be required if you create an environment variable called CLASSPATH. If the JAVAC compile command does not contain a –CLASSPATH option, the compiler looks for an environment variable called—you guessed it—CLASSPATH. The following two statements, for instance, are in my AUTOEXEC.BAT file:

```
SET CLASSPATH=%CLASSPATH%D:\java\jt00\lib\jt400.jar;
SET CLASSPATH=%CLASSPATH%D:\java\Swing\swing-1.1beta2\swingall.jar;
```

EXECUTION

Once the Java source files (.JAVA suffix) are compiled into executable Java byte code (.CLASS suffix), those class files that contain a MAIN function may be executed. But before the MAIN function can be executed, the DOS PATH and CLASSPATH environment variables must be set. The PATH environment variable qualifies the location of the JAVA.EXE file that starts the Java Virtual Machine (JVM), which then executes the Java class specified as a parameter.

The JVM uses the CLASSPATH environment variable to find the packages specified in the IMPORT statements of the various classes used in a Java application. For instance, to execute the ToDoApplication of chapter 4, you would use the following command in a DOS window after you change your current directory to the directory that contains the TODOAPPLICATION.CLASS Java byte code file:

```
java ToDoApplication
```

DEPRECATION ERRORS

You will notice that some of the make batch files will generate Java deprecation warnings, or warnings that are issued when you use functions of classes that have been flagged as obsolete. In some circumstances, the classes of this book use such "obsolete" functions because they made the code easier to read and understand. For instance, Java's JAVA.UTIL.DATE class has now been effectively replaced with the JAVA.UTIL.CALENDAR class. Although the calendar class's implementation is far superior to that of the date class, it more difficult to use and understand.

I leave it to you, the reader, as an exercise to replace the deprecated functions used in this book with the new recommended functions. To find the recommended replacement strategy, review the HTML documentation for the class that contains the deprecated function. That document will suggest a replacement function or class.

GLOSSARY

Learning a new language poses enough of a challenge without being bombarded with a completely new set of terms. With the aid of this glossary, you will, hopefully, understand the terms used as field and function names in the ridiculous AMETHODBYANYOTHERNAMEWOULDBEEASIERTOUNDERSTAND Java class shown in Figure G.1.

Object-oriented programming concepts can be far more complex than those covered in this glossary, but gaining an understanding of vocabulary should be your first step to understanding the basics concepts of object-oriented programming. This glossary should become a handy reference as you read more about Java in *AS/400 Internet Expert* and in other sources of Java literature.

Books such as *You Just Don't Understand* by Deborah Tannen and *Men Are from Mars, Women Are from Venus: A Practical Guide for Improving Communications and Getting What You Want in Your Relationships* by John Gray explain that although different people might use the same words, they really have very different meanings.

Java takes this phenomenon to a new height. When you hear *class*, you might picture students, desks, and the like, when you should envision a set of business entities grouped together because of their common attributes. Although some Java terms do relate to concepts you're already familiar with, the new terminology can throw you off. For instance, you probably already know what a function is, but you might not know that a class method is basically the same thing.

All this new object-oriented vocabulary can be the first stumbling block to learning Java. Not only do you have many new words to learn, but many of these terms, such as *method* and *function*, are interchangeable, as the ridiculous Java class example in Figure G.1 illustrates.

```
class aMethodByAnyOtherNameWouldBeEasierToUnderstand {
        int dataMember;
        int field;
        int classVariable;

        void method(int parm1, int parm2) {}
        void operation(int parm1, int parm2) {}
        void function(int parm1, int parm2) {}
        void memberFunction(int parm1, int parm2) {}
        void behavior(int parm1, int parm2) {}
}
```

Figure G.1: This hypothetical Java class shows the ambiguity of many object-oriented programming terms.

Even worse, the same term can mean two entirely different things. This short glossary helps you get your foot in the door by illuminating these new and confusing terms. The words are grouped by synonyms.

OBJECT

An *object* is the basic building block of any object-oriented application. Java objects are designed to represent the entities (for AS/400 programmers, business entities) that a Java application will control—for example, customers, purchase orders, and inventory items.

CLASS/ABSTRACT DATA TYPE

A Java CLASS is a template that lets you create objects with similar features; it is the Java code that embodies all the features of a particular set of objects. Take, for example, a program variable called PO. You can declare that PO variable to be of the purchase order class type. Once you've defined PO as a purchase order class item, it becomes a purchase order object, which means it has all the attributes defined in the purchase order class. The purchase order object can then invoke all the purchase order class operations (or functions) that have been defined by the class template. A class is also known as an *abstract data type*.

Once an object variable is created and typed as a class, the object can invoke functions defined in its Java class. The syntax to invoke a class function is simply the class variable name, the dot operator (.), the function, and any required arguments:

```
PO.addLineItem(itemNumber, quantity);
```

CLASS METHOD/FUNCTION/ FUNCTION MEMBER/OPERATION/BEHAVIOR/MESSAGE

All these terms mean basically the same thing; it's no wonder it takes time for people to learn object-oriented programming!

Although object-oriented programming purists maintain that *function* does not adequately describe what a *class method* does, I believe that the two terms are interchangeable. Class methods (or functions, if you prefer that term) are integral parts of a class. Functions manipulate the state of an object. For example, the function ADDLINEITEM will add an additional line item to a PO object.

The term *function member,* or member function, is simply a qualification of the use of a function where the word *member* explicitly states that the function is a part of a class. If you work in Java, you don't really need this term, but you might run across it in C++ and other languages that allow you to violate object-oriented techniques.

The term *operation* is sometimes used in object-oriented parlance because of its historical relationship with data types. Basic numerical data types—such as integer, float, zoned, and packed—all have implicit operations that may be performed on them (e.g., addition, subtraction, multiplication, division, and assignment). Similarly, Java classes (also called abstract data types) contain explicit operations that can be performed on objects of that class. For example, a purchase order object could have operations such as DELETE, ADDLINEITEM, and REMOVELINEITEMS.

Object-oriented programmers use the term *behavior* when thinking conceptually about objects and their functions: An object has identity, state, and behavior. The identity of an object is similar to the key of a relational database record. The state of an object is stored as a set of values in the object's class fields, just as a relational database record stores values as database fields. In object-oriented programming, objects, unlike relational database entities, also contain behaviors. When object-oriented programmers design Java classes, they shape the behavior of an object by defining class functions coded to simulate the behaviors of a real-world entity. A purchase order object would have behaviors that include adding line items and removing line items.

Message is yet another, albeit less frequently used, synonym for method. You will run across it in pure object-oriented literature, so you should know what it means. When object-oriented technology was in its infancy, programmers used to say that objects communicated with each other through messages. For instance, a purchase order object might send a message to a customer object requesting that the customer object return a credit limit to see if the purchase order should be allowed. In reality, those messages were implemented as simple class function calls. The following Java code snippet shows how a purchase order object with the variable name PO would invoke the customer object's check credit function:

```
po.customer.checkCredit();
```

DATA MEMBER/ATTRIBUTE/CLASS FIELD

Data members and *function members* are the components of a class. Data members describe an object's attributes and function members define the actions allowed to be performed against an object. A purchase order class might have data members such as the purchase order number, a due date, the customer's number, and a list of the purchase order's line items; and it might have function members such as add, change, and delete. A class is somewhat like a relational database (RDB) record format in that it also contains data fields (analogous to data members) that make up an entity. A class, however, also contains functions that operate on those fields. It takes both data members and function members to make up a class.

Like other object-oriented terms, *attribute* is borrowed from relational database design. For example, the attributes of a customer class would include address, credit limit, and Social Security number.

I credit IBM for initially using the term *class field* in the context of Java objects. Because AS/400 programmers are already comfortable with the idea of business entities being in a database record format made up of fields, IBM uses class field rather than data member or attribute.

PARENT CLASS/SUPERCLASS

In object-oriented programming, you can derive classes from other classes. For example, a purchase order class could be derived from an order class. ORDER is the *parent class* or *superclass* of the purchase order class. A class called WORKORDER could also be derived from the same parent class. The ORDER class might be a general class containing class fields and class functions that relate to an order, regardless of whether it is a purchase order or an internal company work order.

SUBCLASS/DERIVED CLASS/INHERITANCE

If an order class is the parent class of a purchase order class, then the purchase order class is a *subclass* or *derived class* of the order class. A subclass *inherits* all the fields and functions of its parent class but adds other fields and functions as well. For example, a purchase order would inherit an order date and a list of line items from the order class and then extend the class by adding a vendor number and shipping details.

INTERFACE/JAVA INTERFACE/SIGNATURE

The set of public functions of a class is said to be the class's *interface*. (Public functions are available whenever a class is used, whereas private and protected functions are only available within that same class.) By looking at the public functions of a class, a Java programmer can, without necessarily understanding the full complexity of the interface, understand how to use that class. The JAVAP.EXE tool that comes with Sun's Java Development Kit can be used to display the public functions of a class.

To add to the confusion, Java uses a construct known as an *interface*. This construct, like a Java class, is a list of functions tied together as a named unit. Stated another way, a named set of codeless functions is a Java interface. Just as a Java class has a class name, a Java interface has an interface name. Java interfaces and classes differ mainly in that an interface has no code implementations for its functions. You can use an interface's functions only after you define a class that implements the interface. The following purchase order class derives from the order class and implements the print interface:

```
class PurchaseOrder extends Order implements PrintInterface {...}
```

The print interface might list several functions, such as PRINTHEADER, PRINTDETAIL, and PRINTFOOTER. The purchase order class would have to provide Java code for each of these three functions in order to use any one of them.

A *signature* is the combination of a function name and its list of function arguments and their types. The term *signature* is used because, in Java and most object-oriented languages, several different functions in the same class may bear the same name, as Figure G.2 shows.

```
class PurchaseOrder {
    ...
    public void addPOLineItem(int ItemNumber, int Quantity) {}
    public void addPOLineItem(POLineItem aPOLineItem) {}
    ...
}
```

Figure G.2: Functions with identical names (even within the same class) can have different implementations determined by the number and type of arguments they take.

The number and type of arguments differentiate the implementation of identically named functions. Thus, a function name *and* its arguments comprise the signature of that function.

The interface to the purchase order class excerpted in Figure G.2 includes several ADDPOLINEITEM functions. The first ADDPOLINEITEM function takes two integer arguments. The first integer argument contains an item number and the other integer holds the item order quantity. That ADDPOLINEITEM function then builds a purchase order line item (POLINEITEM) object using the item number and quantity value. The second ADDPOLINEITEM function takes only one argument– a purchase order line item object. That second function doesn't have to build a purchase order line item; it only has to store it.

IMPLEMENTS

The Java class code for a function makes up the *implementation* of that function. To implement a function means to write code for that function. As explained, Java has a construct known as an interface, which is a named set of functions. A class may be defined to *implement* that interface by providing Java code for each of the functions declared in the interface, as shown in Figure G.3.

```
interface PrintInterface {
  // a list of functions with no code implementation
  void printHeader ();
  void printDetail();
  void printFooter();
}

class PurchaseOrder implements PrintInterface {
  // PO specific code
  Integer PONumber;
  Vector POLineItems;
  ...
  // code implementations for the PrintInterface interface
  void printHeader () {
    System.out.println ("\nPO No:" + PONumber+"\n");
  }
  void printDetail(){
    for (int i = 0; i < lineItems.size(); i++) {
      POLineItem lineItem = (POLineItem)lineItems.elementAt(i);
      System.out.println ("\nLine Item:" + LineItem.ItemNumber);
    }
  }
  void printFooter() {
    System.out.println ("\n * * * End of PO * * *");
  }
}
```

Figure G.3: The PURCHASEORDER class provides code implementations for functions listed in the PRINTINTERFACE interface.

VISIBILITY/ACCESS SPECIFIER

The data members and function members that make up a class might not all be *visible* (available) to the programmers that use that class. Visibility is explicitly set with the Java reserved words *public, protected,* and *private.* These reserved words are known as *access specifiers.* The purchase order class's ADDLINEITEM function might have an access specifier of public, but its ALLOCATEINVENTORY function might have a visibility of private:

```
class PurchaseOrder {
  public void addLineItem(int ItemNumber, int Quantity) {...}
  private void allocateInventory() {...}
}
```

With visibility set to private, the ALLOCATEINVENTORY function is accessible only to functions of the purchase order class itself. In other words, ALLO-CATEINVENTORY is designed for internal use only. A program with a variable typed as the PURCHASEORDER class could invoke the ADDLINEITEM function but it could not invoke the allocate function. That program wouldn't even pass the Java compiler:

```
PurchaseOrder PO = new PurchaseOrder();
PO.addLineItem( 549, 3); // compiles OK
PO.allocate();  // compile error: function inaccessible
```

INSTANTIATE/CREATE/CONSTRUCT

A Java programmer uses a Java class as an abstract data type to declare the type of a program variable. Before that variable can be used, the program must first *create* the object that the variable is to reference. Prior to the object's creation, the variable is a reference to nothing. If a variable is used before it is assigned an object reference, the Java Virtual Machine returns a message that says the variable contains a null reference.

Objects are created with a process known as *construction.* Every Java class has a special constructor function, which bears the same name as its class. An object is created by using the Java keyword NEW, followed by the name of a class's constructor function and its argument list. The object returned by the constructor function is said to be an instance of its class. This process of creating an object instance is referred to as instancing or *instantiating* an object:

```
PurchaseOrder po = new PurchaseOrder(1298, aCustomerObject);
```

The purchase order constructor (as invoked with the NEW operator in the code snippet) would have been implemented with the Java code that set the initial values of fields in the newly created object. For example, the purchase order constructor first sets its due date attribute to be equal to 12/98 and then sets its Customer attribute to reference the passed Customer object (ACUSTOMEROBJECT).

ASSOCIATE

Associations represent relationships between instances of classes (e.g., a purchase order exists for a specific customer). Java associations are very similar to file relationships in a relational database. For instance, a purchase order record typically uses a customer number as a foreign key to retrieve information from a customer file. A purchase order class associates a purchase order object to the customer object with a class field that contains the customer's number. That customer number can then be used to retrieve the proper customer object from the customer class, as Figure G.4 shows.

```
class PurchaseOrder {
  int CustomerNumber; // association field
  ...
  void printCustomerAddress() {
    // get a customer object from the customer number
    Customer cust = Customer.getCustomer(CustomerNumber);
    System.out.println (cust.addr);
    System.out.println (cust.city + ", "+cust.state+"
"cust.zip);
  }
}
```

Figure G.4: Objects of the purchase order's Java class are associated with customers through the GETCUSTOMER function.

Neither a relational database purchase order record nor an object-oriented purchase order class would contain all the information relating to the customer (such as name, address, and credit limit). Both Java classes and RDB records simply store a field used to retrieve the associated customer from the CUSTOMER class or the RDB customer file.

CONTAINMENT/COMPOSITION

A business entity consists of many parts. For instance, a purchase order is comprised of one or more line items. The purchase order class might be designed to *contain* an array or vector (a vector is a dynamically sizeable array) of line item objects:

```
class PurchaseOrder {
  Vector POLineItems;
  ...
}
```

The vector of purchase order line items is part of the *composition* of the purchase order class. In other words, the structure of a purchase order object as defined in the purchase order class is composed of a set of line item objects. That vector of line items is also said to be *contained* in the purchase order object.

PERSISTENCE

The ability for an object to maintain its state across program invocations is known as *persistence*. Today, when implementing a Java application on the AS/400, you make a Java object persistent by writing the state of an object (i.e., the value of the fields of that object) to a record in a DB2/400 file. On other platforms, you could also make an object's state persistent with the use of a relational database. Storing objects in relational databases, however, is not natural to an object-oriented environment—it requires additional programming effort and can exert a negative impact on performance.

Java objects can be made persistent more naturally with other types of databases such as object relational databases, object-oriented databases, and a Java mechanism called *serialization*. Fortunately, IBM is working on object persistence for the AS/400 that will perform well and be easier on programmers.

REFERENCE LIST

Booch, Grady. *Object-Oriented Analysis and Design with Applications,* 2nd ed. Menlo Park, Calif.: Addison-Wesley, 1994.

Coad, Peter. *Java Design: Building Better Apps & Applets.* Upper Saddle River, N.J.: Yourdon Press, 1996.

Cohen, Shy. *Professional Java Fundamentals.* Birmingham, Pa.: WROX Press, 1996.

Englander, Robert. *Developing Java Beans.* Sebastopol, Calif.: O'Reilly & Associates, 1997.

Flanagan, David. *Java Examples in a Nutshell.* Sebastopol, Calif.: O'Reilly & Associates, 1997.

Flanagan, David. *Java in a Nutshell.* Sebastopol, Calif.: O'Reilly & Associates, 1997.

Fowler, Martin. *UML Distilled: Applying the Standard Object Modeling Language.* Menlo Park, Calif.: Addison-Wesley, 1997.

Gamma, Erich et al. *Design Patterns: Elements of Reusable Object-Oriented Software.* Menlo Park, Calif.: Addison-Wesley, 1997.

Gosling, James. *The Java Language Specification.* Menlo Park, Calif.: Addison-Wesley, 1996.

Gutz, Steven. *Up To Speed with Swing: User Interfaces with Java Foundation Classes.* Greenwich, Conn.: Manning Publications, 1998.

Maatta, Bob et al. *Accessing the AS/400 System with Java* (SC24-2152-00). Rochester, Minn.: International Business Machines, 1997.

Maatta, Bob et al. *Building AS/400 Applications with Java* (SC24-2163-01). Rochester, Minn.: International Business Machines, 1998.

Moss, Karl. *Java Servlets.* New York: McGraw-Hill, 1998.

Reese, George. *Database Programming with JDBC and Java.* Sebastopol, Calif.: O'Reilly & Associates, 1997.

INDEX

Note: Boldface numbers indicate illustrations.

Note: Boldface numbers indicate illustrations.

graphical user interface development, *continued*
  listener interfaces, 329-333
  load-all subfiles, 381
  nesting containers with components in them,
    325-326
  page-at-a-time subfiles, 381
  persistence, ISPersistent function, 344
  remote method invocation (RMI), grid
    support, 358
  scroll bars, 372
  source-event-listener model, AWT, 329
  subfiles vs. grids, 355-357, **356**
  summary event handling, 336-337
  Swing vs. AWT, 386-387
  tabbed dialogs, 325, 376-378
  tool tips associated with panels, 373-374
  tree hierarchies, 378-381, **378**
  window-closing events, 333-334, 342
GridLayout manager, 324, **324, 325**
grids, subfiles vs. grids (*See also* JTable grids),
  355-357, **356**

H
HasNext, 300, 304
helper classes, 342-343

I
implementation of a function, 407
implementation of abstract classes, 126-131
implementation of interface, 111-114, **113**
implicit class construction, 106-107
Import statements, 6-7
increment math operator, 36
information hiding, in encapsulation, 86, 89
inheritance, 80, 85, 95-108, 405
  abstraction, 22, 74, 96, 98, 125-134, 402-403
  access specifiers, 92-94, **93**, 100-101, 408
  base class, 100, 127-128
  classes, 96-98, **97**
  constructors, 14, 15-16, 20, 70, 105-107
  default constructors, 107
  descendant classes, 97-98
  explicit class construction, 107
  extending a class with inheritance, 98-101
  implicit class construction, 106-107

interfaces vs. inheritance, 115, 121-123
IS A KIND OF, 102
overloading functions, 104-105, 304-305
overriding, 101-104, 105
parent class, 100, 405
Protected, 100-101
Public, 100-101
subclass, 85, 100, 405
SUPER keyword, 106-107
superclass, 100, 405
initialization
  initialization subroutine (INZSR), 15-16, 20,
    22
  lazy initialization, 252-253
  static initializer function, 275-277
inner classes, 334-335
Inprise, 318, 395
instantiation, 33, 127-128, 408-409
INTEGER, 37-39
Integrated File System (IFS), 161
  applet storage, 54
  Java package storage, 5-6
integrating Java and AS/400 applications,
  211-236
  array creation for parameter list, 211,
    212-217
  call object creation, 212, 217
  converting values to Java data types, 219-220
  data conversion classes, 215-217
  data queues, 227-229, 227
  encapsulating AS/400 program calls, 222-224
  error handling, 212, 218-219
  establishing AS/400 connection, 211, 212
  executing the program, 212, 218
  input parameters list, 214-217
  Java Native Interface (JNI), 225-227
  OS/400 command invocation, 224-225
  output parameters list, 213-214
  path creation to program, 211, 217
  PLIST, 212-217
  program call markup language (PCML)
    program calls, 229-235
  program parameters list, 212-213
  remote program calls, 211-222
  sample listing, 220-222

Note: Boldface numbers indicate illustrations.

Note: Boldface numbers indicate illustrations.

Note: Boldface numbers indicate illustrations.

MIDRANGE
COMPUTING
IIR PUBLICATIONS INC.

Other Bestsellers of Related Interest

Complete CL
The Definitive Control Language Programming Guide—Third Edition
by Ernie Malaga and Ted Holt
This new and updated version of the classic 1992 book brings together the solid basics of CL and the newest innovations to this mainstay programming language. When you have completed this book, you will be able to write simple and advanced CL programs, understand the strengths and limitations of the CL language, develop a good CL coding style, and avoid common mistakes when writing CL. You will learn to manipulate strings with built-in functions and operators, code looping, and decision structures; make procedures communicate with one another via messages; make CL procedures communicate with users; and use data queues and data areas. You also will learn to understand and use overrides effectively, process display and database files, use APIs, and effectively use the QTEMP library. You will be able to avoid the pitfalls of adopted authorities, understand security issues, convert S/36 OCL and S/38 CL to native CL, understand the differences between OPM and ILE, use CL in both batch and interactive processing, compile CL programs and modules, bind modules into programs, and use the interactive debugger. If you are responsible for AS/400 application development or if you are an operator or programmer responsible for AS/400 operations, you won't want to be without this book. 496 pages. Level: Novice to Intermediate.
❏ Book C5001 .... $79
ISBN 1-883884-58-6

Power CL
by Ted Holt and Ernie Malaga
Now you can be a power CL programmer and write more robust CL code than ever before! This new book gives you proven CL programming techniques from experienced pros that take you beyond the fundamentals to a more advanced level of CL programming. Everyone can use a mentor, and this book is like having two—Ted Holt and Ernie Malaga—right at your elbow, offering advice about topics like softcoding techniques, properly using overrides, debugging CL, error handling, and much more! You will learn to write better CL code. The better code you write, the more productive you will be, the more successful your programs will be, and the fewer problems you and your company will have. Use this book to take your career to another level! 350 pages. Level: Intermediate to Advanced.
❏ BOOK C570 .... $99
ISBN 1-883884-41-1

Creating Commands
The Complete Handbook for Developing Powerful AS/400 Commands
by Ernie Malaga
This comprehensive handbook sets forth in concise detail everything you need to know to write simple, powerful commands that would normally take time-consuming, complex programs to duplicate. Creating your own commands has numerous advantages. Commands provide a consistent user interface. In addition, commands provide their own built-in prompt displays, so you don't have to be bothered with the chore of designing your own. Commands also provide extensive, built-in validation checking for parameter values, let you define parameters in any order, and omit those parameters that have default values. With commands, you can define parameter values as a string of characters, even when they are expected to be of other data types. The book includes more than a dozen sample commands that have real-life usefulness. You'll gain an important understanding of security and performance issues as they relate to commands. 145 pages. Level: Intermediate.
❏ BOOK C501 .... $89
ISBN 1-883884-06-3

Open Query File Magic!
A Complete Guide to Maximizing the Power of OPNQRYF, Second Edition
by Ted Holt
OPNQRYF (Open Query File) is the most powerful, most complex, and least documented command in the CL language. You can use it to sort and summarize data, but it can also do much more for you. It allows you to create new fields and assign values to them, perform complex joins of multiple files, create new files with existing and calculated fields, select records (even based on summarized data), and much more! This book explains the ins and outs of OPNQRYF from the basic operations through the most complex mapping and selection parameters. Ted Holt, long known for his ability to teach and show by example, makes the often-complex rules of OPNQRYF easy to understand. He shows you not only the how of OPNQRYF but also the when (when you should use certain functions and parameters to make more powerful and flexible applications for your users) and the why (why you should choose certain options in specific situations).

The book is reorganized to make it more useful not only as a learning tool, but also as a reference for ongoing value. 304 pages. Level: Intermediate to Advanced.
❏ BOOK C590 .... $69
ISBN 1-883884-57-8

Other Bestsellers of Related Interest

The AS/400 & Microsoft® Office Integration Handbook

by Brian Singleton with Colleen Garton

This book takes a detailed look at how you can integrate applications in the Microsoft Office 97 product suite with data from your AS/400. Unravel secrets such as how to use your AS/400's output with your PC's data formatting tools or how to make attractive, professional reports with AS/400 data the easy way. Learn the secret of using visual query tools to point and click the creation of sophisticated information output and how to analyze and summarize the detailed (and often cumbersome) reports from your AS/400. Discover how you can combine the presentation capabilities of Microsoft Office with the database capabilities of the AS/400 to provide your company with the best of both worlds.

In the first sections of the book, Singleton introduces you to the essential knowledge you need to use Client Access as you integrate AS/400 data with the Microsoft Office applications. He covers installing and configuring Client Access, how to provide a seamless method of AS/400 integration with Microsoft Office using ODBC, the network drive functionality of Client Access, and the Client Access Data Transfer Function. He also covers TCP/IP's FTP file transfer function and how to use it to bring data from the AS/400 to your PC.

The remaining sections of the book cover the veritable Swiss Army knife functions of Microsoft Office. 320 pages. Level: Novice, Intermediate, and Advanced.

❏ BOOK C587 ....$79
ISBN 1-883884-49-7

TCP/IP Primer for the AS/400

The Essential Guide to AS/400 TCP/IP Concepts, Configuration, and Use

by Jim Hoopes, Robin Klima, and Martin Pluth

Imagine the rewards you'll reap as you connect your company's AS/400 to any other computer in the world! Wishful thinking? Not at all, since V3R1 when IBM started including TCP/IP free with OS/400. This book will show you how to simplify communications between AS/400s by throwing out SNADS and moving to TCP/IP, improve communications in your AS/400-to-PC environment, and lead your company into a whole new world of bargains and business on the Internet. *TCP/IP Primer for the AS/400* is the hands-on, how-to book you've been waiting for. It begins with the basics and proceeds through the various configuration options, utilities, and troubleshooting skills you need to connect your AS/400 to users within the office and around the world. 370 pages. Level: Novice.

❏ BOOK C561 ....$99
ISBN 1-883884-33-0

The AS/400 Owner's Manual for V4

by Mike Dawson

Midrange Computing's all-time bestselling manual is now V4R2-ready! Designed for AS/400 professionals at all levels, The *AS/400 Owner's Manual for V4* walks you through hundreds of AS/400 tasks from the perspective of how most shops actually work. Cutting through the dozens of parameters and options of AS/400 commands, *The AS/400 Owner's Manual for V4* takes you directly to the results you need. Offering much more than brief, to-the-point instructions, it also includes valuable descriptions that examine why AS/400 managers, administrators, operators, and programmers do certain things on the machine and how the AS/400 works internally. This edition is completely up-to-date for Version 4 of OS/400 and contains a new chapter about the Internet and TCP/IP. Wire-bound and concise, *The AS/400 Owner's Manual for V4* is the perfect workstation tool for anyone who does AS/400 operations, administration, or management. 464 pages. Level: Intermediate to Advanced.

❏ Book C5000..$59
ISBN 1-58347-001-8

AS/400 Primer

Fundamental Concepts and Training for Programmers, Administrators, and System Operators

by Ernie Malaga

A must for every AS/400 shop, this comprehensive, 29-chapter book is perfect for novice and intermediate programmers, as well as system administrators and operators. In a simple, straightforward style, Ernie Malaga not only explains core AS/400 concepts, but shows you—step by step—how to perform 30 essential AS/400 functions, including installation, troubleshooting, administration, operation, programming, and 25 other tasks!

You'll learn the essential technical concepts you need to get you up to speed on all areas of the AS/400. Increased understanding of the AS/400 will boost productivity and put all personnel in your organization on friendly terms with the computer. You'll find the *AS/400 Primer* will be a learning tool and a valuable reference for years to come. As one satisfied reader put it, "If you could only own one AS/400 book, this would be it." Don't power up without it! 435 pages. Level: Novice to Intermediate.

❏ BOOK C507..$99
ISBN 1-883884-25-X

Other Bestsellers of Related Interest

The AS/400 Programmer's Handbook
A Toolbox of Examples for Every
AS/400 Programmer
by Mark McCall

Now you can eliminate hours of time spent researching complex programming techniques. This handy desktop guide provides programming examples for nearly every AS/400 development task you face. No more rummaging around in old code to find and modify a technique you need for a new application. No more writing routines from scratch. This book and companion diskette put dozens of prototypical techniques at your fingertips, ready to key in or insert directly from your development library.

You get more than 70 examples of essential programming techniques using CL, RPG III, RPG IV, command creation, and UIM panel groups. All of the code examples from the book are included on the companion diskette—ready to upload into your development library.

Spiral-bound so it lays flat on your desk, *The AS/400 Programmer's Handbook* is designed as a complete reference for the AS/400 programmer. It's the first place to turn whenever you need help remembering or understanding a coding technique. 400 pages. Level: Novice, Intermediate, and Advanced.

❏ BOOK C585 ....$59
ISBN 1-883884-48-9

Power RPG IV
Advanced Concepts, Tips & Techniques,
Including ILE
by Doug Pence and Ron Hawkins

Before you write your next RPG IV program, make sure you're using the most powerful, code-saving features this potent new language has to offer. This book from Doug Pence and Ron Hawkins gives you practical, hands-on tips, hints, and shortcuts that will save you time and increase the reliability of the code you write. The book includes a valuable chapter devoted to date handling and the turn of the century, which will help you cope with this important event. It also contains a chapter on Integrated Language Environment (ILE) concepts, exploring this vital feature of RPG IV. You get explanations of softcoding function keys, new ways to use the QCMDEXC command processing API, new APIs for ILE, and new utilities to help you work with ILE. Built-in functions such as %ELEM, %TRIML, %TRIMR, and %TRIM also are explained in detail. *Power RPG IV* comes with a free diskette containing 11 useful AS/400 utilities. 477 pages. Level: Intermediate to Advanced.

❏ BOOK C560 ....$99
ISBN 1-883884-32-2

Subfiles for RPG Programmers
A Comprehensive User Guide
by Michael Catalani

Does the word *subfile* scare you? Fear no more! *Subfiles for RPG Programmers* explains everything you need to know about subfiles in simple and concise detail. Whether you're a novice subfile programmer or a seasoned pro, you'll find this book to be an invaluable resource.

Subfiles for RPG Programmers begins with concepts such as subfile record formats and subfile loading, then progresses to more advanced applications. DDS, of course, is at the heart of subfiles, so the author thoroughly explains the DDS keywords and how they apply to subfile programming. He explains and shows you examples of how the RPG code and the DDS work together to make a subfile function with all its built-in power. The more advanced subfile techniques are covered here, too: coding for multiple subfiles on the screen, using OPNQRYF and subfiles, coding message subfiles, and coding window techniques.

To increase your understanding and retention of the information, all theory is backed up with easy-to-understand working program examples. *Subfiles for RPG Programmers* is V2R3-ready and comes with a diskette of all working program examples. 505 pages. Level: Intermediate.

❏ BOOK C517 ....$99
ISBN 1-883884-18-7

The RPG Programmer's Guide to RPG IV and ILE
by Richard Shaler and Robin Klima

Aimed at the experienced RPG programmer, this book will quickly take you from your RPG III skills to writing powerful RPG IV programs. It addresses the differences between RPG III and RPG IV so that you can quickly become a productive RPG IV programmer.

The book contains extensive code examples that compare the two RPG languages and introduces the ILE capabilities that can be used to your advantage.

There are two new chapters on subprocedures. The authors have added a chapter on conditional compiler objects to show you how the old directives have been enhanced and what new directives are available. They have also added a chapter on implementing object-oriented concepts in RPG.

There are also appendixes with utilities and programs that you can add to your copy book and learn from. 368 pages. Level: Intermediate to Advanced.

❏ BOOK C588 ....$79
ISBN 1-883884-56-X

For a more complete list of titles, call 1-800-477-5665, or visit our Web site at *www.midrangecomputing.com*.

MIDRANGE COMPUTING IIR PUBLICATIONS INC.

Other Bestsellers of Related Interest

The Modern RPG IV Language

by Bob Cozzi

Get ready to experience a whole new level of productivity and power on the AS/400! This best-selling book by Bob Cozzi, the world's number one RPG authority, shows you how to exploit the powerful new features of RPG IV, the most powerful RPG language ever created. You'll accomplish more with fewer lines of code—guaranteed! It gives you a structured approach to programming in RPG IV. You'll learn to accomplish sophisticated calculations and algorithms with single, powerful RPG IV statements— calculations that may have required dozens of lines of code and numerous subroutines in earlier versions of RPG. This book gives you the details and the depth of coverage you need. There are comprehensive syntax diagrams for all of the RPG IV op codes. You'll find a list of the new built-in functions and a complete and up-to-date listing of RPG IV keywords and options. Cozzi gives you extensive coverage of the integrated RPG IV date and time support, which is critical as you move your applications into the Year 2000. There are many examples and suggestions for coexistence with RPG III, along with useful coding examples, references, illustrations, and the AS/400 ILE RPG/400 compiler and program binding options.

Packed with information not available in IBM manuals, this book will save you untold hours of research and programming time! If you program in RPG IV or plan to soon, this book is indispensable to your productivity—and to your career!

570 pages. Level: Novice, Intermediate, and Advanced.

BOOK C546 ....$99
ISBN 1-883884-31-4

RPG IV The Modern RPG Language Reference Summary

by Bob Cozzi

Remembering all the new features of RPG IV (and how to implement them) is a daunting challenge. That's why Bob Cozzi created a 95-page quick reference guide as a companion to his RPG IV book. The Modern RPG IV Language Reference Summary gives you instant access to the answers you need to take advantage of the full array of new RPG IV functions. Keep it at your side, and you'll always know where you are in RPG IV! 95 pages. Level: Novice, Intermediate, and Advanced.

BOOK C545 ....$29
ISBN 1-883884-38-1

The Modern RPG [III] Language with Structured Programming

by Bob Cozzi

Whether you're a new programmer or an old hand, this best-selling book will help you write the kind of code that sets you apart from the crowd—powerful RPG code that's easy to use, enhance, and expand. You'll increase your professional value as you apply the principles and ready-to-use solutions that have made *The Modern RPG [III] Language with Structured Programming* the world's most popular RPG III book.

You'll learn about structured programming concepts from the world's number one RPG authority, as well as program design and implementation. Cozzi explains modular programming concepts and implementation so that you can easily write, debug, and maintain truly modern modular programs. He explains how to code and implement traditional RPG database file processing so that you will no longer be constricted by the RPG cycle. He even includes information on database file processing with embedded SQL.

With this book, you learn RPG programming the way it's taught in the computer science curriculums of many colleges, universities, and trade schools, and you'll be learning from the number one RPG expert. 458 pages. Level: Novice, Intermediate, and Advanced.

BOOK C531 ....$69
ISBN 0-9621825-0-8

Introduction to RPG IV

by Bob Cozzi

Now you can come up to speed quickly on the basics of programming in RPG IV—the modern, modular AS/400 programming language that has gained acceptance worldwide. All you need is this easy-to-follow book from Bob Cozzi, the world's leading authority on RPG programming. Rich with practical examples and sample code, this book provides step-by-step guidance to writing structured programs in RPG IV. You'll find out how to create simple, powerful programs with just a few lines of code.

Completely up-to-date with all new RPG IV features, this book tells you everything you need to understand the modern constructs of RPG IV, including figurative and named constants, operation extenders, and free-format expressions. You'll discover how to perform basic programming tasks such as opening files, processing data, communicating with the user, controlling workflow, and calling other programs. You'll even learn how to set up a development environment, including the integration of RPG IV and DDS! This book opens the door to the world of programming in RPG IV. 304 pages. Level: Novice.

❑ BOOK C577 ....$59
ISBN 1-883884-46-2

For a more complete list of titles, call **1-800-477-5665**, or visit our Web site at **www.midrangecomputing.com**.

ORDER FORM

5 Easy Ways to Order!

BILL TO:

Name _____

Title _____

Company _____

Address _____

City _____ State _____ ZIP _____

YTQBZ

SHIP TO (if different from above):

Name _____ Title _____

Company _____

Address _____

City/State/ZIP _____

FAX
this order form to 760-931-9935,
24 hours a day, 365 days a year.

MAIL
your order to: 5650 El Camino Real,
Suite 225, Carlsbad, CA 92008

EMAIL
your order to
custsvc@midrangecomputing.com.

PHONE
toll-free 1-800-477-5665
(Mon. - Fri. 6 a.m. to 5 p.m. PST).

ONLINE
ordering is available at
www.mc-store.com.

ITEMS ORDERED:

Item No.	Description	Price	Quantity	Total Price

Subtotal	
Add 7.75% sales tax (CA residents only) or 6.25% sales tax (TX residents only)	
Shipping/Handling—$6.25 per item (UPS ground, continental U.S. only)	
Total	

ADDITIONAL INFORMATION:

Daytime Phone (required to process order):

(_____) _____ - _____

Fax (_____) _____ - _____

Email _____

* Note: All prices are U.S. only. Please call for orders and prices outside the U.S. Prices Subject to change.

BILLING INFORMATION:

☐ Payment Enclosed (Make check payable to Midrange Computing.)

CREDIT CARD: ☐ VISA ☐ MasterCard ☐ AmEx ☐ Discover

Card # _____ Exp Date _____

BILL ME, P.O. # _____

Signature (required) _____

Priority code: YTTAZ